Praise for *Emigrants*

'James Evans has written a marvellously engaging and comprehensive account of this ambitious undertaking and the men and women who accomplished it, often with the odds stacked against them. Here he tells the exciting, sometimes heartbreaking stories of the pioneers and explains what kind of world they dreamt of creating. It was one in which individual liberty and freedom was cherished: both became part of the modern American mindset'      Lawrence James, *The Times*

'Otto von Bismarck was once asked to identify the pre-eminent fact in modern world history. That America spoke English, he replied. In *Emigrants*, James Evans attempts to explain how and why that happened... Evans' book is an eloquent testimony to the fact that the commodity America has always traded in, above all others, is hope'

Mathew Lyons, *Financial Times*

'What led a person in seventeenth-century England to get on a ship bound for the Americas? James Evans attempts to answer that question by exploring both the push and pull factors involved... His descriptions are vivid... and he relates in a readable style the lives of people who chose to make the journey'      Katrina Gulliver, *The Spectator*

'Engaging... Evans is vivid on the risks of going to a land that, for a good portion of the century, had little to recommend it... Brisk, informative and... eye-opening'      Tim Smith-Lang, *Daily Telegraph*

'Why this book is such a gripping and enjoyable read is that Evans does not focus on the great and the good of history, but on the ordinary men, women, and children who migrated, with their hopes, fears, and desperation. Through primary sources of diaries, court hearings, and letters, Evans tells their stories, which sometimes inspire you with their heroism, and sometimes make you weep over their tragedies... In a lucid, well-written, and solidly researched analysis, he teases out the mixed and complicated reasons that so many people were compelled to make the risky sea voyage to a perilous wilderness'

The Ven. Dr Lyle Dennen, *Church Times*

James Evans completed a doctorate at Oriel College, Oxford, following a first-class degree and a Masters in Historical Research. He is a writer and producer of historical documentaries for the BBC and Channel 4, and the author of *Merchant Adventurers: The Voyage of Discovery that Transformed England*. He lives in London with his wife and children.

@JamesEvansUK

# Emigrants

## Why the English Sailed to the New World

### JAMES EVANS

WEIDENFELD & NICOLSON

First published in Great Britain in 2017
This paperback edition first published in 2018 by Weidenfeld & Nicolson
an imprint of The Orion Publishing Group Ltd
Carmelite House, 50 Victoria Embankment
London EC4Y ODZ

An Hachette UK Company

3 5 7 9 10 8 6 4 2

Copyright © 2017 by James Evans
Maps © 2017 by John Gilkes

A CIP catalogue record for this book is
available from the British Library.

ISBN (paperback) 978 1 78022 103 8
ISBN (audio) 978 1 4091 7744 9
ISBN (ebook) 978 0 297 86691 6

Typeset at The Spartan Press Ltd,
Lymington, Hants

Printed and bound by CPI Group (UK) Ltd,
Croydon, CRO 4YY

MIX
Paper from
responsible sources
FSC® C104740

www.orionbooks.co.uk

This book is dedicated with love to Nicola and my three children, who made the long, at times arduous – if perhaps not dangerous – journey with me.

# CONTENTS

*List of Illustrations*   xi
*Maps*   xiii

Introduction   1

I FISH   15
II GOLD AND SMOKE   51
III EQUALITY BEFORE GOD   95
IV KING   140
V FUR   170
VI LIBERTY   205
VII DESPAIR   237

Conclusion   266

*Notes*   272
*Bibliography*   292
*Acknowledgements*   304
*Index*   307

# LIST OF ILLUSTRATIONS

Wenceslaus Hollar, *Three Ships in a Rough Sea*, c.1664. Courtesy of the Thomas Fisher Rare Book Library, University of Toronto.

Portrait of Sir Humphrey Gilbert, English school, 16th century. © National Trust Photographic Library / Bridgeman.

Plan of Dartmouth, 1619. Reproduced with the kind permission of Devon Archives and Local Studies Service.

John Guy meeting the Beothuk in 1612, engraving by Matthäus Merian, from Theodor de Bry, *America*, 1628). Courtesy of the Huntington Library, San Marino, California.

Title page to Richard Whitbourne, *A Discourse and Discovery of Newfoundland*, 1620. British Library, London / Bridgeman.

Captain John Smith, engraving, c.1624. Courtesy of the Huntington Library, San Marino, California.

Cupellation furnaces, engraving from Georgius Agricola, *De re metallica*, 1556.

Title page to Georgius Agricola, *De re metallica*, 1556.

A tobacco plant, illustration from Matthias de Lobel, *Plantarum seu stirpium*, 1576.

Frontispiece and title page to Giles Everard, *Panacea; or the universal medicine, being a discovery of the wonderfull vertues of tobacco*, 1659. Courtesy of the Royal Physicians of Edinburgh.

Portrait of James VI and I, Daniel Mytens the Elder, 1621. Photo © Ann Ronan Pictures / Print Collector / Getty.

Illustration from *A Declaration for the Certaine Time of Drawing the Great Standing Lottery*, London, 1616. Courtesy of the Society of Antiquaries, London.

Simon van de Passe, *Matoaka Alias Rebecca*, engraving 1661. Courtesy of the Library of Congress, Washington DC.

Portrait of Edward Winslow, school of Robert Walker, 1651. © Courtesy of the Pilgrim Hall Museum, Plymouth, MA, USA.

Portrait of Anne Dudley Bradstreet, etching by an unknown artist. © Granger / Bridgeman.

Portrait of William Laud, Archbishop of Canterbury, Anthony van Dyck, 1633. © Lambeth Palace, London / Bridgeman.

Emblem from *A rot amongst the bishops*, Thomas Stirry, 1641. © Used by permission of the Folger Shakespeare Library.

The Short Parliament assembled at Westminster in April 1640, English school, 17th century. © Museum of London / Bridgeman.

Atrocities of the Irish rebellion, woodcuts from *The Teares of Ireland*, James Cranford, 1642 © British Library / Bridgeman.

*The Kingdom's Monster Uncloaked*. Woodcut from c.1643. © British Library / Bridgeman.

Execution of King Charles I from a contemporary broadsheet. © The Art Archive / Rex / Shutterstock.

Ralph Hall, *Virginia*, engraving, 1636. Courtesy of the Huntington Library, San Marino, California.

A North American beaver, illustration from Louis Armand de Lahontan, *New Voyages to North America*, 1703. Courtesy of Library and Archives Canada.

A scene in a seventeenth-century coffee house from the fourth edition of William Hickes, *Oxford Jests*, 1688. © British Library / Bridgeman.

The Duke's Plan of New York, English school, 1664. © British Library / Bridgeman.

William Penn in armour, English school, 1666. Courtesy of the Historical Society of Pennsylvania Collection / Bridgeman.

First page of William Penn, *A Further Account of the Province of Pennsylvania and its Improvements*, 1685. © 2017 Photographic Unit, University of Glasgow.

Wood engraving of Mary Dyer escorted to the Boston gallows, 19th century. © Granger / Bridgeman.

An indentured servant agreement, 1627. © Virginia Historical Society, USA / Bridgeman.

Plague of London, 1665. Contemporary woodcut. © Granger / Bridgeman.

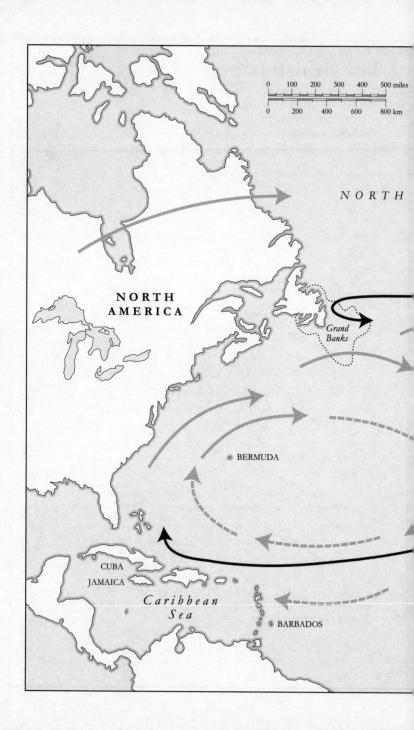

NORTH

NORTH
AMERICA

Grand
Banks

BERMUDA

CUBA

JAMAICA

Caribbean
Sea

BARBADOS

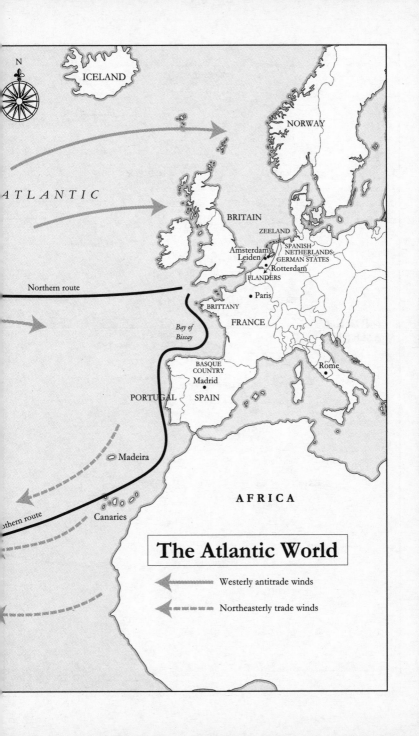

N

ICELAND

NORWAY

ATLANTIC

BRITAIN

ZEELAND

Amsterdam  SPANISH
Leiden  NETHERLANDS
GERMAN STATES
Rotterdam
FLANDERS

Northern route

• Paris

BRITTANY

FRANCE

Bay of
Biscay

BASQUE
COUNTRY

Madrid  Rome

PORTUGAL  • SPAIN

Madeira

AFRICA

outhern route

Canaries

## The Atlantic World

Westerly antitrade winds

Northeasterly trade winds

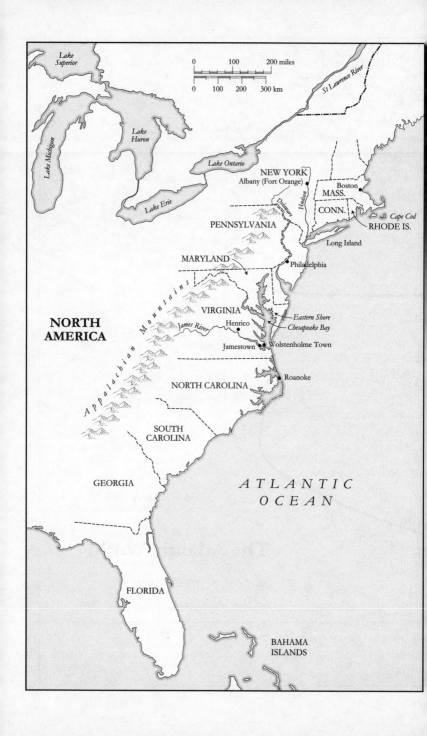

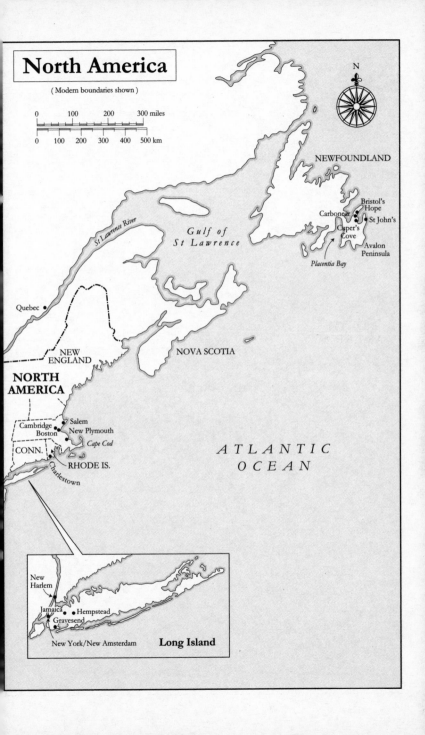

# North America

( Modern boundaries shown )

0    100    200    300 miles

0    100   200   300   400   500 km

N

NEWFOUNDLAND

Bristol's
Hope
Carbonear
St John's
Cuper's
Cove
Avalon
Peninsula

*Placentia Bay*

*Gulf of
St Lawrence*

*St Lawrence River*

Quebec

NEW
ENGLAND

**NORTH
AMERICA**

NOVA SCOTIA

Salem
Cambridge
Boston
New Plymouth
*Cape Cod*

CONN.

RHODE IS.

*Charlestown*

*ATLANTIC
OCEAN*

New
Harlem

Jamaica
Gravesend
Hempstead

New York/New Amsterdam    **Long Island**

# Introduction

In countries like Great Britain or the United States of America, most talk nowadays, where the movement of people is concerned, is not about *emigrants* but about *immigrants*. Britain has become a fortunate place – a country that many more people want to enter than to leave. A quick internet search returns five million results in the United Kingdom for 'emigrants', but more than twenty-two times that number, 113 million, for 'immigrants'. Things were different four hundred years ago, and many more people looked to leave England than move to it.

As a direct result of the truly astonishing levels of emigration from England, the seventeenth century witnessed an unprecedented realignment of world geography – in terms, that is, of its human population, of where it lived on the earth, and of what it knew about it. Thousands upon thousands of men, women and children who were born on the eastern side of the Atlantic began life anew on its western side, in a region that they knew very little about: in America.

It is a few of these stories which dominate the pages ahead – of the self-taught Puritan Robert Cushman, unimpressed by social standing, of the remarkable poet and pioneer of female equality Anne Bradstreet, of the tobacco farmer John Rolfe, famous for marrying a Native American woman known as Pocahontas, or of the charismatic and passionate Royalist Henry Norwood. It was emigration which would have dominated the consciousness of the English, deafened as they were by the chatter and hubbub and beseeching – by the 'such loud noise' – of crowds who clambered onto ships to leave the country, of what one charter then called 'the multitude of people thronging thither'.[1]

While other European countries were certainly involved, it was the people of England who were in the forefront of this massive realignment. Often, having moved within England, to towns, to cities, and in particular to London, the capital city, they then moved onward, far across the sea. Although many died soon afterwards, because mortality rates among those who went were terrifyingly high, so many did go that the alteration became permanent, with effects which have shaped and defined our world ever since.

The truly remarkable nature of the shift which took place is not nearly, though – certainly not widely – as appreciated as it should be.

It was not that humans first came to live in places where humans had not lived before. For many thousands of years there had been men and women on both sides of the Atlantic: ever since the days when land connections existed, far to the north, between the European and the American continents, as well as between America and Asia, allowing migration overland. Until approximately 10,000 years ago, when the melting of polar ice caps flooded these land corridors, plunging footprints beneath the waves, a significant exchange of populations – of both flora and fauna – clearly took place, as is obvious now from substantial similarities among life forms. And included in this exchange, of course, were people.[2]

Nor was it, indeed, that the seventeenth century saw any fundamental new beginning. It was not then that the American continent first entered European consciousness. Viking ships, many hundreds of years earlier, had crossed the Northern Atlantic from Scandinavia, even if the settlement that these wide-roving Europeans had established – on territory that they called 'Vinland' – had not proved an enduring one. And it was also over a hundred years before the seventeenth century that another European explorer known to Englishmen as Christopher Columbus discovered (insofar as the people of Eurasia were concerned) the American continent.

While Columbus reached islands in what we now call the Caribbean, far to the south of what we think of as the countries of Canada and the United States of America, another sailor from Italy, a man the English called John Cabot, followed soon afterwards, much further north. When he dropped anchor, he did so in cooler, very different territory – not far from where the Vikings had landed centuries earlier – by the island that we now call Newfoundland. Neither man appreciated, though, what in fact they had found. Both thought that the globe was much smaller than it really is. Both thought that the land they had reached was an outlying, hitherto unknown fragment of Asia – that the large islands of Japan must lie nearby. Today, of course, the island on which Cabot landed is a part of Canada, its very name describing what it was to the men who then saw it: New Found Land.

The discovery of America was one thing, and it was a momentous thing, of course. But substantial settlement was quite another. And it was this that made all the difference, if these European voyages were not to go the way of the earlier Viking ones: to vanish into the thick mists which all too frequently cloaked the north-east American coast, leaving only clues, before a definite rediscovery by archaeologists. The century after Columbus and Cabot – the sixteenth – was a time of further exploration, as well as of a number of tentative, often unsuccessful attempts to colonise this astonishing new territory which (as it soon became apparent) was not Asia at all but an entire, hitherto unsuspected continent: a place both 'vast and unmeasured'.[3]

While the Iberian nations – Spain and Portugal – did become established in Central and South America, causing grievous suffering both through deliberate violence and the unwitting bequest of infections against which the American natives had no resistance, the much weaker efforts made by England and France further north in the course of the sixteenth century proved less enduring, as well as less immediately fruitful. In places like Roanoke, famously, on the shore of what is now North Carolina, an effort was made in the time of Queen Elizabeth I – the first such that England did make – to establish a colony upon the shores of what were called these 'remote heathen and barbarous lands'.

There, in the course of the 1580s, on the precarious, far-flung edge of a strange and unknown territory, over one hundred men were left, to establish a settlement and build a fort, while they awaited further supplies. But first Sir Francis Drake removed – rescued – most of the desperate group. Then, when relief did arrive for the remaining fifteen, it was found that the colonists had entirely disappeared, with the haunting exception of a single skeleton.

Subsequently a second group of settlers was left, nervous and uncertain, also to await contact from England. But this time (whatever the intentions) the impending Armada, and the subsequent war with Spain, caused significant delays to transatlantic shipping. And by the time that assistance did arrive, these men, women and children had also vanished.

Along with their settlement. While artwork and writing of a high quality does survive from the venture, taken home before disaster struck, the encampment itself had disappeared, like its predecessor, into mysterious oblivion, known simply to history as the 'lost colony'.

Among its members was one young girl, born to parents Ananias and Eleanor, the latter of whom was the daughter of the colony's governor. The baby's name was 'Virginia Dare' – her surname sounding suitably intrepid, her first name given in honour of the colony in which she saw the light. Virginia has the honour of being the first English person to be born in America. But almost certainly she did not survive early childhood: a symbol – apt, perhaps – for a cultural arrival which, while decisive once it was allowed to reach maturity, was in the short term sadly doomed.

Nobody, in 1600, would have thought of America as an English region. The Atlantic world was dominated by the Spanish and Portuguese, and any attempt to join them – even by a colony much further north – required the naval strength to resist their inevitable challenge. In this respect England had indeed grown stronger, more determined, as well as more fiercely anti-Catholic. The numbers of the English population swelled, even if life there, for many, was bleak, and grew bleaker.

Still, people in England persisted – at least once the culmination of the long war with Spain allowed. The failed attempts of the sixteenth century were followed by successes. Although fears persisted that England's small population could ill afford to spare significant numbers of colonists, old laws restricting emigration from England were abolished. A fourteenth-century statute which forbade 'the passage utterly' of any except 'Lords and other Great Men', along with notable merchants and the king's soldiers, 'without the King's special licence', was repealed in 1606.[4]

In the seventeenth century England proved pre-eminent above all other countries involved in this business of settlement. And even though by then King James I had travelled down from Edinburgh to become King of England as well as King of Scotland, though he also ruled over the principality of Wales, and while the brutal colonisation of Ireland had already begun – though he conjured an old, mythological concept of 'Great Britain' – it *was* largely England, rather than Britain, which was responsible for the early peopling of America.

The concept of 'Britain' bore little meaning in reality. The countries of the British Isles were divided, and widely different. They were certainly not a united kingdom. And it was many years later that significant emigration did take place to America from Scotland and Ireland in particular, while colonists from England declined. Other nationalities have also followed, some voluntarily, others – in the obvious case of African slaves – not voluntarily at all, but it was England which in the seventeenth century was the pioneer of mass migration.[5]

It is difficult to be precise about overall numbers, when nobody counted. Not until late in the nineteenth century was any careful attempt made to monitor those who went.

It was always the case that authorities in the place of destination were more interested in arrivals than the country of origin was in departures. And eastern America was pretty remote from England, even given that the 'plantations' there were not at the time considered 'foreign' territory but part of an English 'empire'. There were certainly plenty of people whom the English government much preferred were in America than causing trouble at home in England. (The 'offals' of our people, they were called.) In any case, there were certainly no immigration checks in the seventeenth century.

Almost 380,000 people are thought to have sailed west from England across the Atlantic to America during the seventeenth century. Perhaps 200,000 of these went to the Caribbean, leaving the rest to begin a new life in the North American colonies. From a total population that was only about five and a half million, it was a colossal number, especially given that as many people also travelled the shorter distance to Ireland, where English colonialism began and substantially dwarfed the flow to America during the first decades of the century. Twice as many emigrated from England as from Spain – the next biggest European exporter of people – over the same period. The number of emigrants was *forty* times that of another maritime Atlantic power (and one with a much larger population): France.[6]

The massive emigration which then took place from England to Ireland and to America was labelled the 'swarming of the English' – an allusion to the image of bees in a hive which was commonly used in discussions of population. In particular, in less than fifteen years, from the late 1620s to the early 1640s, some 80,000 English left their homeland, almost 60,000 of them to cross the Atlantic: more than the number of Spaniards who had done so during the entire previous century. Emigrant numbers from England, moreover, were higher in the seventeenth century than they were in the eighteenth, a time when the overall population was larger. Today the number of their descendants, of course, is vastly bigger still. In one census conducted over thirty years ago at least forty million citizens in the US claimed ancestry from an English migrant. Very many more are in Canada. Historians, bowled over by the sheer magnitude of the events, have talked in awe of what was unquestionably a 'huge flow of people'.[7]

With them – much more significant in the long run than the hoes, the shovels, the animals, than any of the heavy, ornate, dark-wood chests crammed with personal possessions that were stowed in the hold – the seventeenth-century emigrants brought to America the English language, English law and English culture. And there they have remained predominant ever since, in spite of particular tensions during and after the struggle for American independence: the differences from those of England being more apparent precisely because of the very significant similarity. It has been noted that, almost uniquely, English emigrants did not have to worry about fitting into a different linguistic environment – that they wrestled far less than did other emigrants with the problems of identity which often were (and are) felt by the expatriate. They moved, very largely, within a world that spoke English.

The great nineteenth-century German politician Otto von Bismarck was asked what he thought was the pre-eminent fact in modern world history. Many might hesitate when faced with a question like this, but Bismarck answered emphatically. It was, he said, that America – by which he meant the United States of America – spoke English. Few, after the events of the century that followed his own, would be inclined to disagree. And Winston Churchill, for one, said that he had often cited Bismarck's comment with approval. It assuredly isn't because of England now that English has become the global *lingua franca* that it has, used by some billion people worldwide.

Perhaps indirectly, though, this *is* England's legacy: the long-term impact of those countless thousands of seventeenth-century English emigrants, as well as of the many more who followed during the years afterwards. It is more than suggestive that some words which now seem distinctively American – like 'fall', for instance, referring to the season of autumn – were in fact commonly used in seventeenth-century England. While subsequently they fell into disuse in the mother country, in America they continued to form part of daily speech. Sometimes American English is more English, historically, than English.[8]

What did those who set out from England during the seventeenth century expect to find in northern America? Things changed a good deal, of course, as the century went on. Times were much harder, the settlements much more fragile and tenuous, early in the century than they were during its second half, by when it was clear to friend and foe alike that these colonies were here to stay.

For anyone considering emigration from England, the availability of informed material increased very significantly. Those who had had nothing to go on apart from the dubious, untrustworthy reassurances of company propaganda or of emigration agents had access later to a wide pool of general knowledge, which filtered into the public domain even for people who could not read.

Expectation was one thing, and reality another. But it is doubtful whether it was ever quite true that settlers encountered what the early Puritan leader William Bradford had called in New England a 'hideous and desolate wilderness'. He was in a position to know, of course, but his description is not wholly plausible all the same. The coastal region in which he arrived had been much exploited by Native American communities, even when many had recently perished as a result of European diseases. Land had been cleared. Crops had been grown. The 'Pilgrims' stepped ashore on a hillside from which trees had been methodically removed, on which they were able almost immediately to plant peas, corn, barley and wheat. The few Native American survivors seem even – after earlier encounters – to have spoken a little English. Some English men and women did learn local languages, but many others found it a difficult, thankless task, and even those like William Penn who subsequently made a genuine effort seem to have abandoned the attempt.

Experience of the American coast as it was then was all relative, though. For the early arrivals the land no doubt did seem vast, thickly forested and relatively untamed in comparison with England, much more 'full of wild beasts' than the homeland had been, and certainly more full of 'wild [aboriginal] men': an entirely new phenomenon, even if there were significantly fewer of these men than there had been. The Chesapeake Bay region was, just like that of New England, comparatively wild for the English men and women who arrived there for many decades after their first appearance, even as the small English settlements gradually became a little less vulnerable. By mid-century, though, both Virginia – and America in general – did seem that 'brave and ample theatre', where land and opportunity were in abundance, of which some enthusiasts spoke.[9]

The fact, however, that plenty of emigrants, having failed for one reason or another to depart from England in favour of one settlement, then left again for another that was quite different, does suggest that only rarely was the precise nature of the destination the compelling factor. Most, in truth, were simply anxious to leave England. The *push*, generally, was more significant in their decision than the *pull*. The mere possibility of improvement was enough.

Certainly the premise of this book is precisely that, while a great deal has been written (especially – a fact which is scarcely surprising – by scholars in America) about what became of early American colonists *after they arrived*, along with a great deal about the fate of these settlers *in aggregate*, about what became of the early colonies, much less has been produced for the general reader about the reasons which prompted people to undertake such an extraordinary relocation in the first place. Because extraordinary is, without question, what it was.

To emigrate across the Atlantic is not a decision that would be undertaken lightly even today, at a time when the journey holds few terrors, when return is relatively straightforward, when constant communication with family or friends – along with repeated visits in either direction – is easy; and when more is known now about life in the US or in Canada than was known then about life in a neighbouring county. In the seventeenth century the decision was life-changing. Whether or not it was intended as a final move, final it was known that it could be, and final of course it very often was.

Many of those whose stories are told in the pages ahead – the poor, desperate adolescent Richard Frethorne, whose parents did not live to read the letters that he sent home, or Anne Bradstreet, who solved that problem by leaving the country along with her husband and her parents – never did return to the land of their birth. Many, even if they survived to live for some years in America, did not expect ever to see England again.

Aware as they were of the risks, their departure was often accompanied by an emotional farewell to a land, to everything and to everyone that emigrants had known: by the decision – as one emigrant wrote emotionally to his father from 'aboard a ship at Gravesend' – to 'bid adieu to the old world, or shake hands with my native soil forever'.[10]

The purpose of this book is to explore some of these emigrants' motives in going – to look at some of the major reasons for leaving England, and to explore the stories of certain individuals which illustrate these reasons. It is true, of course, that everyone's motives were slightly different, but that doesn't make pointless the attempt to group them, and to generalise.

Today, many people in England know about the role that was played early in the seventeenth century by religion. They have heard about the Puritans, have heard about the 'Pilgrim Fathers', sailing, in a remote time, on board a ship called the *Mayflower*. They know that these people were looking for somewhere to practise their strict, austere, whitewashed religion, which was persecuted in England. They have heard John Winthrop's phrase 'a city on a hill', used to describe the manner in which many in his homeland would watch the fate of Boston – the settlement in New England as opposed to the Lincolnshire port – in order to see how its residents' assumption of divine favour would play out in the world.

Often, though, religion was not the reason which prompted English men, women and children to emigrate. Or at least it wasn't the principal reason. Some went to fish – astonished by this teeming resource in the western Atlantic, at a time when European stocks were much depleted, thinking that while many crossed and re-crossed the ocean to do so, there might be a benefit in staying to live. This at least was what some fishermen and propagandists like Richard Whitbourne – himself an early emigrant to Newfoundland – fervently believed. Many, by contrast, went to America in search of more instant wealth, consumed by what one man called the 'sweet scent of riches and gain', at the expense of 'justice and equity', haunted by the same lustful idea that led the explorer Martin Frobisher and his crew to dig up tons of worthless rock in the cold of the north because it glistened like gold.

Numerous colonists in Virginia neglected basic agriculture in favour of this delusionary quest, frustrating those who would have them work to provide sustenance for the settlement. They left England, it was complained, purely 'for gain's sake', while company men in London who were anxious to encourage emigration did little to suppress this dream. In his 'Ode to the Virginian Voyage' one official poet hailed the attempt 'to get the pearl and gold, / And ours to hold / Virginia, / Earth's only paradise!'[11] Preachers, on the other hand, were unconvinced, railing against the same tendency: against what they saw as the 'excessive covetousness of some'. Later in the century one man criticised those he called 'juggling parasites whose tottering fortunes have been repaired and supported at the public charge'. Many of those who left England for this reason, of course, did not plan a permanent emigration. They viewed America 'not as a place of habitation but only of a short sojourning'. What they envisaged was a smash-and-grab – 'a present crop' – followed, soon enough, by 'their hasty return'.

Often, though, reality refused to comply, and no 'hasty return' was ever possible. As far as the colony as a whole was concerned, great reserves of gold or other precious metals never were found, but the dream was replaced by another which was condemned by many as being similarly empty, or indeed even more so. Bullion, then, was seen as true wealth.

What, by contrast, could be more profligate or more pointless than money spent on smoke: the very definition of something that was short-lived, that formed in the air then quickly vanished? But tobacco, as it turned out, was a genuinely prized commodity, which did, for all the health problems familiar to a later age, provide succour and support to the colony and allow it to do what was envisaged in earlier plans, to 'take fast hold and root in that land'.[12]

Many colonists certainly did leave England for the sake of a Puritan-ical religion which found little support at home, expecting to be able to practise it freely, away from a country that seemed doomed by its hostility and by its wrongful, satanic forms of worship. And this was particularly true of those who travelled to New England: who were not, admittedly, anything like as numerous as those who went to Virginia, but who were a very sizeable number all the same. A great number of such Puritans did emigrate in the course of the 1630s, when a sort of intense fever struck and emigrants persuaded each other to go. No period better illustrates the importance of such contagion, when thousands upon thousands of like-minded people took ship from England every year – a *hegira*, as the wave has been called, in suitably religious (if not suitably Christian) terminology.

Others, meanwhile, felt obliged to leave the country less because of religion than because of the appalling, mundane chaos into which it descended in the course of the 1640s, even if such chaos did seem to bespeak a land which God had abandoned. While many Puritans felt impelled by the disorder to return, to fight for what seemed a holy cause, before long Royalists who could not abide the defeat, and execution, of the king, or indeed the decade of Republican rule which came afterwards, left the country. Some exited, then returned. Others emigrated for good.

Some were drawn to America not out of a lust for precious metals but the hope, nevertheless, that valuable commodities which had become very hard, or even impossible, to obtain in the wild in England would prove much easier to secure on the other side of the Atlantic. Wood and land were both commodities in short supply in Europe but abundant, almost limitless, in America. Fur was another, and the fur of one animal – the beaver – in particular. Many years earlier it had been hunted to extinction in Europe, but its pelt proved a material much coveted for its unique waterproof qualities, especially once the unpredictable dictates of fashion rendered the 'beaver hat' a sought-after accessory.

Some emigrated to America, in the course first of the Republic and then of the restored king, Charles II, because of the freedom that they could find there to practise their own religion, as the Puritans of the 1630s had done, but with a fundamental difference which has influenced American thinking ever since: because, unlike the Puritans, a man like William Penn believed in extending this freedom to all men, as a matter of principle. He wished not to impose any faith, but thought that conscience should be a purely personal matter, left to the individual. This is a distinctively modern idea. While it is found among some during the latter half of the seventeenth century, it was rare indeed during its first half, and even those with clear ideas that the established thinking was wrong were unlikely to argue that no one could know with certainty and therefore that none could dictate what others were to believe.

In spite of all these reasons for emigrating, there is little doubt that the majority who went from England to America during the seventeenth century did so for none of them. They were, as it was said of one ship-load, 'mostly miserable poor people'. They went simply because they were desperate, and because this was a course, perhaps the only course, which offered some hope. England, then, was a dreadfully difficult place in which to scratch a living. Its rising population – what one Londoner called the 'late unspeakable increases of people' – at a time when the economy was stagnant, only made it more so. Increasingly, the majority of opinion (certainly of published opinion) backed a 'diminution of the people', by transplanting 'no small number of them' into 'some other soil'.

People were driven to emigrate both because of their dire state, and also, of course, because emigration was possible, even relatively straight-forward. Ships crossed the Atlantic in increasing numbers, with space in the hold for passengers. And the device of the indenture allowed poor men, women and children to have their ocean passage paid for them by others, in return for a guaranteed period of labour. Among the plantation-owners already in America, it was labour that was urgently required. Servants, it was said, were how wealth was assessed: the more one had, the richer one was. It was the demand for this – for cheap, physical, manual work – that helped to ensure that a great many of those who went were teenage boys, who could be indentured for longer than could men in their twenties, with the potential for longer spans of effort.[13]

Nevertheless, those who did leave England were not in fact the most desperate. Because such a decision to relocate without any likely return, to undertake a long voyage, with all the uncertainty that accompanied it regarding a subsequent new life, did require gumption, did require a certain energy, did require a certain lively, youthful disposition. Those it marked out were, as was said, among the country's more 'vivid people'. The move perhaps did ensure, as one New England colonist declared with a somewhat pious, self-congratulatory air, that 'choice grain' was sent 'into this wilderness' – not, as the phrase intended, in any religious sense, but in terms purely of a determination to improve one's lot.

A few, of course, were pulled back by an affection for their native soil which might not have been logical in the circumstances – for what, after all, did most of these people owe to England? But it was the sort of instinctive comfort, as one early proponent of emigration put it, which was felt by 'a snail for his shell', the security of the known – even when what was known was a devil.[14]

Certainly it is impossible to reduce the reasons for the large-scale emigration from England to a single factor. Historians have tried. But they have largely abandoned the attempt. They agree that, in general, looking at the history of English migration, multiple factors were at play, different in different cases.

What certainly was paramount, though, was both the desire to move and the *possibility* of moving. There needed to be ships sailing to America. Emigration was always more likely from London or from Bristol than it was from Switzerland. It was immensely important, naturally, that no part of England is far from the coast. But this alone is not enough. For why were rates of emigration so much higher in England than they were, for example, in maritime France? Besides ships, there needed to be ship-owners, or ship captains, looking to fill holds which were in need of (preferably lucrative) ballast. There needed to be affluent men – either in England or in America – who were willing to fund the move.

To separate motives here is not to suggest that those of a large group were ever entirely one-dimensional, even though at times one factor could dominate the thinking of a particular individual or group of individuals. It is simply a way of illustrating some of the powerful factors which were at play.

What is also true is that the emigration of often very ordinary people from England altered the complexion of global politics in a way that still fundamentally shapes events today. The fact that so many left England to seek a new life in North America has defined our world ever since.

The United States of America, as it has long been known, is predominantly English-speaking – predominantly Anglophone, and predominantly Anglophile, with profound cultural as well as linguistic ties to its 'mother country'. The 'special relationship', however much more it means to those in our small island, haunted by delusions based upon former grandeur, than it does in America, has genuinely been of massive importance. And this, the *Englishness* of America, as opposed to purely its language, is, just as Bismarck noted, perhaps the single most important factor in modern life.

# I

# FISH

In the north Atlantic the wind and weather were rough. Supplies dwindled. And as they did so the crew members on board the small ship – small even by the standards of the late fifteenth century – grew increasingly restive and short-tempered.

Once already the captain, a Venetian whose name was anglicised to John Cabot, had led a voyage west from England which had had to be abandoned mid-ocean as the result both of bad weather and of a doubtful, hungry, grumbling crew. Cabot was a mild man, of 'a gentle disposition', not the sort to confront a restive (albeit subordinate) crowd. He must have feared now that the same outcome seemed likely.

Suddenly, however, there were shouts of excitement, as signs were noticed that the deep ocean floor had reared up, that the water had become much shallower as they moved over what was later called 'some vein of mountains within the sea'. After weeks unaccompanied by birdlife, gulls now circled and called overhead, a sure indication of land nearby. And men saw and heard – what the gulls saw and heard – the sporadic splash, as silvery fins broke the surface, drops of water glistening, airborne, in the sunlight. Here (what they could not have known), warm water flowing northward collided with cold water travelling in the other direction, above an underwater mountain range known as the 'Banks' which extended for hundreds of miles both north to south and east to west, creating an extraordinarily fertile haven for aquatic life. The crew demanded a chance to pause and to lower the sails. To drift, and to fish.

Cabot, his English inflected with a strong Mediterranean accent, was now more obsessed than ever with pushing onward. His mind was consumed with what to him were 'greater things' than seafood – with a passage to the east of the world, via the west. A passage of which he had dreamt for so long. This, he thought, would lead English sailors for the first time to markets of astonishing wealth, to a place where, he felt sure, 'all the spices of the world, as well as the jewels, are found'. If land was now close, as the seabirds indicated that it must be, then this, surely, was Asia, closer to England (just as Cabot had predicted) than to other, more southerly European rivals. And nearer if one sailed west from Europe than if one sailed east, round the southern tip of Africa and India.

Incalculable wealth – and vast rewards – awaited. And Cabot was a man who, for all his reputation as one of Europe's leading sailors, for all his useful contacts in the Italian banking and religious communities of London, was poor, and in flight from creditors. Still, he did not risk overruling his crew, and he allowed them the chance briefly to drop fishing lines from the decks. Not only were they hungry. Many of them were also sailors from Bristol who had taken part in earlier fishing voyages which had set out from this western English port, heading past Ireland and into the Atlantic. As a result these men were intensely aware what a rich catch here would mean. And when they were permitted to fish, they were more astonished than they had dared to hope. Huge codfish pulled at the lines as soon as they were cast. The number, and the sheer size, of the fish that were landed were hard to believe. Great flanks writhed and flipped on the deck, lidless eyes grew more bulbous, as the creatures slowly suffocated. It was a huge and easy haul.

Onward, a little further to the west, they did come across land which emerged from the mist – new land, New Found Land, just as the presence of seabirds had suggested that they might. This was the first sight that Englishmen had of a new continent which soon was to become known in Europe as 'America'. Steep, tree-clad hills, quite unknown to the English, unmarked on their maps, reared up from the water. And Cabot, just like Christopher Columbus before him, further south, assumed that this, far from being an unknown continent, was Asia – that this was the land, as he put it, of 'the Great Khan'. Through him, one diplomat wrote home on his return, the English king had 'acquired a part of Asia without drawing his sword'.

Cabot and his men followed the coast south for hundreds of miles. They looked for the great island of Japan, fabled for its wealth, and for other thickly populated centres of Asian civilisation. But when, reluctantly, he ordered that they turn back, they had seen no one. What they had noticed, however, when they landed briefly, were trees whose bark had been 'notched', along with snares to catch game, as well as a needle which had evidently been used for making nets. So they assumed, rightly enough, that this land did have human inhabitants.

This, insofar as Cabot was concerned, was the exciting news with which the ship turned and sailed back to England. He had found a 'new isle'. A vast one. Stretching hundreds of miles across the Atlantic. And soon, for certain, he would discover other, yet richer lands. But for many of the crew it was not the territory but the creatures which lived in the water that were the truly exciting discovery, and it was with accounts of these that they regaled their listeners.

'They affirm', said those to whom they spoke, 'that the sea is full of fish, which are not only taken with a net, but also with a basket.' The basket was simply weighted down, 'a stone being fastened to it in order to keep it in the water'. 'They took so many fish', they promised, breathlessly, that 'this kingdom will not longer have need of Iceland' – the northern island whose offshore waters were currently the dominant location for fishing.

For all that the English flag, along with the arms of the country's king – Henry VII – were thrust then into American soil, in fact England, 'this kingdom', was slow to exploit its discovery.

Instead, for many years, the rich fishing grounds were harvested by other vessels, manned by other sailors, from elsewhere in Europe. Unlike his father, Henry's son, Henry VIII (who became king in 1509) had little interest in exploration. He 'cared little', it was said, for 'such an enterprise', much preferring to jostle with rivals on the thrones of Europe. He had no use for a new world which wasn't going to enrich him instantly, when there was an old one – large enough even for him – in which to domineer.

Henry VIII was an imperious, assertive personality, and this was a mentality which infected those beneath him. In Newfoundland the English initially took only a small piece of 'the manifold gain which the French, Bretons, Basques, and Biscayans do yearly return'. To the Portuguese also, meanwhile, this quickly became famous, and much visited: *terra do bacalhau* – the land of the codfish. By 1580 one Elizabethan writer estimated that the annual French fleet to Newfoundland consisted of as many as 500 ships, a number which dwarfed the English total.[1]

The pattern of settlement, the weight of tradition, as well as the habits of fish themselves, dictated that England's *eastern* coast, historically, had been a more significant resource than the waters to its west. And here, even so, it was fishermen from elsewhere in Europe who had tended to be pre-eminent. Each year the 'silver darlings' – 'herrings', as they are generally called now – followed the eastern coastline southward. Thousands upon thousands of them flitted in a vast, glittering, shimmering mass, close to the surface, drawn instinctively to spawn in the shallower water which sat on the North Sea shelf.

As they moved they were tracked and pursued by hundreds of small boats which drifted after them with the current, their nets spread wide in the water. For centuries, this was an annual event in medieval and early modern England. At 'Bartholomew tide', late in August, the fish clouded the water off the coast of Yorkshire, opposite Scarborough. Six weeks later, by the festival of 'Hollantide Eve', old Halloween, when groups of children chanted and battered doors in the dark by the flickering light of lanterns carved from turnips, the 'darlings' swam in large numbers near the mouth of the Thames. In east-coast towns like Yarmouth, huge 'fish fairs' which lasted for over a month were held each year in the autumn.

'He that will buy herring', noted one English merchant manual in the fifteenth century, 'may go into the east part of England, for there', it said, the fish could be bought 'in most plenty'. Go to Scarborough, or Yarmouth, it urged, or to 'other diverse towns in Norfolk and Suffolk'. In Yarmouth, for instance, from the end of September until the middle of November, the old medieval marketplace resounded during the shortening autumnal days with shouts and hubbub, and smelt strongly of fish, while the herring swam nearby. For the counties on this side of England the sea was a defining fact of life: the 'nigh and necessary neighbour on the east'.

Still, it was not the English who dominated this water. While the fair at Yarmouth was overseen by the Cinque Ports, and while tiny houses used by sailors and fishermen clustered by the port-side, most of the merchants who visited them and who lodged with local families for the duration of the fair were not Englishmen but foreigners. Before the rise of the Dutch, it was the Hanseatic merchants of the northern German cities who were pre-eminent in the North Sea region. It is telling that on one sixteenth-century map of Europe this body of water was marked not as the 'North Sea', but as the 'Oceanus Germanicus'.

One English writer who lived nearby, meanwhile, remarked on the 'great numbers of the fishermen of France, Flanders and of Holland, Zealand and all the low countries' who visited Yarmouth late each year, drawn by the 'taking, selling and buying of herrings'. And another man brought up in the region, in the Suffolk coastal town of Southwold, who had lived as 'a fisherman's son by the seashore', and who recalled a childhood devoted to what he called 'fisher affairs' (remarking that he knew much more about 'nets, lines and hooks' than he ever did about rhetoric, logic or learned books), remembered watching as Dutchmen sailed into Yarmouth from the waters close by, their boats laden with barrel-loads of herring.

He was reminded, he said, of the taunts that they yelled at local Englishmen as they sailed home afterwards with English gold. They would be only too glad, they shouted, to sell them their new shoes, when they had worn out and were second-hand. This domination of sea-fishing by outsiders was, the writer considered, a disaster for the English. England abounded in natural resources. In fish that swam off the coast. And in coves, and harbours. He urged his countrymen to back what he regarded as an invaluable national industry.[2]

Nor was he the only one. For decades many had bemoaned the fact that England seemed to be languishing as a sea power. And in an age when fishing vessels, and the men used to sailing them, were routinely pressed into naval service as occasion demanded, this was a concern not simply of economics but one of national defence. Among the fishing boats that he saw, one merchant wrote regretfully, there was 'never an English mariner': a 'wonderful discommodity', he added, 'to this realm'. Late in the reign of Henry VIII an Act for the Maintenance of the Navy had similarly lamented the decline of English shipping, the impoverishment of those who depended upon it and the 'ruin and decay' which affected those 'towns, villages and habitations near adjoining unto the sea coasts'. The fishing industry was, it was often pointed out, a 'nursery of seamen'. And as such it needed to be protected.[3]

*

Gradually, though, a shift did take place – a shift which proved hugely important not only for England's economy, but for the country's role in north America.

Anthony Parkhurst was typical. He began life in the east of the country. He spent his childhood in a village nestled in the downland of Kent, not far from Folkestone. He was funny and self-confident. While working as a junior diplomat in Spain he impressed his superiors sufficiently to secure a place on the long English slaving voyage which sailed in the autumn of 1564 first to Africa, before crossing the Atlantic to America, pressing hundreds of slaves on board a ship named in honour of the figure at the heart of the Christian religion, to sell them in the Spanish colonies. Afterwards Parkhurst and the other English crew moved north, to anchor off the small French settlement in Florida. Then they drifted slowly further north, beset by unfavourable (indeed barely discernible) winds.

As the surface of the water gently rumpled and rolled, waves did not break against the wooden hull or send spray across the deck. Men who were used to the rapid lift and heave of the planks beneath their feet felt strangely disorientated by their stillness. Barely a breath of wind disturbed the full expanse of sails, which hung unfilled. As food supplies dwindled, for a month the ship was pinned to the western flank of the Atlantic. The crew began to despair that they, just like the slaves they had not deigned to consider, were destined never to see homes or relatives again. All were in, it was said, a state of 'great misery'. In desperation, they collapsed on the deck in 'fervent' prayer. And God, it was later reported, heeded their call.

He sent a 'prosperous wind', which blew them north, far up the American coast, to the Banks. Here the ship's crew saw other European boats fishing. (The secret of the area's marine abundance, discovered seventy-odd years earlier by John Cabot, was now out.)[4] And they heard, and watched, the gulls overhead – birds familiar enough to the men of northern Europe, unlike those further south – circling and crying and suddenly diving as men tossed entrails into the water, the 'offals and garbage of fish' left 'floating upon the sea'. When the wind dropped once more the men on board, increasingly desperate for food, took the opportunity to fish likewise, as they had seen others do.

Just like the men on board Cabot's boat decades earlier, they were astonished by the number and the sheer size of the huge fish that pulled at lines as soon as they were cast. The easy haul, as the crew later admitted, 'greatly relieved us'. And later, on their way homeward, they obtained more from two French ships which had also been fishing over the Banks: 'so much fish', they remembered, 'as would serve us plentifully for all the rest of the way'.

It was an experience which made a very lasting impression on Parkhurst. When the crew returned to Padstow on the north coast of Cornwall, their vessel was loaded with all sorts of riches: with 'gold, silver, pearls and other jewels', all in 'great store', fulfilling the greediest hopes of the expedition's investors. They may also have brought from the 'New World' the first sample of tobacco to reach European shores. But none of these excited Parkhurst's fervour in comparison with the glint and sparkle of sunlight on thousands upon thousands of silver fins and flanks flitting through the water as the gull flocks wheeled overhead.

On his return to England he embraced the life of an adventurer and an explorer, realising what riches were to be had by the English if they would only venture out into the wider world. He was determined to exploit the seas off the cooler extremity of northern America which, just as Cabot had long ago reported, 'swarmed with fish'. This resource – relatively untapped by the English – seemed a gift from a beneficent God.

Parkhurst fell out with his father, who perhaps imagined his son plugging away at something less uncertain. He bought himself a ship. And he moved west, away from the more densely populated southeast corner of the country to Bristol, where he decided to work as a merchant.

A decade later, in four successive years between 1575 and 1578, Parkhurst used his ship to catch fish in the same waters off Newfoundland that had so amazed him as a young man. And while most ship-owners sent others to do the actual business of gathering resources and trading for them, he, rather unusually, travelled himself. When he did sail back, furthermore, to the coast of northern America, he took the opportunity to explore what was to him (as it was to most of his countrymen) an entirely new landscape.

Many of the European fishermen who visited the Banks during the sixteenth century used salt to preserve fish 'wet' in their hold prior to returning directly home – never setting foot, in other words, on American soil. The English, though, did not possess the same natural deposits of salt as were cheaply obtained further south. And as a result they were more prone, like other northern nations, to preserve fish by salting it only lightly before stacking it on wooden 'flakes', or racks, to dry in the cool wind and the sunshine. This meant coming on shore. It meant spending time, in other words, in America.

As a result, Parkhurst found himself for long summer weeks, in the latter half of the 1570s, on Newfoundland. The south-east corner of the island, which the English then explored, was largely uninhabited by people. Firs clung to the granite hillside, dank and grey in the fogs which all too frequently cloaked the shoreline, well watered by the regular rainfall. Inquisitive bears learnt to resist their curiosity (and the tempting whiff of seafood) as muskets were fired in their direction. And for days, as a result, Parkhurst was able to roam far, accompanied only by his dog, exploring Newfoundland's coasts, its woods and its hills. He searched 'the harbours, creeks and havens and also the land', he said, 'much more than ever any Englishman hath done' (though there was not, it is true, a great deal of competition). This was some thirty years before the English established Jamestown.

He fashioned a primitive fish spear, banging and straightening metal hooks and attaching them to the end of a long wooden pole. And he found that in half a day, paddling in the cold, shallow coastal water, he could kill enough lobsters to feed 300 men. The fish he caught he piled up in great flapping heaps on the shore, and if one started to wriggle its way slowly back towards the water he had trained his dog to pick it up and bring it back. Some of the edible aquatic life – the crabs, for instance – came themselves, unsuspectingly, and could simply be swept with Parkhurst's broom into a pile while his canine friend watched attentively, learning, no doubt, to avoid the nip of a salty claw on his nose. Parkhurst noted that he didn't even need to get his feet wet. Squid, likewise, he said, fled the shoals of aggressive cod further out and were 'driven dry by the surge of the sea on the pebble and sands', where they could be scooped up like wheat in a shovel.

Parkhurst had a wry sense of humour. He told interested questioners with a straight face that on his travels he had seen mussels and oysters which grew on the branches of trees – only confessing afterwards, in response to looks marked by scepticism as well as wonder, that while he was not technically lying, these were boughs which hung low, in the sea. And he teased his old friends, and those who sailed with him, by assuring them that he knew how to cast spells upon the sea-life, which then obeyed his commands to come forth from the water provided that the commands were given in the name of England's five (Cinque) ports. 'The virtue of the words', he confessed to the older Richard Hakluyt, a man renowned, like his young nephew, for his interest and expertise in geography and trade, was small, while the nature of the fish themselves, to a European, was genuinely 'great and strange' – though creatures of the North Atlantic were, in fact, a good deal more familiar than those encountered by European nationals much further south, in the Caribbean for instance.

As it happens, the English *were* just beginning, belatedly, to appreciate the region's potential, long after Cabot and his men had pointed it out to them. Only now, in the late sixteenth century, were techniques and knowledge both of boat-building and of navigation, beginning significantly to improve. During the short period that he was going there, Parkhurst noted that the number of English fishing boats crossing the Atlantic to Newfoundland increased substantially. 'Thanked be God', he declared, the trade of fishing in the course of the last five years had been 'well amended'. While there was annual variety, on average each year's fleet had grown more than tenfold, from 'four sail of small barks' to forty, and each of these latter ships was so large that as many fish were packed in one as could fit before in the entire fleet. Which was not to say that there was not room for further improvement: 'our trade of fishing', he wrote, could 'be made twice, yea thrice, as good as yet it is'.

The real increase which had taken place, however, had been brought about primarily by 'western men': by the merchants and fishermen of Cornwall, Devon or Dorset, who were ideally situated among the English to take advantage of this rewarding new region for fishing.

During the sixteenth century a tilt took place, which saw population move not only towards the capital in London but also from the east of the country towards the west. And since his move to Bristol, of course, Parkhurst had become a 'western man' himself.

In the past, western men had tended not to fish full-time. Farmers took to small boats in local waters – during breaks in the agricultural season – to supplement their diet. They dredged river estuaries for shellfish and paid local lords, or local towns, a premium for access to the water and for use of the shoreline. But they were not full-time mariners. The region's population was relatively small. And communities lay low, concealed by hills where they were not visible from the sea, sheltering from the threat posed by armed ships full of marauding foreigners.

As migration increased, life in the south-west began to change. In a prelude to what happened in Newfoundland, small congregations of men who stayed here to fish by the coast for the season solidified into permanent villages and towns defined by the marine activity which had guided their inception. As herring ceased to be the staple it had long been – a fact which had favoured the east coast, on the North Sea, where that fish tended to congregate – archaeological remains confirm a dramatic growth in the diversity of fish eaten in the west, and an end to reliance on herring imported from the east. Along the coasts of Devon and Cornwall, masons and carpenters worked as new quays and jetties were erected. And men built special cellars or houses, known later, with appropriate reverence, as 'fish palaces', in which they cured local fish.[5]

Not many in the west, initially, could afford the larger boats, or the longer timespans, needed to exploit distant fishing grounds like those near to America. But they went to the coast of Ireland. And a few did remember great voyages launched from this part of the country – like those led by John Cabot – and spoke in awe of the richness of the western Atlantic. For decades it was largely foreign fishermen who had followed this lead. But the memory remained strong. As did the sense of entitlement to what seemed, initially (and this of course was what was thought to matter), to have been an English discovery.

For most fishermen from the West Country the waters off New-foundland were a spectacularly rich resource, to be harvested prior to sailing back to Europe with their catch, and Parkhurst testified to the growing numbers of men who went. When Sir Walter Raleigh, a western man himself, spoke on the subject in Parliament he referred to the fishing trade in the western Atlantic as vital to his region. He called it, indeed, the 'stay' – the prop – 'of the West countries'.

For Anthony Parkhurst, though, a man who was ahead of his time, moving west within England was merely the beginning. He thought that men (and women too) should keep moving. From the west of England they should sail further in the same direction, towards the setting sun, into the Atlantic. Not simply to fish, but to live. Englishmen, he believed, should colonise this new and seemingly empty land. They should take with them their important possessions, and should stay. As he paced the landscape of Newfoundland he picked up information, whenever he could, about the island and its climate, both by personal observation and from the fishermen of other European nations whom he met there: from the French or the Portuguese, for example, who had been significantly faster than the English to exploit the wealth of these American waters. And what he found, he professed, greatly encouraged him.

On his return to England Parkhurst eulogised about Newfoundland to anyone who would listen. He told of the 'fertility and goodness' of its land as well as of the extraordinary riches in the surrounding water. Cereal crops flourished there, he said (rather untruthfully). Sweet fruits grew naturally. As did trees which were good for firewood and for building boats, two uses which had made the English acutely conscious of their own diminishing timber supplies. And he urged a few eager propagandists to encourage the English to go – not simply to fish and to sail back, but to *emigrate*.

People exaggerated regarding the place's cold climate, he said. It was not, in reality, 'so cold as foolish mariners do say'. They were misled by ice which drifted south, far out at sea. Bergs, he insisted, spoke more of the regions from which they came – of the freezing 'north parts of the world' – than they did of Newfoundland itself. In the summer, Parkhurst said, it was actually rather warmer in Newfoundland than it was in England. And even in winter it wasn't so bad (though it must be admitted that he wrote, very probably, without having remained through the close of the year himself).

*

For almost a century now the presence of land over the great ocean to the west had been known. Men in England had gradually come to recognise that what lay there was neither Asia nor the cluster of islands en route to Asia, as had been assumed. They talked, as the close of the sixteenth century approached, of a 'now supposed continent', of 'vast countries'. Of a land 'described to be bigger than all Europe'. And they exchanged hushed assurances of a previously unsuspected territory whose regions rearing up to the north were even larger than the huge and wealthy expanses explored and claimed by the Spanish in the south.

The geography, though, did remain profoundly uncertain: uncertain for all Europeans and particularly for the English, who had been slower than other Atlantic powers of the old world to ascertain what it was exactly that Columbus and Cabot had found. America, they admitted, was a region 'not yet perfectly discovered'. It was a land of which God had granted them only what was called an 'obscure and misty knowledge' (a well-chosen metaphor for the fog-cloaked coastline of far-northern America). Most of what *was* known they had learnt through the explorations of other Europeans, like the French. The planting of what was truly 'a Christian habitation and regiment' had, it was admitted, yet to be properly attempted.

Englishmen piously observed that when efforts had been made by others in northern America – by the Spanish, for instance, or by the French – their success had been decidedly limited. Even those who might be deemed to be, in God's sight, 'both religious and valiant in arms' (French Protestants, for example) had been dealt an outcome which was, it had to be admitted, 'hard and lamentable'. It seemed plain enough, to English writers at least, that God had 'prescribed limits' – that clearly He had in mind a region which would be settled by England. (He was, by inclination, English, after all.) Only this, surely, could explain why His 'powerful hand' had withstood the attempts made in the north by other nations. He might tolerate – He might even bless – Spanish incursions and control in the Caribbean, or in America to the south: regions which they had been the first from Europe to discover. But He evidently didn't care for them straying north of Florida. And He made His displeasure plain.

As for the dastardly French, they had no just claim. All that they had done was attach Francophone names to 'countries, rivers, bays, capes, or headlands' previously discovered by the English – even if their explorations had been more thorough, and more widespread. No wonder then that God had not permitted them, for all their many attempts, to establish what was to the English 'a possession permanent upon another's right'. It might be impossible for mankind to speculate as to His intent for what was now, it seemed certain, the 'last age of the world'. But this didn't stop observers in England from trying.

It was true that, after her initial flourish under Cabot's guidance, England had participated in fishing on the Banks only tardily and insignificantly by comparison with her European rivals. While the number of English boats had increased belatedly, from the neighbouring countries of Catholic western Europe – from France, Portugal or Spain – they had come, for a long time, from 'all parts'. For Europe in general, and for its Atlantic powers in particular, the ocean adjacent to northern America had become, as one English visitor wrote, 'the most famous fishing of the world'. And whereas before, in the competition for herring in the North Sea, or for cod when men sailed north to Norway or to Iceland (largely, again, from England's east coast), the rivalry had for the most part been with other powers which were, or which became, Protestant, now – after the Reformation – it was with *Catholics*.

How should this confrontation in the New World be interpreted? In England men wondered whether Christianity would spread from south to north in America, just as it had done in Europe – with Catholic religion, first, in the south, before true, Protestant faith washed over it from above. And only then, it was guessed, when all the world had heard the true message of the Gospel, would Christ return, as the Bible had foretold.

Certainly, it is essential to understand the encouragement that was given to the English to expand westward in the context of the deep religious chasm – between Protestant and Catholic Christianity – which had torn open across Europe. The more America's size, and importance, became clear, the more, for religious reasons, it seemed to matter.

One of the men who listened avidly to what Parkhurst had to say was an adventurer by nature and emphatically a 'western man' himself, who typified the shift of maritime activity from the south and eastern coasts of England towards the country's west – as the English began to look in that direction, over the Atlantic, across what no longer seemed a deep, limitless and dangerous ocean and became instead a large body of water which led to America.

Sir Humphrey Gilbert was a seaman and a gentleman from Devon. He was a tall, clever man, with hard eyes and a hard streak. He was always looking for a way in which the English could reach out from their small island to become – what as yet they were not – a major power in the world. The half-brother of Sir Walter Raleigh, he had seen, just as Raleigh had, the impact that fishing in the New World had had upon his part of England.

He dwelt upon Parkhurst's ideas. He thought about the new division which had opened up in Europe between a Catholic south and a Protestant north. He had fought personally against the Spanish in the Netherlands, where England had backed the rebellious Protestants who were attempting to cast off Spanish rule. And what he suggested to his queen was a means by which he thought she could, across the ocean to the west, further 'annoy the King of Spain'. This sort of 'western enterprise' ought to prove, as one of Elizabeth's chief ministers had observed, 'generally beneficial to the whole realm'.[6]

Already the rivalry between Protestant England and Catholic Spain – the rivalry which in a decade would see the great Armada of Spanish ships moving up Europe's west coast to mount what was planned to be a full-blown invasion – had begun to escalate. The days when Spain and England had been allies, when Henry VIII had been married to Catherine of Aragon, seemed distant now. In 1559 the two dominant powers on the Continent, France and Spain, both of them Catholic, had put their own bitter rivalry for a time to one side, as Europe split upon religious lines.

At first Elizabeth, England's queen, was conciliatory, and sought to avoid entrenching the division. Unlike her father, she didn't care much for warfare, which to her seemed costly and unpredictable. But when in 1570 the pope excommunicated her, the rift solidified. And for England serious rivalry was becoming more feasible: a country weak and unruly on her accession was becoming stronger and more confident. And in any case English men and women now had no choice: they had to back their queen, or back the pope. They could not do both.[7] While she didn't naturally warm to warfare, moreover, Elizabeth did like those bold subjects of hers who would undertake privately to harass Spanish fleets, either across the Atlantic or as they returned to Europe.

Sir Humphrey Gilbert was both a dauntless soldier and a man of intellect and ideas. He was described as 'choleric' – bold, intense and impetuous. (His buccaneering personality is clear enough in a motto that he chose for himself: *mutare vel timere sperno*, I scorn to change or to fear.) He said what he thought.[8] He was smart and remorseless: a man who while attempting to quell the rebellious Irish had found that making them approach his tent through an avenue of the decapitated heads of their relatives had helped to concentrate minds, which no doubt it did.

He had a particular interest in the developing sciences of geography and navigation, and in the discovery of unexplored regions of the world. In fact, they obsessed him. He wrote about them, discussed them in private, and was willing to debate them in front of the queen. But he loved action as well as debate, radical and decisive ideas as a basis for similar conduct. Not only did he propose a means of annoying the King of Spain, but he volunteered to do the annoying himself. 'I will do it', he promised, 'if you will allow me.' He had endeared himself quickly to a queen who liked men like him.

To Gilbert, the Spanish king was a principal supporter of the Catholic Antichrist. It made no sense to think of him as a man. He was the puppet of diabolical forces who, as the 'chief maintainer of the Romish religion', was 'wholly addicted' to that agent of the devil, the pope. It was he who had sworn to protect the Catholic Church and all those who followed it – the 'whole troop of Papists' – and whose 'malicious disposition' towards Elizabeth was increasingly plain. With the Spanish, England could not maintain any sort of amity. 'So long as they be of that religion and we of ours', Gilbert wrote, 'there can be between us and them no good friendship.'

It was true that at times realpolitik had dictated otherwise. It was the case, for instance, that states of western Europe had collaborated even with that 'professed and obstinate enemy of Christ', the Turkish sultan. But the King of Spain, nevertheless, was 'an enemy to all others that be not of the same religion'. No Christian prince, Gilbert insisted, should combine with 'such as are at open and professed war with God himself'.

And the best way for England to annoy him, Gilbert suggested, was to strike a blow at Spanish power in the New World – for England to stake clearly its claim to the northern regions of 'America', not simply by trading, but by expelling outsiders. The right strategy, he argued, was for the English to establish *colonies*: permanent outposts for trade and for plunder. Settlers would leave their overcrowded home. And they would fashion a new England across the Atlantic.

While initially foreign navies in Newfoundland would be much larger than the English, it was to be remembered that as soon as these foreign boats arrived they would quickly disperse along the coast, pausing in scattered havens and harbours to fish. Moreover, the broader Spanish Empire in America could wait. Newfoundland, Gilbert felt, was the place to start. 'Let us first do this', he wrote, and 'we will next take the West Indies from Spain', with all their mines and their precious metals.

For ultimately, if God provided the outward motive, and a young but fast-developing nationalism a more underlying one, it was fish, more prosaically, which offered the means and often the true rationale. It was the fish which had induced foreign navies to travel to North America in the first place, where wealth had quickly been found in the water but not yet, as was hoped, in the soil. As the population in Europe grew from the end of the fifteenth century to the middle of the sixteenth, so there was a strong impetus for fishermen to push further into the Atlantic in search of new fishing grounds. While fishermen did not tend to record their explorations, preferring to keep them secret in order to suppress unwanted competition, the boost to a nation's geograph-ical and maritime expertise was paramount. And it was the fish which meant that the great ships, of Spain, of Portugal, or of France, would be scattered and unprotected once they were close by America.

Whatever the outcome in grand geopolitical terms, or the help which it offered in fulfilling a divine plan, an English venture would be worth-while for the simple reason that the fish which abounded in these waters were a highly lucrative product. As its population grew, Europe craved the protein that it provided – often cheaper than alternatives, and free from religious rulings. (The consumption of fish, unlike that of meat, because fish were cold-blooded, was not legislated against by the pope, and was permitted on what had proved a growing number of holy, or 'fish' days.) It was North America's fish which, as Gilbert himself wrote, were 'a principal and rich and everywhere vendible merchandise'. It was the fish which could be sold easily, and sold, when they were, for 'great gain'. And indeed the profit derived from fish would cover the other expenses incurred by an early expedition: the costs of shipping, the food, the munitions and even 'the transporting of five or six thousand soldiers'. The one thing to guard against, Gilbert warned, was uncertainty or hesitation. For it was delay, he argued, which prevented, too often, 'the performance of good things'. The moment should be seized by decisive action. For 'the wings of man's life', he wrote portentously, 'are plumed with the feathers of death'.

Both the queen herself, and those around her, were impressed by Gilbert's argument. He was granted a royal patent, which ran from the Cape of Florida in the south and along the entire eastern flank of northern America. It entitled him to colonise these new regions: to 'inhabit, people and manure the said islands, lands and countries'. He could take with him as many of Her Majesty's subjects as were willing to go, provided only that they weren't fugitives from the law. And he, and fellow leaders, would enjoy complete authority to execute laws of every kind, 'ecclesiastical, temporal, political, martial and civil'.

There was only one stipulation. These laws should not be opposed to the true Christian religion – the true *Protestant* religion – as it was now practised by the Church of England.

Elizabeth's government was attracted, naturally enough, by the prospect of England growing 'great by means of navigation'. And they liked the idea not only of robbing the Spanish at sea but of gaining what was called 'a footing on the coast' in the New World.

The Spanish ambassador was quick to warn his master that this was what was intended. The only way to put a stop to what he called such 'barefaced' impertinence was, he suggested, for captured English crews to be dealt with mercilessly. Not a man should be left alive. All should be thrown into the water – 'sent', as he put it, 'to the bottom'.

Spain, furthermore, was not England's only European competitor with an interest in her plans. Gilbert played his cards close to his chest. He didn't trumpet his intentions. The French ambassador considered him 'a very shrewd man', and reported that he would lead a voyage to American lands in the same latitude as England, just as Newfoundland is. Here, he wrote, 'empires and monarchies may be built up', though probably there was room enough, he thought (as for a good while there was) for the French and the English alike. At home in Devonshire Gilbert prepared to head into the Atlantic: 'ready', as one observer put it, 'to cross sails'.

The elements though, in spite of 'the true Christian faith or religion now professed in the church of England', were not kind. God, it was later written, did not favour the attempt – though this did not provoke any doubts about doctrine. Winds were contrary. And personal animosities and ambitions wrought havoc, with greed driving the venture just as surely as did anti-Catholic feeling. But Gilbert was unchastened – to be chastened was hardly in his personality – and his outraged self-confidence won the day.

Elizabeth put to one side her fears that he was 'of not good hap by sea'. And he secured a new patent for what was called 'so worthy and commendable an enterprise', though he did narrow his focus, concentrating upon the colonising side of his voyage – the 'discovering and habiting' – as opposed to the martial confrontation with Iberian shipping. A stream of Protestant arrivals – *English* Protestant arrivals – would create in America, documents daydreamed, a New England.

Those entitled to substantial land would become a new elite. They would build themselves a house in the province's principal city, besides their large estates outside it. Country parishes, three miles square, would be centred upon a church. And the whole colony would be protected by a navy and by soldiers, who would be equipped with horses (when, it was noted, in a rare concession to realism, 'God shall send sufficient horses in those parts'). And there were incentives to encourage lasting residency. One agreement, composed the year before, referred not only to the added privileges which would be enjoyed by all who wintered there – those who didn't cut and run before the weather grew cold – but also to the need for 'special privileges to encourage women to go on the voyage'. Rival merchants noted that the men, women and children who went to live (as opposed to those who went merely to trade) would be bound to remain there for ten years at least.

And it would, in northern America, it was remarked, be the proceeds of fishing which could initially be relied upon. Preliminary agreements formulated by Gilbert with the Merchant Adventurers of Southampton, who had signed up to take part, mentioned specifically the fish and fishing to be carried out in the area as being exempt from the payment of customs. In the list of 'fishes, goods, bullion, wares or merchandise' which the men might hope to acquire, it was the 'fishes' which came first.

Influential sea captains, close to the government, wrote at length in support of the venture. Trade in America, it was argued, would be sure to increase with time. Proper exploration of the land would naturally take place in due course. But initially it would be the fish in the north which would keep the colony going. Even if at first nothing was to be found but 'the bare fishing', this alone would support an annual visit by at least half a dozen of Her Majesty's finest ships.

And so, on 11 June 1583, Sir Humphrey Gilbert and his men lifted their anchors and raised their sails once again, ready to make for what one poet called Newfoundland's 'plenteous seas and fishful havens'.

When, after a difficult voyage, the continent duly emerged from the 'great haze and fog' which hung, as it often did, upon the coast, the men found English ships as well as about twenty Portuguese and Spanish vessels in the huge bay of St John's – one of the best of what was a series of 'large and excellent bays' – near the southerly tip of the island of Newfoundland.[9]

So many English fishermen now went there that Gilbert and his men had sailed by a regular route which had become known as 'the trade way'. And in St John's it was the English who were routinely now recognised as the 'Admirals' of the harbour: who passed judgement in any dispute among the fleet of fishermen of different European nations which dropped anchor in these waters.

From the English ships as well as from the foreign ones, men rowed promptly over in small boats to learn what it was that Gilbert intended – enquiries which he met by brandishing the patent he had from his queen. The fishermen from England, at least, declared themselves well satisfied. As, of course, they had to. Each ship fired its cannon in welcome, the noise reverberating from the fir- and spruce-clad hills which formed the backdrop to the bay. And the English boats in turn assembled feasts for Gilbert's crew, who were more than happy to be indulged after the seven weeks which comprised what they called their 'tedious passage through the ocean'.

Early in August Sir Humphrey swaggered ashore. Here, on a land where through much of the year only 'wild beasts and birds' made their homes, now, in the summer, the place was busy. And two of the men who watched, and who knew Gilbert as a prominent individual in their own western region of England, believed, already, that their countrymen should seek to create permanent settlements on this island off the shore of America.

One was Anthony Parkhurst, whose wildly enthusiastic conversation about Newfoundland had probably inspired Gilbert to sail here in the first place. The other was also a West Country seaman – a tough and experienced fisherman and captain called Richard Whitbourne, who had learnt to sail using the small boat his father had kept by the Devon shore. He was sufficiently educated to publish books, and later became, like Parkhurst, a leading propagandist for English settlement in Newfoundland, a place, he said, where he had spent longer than anywhere else abroad. Of Gilbert's claim to the territory on behalf of Queen Elizabeth, 'I', Whitbourne wrote later, 'was an eye-witness'.[10]

Both applauded with unfeigned enthusiasm when Gilbert proclaimed English ownership: when he announced what, with hindsight, was the birth of a British Empire, in a cold and unpopulated corner of North America. Here, before Jamestown, before Virginia, the empire which would come to control so much of the earth's surface had its inception. By this means, Gilbert's supporters declared, Christian religion – Protestant religion – was advanced in what were called 'those paganish regions'.

A formal tent was erected, and all present – English and foreign fishermen and shipmasters, Parkhurst and Whitbourne among them – were summoned to watch as Gilbert ceremonially took possession of these lands on behalf of his queen. A rod was invested in him. And a piece of the local turf (a symbol of the ownership of the land) was cut and presented. In a loud voice his royal commission was read out, interpreted for the benefit of anyone who did not understand. Gilbert's right to ordain laws was decreed, while three, he announced, became active immediately: religious worship from now on would be practised according to the laws of the Church of England; Her Majesty's ultimate right to the land was to be honoured and upheld; and any who spoke or wrote against her should not only have his ship and goods confiscated, but should also 'lose his ears'.

Those watching assented, probably feeling both that they didn't have much choice, and that in any case the proclamation was unlikely to mean a great deal in the long run. The arms of England, pre-engraved on lead and then strapped tightly to the end of a wooden pillar, were thrust into the soil nearby. Approximate maps were drawn. And the land here and round about, along what were 'very many goodly bays and harbours', the like of which was not, it was thought, 'to be found in any part of the known world', was parcelled up and allotted, by Gilbert, to his men, and to the Englishmen in general: to Parkhurst and to Whitbourne as well as to many others.

In future, all were told, they would be assured grounds upon which 'to dress and to dry their fish', where the best of these had been claimed in the past by the year's first arrivals. They would need only to pay a small rent to Gilbert, and to make good their claims by a regular, and ideally a permanent presence – maintaining year-round 'possession of the same'. And while it was true that the weather here in winter was tough for the latitude, 'more cold', as one chronicler who was present put it, 'than in countries of Europe, which are under the same elevation', the difficulties, it was felt, should not be overstated.

Certainly it was a climatic discrepancy which, given that New-foundland was not more northerly than England, men struggled to understand. No doubt land on the coast, this chronicler speculated, was subject to the greatest extremes, since presumably the sun's strength was weakened by its long daily passage from east to west over the ocean – the journey across water moderating its heat by 'moist vapours'. It was true that men near the shore in Newfoundland at the close of the year had found very deep snow. But this was 'no marvel'. Parts of Europe, after all, saw the same. Only a short way inland, it was confidently surmised, beyond higher ground which would act as a barrier against extreme weather, things would surely be more tolerable.

In any case, extreme as the cold was, it was hardly worse than in, say, Sweden or Russia – countries which were well populated, and where winter temperatures were simply countered 'by the commodity of stoves, warm clothing, meats and drinks'. These simple resources could easily be made available in Newfoundland. And this defect of cold weather here nature had amply recompensed by the 'incredible quantity' of fish which swam in these parts.

The sense was already strong – a sense which would burgeon with the empire – of a beneficent guiding presence which laid all of creation at the service of mankind, and at the particular service of his chosen people, the English. The 'magnificent God' had filled the earth with all manner of creatures, only a tiny proportion of which were yet used. Men were too lazy. In an England which was overcrowded, which was 'pestered with inhabitants', they lived and died, often 'very miserably'. The fact was bemoaned not only at the end of the sixteenth century but for much of the century which ensued as well. If only, this man wrote, having visited Newfoundland, 'we had intent there to inhabit'.

Gilbert himself was similarly impressed. Before, he said, he hadn't felt sure about these 'north parts of the world'. He had seen them as a worthwhile English possession, where ships could restock, en route to the south. And indeed he had planned to do this himself. But this voyage had transformed his outlook, winning his heart away from the south of the continent. Now, he said, 'his mind was wholly fixed upon the Newfoundland'. Now, he declared confidently, he was 'a northern man altogether'.

Gilbert, though, never had a chance to return. He insisted upon sailing back to England in a smaller boat – in what was termed a 'pinnace' – in which, he said, he had endured 'so many storms and perils'. He felt a loyalty to it. But this time, the boat, named the *Squirrel*, was too heavily laden, with artillery, fishing nets and paraphernalia, as well as other goods – 'too cumbersome for so small a boat that was to pass through the ocean sea at that season of the year'. As had been anticipated, strong storms blew up. The roughness of the open water was 'terrible'. Men who had been sailors all their lives complained that they had never before seen seas more outrageous.

After Gilbert's boat survived one onslaught, witnesses observed him sitting in the stern, calmly reading a book. Subsequently he was heard calling out to the crew on a fellow ship, in what sounds like an acceptance of his fate, that men were just as close to heaven at sea as they were on land. And when the next tempest came the *Squirrel* was duly overwhelmed, the watching crew noticing, with a grim fascination and admiration, that the lights on board suddenly extinguished. Since the general and his men were never found, it was presumed that they had been 'devoured and swallowed up'.

Those who remained on Newfoundland could only hope that 'fruit may grow in time of our travelling into those north-west lands'. Certainly Parkhurst and Whitbourne were two who were, if anything, more determined than ever.

Tensions between Protestant England and Catholic Spain continued to mount. Throughout English society paranoia against Catholics became widespread. The Spanish ambassador in England reported to his king that all Catholic priests had been ordered by Parliament to leave the country within forty days, or be hanged without trial. And at the Spanish court planning was already under way for what was called the 'enterprise' – the invasion of England – which hoped to remove Elizabeth, the 'English Jezebel', and restore true religion to this troubled and troublesome northern island.

England, meanwhile, despatched an armed naval expedition to Newfoundland which seized Portuguese ships in particular (the monarchies of Portugal and Spain now being united) since they tended, more than did the Spanish, to fish in the same bays as the English. Richard Whitbourne recalled the unusual visit of naval vessels to the island – of what he called 'diverse good ships', as opposed to the smaller fishing boats. Many Iberian vessels were then seized. And the combined fleets of Portugal and Spain were deprived of vast quantities of the dried fish on which they relied for provisions.

The Spanish government was obliged by this move to take precautionary action, forbidding their ships from sailing to Newfoundland. And even when they did return, they tried harder to avoid any regions that were frequented by the English. Portuguese fishing in Newfoundland, meanwhile, never did recover. English dominance there in future was guaranteed, while the kidnapped fishing vessels were of course no longer available to join the vast Spanish fleet which was being prepared to sail against England.

Shortly afterwards Richard Whitbourne – still, then, a young man in his twenties – led his own ship as part of the western wing of the English fleet which confronted the vast navy (130 ships) that comprised the Spanish Armada. He saw the distant glint as fires lit on the English cliff-tops sent the alarm rapidly round the east coast and up to the north of the country. And he remembered in the aftermath of this seismic moment, watched anxiously by a divided continent, that he had been commended by England's Admiral of the Fleet for the manner in which he had conducted himself – his contribution recorded in a special book that was kept at Whitehall to honour those many Englishmen who had helped to resist the Spanish.[11]

Whitbourne, like Anthony Parkhurst, was a 'western man', this time by birth rather than simply by inclination. He was the son of a yeoman farmer, and he passed his childhood at Exmouth, on the mouth of the River Exe, on Devon's south coast, within earshot when high winds threw the waters of the Channel into foam. As a boy he watched as men ran, shouted and launched boats into the sea. He probably had an early taste himself of life in the water, by sailing near his home in a small boat owned by his father, delivering agricultural goods, or netting local fish, before he turned full-time, like many others in the region, to the ocean.

From at least his teens he served as an apprentice on board ship. Later he recalled the early travels which had taken him all over Europe and beyond: to France, Spain, Italy, Savoy, Denmark and Norway, to the Canary Islands, as well as to 'Spruceland', as he called Poland, and 'Soris Hands' (the Azores). 'Most of my days', he wrote, had been spent 'in travel, especially in merchandising, and sea-voyages'. In 1579, aged only eighteen, he crossed the Atlantic in pursuit of whales, and of trade with the American natives, even if he complained that some of the company didn't take to the literal hardship involved – to the detriment of the enterprise. They 'loved soft featherbeds', he wrote in bafflement, 'better than hard cabins, and longed rather to sit by a tavern fire, than to have the cold weather blasts of those seas blow on their faces'.

Having spent so long on Newfoundland, Whitbourne claimed he knew the place just as well as he did his homeland. And over this period he had seen the English become dominant in the south-eastern corner of an island which sat, conveniently, midway between England and Virginia. He had fished there, chased whales and brought barrels of train oil – extracted from their blubber – back to Europe. And the more experience he had of it, he said, the more he liked it. To him

Newfoundland seemed a place that his countrymen and countrywomen might inhabit.

He admitted that it wasn't easy 'to persuade people to adventure into strange countries', and particularly not 'to remain and settle themselves there'. But he could only remind his readership what 'infinite riches and advantages' the Spanish and Portuguese had derived from the planta-tions that they had established in America and elsewhere. An orderly English colony in Newfoundland would be, he thought, an 'everlasting good'. It would draw away the poor who, whatever their instinctive reluctance to emigrate, proved 'burdensome' to a home country widely held to 'overflow with people'. And it would be of benefit not merely to certain, maritime regions but even to those counties 'remote from the sea-coast' – not that any counties really were remote, in this 'nation of the sea' where no one lived 'further than 100 miles from the sea-side': 'no great journey'.

In the spring of 1603, early in the new century, Queen Elizabeth died – standing, resolutely, for hours before at last her will gave way and she lay down on the cushions provided for her. It may simply have been age, accompanied by the low spirits which followed the deaths of many who had been close to her (a common enough combination). Or it may have been the lead which was a key ingredient in the white make-up that she plastered habitually onto her face. We cannot know.

Either way, she submitted calmly in the end, 'like a lamb', and in a variety of ways her demise signalled the passing of an era, not least in terms of the long-running war between Protestant ('Anglican') England and Catholic Spain. Immediately James, the Stuart successor whom Elizabeth had never named directly, sued for peace with Spain. And the following year a settlement was signed.

Letters of commission to privateers were cancelled. Countless sea captains who had profited from robbing the Spanish in the name of their country and of true religion found themselves suddenly kicking their heels and looking for employment. Money which had been eagerly invested in the quick returns offered by privateering became available for other causes. English fishermen could now sell dried cod at much lower risk in the Mediterranean markets where demand was strongest.

Over the subsequent decade, as a result, the number of Englishmen sailing across the Atlantic to Newfoundland – to waters which were, as Whitbourne wrote, 'so rich' – grew. In 1615, when he was tasked by the High Court of Admiralty with looking into abuses alleged against the English fishermen there, he estimated that there were now, annually, around 250 English ships in those seas.[12] Averaging out their size, he guessed they carried a total of about 5,000 persons. And this took no account of dependants: of the servants of ship-owners and masters, or the families of mariners. Then one had to remember also those who were employed by the industry remotely: the 'bakers, brewers, coopers, ship-carpenters, smiths, net-makers, rope-makers, line-makers, hook-makers, pulley-makers', in addition to 'many other trades'. For all these people and their dependants their 'best means of maintenance', he argued, came from 'these Newfoundland voyages'.

It was impossible not to be impressed that by fish alone – in fact by only one species of fish: cod – so much could be earned (well over £100,000, Whitbourne calculated), while no English coinage was expended, and so many were involved in the supply of related commodities. The trade was, he concluded, 'a great benefit to all your Majesty's Kingdoms in many respects'. Englishmen and women who had lived on Newfoundland itself, meanwhile, had found, he argued, not only that it supported a 'great trade of fishing', but also that its soil was fertile, and that its coasts were safe. Newfoundland, he wrote, lay 'with open arms towards England, offering itself to be embraced, and inhabited by us'.

Men could go either way after the peace with Spain. On the one hand, the protracted effort and organisation involved in leading a colonial settlement became more appealing than it had been. And on the other, a number of semi-legal privateers who could claim to have been doing their country proud (while happening to become rich in the process) became simple, unabashed pirates: not always unwillingly. It was scarcely a coincidence that the early decades of the seventeenth century saw some of the first, concerted attempts at colonisation severely disrupted by the hostility of renegade Englishmen. In spite of the attentions of men like Parkhurst, Whitbourne himself, or Sir Humphrey Gilbert, Whitbourne wrote later that Newfoundland had never been given serious enough consideration as the location for an

English colony. It had never, he wrote, been 'looked into by those discoverers as it deserved'.

In the course of a long career, Whitbourne remarked, he had been lucky enough to avoid shipwreck, but had suffered nevertheless 'great losses by pirates and sea-rovers'. (Life, he admitted, had been a mixture of 'crosses and comforts', even if, in his case, fortune had permitted the latter to outweigh the former.) In southern Newfoundland English fishing, and settling, were compromised in particular by 'that famous arch-pirate' called Peter Easton, who had flown the English flag as a privateer before continuing to rob, more indiscriminately, when the royal commission to assault the Spanish was withdrawn – attracting a community of piratical renegades, who were 'emigrants' from England themselves.

More law-abiding English colonists despaired of Easton's 'damnable course of life'. And Whitbourne was himself in fact taken captive by Easton for eleven weeks. 'I did persuade him much', Whitbourne wrote later, 'to desist from his evil course.'

Newfoundland's particular importance for business interests in England's West Country – expressed in the careers of Anthony Parkhurst, Sir Humphrey Gilbert and Richard Whitbourne – remained strong. When King James I granted a patent for colonisation in 1610, it was to a group who called themselves the 'Company of Adventurers, and Planters of the City of London, *and Bristol*, for the Colony or Plantation in Newfoundland'.

John Guy, the man who was the first colonial governor there – firm, practical, ungiven (as were some early admirers of Newfoundland) to flights of romantic fantasy, his hair long and his beard neatly trimmed – was himself a well-known merchant from Bristol, as well as its former mayor. Later in the seventeenth century one biographer called Guy 'the wisest man of his time in that city' – the very place from which John Cabot had first sailed to Newfoundland more than a century previously.[13]

As well as being mayor, for over twenty-five years Guy served on Bristol's Common Council, from the final year of Elizabeth's reign until the start of Charles I's 'personal rule' in 1629. In 1606 – and though his birth date is not known precisely, he was probably then in his early thirties – he was Bristol's main subscriber to what was called the 'North Virginia Company', the northern counterpart to the southern company which backed the settlement at Jamestown. In 1608 he visited Newfoundland. He was highly and widely respected: a man, it was said, 'very industrious and of great experience'.

That year, having now been to the island himself, he wrote a pamphlet which echoed the calls for settlement made already by Anthony Parkhurst and Richard Whitbourne: calls which hoped 'to animate the English to plant in Newfoundland'. Although the document has now unfortunately been lost, clearly it seconded many of Parkhurst and Whitbourne's arguments.

With the coming to the throne of James Stuart, and the end of the long war with Spain, the establishment of colonies was then a subject much discussed in England. It was only months since the English, with very high expectations, had first landed in Virginia. And it was in large part as a result of Guy's document that this 'London and Bristol Company' received its formal charter, 'confident', as it was said, that Newfoundland was 'habitable in winter'. For significant attention was paid in particular (as ever) to the island's latitude. How could it be colder, men reasoned, as in the fishing community it was widely rumoured to be, when parts of it lay 'more to the southward than any part of England'? Fishermen tended not to remain all year round. Plainly they were talking nonsense.

The principal reason to settle Newfoundland, however, did have, as the company's patent itself made clear, to do with the fish: it was in order 'to secure and make safe the said trade of fishing to our subjects for ever'. And who was there on the island to dispute it? For over a century Europeans had been fishing offshore. But the land itself – particularly the south-eastern tip in which the English were interested – remained largely uninhabited. (Native American communities congregated, as Whitbourne had noted, in the north and west of the island.) It was, the patent proclaimed, 'vacant and not actually possessed', 'destitute and desolate of inhabitants', though it – like everywhere on earth – had been (of course) 'from the beginning created for mankind'. To populate it would be praiseworthy. It would be 'a matter and action well beseeming a Christian King'.

So, that same year, in 1610, Guy assembled a group of thirty-nine colonists, and together they set out from Bristol in a single ship. (They sent it back laden with trees, pinewood in particular being widespread in Newfoundland, and ideal for sawing, the hills on the island 'full of woods', while back in England wood in general was now sparse.) The colonists were tradesmen or farmers, all, it was said, 'of civil life', and it is to be assumed – simply on the basis that they signed up for such an uncertain undertaking – that things were not going well for them in England. One can deduce from the equipment they needed, and from the tasks that they were required to perform, the professions from which some of them came.

A list of provisions which were left with them the following year mentions tools for a smith, tools for a cooper, tools for a mason, tools for a carpenter and for a sawyer, powder and muskets, saws, hatchets and axes, beds and bolsters, linen, pewter and clothing, shoes, fishing nets and boat sails, as well as a Bible, a book about medicine and numerous other items. With Guy went his immediate family, as well as his brother. They took grain. And animals: 'hens, ducks, pigeons, rabbits, goats, cattle', as well as 'other live creatures'. One of the emigrants had smallpox and soon died of the disease, although luckily he did not infect anyone else. For which, Guy proclaimed, 'great thanks' were due to God.

When they arrived the colonists found seasonal fishing boats from Europe still in the harbour, though these had now finished fishing and were waiting for the right wind to blow them back east. With them the group took long and detailed instructions – to fortify a settlement on the island's south-eastern 'Avalon' peninsula known as 'Cuper's Cove' (and subsequently as 'Cupid's').

At first their presumptions were justified, by conditions that were mild. For the first couple of months, Guy wrote – admittedly in August and September – the weather was 'so temperate as in England, and rather better'. Even afterwards, in October and November, conditions, he reported subsequently, were 'warmer and drier than in England'. Colonists were favourably impressed: 'much confirmed', he said, 'in a good concept of this climate'. Guy mentioned that he himself had measured the colonists' latitude on what he called a 'hot and most fair, clear, sunshining day'. And there were many of these. In general the climate should, he thought, 'draw inhabitants' to the island. He admitted, though, in an early letter, that he had not yet experienced the worst of the winter of which such hardship had often been spoken. With a little trepidation, he promised to write further, 'when experience of the winter season is made'.

Fearing the worst, even if they hoped it was mistaken, the group's first priority after landing on Newfoundland was to build somewhere in which they could live. They worked frantically as the hours of daylight shortened, and by the beginning of December had finished the first basic dwelling house. Only then was work begun on the frame of what was described as 'a far greater and fairer' house, in which the community could live in due course. Men worked desperately hard in addition to build a storehouse in which to keep the colony's provisions. And a workhouse which would enable them to make boats – six fishing vessels, along with a larger boat in which to 'sail and row about the headlands' – as well as other things, in the dry, even when the weather was inclement.

Around these buildings they fashioned a rectangular, stockaded enclosure, '120 foot long and 90 foot broad', nervously uncertain then about aggressive wildlife or Native American raids. A platform was built 'of great posts and rails', from which three guns could sweep the harbour while two smaller 'flankers' were also able to 'scour the quarters'. Beyond the enclosure, ground was cleared before it became too hard with the frost, to allow the sowing in the spring of 'corn and garden seeds'. A great deal of wood was cut – sawyers being kept busy both by the demand for planks for construction as well as by the need of the 'collier' to burn wood for charcoal. Each afternoon it grew darker earlier, while the temperature dropped, and inevitably, in the small colony, anxiety grew.

Mercifully the settlement's first winter was mild, and Guy was able to report that his initial experience of the cold season in these parts had been a pleasant surprise. While large bergs of frozen ice had been seen far out at sea, they had not approached the shore. Each morning, Guy said, he had walked out with his dog (because he too, like Anthony Parkhurst, had travelled to Newfoundland with his faithful friend) to a nearby brook in order to wash. And not once during the whole winter, he wrote, did they find that the water had frozen solidly enough for the dog to be able to walk over it. Snow, apart from where it had drifted, 'was never above eighteen inches thick'. At no point, he reassured company leaders, in spite of their prior trepidation, was the community seized by 'fear of wanting wood or water'.

In fact, he said, there hadn't been any month of the winter in which the colonists had not travelled, by land or water. And sometimes, indeed, groups had even lain at night 'in the woods without fire', receiving 'no harm'. There had not been fifteen days during the whole winter, Guy reckoned, when conditions had made it impossible for the company to work outside. Far from being confined to the middle months, ships could sail to and from England 'at any time of the year'. 'The doubts that have been made of the extremity of the winter season in these parts of Newfoundland', he concluded, 'are found by our experience causeless.' Seafaring men who had spoken to him, Guy said, and seen 'what a mild winter' the colony had had, were highly impressed. In fact they began 'to be in love with the country', and to talk about settling themselves.

One reason for the construction of the colony's defences had been 'the fear of wild beasts'. Bears were known to inhabit the woods. And while they tended to be timorous where people were concerned – hardly inured to regular contact – it was certainly feared that they might kill domestic animals. As it happened, though, this concern too was found 'almost needless'. (Guy's successor called the creatures 'harmless'.)[14] In fact, Guy noted in May the following year, 'our great ram-goat was missing fifteen days in October, and came home well again and is yet well with us'.

In general, the animals taken across the Atlantic on the English ships thrived in their new home. Of the goats, Guy reported, 'one lusty kid' had been weaned in the dead of winter. Pigs prospered, while pigeons and rabbits were also, he said, doing 'exceeding well'. Not only had the poultry laid plenty of eggs but in mid-May there were 'eighteen young chickens that are a week old, besides others that are a hatching'. And meanwhile the indigenous wildlife proved similarly attractive. The sea, of course, was 'most admirable', Guy's successor expostulating that he could not 'comprehend or express the riches thereof' – 'cods so thick by the shore that we hardly have been able to row a boat through them' – but creatures abounded in the air and on land too: ducks, deer, geese, grouse, partridges, hares, as well as numerous other birds.[15]

The subsequent winter was a little colder. One colonist reported that conditions were 'somewhat more intemperate than [they] had been the year before'. But nevertheless, they were not, he added, 'intolerable, nor perhaps so bad as we have it sometimes in England'. During 1612 sixteen women were shipped out to join the original male colonists, with a clear mind to the colony's long-term viability, along with other apprentices. Some of the settlement's apprentices claimed that Guy could rule harshly. But he might of course have been entitled to do so. Some, Guy claimed, were a hindrance to the colony, expecting provisions, and wages, while offering little in return. He referred to 'such others as are not fit longer to be entertained here', and to sending them home, 'that the unprofitable expense of victuals and wages might cease'. It is difficult to think that the ruling of such a colony – clinging bravely on, on the edge of the known world – could have been anything other than firm, and Guy, as such, should be given the benefit of the doubt.

On the downside, the land was much less fertile than those who had emigrated had been led to expect (for all Guy's early praise of the 'fruitfulness of the soil'). The climate meant that crops, unlike root vegetables, failed to ripen. But allowances could be made, and the right things grown. Soon, Guy predicted, with a little work – with both 'husbandry and fishing' – the colony would be 'able to support itself'.[16]

It did turn out that their induction to winter in the region had been misleadingly mild. In 1613 that season was much harder than it had been. Moreover, pirates – led by Easton – presented a serious problem, and had to be paid 'protection' (in animals) not to attack the colony. They did feel some sense of national allegiance, and so were particularly savage towards the French who they encountered. But they menaced the English too.

Furthermore, a recurrent rivalry emerged between colonists and the 'migrant' fishermen – those who came and went each year, and who could not but suspect that the colony represented a serious challenge to their livelihood. Guy might in fact have desired that that challenge was more serious than it was: he felt that colonists failed to give fishing the emphasis that it deserved, and that they scorned, as his successor put it, to 'turn a fish' – to turn it to dry, that is, in the cool wind. For decades, though, this animosity continued, the subject of hearings and judgements in England.

Fishing interests there were voiced loudly – migratory fishing interests, that is – and it took calm voices to insist that in reality 'planters are not so bad as the merchants make them', and that training for life at sea, and the demand for English goods, were fostered among Newfoundland colonists just as much as they were in the West Country. In reality the two industries, colonial fishing and migratory fishing, were co-dependent as well as competitive.[17]

The fundamental difficulty was that the way in which the company was set up meant that colonists not only had to make the settlement pay for itself, but also to make it pay a dividend to its shareholders back in England. As a result, when it was on the edge in any case, it struggled financially. Guy himself became demoralised. As a successful merchant he was accustomed to ventures that returned a fast profit, and even when he had steeled himself for things this time to take longer, the substantial absence of progress, combined with the lack of understanding from some in the company who had not been to America themselves, was profoundly frustrating.

In 1615 he withdrew from the company, taking investors with him (who turned instead to a nearby colony that was given the transparent name, 'Bristol's Hope'). Guy himself, meanwhile, had already returned to England. And back in his home town in the West Country, he served again as mayor, and twice as a Member of Parliament early in the 1620s. The fact that his replacement at Cuper's seems to have been chosen for his particular experience of combating pirates suggests the scale of the nuisance presented by Easton and his crew. In general, as a profit-making enterprise run from England, the venture did not flourish, and English backers pulled out. But the settlement survived, as did individual emigrants, even when they moved to build other settlements nearby.

Thus, after John Guy's return to England, his extended family – which had thrived early on with the birth of a son to his brother Nicholas – continued to do well in the New World. Nicholas moved from Cuper's first to the successor colony of Bristol's Hope, when that was established in 1618, before moving again around a decade later. In a letter written in 1631 Nicholas said that his family was now settled and flourishing at a settlement called Carbonear, on the same bay, twelve and a half miles north of Cuper's as the crow flew (longer by water), where he requested help both with fishing and with tending cattle. From the milk that they gave him he made butter and cheese, selling them or giving them to his neighbours. Labour, he said, was his one urgent requirement here in the New World – a need that was felt by colonists in other parts of America: there was a 'want of men to till your land'.

A census taken later in the century, in 1677, lists both Jonathan Guy, a son of Nicholas, as well as another Nicholas Guy, probably Jonathan's son – his namesake's grandson. Both lived on Newfoundland with their families. By this time Jonathan was doing well. He owned four dwelling houses, two boats and a vegetable garden, as well as seven cattle, eleven sheep and three pigs. Names in the census suggest that more than twenty families in the south Avalon region of Newfoundland had reproduced themselves before 1670.

In general, settlement persisted even after the demise of official interest. Some colonists, it seems, continued to live at the original site that John Guy had overseen at Cuper's. Though little material of a documentary nature remains, archaeologists have found evidence that the structures built by the first colonists continued to be inhabited, and used, until fire destroyed them decades later in the 1660s. And many others lived, just as Nicholas Guy and his family did, at newer, successor settlements nearby. When one civil servant in London tried to estimate the winter population of this area of Newfoundland in 1660 (it was significantly boosted in summer by the annual arrival of migrants), he put it at 180 families – 'families' in the broad sense of households which included servants – making perhaps in the region of 1,500 individuals.[18]

One man who was heavily involved early on in supplying, and even governing, these successor settlements was Richard Whitbourne. The precise process of settlement in these early colonies is shrouded at times in the Newfoundland fog. Fishing colonies, rather like fishermen themselves, were not always careful to leave records. But increasingly it is apparent that English men, women and children did live there permanently, laying the basis for what later in the century became successful colonies.

Only known for certain is that by the time censuses of the English communities began to be taken in the 1670s, settlement was well established, while memories, and traditions, remained of houses that were 'already built' by the 1620s, and which dated probably from the decade before that. It may be true that residency, as opposed to seasonal migration, did not provide a clear economic advantage: that savings were often eroded by the costs of overwintering and of an unproductive period. But settlements were not driven purely by economic imperatives. The rivalries with Easton's pirates, with native 'Beothuk' communities who were eager to seize any unguarded iron commodities (a material to which they did not otherwise have access), and with the French fishermen based further west in Placentia Bay all illustrated this plainly. Permanent English communities during the seventeenth century were justified, for instance, by the presence of the French, and vice versa.

The English settlements, moreover, encouraged one another. And by this means the process of colonisation acquired a momentum that was difficult to arrest. As the resident population expanded it also became harder and harder for a migrant fisherman to secure the coastal space that he needed, even if the fish themselves – swimming in open water – remained an accessible resource. Lacking the supplies of salt that could easily be obtained by other Europeans, access to the shore was necessary, but it was increasingly difficult for fishermen who did not also live on Newfoundland. It is telling that, decades later, after all French settlement was banned, fishermen in France made it plain that they regarded settlement by the English here as constituting a significant competitive advantage.[19]

There is no doubt, though, that the growth of the European presence each summer, as both migrant fishermen and the fishing servants who helped and worked with the resident colonists arrived, provided a significant boost to the colonial presence in Newfoundland – as well as stirring up rivalry and animosity. Not until perhaps 100 years later, towards the end of the eighteenth century, was the native population of Newfoundland sufficiently large to meet the fishing industry's demands (and it was then that the English migratory fishery began its final, irrevocable decline).

Newfoundland, moreover, became an integral part of an Atlantic trade network, as ships which went on to buy 'sack' (wine), as well as fruit, oil and other commodities which required a warmer climate than England could offer, took the opportunity first to head west across the Atlantic to pack their holds with dried cod from Newfoundland, in the knowledge that the fish was highly popular both in the Mediterranean and in Atlantic islands like the Canaries, Madeira and the Azores. It was a lucrative, important, 'triangular' trade. Increasingly, towards mid-century, English ships or 'bottoms' superseded those which were Dutch, French or from other countries. (One petition in 1639 boasted that English companies had 'of late procured almost all the trade from Newfoundland from the Dutch'.) And this demand for dried fish proved a significant boost to the fishing upon which the English colonies in Newfoundland were based.

In addition, the demand for further emigration from England to work in the colonies could be met at the same time, since the ships were not during this outward voyage heavily laden.[20] The fishing settlements, moreover, were a useful stop-off point for those who were on their way to other parts of North America, and this is what they were for many of the English: a station on their journey west.

# II

# GOLD AND SMOKE

At the end of July 1607 – the summer before John Guy made his exploratory voyage from Bristol to Newfoundland – a man with one arm sailed east into the Channel from the Atlantic. Passing the citadel and four towers built, in the aftermath of the Spanish Armada, under Queen Elizabeth to guard the entrance to Plymouth harbour, the crew on his ship dropped anchor, then rowed him ashore. Tightly clutched under his good arm was a small wooden barrel containing American soil.

After weeks at sea, the captain's beard was thick and unkempt. He was almost fifty – old for the time, and old, certainly, in a profession in which few lived to what was called 'grey hairs'. The hair on this man's cheeks and head, though, was dark but also substantially grey. His round face was etched with deep lines. And his leathery skin betrayed years braced against saltwater spray whipped across decks by ocean gales, or steeling armed men to board enemy ships.

No sooner had Christopher Newport clambered ashore and taken his first, stiff steps back in England, than he went to see about arranging for the despatch of an official messenger, knowing that conditions here in Plymouth – the wind, and the tide – prevented him sailing on immediately up the Channel towards London. Within hours of Newport's arrival a rider was despatched through the town gates galloping northeast towards the capital, with a secret letter concealed in his clothing.

Carefully sealed to ensure that it was not read, the hastily penned message was addressed to Robert Cecil, the clever, short and hunchbacked chief minister of King James (the man the king referred to with affectionate, if hurtful, admiration as his 'little beagle' and his 'pygmy', and Elizabeth had labelled her 'little elf').[1] 'This day', wrote Newport, he had arrived 'here in the sound of Plymouth'. He came fresh from

America, from the exploration with which he had been tasked: 'the discovery of that part of Virginia imposed upon me'.

In ecstatic tones he conveyed to Cecil good news – 'glad tidings'. Everything, he reported, had turned out just as investors and organisers had hoped.

Having accustomed himself once more to the feel of land which did not plunge beneath his feet, and arranged for the message to be taken quickly to London, Newport set off on another mission that he had in Plymouth.

Still clasping his precious barrel of earth, he began to walk briskly through the narrow streets of the port, making purposefully for the substantial local residence of the governor of Plymouth Castle. His mind was set, and for all their diverting interest after weeks at sea, he paid little attention to the local residents, the children or the animals – to all the shouts and smells of town life – as he made for the fort, newly built, which stood on the sea-cliffs just outside town.

The governor was a local man well known to Newport. Boasting the unusual, un-English-sounding name of Fernando Gorges (a family affectation, their surname being Russell until they changed it for an older, extinct, more exotic-sounding moniker), he had risen to eminence as a soldier fighting the Spanish on the European mainland. As the massed ships of the Armada sailed towards England back in 1588, Gorges himself had lain, unaware of events, in a Spanish prison, released only in return for Spanish prisoners who were captured after this failed attack – so it was scarcely surprising that he remained anxious himself, long afterwards, for the 'release of our poor men that are prisoners in Spain', who found themselves, just as he had done, in the hands of these unbelieving Spaniards 'who delight themselves in doing wrongs to all and right to none'.

Towards the end of Queen Elizabeth's reign Gorges had been rewarded for his loyal service with the governorship of the new fort at Plymouth, a place which was increasingly prominent both as an outpost against the seaborne Spanish threat (it was here, on the cliff-top known as the 'Hoe', that Sir Francis Drake had famously played bowls while waiting for a tide which would allow him to confront the Armada), and as one of England's western ports well situated for voyages across the Atlantic. Gorges had also become, since 1604 brought the end of the long war with Spain, a fervent advocate of English colonisation in America, and he was directly involved in the enterprise with which Newport had sailed.

When Newport first called, Gorges was not at home. Newport spoke with a servant, however, and the message that he had visited was passed on. When Gorges came back soon afterwards he was delighted to hear of the one-armed sailor's return, and quickly sent word in order to arrange another meeting. In the course of the day or two before Newport left, the two men did manage to see one another. And when they did Gorges listened, with mounting enthusiasm and excitement, as Newport recounted his experiences in mainland America. Soon afterwards Newport set sail once more from Plymouth towards London, following the English south coast east, before heading north and west into the Thames estuary.

Subsequently Gorges drafted a letter of his own to Secretary Cecil in London. Having spoken with Newport, he wrote, he 'understood so much by him' that it was clear that the venture's supporters in England had every reason to be hopeful. The harbour which the colonists had visited was 'commodious'. The country was fertile. And the climate was healthy. It was true that the local people were numerous and aggressive – an undoubted inconvenience – but as long as the colony was quickly and well provided, there should not, he felt sure, be any insuperable problem. In fact, from the point of view of colonisation, he wrote, there would be 'no doubt of success'.

Gorges made no mention of specifics, and certainly not of precious metals. He did not wish to pre-empt. (Or if he did wish to do so, he managed to restrain himself, on the basis that certain news was not his to convey.) Besides, tests, as Newport had made clear during the discussion between the two men, had yet to be performed. 'I cannot as yet', Gorges wrote, 'give any assurance of the particulars of the estate of the country where we have sent our colony.' But there can be little doubt that this is exactly what the two men did in fact discuss, as they peered together in greedy but doubtful wonder at Newport's precious barrel of glistening earth.

'If I be not much deceived', Gorges predicted to Cecil confidently, the land explored by the English across the Atlantic in America would prove well worth protecting. There was, he said – knowing that Cecil would be sure to catch his drift – 'the possibility of great good to be done in the place where they are'. He was right, of course, though not in the manner in which he intended.

By the time he received Gorges' letter, Cecil had seen already the urgent, and more direct, message from Newport himself. He and his fellow colonists, Newport had written, had performed their duties 'to the uttermost of our powers'.

Months earlier, before embarking in England, Newport and his fellow leading men had been presented by the company hierarchy with a document which pretended not to dictate, but whose tenor was unambiguous. They called it 'Instructions given by way of Advice'.

Among other things, this pamphlet recommended some key criteria for the choosing of a site for a settlement. It should be on the banks of a navigable river, but out of view of the coast, where other European ships – the 'all devouring Spaniard' in particular – would not be able to spot and attack it.[2] Ideally this river would flow towards the eastern American coast from the north-west, leading, if it was followed upstream, towards the 'other sea' (because the English knew, now, that mainland America, even if it was surrounded by islands, was a continent in its own right which would need to be crossed before they could set sail again towards Asia). From the outset the priorities of many in England who were instrumental in the establishment of the colony were plain. They hoped not only to build a lasting, self-sustaining settlement that would comprise a part of an English empire, but also – as was certainly the case with Newport himself – to find, and to harvest, one or more sources of rapid wealth.

Three ships were obtained and prepared for the venture, of which the largest, commanded by Newport himself, who led the whole expedition across the Atlantic, was a cargo ship hired for the occasion and well able to stow large quantities of valuable commodities. But winter conditions in England caused significant delays, and it was not until late in December 1606 that they were able to head down the Thames from London. And then, for six interminable weeks, further bad weather – 'unprosperous winds' which blew eastward up the Channel – kept the ships pitching violently only a short distance from the Kent coast, unable to make any progress towards America. (Their priest, Robert Hunt, was so nauseous, 'so weak and sick', that few were said to have 'expected his recovery', impressed as they all were by his fortitude and his determination not to return to England.) It was the middle of February before they were finally able to sail. And by then frustration had overspilled into fierce rows among the men.

As the weeks ticked by, furthermore, the crews had naturally had no choice but to consume their supplies. And as a result Newport was compelled to order a pause in the Canary Islands where they might purchase more, a necessity which caused further delay, before the ships anchored again, after crossing the Atlantic, in the Caribbean, where natives, relieved to find that the crews were not Spanish, offered 'sundry fruits' including plantains, potatoes, 'pines' (pineapples) – and tobacco, a commodity with which many of the English were not at first familiar. In general, though, the natives of the Caribbean were shy and kept a distance. The springs were warm. And the sun shone on a calm blue sea. It was a wrench to leave, and it was the end of April 1607 before the shoreline of Virginia was finally sighted: a coastal plain, low and thickly carpeted with trees, smudging the early-morning horizon as the sun rose behind the backs of men who peered across their bows in the gloom.

The first site proposed for a settlement was rejected on the basis that it was too visible from the sea and too vulnerable to bombardment. (The threat posed by roving French or particularly Spanish fleets was at the forefront of men's minds, especially since many of them – like Newport himself – had been accustomed to military confrontations with the Spanish, on sea and on land.) Instead, the party moved upriver, inland, pleased to note that as they did so the water remained deep enough for even the largest ship.

Around sixty miles upriver was a low, marshy island or peninsula, connected to the bank by only a thin strip. Hard by it, the river remained deep, meaning that unlike at Roanoke, where ships had been moored some distance away, large craft could be tied to trees directly adjacent – a significant advantage. Visibility up- and downstream was good. And the land itself, critically, was not at present occupied by Native Americans, those strange locals of whom the English were aware but who, they admitted, 'we neither knew nor understood'. It seemed 'the most apt and securest place', Newport thought: 'a very great place', as one sensible leading colonist put it, 'for the erecting of a great city'.[3]

The fact that there were serious shortcomings – that the site was, for instance, a rather sweaty, unhealthy spot, precisely the marshy, 'low or moist place' that the company had encouraged the settlers to avoid – was overlooked. The emigrants were pressed for time. It was May: the original instructions for the expedition had assumed that Newport would have finished his preliminary explorations by now and be ready to set sail on his return voyage to England. Anxious to fulfil his tasks prior to doing so, Newport left some of the men on board to work at building a settlement, felling trees and tilling soil. Many continued to live in tents, or in the open 'under boughs of trees', as opposed to in slightly more permanent and protective wooden houses. And he led a party (made up substantially of the crewmen whom he most trusted) further upriver.[4]

The heat, as he did so, was intensifying daily, as late spring gave way to a muggy summer. Newport, however, vowed that he and his men would not return until they had discovered 'some issue' that was likely to excite investors back in England: the head of the river, an inland lake from which it flowed, the 'sea again' (the Pacific), or the Appalachian mountains, which, surely, would harbour precious ore. Things in Jamestown, meanwhile, were far from easy. Not only did temperatures climb, but drinking water was scarce. (River water that had tasted palatable became increasingly saline, brackish and unpleasant as time passed.) And a fast-growing number of mosquitoes, breeding in the warm, marshy conditions, hummed and whined in thick clouds.

Colonists began to expire, daily, of fevers and other ailments.[5] On 6 August a man called John Asbie died of dysentery. Three days later, on the 9th, George Flower died 'of the swelling'. William Brewster ('gentleman') – so taken with the region's potential – died on the 10th. Three men died on the 14th. Two more died the following day. And for weeks the grim roll call went on. By disease, by war, or by famine, it was recorded, 'our men were destroyed'. (By the end of that year only around forty of the original 105 colonists remained alive.) But knowing how important his task of exploration was to senior company members in London, and sharing their fixation with instant riches, Newport felt that he could not head back without having at least attempted the discovery of significant wealth, or the route to significant wealth, with which he could regale the English leadership.

For all the re-provisioning at islands en route, the colony's supplies were once again running low, and men put pressure on Newport when he returned from his expedition to head home to collect more – supplies which might have been cheap and exhaustible but which were a good deal less fanciful than the jewels or precious metals whose existence possessed him. There had been no chance yet for the agriculture which might make the English self-sufficient, and which should, some believed, have been given a rather higher priority than it was.

Foolishly, furthermore, as the settlement was built, it was decided that it could dispense with fortifications against nearby Native American communities in favour of the appearance of trust. It was a high-risk tactic. Other leading men could scarcely believe that guns remained packed away in crates, while walls and bulwarks went unbuilt. Among them was the bullish and practical soldier John Smith, a squat man with dark hair and a thick beard, who entirely failed to be impressed, as men then usually were impressed, by the hierarchy of class, and who as a result made enemies of other leading men (of 'them who were called the better sort', as he referred to them contemptuously).[6] Why, he thought, would the colonists at Jamestown not take such a basic precaution as properly to fortify their habitation?

Smith was an experienced and resourceful soldier, having fought for the Emperor of Austria against the Muslim Turks in south-eastern Europe. In England he lived in rural Lincolnshire, a backwater, far from the aristocratic world which existed in metropolitan London and at certain country estates. Having escaped from captive slavery on the Continent, he returned home, dedicating himself – in 'a little woody pasture' – to the study of explosives and ballistics, as well as to horse-riding and other martial accomplishments. He had a deep, personal interest in this sort of practical knowledge, rather than in the theoretical skills of grammar, rhetoric and ancient languages which tended then to be valued.

Many of the so-called 'upper' classes, he grumbled, did not even go this far: did not value education at all. Not only did he find most of the 'gentlemen' on the voyage to Virginia lazy – wedded to their 'accustomed dainties', their 'feather beds and down pillows' – but they were incurious. 'They never', he complained, 'adventured to know *any* thing.' To him their self-satisfaction was infuriating, and wholly unjustified. Even the better ones, who were willing to stick at a task after something like an axe had 'blistered their tender fingers', could hardly compete with men who were used to working.[7] As a soldier he felt that it was the practical skills to which he had devoted himself which might at any point prove invaluable. And as it turned out, of course, he was right.

The distrust was mutual, and leading colonists hoped to remove Smith from the picture. Newport, indeed, had planned to execute him on the voyage before the party had even reached Jamestown, though Smith had resolutely refused to play along with this scheme, surviving and having the sentence revoked.

Christopher Newport's own preoccupations did not concern the settlement or its defences. With forty men, the instructions from the company leaders suggested, while their brethren worked at building a permanent colony Newport should head upstream to explore the wider region. 'Two months', it was said, the party could spend in discovery of the river above them, and of the country round about.

Having travelled a good way, half of this group ought then to be tasked to build temporary shelters on the banks, while the other half would make on foot towards any 'high lands or hills' that they could see in the distance. Presumably the exploration party would include John Martin, a prominent crew member who as the well-meaning if rather malleable son of an eminent and trusted London goldsmith and Master of the Royal Mint was supposedly well practised at identifying ores. At altitude in the wilderness, the architects of the English venture in Virginia believed that they would be likely to find gold or other valuable natural deposits.

Why? In a work that was much consulted at the time, one Spanish Jesuit named José de Acosta had offered his reasons for thinking that the Indies in general, and barren, mountainous terrain in particular, would prove the place to search for such commodities. He was someone to whom people listened, who could point to his own experience to show that he knew what he was talking about. Not only had he lived in southern and Central America himself, but when he did return to Spain late in the sixteenth century, it was on board a ship whose hold contained twelve chests of gold, two of large emeralds and millions of pieces of silver, as well as other products of great value.

In part, his thinking was fatalistic and unhelpful. The location of such precious stuff, he argued, was simply 'the will of the Creator', and therefore unfathomable. There was little point in trying to guess: he had simply 'imparted his gifts as it pleased him'. But the writer did then turn to what he called an additional 'philosophical reason' why barren hills and mountainsides were likely to be the best places in which to look. And these were the passages which grabbed his readers' attention.

Metals, gold and silver in particular, he wrote, tended to grow (the assumption always being that they germinated and expanded in the same way that plants did) in land which otherwise was 'barren and unfruitful'. For God had divided His attentions. And while in fertile land He had concentrated on propagating the 'fruits' necessary for life, it was in this high ground – 'very rough, dry, and barren (as in the highest mountains and inaccessible rocks of a rough temper)' – that men would find valuable mines. And of course this very fact could, if the wealth had been discovered already, make these places 'pleasing and agreeable' and 'well inhabited with numbers of people'.[8]

With them, the English exploring in Virginia would carry compasses. And they should take careful notes as they went of the distance travelled in each direction, lest any Native Americans whom they had employed as guides ran suddenly away, 'in the great woods or deserts', leaving the English desperate, stranded and unable 'to find a passage back'. Most importantly, the party would also be sure to carry 'half a dozen pickaxes', with which to attack any promising patches of earth, and to 'try if they can find any mineral'.

Substantially, in other words, the duties of which Newport spoke afterwards consisted of two things (aside from the safe establishment of a colony, which was always considered as a means to an end). First, the men would look for a short route across America to the Pacific, as the Spanish conquistador Vasco Núñez de Balboa had found in Panama, when the 'other sea' had been spotted glinting in the distance, from a mountain-top in Central America. And second, the men would search, within America, just as Balboa had in fact been doing at the time, for natural sources of valuable 'minerals'.

And so, in a frantic attempt to fulfil their instructions, a largish group under Newport's command – though not as large as instructed, consisting of twenty-three men rather than forty – pushed inland from the coast, rowing and sailing their smaller boat, or 'shallop', upriver, towards hills that they could see silhouetted in the distance against the horizon: the 'gold-showing mountains', as the Appalachians were optimistically (and for no good reason other than general prior presumption) described. In the end John Martin was not, in fact, one of the party, probably because he was unfit to go, suffering repeatedly in America from poor health. The river here continued to be wide, and to boast a deep channel. It ran almost 200 miles inland. And three-quarters of this distance, Newport reported – well beyond the Jamestown settlement – it was navigable by 'great ships'.

Their journey was dominated by encounters with local Native American tribes, some of whom the English had come across already at Jamestown. Of these, there were tribes which were friendly, or which seemed it, and there were others which were overtly hostile and dangerous. Some of them painted their bodies using a red dye: 'very beautiful and pleasing to the eye', the English commented. (And it was this, rather than the natural colour of their skin, which gave them the lasting nickname 'Red Indians'.) Occasionally, also, they used a blue colouring which the English greedily presumed – on little evidence once again beyond their own fond imagining – to be 'silver ore'.

As they advanced upstream, some of the natives they met, such as one helpful leader who they dubbed the 'Kind Consort' (not knowing his real name), proved willing to help. This man drew for the English a rough map of the region, first scratching it in the sand with a finger on the riverbank, then using a proffered pen on a piece of parchment, once it had been shown to him how these curious implements worked.

Beyond some large falls in the river, this man told them, they would be unable to travel on the water (and they found, sure enough, that 'great craggy stones' here forced the water to fall 'so rudely, and with such violence, as not any boat can possibly pass'). After getting out and walking for a day they would find, the man showed them, that the river forked. And from there, still 'a great distance off', were the mountains he called 'Quirank', where rocks would be found rich in seams of what he knew as 'caquassan' – a Native American word for red earth, which the English took to connote either copper or perhaps, better still, gold. And just beyond the mountains, he seemed to say, lay 'that which we expected' – a large saltwater lake, from which might flow another river, the English fondly imagined, which headed westward towards the Pacific.

While some other native communities were friendly enough, they were noteworthy more for their customs than for any similar assistance. The Englishmen watched 'their dances', they wrote, in which natives gyrated frenetically, 'shouting, howling, and stamping against the ground', making a noise 'like so many wolves or devils'. And the English took tobacco, as they were invited to do, inhaling the smoke through a large clay pipe fixed to a copper bowl in which the leaf was burnt. They learnt, too, of grievous wars between the diverse Native American tribes. And eventually, sensing vehement hostility to their proceeding further inland, Newport agreed not to go on, but to return instead to Jamestown, in spite of the fact that nothing of great worth had been discovered – no gold, and no sight of the south sea or of another river which might lead that way.

Perhaps he had a strange feeling that he should return. John Smith, one of the colonists who travelled with Newport, wrote later of sensing 'some mischief at the fort'.[9] (In truth, without arms or defences, it was not really a fort at all.) And when the party did duly get back, what they found was a scene of carnage. Hundreds of Native American warriors had attacked the settlement only the day before.

Jamestown had been woefully unprepared for the large-scale assault. Men who had been labouring were caught by surprise. Without weaponry in the town itself, frantic use had been made of shipboard cannon, which, thankfully for the colonists, were close at hand. It was the firing of one of these guns, leading to a cacophonous cascade of branches when its projectile crashed into a tree, which caused the attackers – much more numerous than the defenders – to flee, and which saved the English settlement from total obliteration. Otherwise, Smith observed, 'our men had all been slain'.[10]

Furthermore it was only after this attack, he commented, that the signal change of heart occurred which did lead to the building of true fortifications. 'Hereupon', he observed wryly, the leadership 'was contented the fort should be palisaded', while the faith in an appearance of trust vanished, and men were 'armed'. Even then, though, most of the actual work was in fact done not by 'gentlemen' but by the seamen who had sailed the ships. They, it was remembered, did 'the best part thereof'.

And it was then, ironically, rather than during the expedition towards the mountains, while renewed digging to construct ramparts was taking place along the borders of Jamestown itself, that sparkling golden crystals were discovered dotted within 'turfs of earth' which underlay a small, fast-running stream. This time the sickly John Martin was on hand to offer his opinion. And with barely suppressed excitement he was promptly summoned. Under his supervision, samples of the soil were duly taken.

Martin quickly assembled the special apparatus that the Englishmen had shipped from London in order to conduct 'assays', or tests, of any promising ore. Extraordinarily, the technique for doing this has hardly changed since, in many hundreds of years, from a time when 'scientific' knowledge seems unrecognisable in its crude simplicity and inaccuracy. And from the sixteenth century a growing number of treatises offered directions and insight into the 'hidden secrets' of this 'ingenious mystery' – this 'ancient and profitable art' which had led to 'great and mighty trades' and to the creation of countless towns and cities.[11]

Carefully, a small portion of the earth to be tested was weighed. The sample was wrapped in a thin sheet of lead foil, and then placed in a small dish or 'cupel' made from bone ash, which was put into a small furnace. Here it was heated, using charcoal, to extremely high temperatures at which most metals and impurities would oxidise and be absorbed by the cupel. Critically, though, neither gold nor silver would. It was their resilience in the face of such treatment by 'fire' which constituted the basis of the test (and which formed in part the reason for their great value). These two precious metals, often found together and needing a subsequent process of separation, would be left, as molten droplets, in the bottom of the bowl, from which they could then be removed and weighed.

Martin's initial reaction was favourable. He had, he thought, succeeded in extracting gold. Fellow colonists looked on, listening with hungry expectation. And this fact 'stirred up in them', it was said of all the surviving colonists who crowded eagerly round, 'an unseasonable and inordinate desire after riches' – so many of them having come to America with little else in mind. A small barrel was brought to the site, and into it soil containing the sparkling crystals was eagerly spaded. Newport, Martin declared, could ship it with him back to England, in order to show the expedition leadership what they had found, and to allow for more thorough testing to take place in the hands of experts in London.

It was a find which profoundly coloured reactions to America in general. This, Newport assured Cecil in his letter, was 'excellent country'. And it was a land which now he could confidently declare to be 'very rich in gold and copper' – on, it has to be said, somewhat limited evidence. (This, of course, had been the general hope and expectation among Virginia Company investors, satirised in a popular play called *Eastward Ho* that was printed in 1605: gold, a captain in the play promised, 'is more plentiful there than copper is with us'; everything that American natives used, their 'dripping-pans and their chamber pots', was 'pure gold', while at the same time rubies and diamonds were gathered, like pebbles, 'by the seashore'.)[12] Newport carried with him, moreover, a letter, in which he had had a hand himself, which was signed by the entire Council in Virginia before being addressed to the leadership in England. The colony, this letter promised, would soon 'flow with milk and honey', provided only that the Spaniard, with his heretical, 'ravenous hands', was kept off.

Nor was the opinion unsupported. One private spy among the colonists, whom Cecil had appointed to report directly back to him, was similarly entranced, handing a letter in secret to Newport for the captain to bring home. It was a description which did nothing to dampen enthusiasm among the London government. 'Such a bay, a river and a land', it hymned, 'did never the eye of man behold.' The account would have been longer, it noted, but Newport himself would convey the same findings 'better', ever, 'than I can'. America would surely in time become 'the most stately, rich kingdom in the world'. 'At the head of the river' where the colony had been built, the letter promised, lay 'rocks & mountains, that promise infinite treasure'. It scarcely mattered what the Spanish had discovered further south. King James would live to see England 'more rich, & renowned, than any kingdom in all Europe'.

This was not untrustworthy promotional literature intended to persuade others to emigrate. And it was certainly the stuff that leading men in England wanted to hear, and that they desperately wanted to believe. Independent sources concurred. So why would they not grant them credence?[13]

Newport's own excitement now, on his return to England, was quickly adopted by those who had collaborated with Cecil on the project.

Sir Walter Cope was a capable man who had worked under Cecil's father, Lord Burghley, and who was well liked, and leant upon, by his son Robert Cecil. His connections to the Cecil family had secured Cope election to Parliament, a process which depended much more on good establishment contacts than it did upon popularity with voters, and Cecil had provided assistance in the building and decoration of Cope's rich house in Kensington, on which no expense was spared and which became known, aptly enough, as 'Cope Castle'. Here, observers commented rather bitterly, Cope grew 'more and more into the great lord'. His position, however, was never secure. His debts mounted. Having risen from little on the backs of the Cecil family, he yearned for riches and for an established position. But the anxious, haunted look in his portrait at Hatfield House (ancestral home of the Cecils) reveals a man who was profoundly insecure, and conscious that his gains – too dependent on others; too lightly, too undeservedly won – might just as rapidly be lost.

Cope had invested in a number of ventures which promised vast returns but which failed all too often to meet expectations. When the prospect emerged of gold in the soil in America, a subject on which Cecil, his friend and mentor, spoke rhapsodically and which was talked about more generally with enthusiasm, it seemed too good a chance to pass up, and he became an early investor in the Virginia Company. When Newport's news then reached him, he could not contain his excitement. Here, at last, it seemed, was his personal earthly salvation – the answer to his prayers. It was true that wisdom, he wrote, when he paused to think, cautioned 'slow belief' in such great and unlikely promises. But it wasn't advice that he was good at heeding himself.

'My good Lord', he wrote to his friend and ally, if credence could be given to what they were told (and credence was one thing that he did desperately want to give), 'we are fallen upon a land that promises more than the land of promise'. Never mind milk and honey. This was much better than that. 'Instead of milk', he wrote, 'we find pearl'. Instead of honey, there was gold.

The source for these glad tidings seemed unimpeachable. He had known Newport personally for years, he assured Cecil, and he trusted him. He was familiar with what he called his 'honesty and good deserts'. Newport, he promised, was a sober and entirely plausible witness. He might have brought only 'a barrel full of the earth' – the earth which promised such riches. But across the Atlantic in Virginia (and he could scarcely bear to think of it) there lay waiting to be excavated and shipped 'a kingdom full of the ore'.

Like the contents of a heated crucible, Cope's financial worries melted in front of his eyes. Before him and his fellow investors there lay, he wrote, a 'treasure endless', and his eyes were blinded by the vision.

From the beginning of English attempts to colonise America, the search for precious metals, and for gold and silver in particular, had been high on the list of motivating factors. It had been true for all Europeans, ever since Columbus had sailed among the islands of the Caribbean, 'travelling in search of gold'.[14]

'What is the matter with you Christian men?', the son of one Native American king had demanded then of the Spaniards. Why this great esteem for 'so little a portion of gold', rather than for 'your own quietness'? For the natives who witnessed it, it was entirely baffling. How were they to explain these 'ravening appetites' – this 'greedy hunger of gold' – for which Europeans were willing to sustain 'so many calamities and incommodities', and to live like 'banished men' away from their own countries? 'We suffer from a disease', the Spanish *conquistador* Cortés had joked (or, rather, half-joked) to Inca ambassadors, 'that only gold can cure'. Some natives took them at their word, and Spaniards were found murdered, with melted gold poured down their throats.[15]

The Native American prince's question was no less pertinent for many of those Englishmen who were desperate to get in on the act: desperate to seek, as Walter Raleigh wrote, 'a soil far off', 'new worlds' – 'for gold, for praise, for glory'. The 'discovery of a good mine', or of a 'passage to the South Sea': these enticing visions of great wealth were what drove many of the English who first sailed to America. They didn't imagine settling there permanently. But they did dream of hauling vast riches from the soil, then living like kings from the proceeds – newly rich – in their homeland.

Sir Francis Drake, on visiting coastal California during his circumnavigation in 1579, observed that there was no part of the earth, here in America, 'wherein there is not some special likelihood of gold or silver'. And this was a crucial draw. For 'nothing else', another Englishman had commented late in the sixteenth century, could bring this great new land 'to be inhabited by our nation'. The other things about which propagandists talked were all well and good: a healthy climate, a fertile soil, roots, gums, sassafras. All excellent merchandise, to be sure. But America was a distant place, far across a hostile ocean, and these things were not, in themselves, 'worth the fetching'.[16]

From midway through the sixteenth century, though, as Spanish silver from the New World poured into Europe (especially after the discovery in 1545 of mines at Potosí, in modern Bolivia) the proceeds had funded an unprecedented spending spree. Trades in gold, silver, jewels, silks, spices and other luxuries boomed, in England as throughout the Continent. Traditional hierarchies were challenged. Merchants and investors sought the rich commodities which would make them appear eminent. The reimposition of 'sumptuary laws' – laws dictating what different classes of people were permitted to wear – was a symptom of the concern that new money had undermined the structure and stability which many prized in society. Most (unlike John Smith) did care for the familiar, reassuring hierarchy. Change was unsettling. And old money, of course, never has cared, in general, for the uncouth splendours of the *nouveaux riches*, always too willing, in every age, to forget that its wealth too was once new.

The patent issued by the English government for a new colonisation project in Virginia had expressly permitted the digging and searching for 'all manner of Mines of Gold, Silver and Copper', both in the colony itself and in the unknown 'main lands' which lay behind them. (Copper was the third metal from which money was minted, though it was by far the least valuable of the three.) And no wonder that they permitted them. When enthusiasts had advocated the establishment of

English colonies in America, the presence of precious metals had always been one of their dominant arguments.

In his 'Discourse on Western Planting', written during the 1580s, that passionate 'trumpet' for America Richard Hakluyt had argued that the English queen and her subjects could enjoy not only the great trade exploited currently by the Spanish alone – 'and by customs to fill her Majesty's coffers to the full' – but also 'the treasure of the mines of gold and silver' which this New World offered. Spain's grip on the whole of America, he argued, was a good deal more tenuous than people supposed. In the north, especially, an opportunity existed for England to get in on the act, and he urged them strongly to do so. It wasn't as if the country couldn't spare the colonists. Despair at England's rising population was widespread late in the sixteenth century and during the first half of the seventeenth. England, he wrote, was 'so far from want of people' that sustained settlement was actually something which would do it good.

As in Spain, where the *quinto real*, or royal fifth, had become official policy, the English crown reserved its right only to a fifth of any gold or silver found, and a fifteenth of the copper. But this, of course, could still mean great riches, for individuals and government alike, as the Spanish experience in South America had amply testified. No one in England needed reminding how the wealth both of Spaniards and Portuguese (united, since 1580, under a single crown) had been 'marvellously increased' by trade with what they called the 'Indies', and by the discovery there of vast quantities of precious metals.

Much of this new wealth made its way more or less directly into the vaults of Italian bankers, to pay off debts. Nevertheless, the salaries and supplies of those imperial mercenary armies which marched through central and northern Europe were also funded by American metals. Inflation might, with hindsight, have been the predictable long-term result. But few knew, and fewer would have cared if they had. Gold meant vast and immediate wealth for the finders. And few could turn up their noses at that.

Early explorers and colonists reported being immediately impressed by the possibilities of this new land across the 'Great Ocean Sea', as the Atlantic was labelled on early maps. The English, the Spanish ambassador in London reported with concern to the emperor, were 'mad about the location' that they found in Virginia, and were terrified that the Spanish would eject them. The envoy from Venice despatched similar news to his employers in the Serene Republic after Newport's return: that the English had disembarked in a fertile land, where they felt sure to find 'gold and silver mines', and indeed had brought back 'some of the soil to have it tested here'.[17]

Nor was the choice of Christopher Newport to lead the 1606 venture any coincidence. His career as a privateer during the long Anglo-Spanish war, which had lasted throughout the 1590s and beyond (we are too prone now to forget that the great invasion fleet known as the 'Armada' marked only the outset of many years of conflict), had given him un-rivalled familiarity with the waters of the western Atlantic. He was very visibly marked by the experience. In 1590 he had lost his lower right arm, during a fierce struggle with Spanish treasure ships, near the coast of Cuba.[18] (It was 'strooken off', as it was said at the time, and he was known thereafter as 'Christopher Newport of the one hand';[19] it is even possible that he wore a hook in its place and served as the inspiration for J. M. Barrie's infamous captain, though proof for this appealing tale is unfortunately lacking either way.) But he was not discouraged by his disability, and two years later, in 1592, he played a prominent part in reaping one of the largest hauls that anyone could recall.

The time had come, Newport goaded his crew as a fight with the Portuguese carrack *Madre de Dios* approached – a carrack that had sailed from the East Indies laden with half a million pounds' worth of gems, spices, silks and other precious goods – either to take the carrack, or, if not, to 'end our days' in a good cause. When they did the former, it was Newport who was given the honour of sailing her back to London: testimony to the active part which he had played. It was a windfall which provided a lavish haul to investors, even after crew and captains had made off with substantially more than their share of the booty.

Throughout this long period of war Newport had maintained close links with many of the rich London merchants who sponsored privat-eering voyages (as an excellent source of high returns, albeit at a high risk). He rose rapidly – through contacts and good fortune, but also through evident ability – from apprentice, to captain, to be one of the most eminent seamen of his day. He developed a close association with a family of leading London goldsmiths, the Glanfields, who found no doubt that robbing the treasure fleets of the Spanish or the Portuguese was just as reliable a means as any of securing precious metals.

The men went into business together. With Francis and Richard Glanfield, Newport co-owned a privateering ship, which he sailed often on pirate raids in American waters. When he married (for the third time) it was to Francis Glanfield's daughter, Elizabeth. By the time that he led the expedition to Virginia, Newport was certainly much closer to the precious metal industry, by business and by family links, than most.

Only when the Anglo-Spanish war formally ended in 1604 did Newport's career change fundamentally. Suddenly unable to attack ships in the Caribbean (though some captains, having enjoyed the licence for so long, found that the lure of booty remained hard to resist) he was obliged to take up more peaceful operations. So in 1605 he returned from a voyage with two young crocodiles and a wild boar, alive – and no doubt petrified – in the hold, which he presented to King James, who was well known for his fascination with exotic creatures. Newport himself had been presented with human curiosities from the New World: two natives, who were used, the Spanish ambassador complained, to foster in England enthusiasm for colonisation.[20]

The collection of curiosities, though, never had quite the same draw as the chance of untold wealth, and soon Newport developed an active interest in talk of an English colony further north in America, both to exploit the riches which they would find there, and to look for a route through the continent to the south sea. These were possibilities which certainly did grab him, used as he was to aiming at the acquisition of rapid wealth, not at its steady accumulation through settlement. When arguments between the settlers escalated in the aftermath of the native attack, Newport was one of those accused of affecting more principled motives – of making 'religion his colour' – while his aim in truth was 'nothing but present profit'.[21]

So, while John Smith remained in Jamestown and desperately tried to get the colony established, the precious barrel of Virginian earth was rushed to the best chemical experts in London, including the 'assayers' at Goldsmiths' Hall, with their scales 'pure and clean' and their furnaces ready.

What was their view? Did they agree with the company's 'experts' on the spot – men like John Martin – whose immediate testing had led quantities of the earth to be collected, and who had persuaded an all too easily convinced Captain Newport to ship it home? Could this seed, this 'sperm', as Cope called it, really yield the gold for which he and others too so dearly hoped? Everything would hang on the tests that were now to be done. It would be a tense and extraordinary moment. 'I could wish your Lordship', Cope said to Cecil, 'were at the trial.'

All haste was called for. Initially the 'golden mineral' was carefully wrapped and sealed to prevent tampering or corruption before Cecil could come to inspect it himself. (For some reason social class, and political prominence, conferred a chemical expertise.) But when Cope bent to peer at it closely he couldn't help but be suspicious, and desperately unsure. Was that slight, undoubted sparkle, which glistened within grains of the soil, really gold?

It was not long, as men remembered all too clearly, since Sir Martin Frobisher had plummeted from high hope to the deepest disappointment, while his investors paid, literally, for the mining and shipment of huge quantities of worthless rock. (For leading men then the wasted enterprise had meant the debtors' prison; the dark, shimmering rock itself, of which countless tons had been first dug and then shipped across the Atlantic, had in the end been used only to repair roads in Kent.) Unable to wait, therefore, trials were ordered to be conducted by four separate London experts, a sign of the great importance which was attached to the job, as well as of the deep anxiety which existed not to make a calamitous mistake.

These men, Cope assured Cecil, were the finest that could be found in London: 'the best experienced about the city'. The matter was given total priority, and the verdict quickly relayed. But when the dishes were removed from the furnaces after firing and subsequently inspected, the results were not at all what had been hoped. In vain the refiners looked for any ball of molten gold at the bottom. One modern geologist has suggested that the shining flakes may in fact have been mica.[22] In any case, they had vanished in the heat. So when, on the very next day, 13 August 1607, Sir Walter wrote to Cecil again, his tone this time was markedly more subdued.

Any chief secretary, he began, would be familiar enough with extreme highs followed quickly by disappointment: with hopes raised then, just as suddenly, dashed. Yesterday, he wrote, 'we sent you news of gold'. But 'this day', he continued sorrowfully, 'we cannot return you so much as copper'. The country of Virginia itself seemed to blame. What had appeared the 'land of Ophir' – the legendary, biblical land (for which men still looked) in which the stones, and indeed the very mountains from which they came, consisted of solid gold – resembled rather now the accursed 'land of Canaan'.

'In the end', he lamented, referring both to the fate of the glinting element in the soil when exposed to the fire of the furnace, as well as to the dearest hopes which he, Newport and other colonists and investors in the know had harboured, 'all turned to vapour'. After so much anticipation, the news was crushing.

At first, not surprisingly, Newport felt profoundly deflated. In a moment of deep gloom he declared that he had no intention of going back to Virginia, whatever was expected by his fellow colonists who were fearful of another Native American assault and who were desperately waiting for more men and supplies.

Leading men in London, though, talked him round, convincing Newport that the earth he had brought back to England had simply, in all likelihood, been the wrong sample. 'He found his error', the company treasurer assured Cecil. (Or rather, it was found for him.) What he had brought with him now was simply not 'the same ore of which the first trial was made'. It wasn't that the men had not found gold: they had, of course. The fault in fact was John Martin's, and it was his mistake which had made fools of Newport, of the king, the country and indeed of Martin's own father, the eminent goldsmith, who had looked on as eagerly as any other.

Newport seized gratefully on the idea, and it filled him with a new determination to put matters right. He threw aside his reluctance to go back to Virginia. 'He is now minded', Cecil was reassured, 'to take upon him the present voyage again.' With men and supplies – some sixty new colonists – he would re-cross the Atlantic as planned after all. And this time he would find wealth for real. In fact he was adamant, and rashly he promised Cecil that he would never return to England, would see neither him nor anyone else he knew again, without that which 'he confidently believed he had brought before'.[23]

One interested contemporary, the ambitious diplomat Dudley Carleton (chastened by the fact that it was he who had unwittingly let the house beside Parliament whose vault was stuffed with gunpowder during the famous plot of 1605), penned one of the countless letters he wrote which dealt with the political gossip circulating in a 'misty and unsavoury' capital.[24] Captain Newport had arrived recently from Virginia, Carleton wrote in August 1607. And he – Newport – was full of praise for the air and the soil in America, even if the men no longer had the firm evidence that they thought they had brought with them, of silver or gold. Clearly, by then the initial shock of the failed test had passed, and a determination had set in to try again. The Council, he wrote, planned 'with all diligence' to send much-needed supplies to Virginia.

A ship would return with Newport at the helm. And with it would sail a pinnace – two vessels, a 'double supply'. They duly lifted their anchors and left England on 8 October that year, and on board now sailed around 120 further colonists, taking with them more food and other essentials. Among those who went were not only cloth-workers and apothecaries – those trained in the dispensing of herbal medicines (which in due course, though not yet, included tobacco) – but also two goldsmiths, Richard Belfield and William Johnson, and two refiners, William Dawson and Abram Ransack, whose task it was to assist in ensuring the reliable testing of future samples, which could then be loaded, in bulk, onto the returning ship.[25]

When he managed, finally, to get to see King James – the meeting having been repeatedly and quite deliberately postponed, much to his exasperation – the Spanish ambassador raged that this entire American venture of the English was a 'shabby deceit'. Not only did it trample on Spanish rights in the New World, he claimed: but the men would hardly find in Virginia what they wanted to find, since the land there, he asserted confidently, was 'very sterile'.

The king pretended to agree, and nodded his head wisely. He affected, perhaps actually felt, indifference to the venture (though he did express surprise that Spanish rights were infringed, when Virginia lay so far from the lands which were actually occupied by Spain). The scheme was nothing to do with him, he said. Settlers went to America entirely at their own risk, and any misfortune – such as a Spanish attack – would not be avenged. This official separation from colonial ventures which were run by private bodies was characteristic of early English expansion, and it was certainly useful for the king to be able to deny all knowledge, even if this barely seemed plausible to a Spaniard accustomed to much more direct monarchical control.

Taking the king at his word, the ambassador promptly urged his own king to confront this English presence while it remained small. 'The few who are there', he advised, 'should be finished outright': 'cut the root, so that it would not sprout again.' More clearly than his superior, he saw what a danger this infant settlement might pose in the long term, should it become embedded. In any case, James told the Spanish representative, he had been given the same information about the region which the English had elected to colonise: that the land was barren, and 'very unproductive'. 'Those who thought to find great riches there', he pronounced, 'were deceived'. Perhaps he sincerely believed this to be true.[26]

Still, Englishmen *were* deceived and did think to find great riches, and Christopher Newport was one of them. It was early in January 1608 when his ship arrived back at Jamestown, having stopped once again in the Caribbean for supplies – enjoying, no doubt, the December warmth. (The pinnace which had sailed with her had become separated and was severely delayed.) In Virginia it was the middle of winter now, and it was a winter more extreme, more 'piercing', than those with which the English were familiar. The air was 'bitter cold'.[27] Trees were festooned with ice. Breath clotted and swirled in visible clouds. The ground, especially early in the morning, set white and hard with frost. And little more than a third of the original settlers remained alive.

Immediately Newport set about re-establishing his authority in a colony which was predictably depressed and fractious. (It certainly was not true, as some in England claimed, that the colonists were 'in good health', 'well contented' and 'in love one with another'.)[28] Newport scotched some of the in-fighting which had in fact grown rife among the surviving colonists in his absence. And he tried to energise those who had found easy riches rather harder to come by than they had hoped, and who now were wallowing, idly and hopelessly, 'in such despair'. It was a task which got no easier when fire, days afterwards, devoured the settlement, destroying the primitive, reed-thatched houses which had been built, as well as the supplies which remained in the storehouse, and which left settlers – new as well as old – starving and destitute. After upbraiding him for providing the wrong sample, Newport set John Martin to work leading efforts to provide a batch of earth that did in fact contain gold for him to take back to England, presenting him with the four new men from London who were expert in this line of work.

Newport then became distracted for a while by relations with the local Native Americans, travelling on an embassy to the local chief, Powhatan, who refused to visit Jamestown. But when Newport returned to the English settlement early in March the first thing he did was to go to discover whether Martin had succeeded in his task. The news that he was given, though, was dispiriting. No gold had been found, in spite of (perhaps *because* of) the well-qualified help with which Martin had been provided.

Remembering all too clearly the pledge he had made in England not to return until he had succeeded, Newport began to panic. Everyone in the colony, he demanded, must devote themselves to the search. All should stop what they were doing, however important it might seem: they should stop working to build houses, stop planting corn. Instead they were to spend their days helping to dig for gold. In talking greedily with the refiners and goldsmiths with whom he had voyaged back from England, Newport had acquired a dangerous smattering of knowledge and this mixed, combustibly, with his enthusiasm. 'Till then', noted one observer wryly, 'we never accounted Captain Newport a refiner.'

Those who *were* refiners, of course, and who had been shipped across the Atlantic precisely because of this expertise, were only too eager to foster work which put them firmly at the centre of the stage. These 'gilded' individuals succumbed to Newport's very evident desire to see gold in the glistering earth. They pronounced themselves satisfied. And they made what were called 'golden promises', which allowed loading to get under way and which roused the entire colony to a frenzy.

'All men', it was said, duly became these men's 'slaves in the hope of recompense'. Jamestown was gripped by an insane fever. On every side, one witness later wrote, 'there was no talk, no hope, no work, but dig gold, wash gold, refine gold, load gold'. Such was the obsession, the clamour, that some were driven insane. 'One mad fellow', it was remembered, demanded that if he died he should be buried in the sparkling sand lest this magical earth somehow make 'gold of his bones'.

For no good reason, as the mania gripped the colony, the ship and the mariners waited, in case they be required to ship piles of this glistening soil back to England. For three and a half months they drew wages and consumed precious supplies. Not quite 'all men' were possessed by the fever, though. The down-to-earth Captain John Smith, it seems – 'brass without, but gold within' was how one eulogist described him[29] – was one man who remained resolutely unimpressed by what he called these 'golden inventions'. In fact he soon grew angry and frustrated that so much of the colony's limited food supplies – supplies which undoubtedly *were* precious – should have been consumed by sailors merely waiting to depart.

In any case, if there was so much gold in this land, he reasoned, why then didn't the natives seem to possess it? (In truth, food 'you must know', he declared, 'is all their wealth' – *true* wealth, as he rightly saw it.) In any case, what evidence was there that gold even existed in this earth, whether the natives had discovered it or not? This frantic excitement was all a wasteful and futile distraction. Smith vented his frustration at John Martin, one of the leading men involved. 'I heard him question with Captain Martin', remembered one who was there, 'and tell him, unless he would show him a more substantial trial, he was not enamoured with their dirty skill.' He found it infuriating. 'Never', it was said, did anything more 'torment him, than to see all necessary business neglected, to freight such a drunken ship with so much gilded dirt.'

In his own account, Smith admitted that little concerning the entrails of the earth could be known with certainty. God moved, after all, in mysterious ways. It was true that lands in the same latitude had proved rich in mines. And it was the case that the glistening crust of these American rocks could 'easily persuade a man to believe' that they were valuable, particularly if he wanted desperately to believe this in the first place. But it was clear to him that colonists had allowed themselves to become carried away by their own fond imagination. They collected 'shining stones and spangles' that were carried down by the rivers: 'washings from the mountains'. And they flattered themselves, Smith grumbled, 'in their own vain conceits', that these were what 'they were not'.[30]

When this second ship, with its much larger cargo of alleged ore, arrived back in England tests were hastily carried out once more. But these too showed, of course, that Smith was right to have been sceptical. The dreams of gold which had swept the colony had been simply that: dreams, with no basis in reality. There was, just as Smith had suspected, a good reason why the Native Americans near Jamestown did not use gold and silver in the manner of the natives, say, of the Inca Empire. They did not use it because they did not possess it.

When the pinnace arrived later after a delay in the Caribbean, then prepared to return to England, some – John Martin foremost among them – urged that it too be loaded with earth. Every possible spadeful should be shipped: why be purely rich, when they could be richer? (No word had yet reached Virginia, of course, that the soil, once tested, was not considered to have any value.) But Smith was a forceful character. Passions had somewhat cooled. And this time he was adamant. So cedar wood was sent instead: a commodity which would prove saleable, at least, and of some value.

'I hear not', noted one quizzical London observer when the boat arrived, 'of any novelties or other commodities she hath brought more than sweet wood.' And John Martin had sailed back to England too, thinking of the soil rather than the wood, 'desirous', it was said, 'to enjoy the credit of his supposed art of finding the golden mine' – barely suppressing the images which crowded his mind, the conjured shouts which rang in his ears, appropriate to the return of a hero to his homeland. In this, though, he was to be deeply disappointed, just as investors and officials in the company in London must also have been. For all the preliminary excitement, the sparkle, once again, proved not to be gold.

Over subsequent years continued efforts were made. Newport himself led over one hundred men on a further exploration upriver – though a single individual, Smith grumbled, could have performed the task just as well. Much time and effort were expended on this venture in digging and refining. Now a vein of silver, it was claimed, had been found in that 'crust of earth we digged'. But in truth, Smith later wrote, it was a 'poor trial' and when the men returned, bedraggled, to Jamestown they were 'half sick, all complaining'. Further colonists sent out to Virginia often harboured the same 'great gilded hopes', of gold and rapid fortune. Long before the gold rush of the nineteenth century, 'America' connoted wealth and opportunity. Even a few decades later a ship which carried emigrants to Virginia boasted the name *Golden Fortune*, which spoke eloquently of the hopes of many on board. But often then, as later, the dreams did not materialise, and these hopes too were disappointed.[31]

Further efforts were also made in England: to persuade investors to stump up more money which in the long term, they were promised, would buy them a lucrative share in 'such mines, and minerals of gold, silver, and other metal or treasure' as were found. But, not surprisingly, general excitement and even the belief in such claims dissipated, as surely as did assertions that this was, in other respects, a promised land. Too often these confident declarations had melted into nothing.

Those who invested, or who were involved in the company management, duly became impatient with what they called 'ifs and ands, hopes, and some few proofs'. From being wildly over-inflated, Virginia's reputation suffered a crash. In general, it was said, 'only the name of God' was profaned more frequently 'in the streets and market places of London than was the name of Virginia'.

In the city's taverns the settlement was dismissed as nothing but 'a cloud of smoke' – a metaphor that was in fact more apt than people knew.[32]

By this time the company in London was chronically impoverished: in 'greater straits for money than one can imagine'.[33] Each successive promise of great and instant riches in Virginia had proved a mirage. Selling stock in the company had managed to raise only just over half what was hoped, and many subscribers simply refused to pay the sums they owed, to what seemed a failing enterprise.

In the spring of 1609 the same hierarchy sent a letter to the Lord Mayor of London, who forwarded it in turn to all of the City Livery Companies, requesting that they deal 'very earnestly and effectually' with their members, pleading for investment. Few, however, were convinced. That same year the Virginia Company announced a seven-year moratorium on the paying of dividends. In desperation company leaders urged Newport to find something, anything, in Virginia of significant value: a gold mine, a route to the Pacific Ocean, or even survivors from the old, lost Elizabethan colony at Roanoke. It didn't matter what it was, if it generated wealth and excitement.

When Newport did return to Virginia, he brought with him a barge that could in theory be taken apart, then reassembled beyond the rapids in the James River, to allow further exploration. As it happened, though, the pieces proved far too heavy to carry, even for the 120 men Newport took with him; 500 could not have done so, Smith complained. (And in any case 120 was an absurdly and unnecessarily large number, drawn from a settlement that could ill spare the manpower.) Newport had also shipped an ornate bed from England, to present to Powhatan, the paramount native chieftain. And he brought him a crown: a scheme, dreamt up by the company in London, with which Smith vehemently disagreed. 'By whose advice you sent him such presents', he fumed, 'I know not.' Very probably, he wrote, they would ruin them all ' 'ere we hear from you again'.

These offerings led too, what is more, to a further deterioration in his relationship with Newport. Smith was quite right to disagree. What he called this 'strange coronation', in particular, achieved nothing other than bafflement, and only made relations between Powhatan and the English worse. Bluntly, Smith informed the London hierarchy that he had been 'directly against' the plan, for reasons that now, he said, 'too late', were 'generally confessed'. Was the rumour true, he also demanded to know, that the company had paid Newport £100 per year? If so, the money was wholly wasted. Every shipmaster sent out here, he wrote, 'can find the way as well as he'.[34]

Smith had now been elected Jamestown's president, so popular had his hard-headed, practical and incorrupt approach proved with the settlers themselves. From the directors in London, meanwhile, he demanded a fundamental change in mindset. It was simply not the case, he wrote, that immediate riches – 'present profit' – would be found in Virginia, and it was vital that the company accepted this. They must stop sending out either refiners and goldsmiths, or idle men ('loiterers' as he called them), who thought only of winning easy wealth. What they should provide instead were hard-working individuals with

The later in the year, the stormier the Northern Atlantic tended to be. The crossing might last as little as five weeks, but could take significantly longer.

Sir Humphrey Gilbert envisaged English colonisation of southern North America, but experience of Newfoundland's fish-filled waters turned him into a 'northern man altogether'.

Plan of Dartmouth.

Dartmouth was a major West Country port, increasingly prominent in the fishing trade as England's west came to rival its east.

engraver's impression of the meeting at the end of 1612 between John Guy and the othuk Native Americans who lived on Newfoundland.

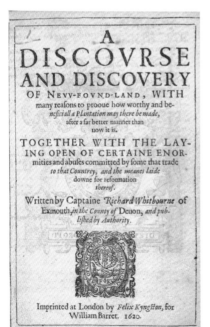

A DISCOVRSE AND DISCOVERY OF NEVV-FOVND-LAND, WITH many reasons to prooue how worthy and beneficiall a *Plantation* may there be made, after a far better manner than now it is.

TOGETHER WITH THE LAYING OPEN OF CERTAINE ENORmities and abuses committed by some that trade to that Countrey, and the meanes laide downe for reformation thereof.

Written by Captaine *Richard Whitbourne* of Exmouth, in the County of Deuon, and published by Authority.

Imprinted at London by *Felix KyngHon*, for William Barret. 1620.

Richard Whitbourne's *Discourse and Discovery*. From the earliest European visits, the seas near Newfoundland earned a reputation for spectacular hauls of cod, which encouraged people from England to settle. Richard Whitbourne was a Devonshire man who served against the Spanish Armada before concentrating on fishing off Newfoundland and colonising the island.

ROUND ASSAY FURNACE.

RECTANGULAR ASSAY FURNACE.

John Smith was one leading early English colonist in Virginia who disagreed profoundly with his compatriots' obsession with finding precious metals.

Cupellation uses high heat t[o] oxidise impurities and base metals, leaving any noble metals like gold or silver in [the] centre of the dish or cupel.

GEORGII AGRICOLAE
DE RE METALLICA LIBRI XII▸ QVI=
BVS OFFICIA, INSTRVMENTA, MACHINAE, AC OMNIA DENI=
que ad Metallicam spectantia, non modò luculentissimè describuntur, sed &
per effigies, suis locis insertas, adiunctis Latinis, Germanicâq; appella=
tionibus ita ob oculos ponuntur, vt clarius tradi non possint.

EIVSDEM

DE ANIMANTIBVS SVBTERRANEIS LIBER, AB AVTORE
recognitus: cum Indicibus diuersis, quicquid in opere tractatum est,
pulchrè demonstrantibus, atq; omnibus nunc iterum ad
archetypum diligenter restitutis & castigatis.

FRO BEN

BASILEAE M▸ D▸ LXI▸

Cum Priuilegio Imperatoris in annos v.
& Galliarum Regis ad sexennium.

Though published in the mid-sixteen[th] century, for almost two centuries Georgius Agricola's *De re metallica* (*On the Nature of Metals*) remained th[e] authoritative text in Europe on minin[g] and refining.

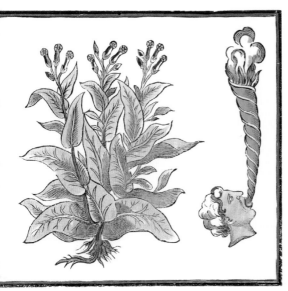

This illustration of the tobacco plant, along with a Native American inhaling its smoke, was included in a work by Matthias de Lobel, a Flemish botanist and physician who worked in England for James I.

*PANACEA,*
OR
The Univerſal Medicine,
BEING
A DISCOVERY
of the
Wonderfull Vertues
OF
Tobacco
Taken in a Pipe,
WITH
Its Operation and Uſe both in
*Phyſick* and *Chyrurgery.*

By Dr *EVERARD,*&c.

*LONDON,*
Printed for *Simon Miller* at the Star in Sᵗ *Pauls* Church-yard, near the Weſt-end, 1659.

bacco was regarded by many as a 'universal medicine' – 'no great friend to ysicians', as one Dutch doctor worried unnecessarily.

James VI and I in 1621, near the end of his life. It was during his reign that the first English colonies in America were established.

The daughter of a Native American chieftain, Pocahontas was captured by the English and converted to Christianity. Her visit to London caused a sensation.

With the Virginia Company desperate for funds, they turned to a device which remains popular today: a lottery.

Edward Winslow lived in Leiden with Robert Cushman, of whom no portrait exists. He sailed on the *Mayflower* and co-wrote an account of early colonial life in America, which Cushman brought to England.

imagined portrait of Anne dstreet by an unknown artist. portrait from life was painted, ich in itself speaks of the uvinistic world in which she d.

Hatred of the ecclesiastical ceremonies and beautification introduced by Charles I's Archbishop of Canterbury, William Laud, impelled many Puritans during the 1630s to emigrate to America.

Laud is here pictured sailing a ship to hell. It was, of course, his enemies who took to the sea, but evidently the pun on a tempest in the 'sea of Canterbury' was irresistible.

humble, practical skills, whose work, while it would not conjure a sudden windfall, might lay the basis for long-term success.

'When you send again', Smith begged, 'I entreat you rather send but thirty carpenters, husbandmen, gardeners, fishermen, blacksmiths, masons, and diggers up of trees' rather than 'a thousand of such as we have'. The colony had no need of any more of those he dismissed as 'lubberly gluttons', and who were only a drain on its limited resources. What the place did need, he maintained, was men who would work. As president, with increased influence over the colony's Council, this was what he decreed: that 'he that will not work shall not eat'.[35]

Popular as he was in Jamestown, Smith's blunt, even belligerent tone – with men who were *clearly* his social betters – was not highly valued among the company hierarchy, and plans were made to replace him, even as his term as president ran down.

Anxious for a significant increase to the English presence in Virginia, a substantial, 'third supply' was organised and despatched. It brought food and many more colonists, as well as new leaders, armed with stronger, more autocratic powers to supplant this troublesome, jumped-up individual who insisted upon dousing all expectation of quick reward.

As he attempted to resist the reorganisation, moreover, Smith was badly wounded in an accidental explosion which tore flesh from his hip and upper leg, leaving him in such agony that he was 'near bereft of his senses'. His practical wisdom, his strong-minded and decisive leadership and his healthy mistrust of the Native Americans were much missed. Those beneath him never doubted that he would share what supplies were available, or that he would go himself wherever he sent his men. And they trusted his judgement, repeatedly proven in the most pressured situations. Soon we all, wrote one, 'found the want of Captain Smith'.[36]

In Virginia itself, Native American tribes, on whom the colonists remained fatally dependent for food, proved increasingly hostile as it became obvious that the English intended to stay put. 'I am told', Powhatan told Smith bluntly (and presciently), that 'your coming hither is not for trade, but to invade my people, and possess my country.' In the short term, this reliance on the Native American communities was one for which the colonists paid dearly. Increasingly, the natives refused to trade with the settlement, thinking to starve them out. And sure enough, during the desperate winter of 1609–10, this tactic wreaked havoc among the hapless English.

In what became aptly known as the 'Starving Time' the grim reaper scythed some 500 colonists down to only sixty. All of the English felt 'that sharp prick of hunger', which none could describe (wrote one who could) 'but he which hath tasted the bitterness thereof'. Without supplies, desperate settlers were reduced to eating first horses, cats and dogs, then the leather of their shoes, and finally each other's corpses. Hunger, it was said, looked 'pale and ghastly in every face'. Nor was fleeing to native villages the salvation it had once been, since Native American communities now were under strict instructions to refuse to welcome the English. No wonder that one colonist was reduced to yelling 'that there was no God' (for He, surely, 'would not suffer His creatures [...] to endure those miseries') prior to heading into the woods to forage for food where he was killed by native arrows, then eaten by wolves.

Illness proved a constant foe in a region which was malarial and unhealthy. (Colonists like Walter Russell, a 'doctor of physic', had their work cut out, though there was little of course that they could do.) Some, in their despair, dug their own graves, and then lay in them. Four-fifths did die. Little imagination is required regarding the state of the remaining fifth who didn't, but they must have envied their deceased brethren. And ships from England bringing further colonists, who were much needed to replace those who had starved, also brought rats, which competed for anything edible which might remain.

It can only be guessed how much better the colony might have fared if led with Smith's emphasis upon self-sufficiency over riches. But some, certainly, felt that it was their bad government, rather than external conditions, which was primarily responsible. 'The occasion' for the calamity, wrote one witness, 'was only our own, for want of providence, industry, and government, and not the barrenness and defect of the country, as is generally supposed.'[37]

Early in 1612 the company was obliged to seek a new charter from the king in London. And when they did so, in serious financial straits, they sought royal approval for the use of a different method of raising funds:

one that was invented in the latter half of the sixteenth century, and which spread the notion of quick and fortuitous wealth, that had so captivated the colonists, to those who stayed behind.

The company could raise extra money, the charter decreed, by the use of lotteries organised all over the country, but chiefly by what was called a 'great lottery' in London. A temporary 'lottery house' was built for the occasion at the west end of St Paul's Cathedral. Posters were mounted across the city to attract attention, decorated with vast, overspilling sacks of coins. Tickets were offered for twelvepence each, and the numbers were then placed into a locked container, with a child – less corruptible, it was presumed – drawing out the winning numbers. The prizes, an array of goods, money, jewels and plate, were donated by the livery companies as well as by wealthy investors.

The first prize was very substantial indeed: 'a thousand pound in plate'. And the first number drawn was that of a London tailor called Thomas Sharplisse, who must have been astonished at the arrival, 'in very stately manner', of all this valuable plate outside his small house. God, to be sure, had listened to his prayers that morning, and had delivered the vast riches which an American gold mine might have been expected to provide. Did he continue thereafter to make clothes? Probably not: we simply don't know. And he would scarcely be remembered by history at all had he not been the winner of the first Virginian lottery.[38]

Sharplisse's chances were improved by the fact that the company did not, for all its promotion, find it easy to persuade people to invest in tickets. Although lotteries were a way of raising money which has proved to have a lasting appeal, this one was in fact slow to become established at the time, particularly when it took place in what was a dubious cause.

The scheme, the company hierarchy admitted, had not 'fall[en] out as our selves desired'. It lamented what it called the 'backwardness' of citizens in taking part. Three thousand tickets for the first lottery had to be disposed of unsold.

There seemed no sign that things were going to get dramatically better. It was true that word reaching the Spanish king still spoke of the long-term threat that the venture posed to his empire, and of the resulting need for action. 'Already', reported one Spanish ambassador in England, 'they have houses and begin another colony in Newfoundland, in those regions where they have their fisheries.' 'Now', he urged, 'is a very favourable time for their punishment.'

Another of his countrymen considered that the English were so desperate to establish a secure footing in America that they would go so far as to 'sell their own children'. But it was also true that often the Spanish dismissed the English venture in Virginia as a pipe dream which was not based on any solid source of wealth, akin to 'building up stones without any foundation'. And they were not wrong to do so, on the evidence that they had. Too many, once easy wealth proved frustratingly hard to obtain, gave up entirely. One English investor lamented that the venture had proved so unsuccessful through what he called 'the extreme beastly idleness of our nation'.[39]

When King James I issued a new royal charter that same year – in 1612 – to a North West Passage Company, the leading members of which had often also assumed key roles in the Virginian venture, it was evidence in part that prominent individuals had come to despair of the wealth that they fondly imagined springing from this particular undertaking – either in gold or in the fabled passage to the east. Always eager to keep multiple irons in the fire, they moved on.

Christopher Newport had himself made his final voyage to Virginia the previous year. He may have been motivated by a difficult relationship with the new, violent and dictatorial governor, less bound than his predecessors like Smith had been by the need to keep other leading men on board. But Newport didn't retire. The simple fact was that he too preferred to work during his final years (until his death abroad during the spring of 1617, for another venture which seemed a more probable source of wealth: the East India Company).[40]

In hindsight, there was much about John Smith's opinion that was well judged. He was right to suspect the ambitions harboured by many of the Jamestown colonists for mines of gold, silver or other valuable commodities. He was right to believe that the English would need to work if they were to build a lasting, solidly founded settlement. But it so happened that those who chased after a dream of quick wealth *were* right in a way that Smith had never suspected: because there was 'gold', or there could be, in the metaphorical sense of rapid wealth, in Virginia. And it did grow in the soil, just as men believed that gold did.

For all the deceptive shimmering in patches of earth, though, this 'gold' was not of the metallic variety, nor was it quite so instant. Seeds would need to be planted.

Among the passengers of 1609's 'third supply' had been one colonist called John Rolfe – a vigorous, good-looking young man from East Anglia who was the only one of two male twins to survive until adulthood.

With his wife, Rolfe embarked early that summer on the *Sea Venture* – the *Sea Adventure*, as she was sometimes appropriately known. She was the largest ship of a substantial fleet. Seven sailed from the royal dockyard east of London at Woolwich, where the huge *Royal Prince*, described as 'the greatest goodliest ship built in England', neared completion, before two more joined at Plymouth, the company having decided that landing colonists in bulk was the only way to counter threats in Virginia posed by disease and warfare.

Of the 150 passengers on the *Sea Venture* some, like the carpenter Nicholas Bennitt, or Rolfe himself, were deemed worthy of a mention on the official list. Others would have been wholly forgotten if they hadn't happened to be mentioned by chance, like the thirty-year-old servant Elizabeth Joons. Most were cramped on board as the ships continued west from Plymouth, heading out into a seemingly limitless ocean, taking a northerly route to America rather than the more southerly one via the Caribbean. As England faded, then disappeared from view, Rolfe shielded the bowl of a clay pipe with his hands and cloak from the wind and the spray which lashed across the bows.

His background was typical of the region from which he came. He was a strict Calvinist, and his writing is suffused with the tenets of Puritan Christianity, while he was also entrepreneurial and hard-working. (We know that his father, also called John Rolfe, was a religious merchant with a keen eye for gaps in the market: a memorial to him in the ancient Norfolk church of Heacham, where he worshipped, praised a man who laboured at the 'export and import of things which England either abounded with or wanted' – and the son to whom he bequeathed his own name shared more than this.)[41] John grew up profoundly familiar with the sea, both from his father's work and from formative years spent at his county's north-west perimeter – beneath vast East Anglian skies stretching above unbroken miles of sandy coastline, next to a grey sea that approached at high tide, then retreated over the great expanse of flat beach into the distance.

Tobacco, at the time Rolfe grew up, was becoming increasingly common, and available, in England. At a young age he was encouraged to try smoking it, and it was a habit to which he became hopelessly addicted. He was only in his twenties when he first crossed the Atlantic to Virginia, and a man who knew him, talking of his relationship with tobacco, referred then – long before the chemistry of addiction was at all understood – to 'the love he hath a long time born unto it'.

At the time he first tried it, and when he asked what this sweetly pungent, dried and shredded brown leaf was, the supply of tobacco in England depended upon Spanish colonies in South America and the Caribbean. But either next to the Thames, in conversation with the increasingly successful tobacco merchants who worked there, or during the time his crew spent in the Caribbean en route to Jamestown, the idea occurred to him of trying to transplant what was a nicer, more popular variety to North America, and then importing the resultant crop to England – if, that is, the plant took to Virginia's soil and climate.

It was only with the discovery of the American continent that this particular plant had come to the attention of Europeans. Christopher Columbus was the first of many* to report in amazement the Native American custom of 'drinking' the smoke given off by its leaves as they burnt. A few decades later, further north, a French explorer wrote (equally incredulously) of seeing natives in modern Canada grinding this 'herb', cramming it into a hollow wooden tube and then lighting it 'with a fire brand' before drawing 'on the other end so long that they fill their bodies with smoke until it comes out of their mouth and nostrils as from a chimney'. They carried the leaves everywhere in pouches and held, he said, that smoking kept them warm and in good health.

England was slow on the draw, so to speak. It wasn't until the 1560s (the decade in which the French diplomat Jean Nicot began a craze for it in France, bequeathing his name to both the plant and to its active chemical ingredient) that the crew on which the fishing pioneer

Anthony Parkhurst served brought a sample of tobacco to English shores. And even then a limited supply meant that smoking remained a peculiar habit restricted for a short time to a few in the sailing community. By the following decade, though, English translations of European medical books were recommending tobacco as a cure for all manner of ailments, including, ironically, bad breath (with some cause, perhaps, at the time) and cancer (with none). Then, in the 1580s, it began to broaden its grip on English society.

In 1586 colonists who were returning from the failed American settlement at Roanoke caused a sensation by smoking tobacco ostentatiously in pipes. (One of them, the early scientist Thomas Hariot, noted that the colonists with him, while in America, had learnt to 'suck' tobacco 'after their [the Native Americans'] manner', continuing to do so after their return. It was 'from that time forward', one eyewitness and historian wrote later, that the substance 'began to grow into great request'.[42] Some took to it because they believed it had health benefits. For others, it was simply 'wantonness'. Both groups relished sucking the 'stinking smoke' through an earthen pipe, then expelling it through their nostrils.

Some lamented that the practice of puffing on the streets became 'so frequent' and that people displayed an 'insatiable desire' for the stuff. Tobacco shops, it was observed, sprang up as commonly in most English towns as taverns. One English gentleman estimated soon afterwards that in London alone there were 7,000 of them. 'Tobacco houses make such a muster', it was said, 'almost in every lane, and in every by-corner round about London.' Sir Walter Raleigh did not, as is often believed, *introduce* the habit, but he certainly did *popularise* it. When he was later executed, after a long spell of imprisonment, an inscription was discovered on the tobacco box that he had been allowed to keep at his side. 'It was my comfort', it read in Latin, 'in those miserable times.'[43]

By the beginning of the seventeenth century antagonists and defenders of this strange custom were vying fiercely in the press. Opponents compared the lungs of smokers to those of chimney sweeps. One declared, with uncanny accuracy – even if his underlying theory was bogus – that regular smoking led to impotence or infertility, rendering men 'incapable of propagation'. (It was an assertion that was repeated, and no doubt observed, one poet noting of the habit that 'it dulls the spirit, it dims the sight / It robs a woman of her right'.) It was claimed too that tobacco left men generally depressed, damaging their 'memory, imagination and understanding'.

And it generally *was* men, initially, who smoked. Another notable opponent was King James, whose 'Counterblast' is well known and often quoted, and who, more significantly, dramatically raised the taxation on tobacco: a move which if nothing else – as countless governments have found since – was a welcome boost to the struggling exchequer, as well as to smugglers of contraband, untaxed product.

But this was one fight beyond even a king. The English press was sufficiently free to allow James's opponents to extol what they called 'the virtues of tobacco'. The addictive nature of the habit saw its practice spread. And a few years later, in 1610, Sir Francis Bacon wrote that the use of tobacco was growing all the time – John Rolfe was only one of a rapidly-rising number of smokers in early-seventeenth-century England – and that it was a custom that was hard to quit.

King James himself soon had no choice but to agree to incorporate the makers of clay pipes, in spite of the bitter taste it must have left in his mouth.

For most of their journey the ships in the *Sea Venture*'s fleet sailed together. But when they were only about a week's voyage from the American colony, signs developed of a brewing storm.

The sky grew black. Clouds, the crew remembered, gathered 'thick upon us', while winds sang and whistled 'most unusually'. For days the sea surged and boiled in the darkness. 'Fury', it was said, 'added to fury.' Seasoned sailors confessed that they had never met anything like it, unable to 'apprehend in our imaginations any possibility of greater violence'. 'All that I had ever suffered gathered together', one sailor remembered, 'might not hold comparison with this.'

While most of the fleet struggled through to Jamestown though battered by towering waves, the *Sea Venture* herself became separated and lost in this 'hell of darkness', the storm having 'beat all light from heaven'. 'Our ship', one West Country passenger recalled, 'became so shaken, torn, and leaked' that the hold filled high over the ballast with sea water, as it poured in much faster than men could frantically bail it out.'[44] Only when the weather began to ease did the ship's captain spy land, in the shape of a small, tree-clad island emerging from the gloom.

For a long time coral reefs surrounding the island had caused it to be spurned by European sailors as too dangerous to frequent. (The 'Isle of Devils', it had been called as a consequence – 'the dangerous and dreaded island'; the most 'unfortunate, and forlorn place of the world'.) But the English now were desperately relieved to have survived at all and took the risk of deliberately grounding their ship upon the reef, before using their small boats to ferry passengers to the land. And what the men, women and children found was far from what the terrifying reputation suggested. 'In truth', wrote one, the island was a paradise. While fellow emigrants on board the other ships thought them lost to the waves, in fact they walked upon 'the richest, healthfullest, and [most] pleasing land' that mankind had ever trodden.[45]

John Rolfe's wife survived the ordeal with him. When they embarked in London she had been in the early stages of pregnancy, and the following year, in February 1610, she gave birth on the island to a daughter. The baby girl was named in honour of the place where she was born: Bermuda Rolfe. Perhaps it was immediately obvious that the baby's life was in danger. In any case, she was quickly christened, as babies generally were to ensure that they did not die without first becoming members of God's Church. The one-armed Christopher Newport had sailed on the ship – as deputy rather than overall captain, perhaps because of his failure to deliver on his previous, extravagant promises – and he stood now as one of the child's godparents. But sadly, like many babies of her era, Bermuda did not survive long, even in paradise, and she was buried on the island, while crew members worked to finish building two new boats in which the colonists planned to sail on towards Jamestown.

It may also have been while he was on the island that Rolfe obtained, and carefully bagged, seeds belonging to a tobacco plant different to those which had previously been grown in North America – unless he had them already, from the Spanish tobacco which was available in England. While the Virginian variety was high in nicotine but bitter – 'poor', wrote one who tried it, with 'a biting taste'[46] – the variety which the Spanish grew and imported to Europe from the Caribbean and from South America had larger, flatter leaves and was milder, more pleasant and commanded a much higher price. It was known as 'Long Tobacco' because of its physical size, and Rolfe, who as a smoker himself was aware how significant the market for it might be in England, determined to try growing it at Jamestown.

When the English embarked nervously again, later that spring, in the two boats which they had built (and named, aptly in one case, *Patience*, and optimistically in the other, *Deliverance*), they arrived at a settlement which could not have been less of a paradise – ravaged, depopulated and run-down as Jamestown then was after the desperately gruelling winter of the 'Starving Time'.

The new arrivals found a place that was 'full of misery'. The gates of the fort hung at an angle from their hinges. Houses had been half pulled down for firewood, to spare men the risk of heading into the woods. And the few survivors were capable only of groaning weakly. In fact, things were so bad that a decision was taken to abandon the settlement – just as the Native Americans hoped – and to make for the fishing grounds off Newfoundland en route back to England.

If this had been what was done, Rolfe's seeds would never have been planted. And it was only the sudden arrival of another fleet of colonists and supplies from the home country which forced a reluctant rethink. With these extra hands a further attempt was made to make this 'noisome and unwholesome place' habitable. A prompt assault on a nearby native town led to it being captured, along with its neighbouring fields.

Rolfe's personal misfortunes continued. Not long after the death of his baby girl, his wife died. It wasn't, of course, the sort of thing that was out of the ordinary, and God, he must quietly have concluded, had His inscrutable reasons. Alone and grieving, Rolfe threw himself instead into his horticultural experiments, working tirelessly. 'No man', it was later said, worked 'to his power.' And the early results, he concluded after trying them himself, were promising, even if they were only on a small scale.

Early in 1614 – a little over six years since the English had first arrived – he sent a first, tentative shipment of this more palatable form of Virginia tobacco to England, where it was well received. The following year he boxed and shipped much more, and sales soared with the supply. 'No country under the sun', it was observed of this

English colony in America, 'doth afford more pleasant, sweet and strong tobacco.'[47] And meanwhile the English in Virginia began to get back on their feet, spreading beyond Jamestown to other small settlements further upstream, under the admittedly draconian rule of a governor who decreed violent and often fatal punishment for the smallest misdemeanour.

Rolfe is most famous these days for the second wife he married in America after the loss of his first. Not a fellow colonist, she was the favourite daughter of Powhatan: the most important Native American chieftain close to Jamestown. She was a young woman now, having been a girl when she first became acquainted with the English, and when she first became a friend in particular of the bluff, bearded colonist called John Smith. He remembered her as 'a child'. But even then her looks were striking, and she had, Smith remarked, 'wit and spirit'.[48] She had often come to the English settlement to play games and do cartwheels with the boys. It seems that she felt a close affinity with the culture and religion of these newcomers from over the sea.

Early in the spring of 1613, though, she was kidnapped by the English – lured, by trickery, onto their boat. The plan was to use her as a bargaining tool: for the return of prisoners, stolen guns and tools, and for obtaining corn which, once again, was desperately needed by the colonists. Investors who learnt of her capture saw it also as a means to secure native help in the search for riches in the ground which, so far, had proved fruitless, but about which – against the odds – they still harboured hope. One observer in England applauded this seizure, pleased to record that finally 'some life' had been put into the venture: 'into that action, that before was almost at the last cast'.

Colonists, he wrote, had 'taken a daughter of a king that was their greatest enemy'. To secure her release, he noted, her father had offered the English 'whatever is in his power, and to become their friend'. Most importantly, what he had promised was to 'bring them where they shall meet with gold mines' – a remarkable offer, even if an alluring one, given the lack of evidence that the natives had gold themselves.[49] It was after this, while she was living as a hostage with the English, that she met one Englishman – John Rolfe – who was unmoved by the search for gold, and who instead busily tended some seedlings which he was the first to plant in North American soil.

The handsome young widower was living in the new settlement of Henrico, over thirty miles upriver from Jamestown, when this Native American hostage was brought to the community under close guard. Rolfe found himself strangely captivated by the young woman. He wrestled with his conscience, and in particular with a biblical injunction (which, as a deeply religious man, he took very seriously) against wedding foreign wives. He sought the permission of his overbearing governor, giving his word that what motivated him was not 'carnal affection', but 'the good of the plantation', 'the honour of our country' and ultimately 'the glory of God', who would surely approve the conversion to Christ of this 'unbelieving creature'. Still, he did admit to himself that his thoughts towards the young woman had become more complex and irrational than he let on: 'so entangled and enthralled in so intricate a labyrinth' that it was impossible to unpick them.

When he obtained the permission that he wanted, she did agree to marry him. She was baptised into the Christian faith, abandoning the religion in which she had been brought up. And she was given a new name, Rebecca, after the Old Testament story in which the arrival of a beautiful foreign servant girl signifies God's blessing, although it is not that name which has stuck. Her formal name among her own people was Matoaka. But it is by her Native American nickname that she is still commonly known: 'little wanton', or Pocahontas.

In the spring of 1614 John and 'Rebecca' married. For a time they lived together in Henrico. And then, in 1616, two years after their marriage, Rolfe brought her to England, where she caused a sensation, leading her husband into social circles much more rarefied than those to which he was accustomed – dazzling and impressive to Rolfe, who was not, presumably, as resolutely unimpressed by class as was Smith.[50] The son they had already had together, whom they christened Thomas, was the physical embodiment of a peace which held for some years between the English and the Native American tribes close to Jamestown under Powhatan's authority.

She was, John Smith wrote, 'the first Christian ever of that nation, the first Virginian [who] ever spake English, or had a child in marriage by an Englishman'.[51] But highly significant as this was, and for all her value as a symbol of that much-repeated English intention to convert the heathen natives to Christianity, Pocahontas sadly died, at Gravesend, before she could return to her American homeland.

It was while he was in England that Rolfe was moved to combat talk that Virginia was ill-suited to colonisation. The colonial cause had been, he insisted, 'so much despised and disgraced', with 'ignominy, scandals and maledictions' wrongly heaped upon it. It was for this reason that he wrote and published a work entitled *A True Relation of the State of Virginia*.

In fact, notable as his marriage to Pocahontas certainly was, Rolfe's most lasting contribution to the success of English colonisation in Virginia was very different. Also stowed in the hold of the ship in which he sailed with his wife to England were barrels of tobacco, that 'esteemed weed', which he had grown himself and which he had first imported into England two years earlier, in 1614. He named his product 'Orinoco' tobacco, in honour of Sir Walter Raleigh's quest for genuine gold in the mythical city of El Dorado, located, it was thought, up the Orinoco River in Guiana – as well as in tribute to the prominent role that Raleigh had played in popularising the use of tobacco in England.

This different variety proved immensely popular. It was cheaper than the contraband Spanish product. And it was fundamentally nicer than the kind which grew naturally in North America. Rolfe himself had developed a plantation called Varina Farms, upstream from the first colonial settlement at Jamestown, where he lived with Pocahontas and their baby son Thomas. There the plant thrived. With a little more trial and experience at cutting it, Rolfe wrote, it would rival the best West Indian crops. And the model was quickly copied, as cultivation of this variety of tobacco in Virginia expanded.

As it did so, plantations appeared along the James River. Wharfs were built for its easy collection and shipment downstream. And groups of tents and makeshift shelters were erected prior to being abandoned for low, primitive but more permanent shacks. Some subscribers to the company lamented how quickly the colony became dependent upon tobacco cultivation. This was not the form of wealth that they had imagined, and they worried that it might prove insecure. But demand for the product only grew, and supply expanded to match it. English investors in general were simply delighted that a profitable trade with Virginia had been found which might secure the colony's future.

Over the ensuing half-century growth of the English settlement continued apace, matching the increased consumption in England of its principal product, which had at last begun to place the colony on a viable footing after the doomed search for gold during its early years had left it floundering. It has been estimated that in the late 1620s, fifteen years after Rolfe grew his first crop, almost half a million pounds of tobacco was imported yearly into England. Prices fell, but demand went dramatically up. By 1670 half of the adult male population of England used small pipes made from clay to smoke tobacco on a regular basis.

In Virginia, seeds were planted just after Christmas, before the young plants were painstakingly transplanted to the main fields in the spring. Over the course of those same decades the use of white indentured labour – of servants who pressed onto ships because they were desperate, and because life in America offered a possible way out – was largely replaced by an even cheaper source which now haunts the imagination of America and the wider world: slavery, which saw thousands of black Africans shipped to America and sold to planters. By the end of the seventeenth century it was these men and women who constituted the majority of the unfree labour force in America.[52] Rolfe himself documented the beginning of the practice, recording in 1619 that a passing Dutch ship had 'sold us twenty niggers', but slavery smacked at first too much of the east – seemed an alien, unchristian practice, in factual if not in moral terms – and it was decades after his time that it became a regular and widespread trade.

After the death of Pocahontas in England in 1616, Rolfe devoted himself to the cultivation of this new commodity, though he served the Virginian colony as an administrator. A few years later, in 1619, he remarried again, while his son Thomas grew up with Rolfe's uncle in England, until he returned to Virginia – which he must have regarded as something of a homeland – as an adult. Not long afterwards, in 1622, after a long period of peace between the English colonists and the Native American tribes, cemented by Rolfe's marriage, there came a devastating attack in which numerous of the English colonists died. (By then Powhatan, Pocahontas's father, had died.) Rolfe died that year too, although the fact that he had described himself as 'sick in body' makes it possible that the cause of his death was illness rather than violence.

However his end came, Rolfe had certainly done, by then, more than anyone to ensure that the English presence in Virginia would prove a lasting one. He was a gentleman, as one writer put it, 'worthy of much commendations'. When women were shipped across the Atlantic as prospective mates for settlers (who initially were all male), their passage was often paid for not in money, not in gold, but in tobacco.

It was tobacco, it has been observed, which 'sealed the success' of early English settlement in America.[53]

During the years after he left the permanent employment of the Virginian Company, John Smith continued to take a particular interest in the fate of the English living in America.

From a distance he watched the first establishment of one new colony in particular – that of the Massachusetts Bay Company in New England – an area which he had explored some years after his time in Virginia, and about which he had written. (Ostensibly, the purpose of the venture had been similar: to look for gold and copper, and only if this failed to fish; in reality, though, Smith was cynical. The promise of gold, he claimed, had been made purely to attract investors, and not because of 'any knowledge [the master] had at all of any such matter'.)[54] In fact he had put himself forward to the company as a military leader, though ultimately he was not chosen. Probably, by then, he seemed past it. Though only in his early fifties, his experiences, as well as the toughness of the time, had aged him markedly. He complained of constant pain in his 'bruised sides': the site of the accidental injuries which he received in Virginia. And he died soon afterwards, in 1631.

Watching this subsequent venture, though, he wholeheartedly applauded the fact that this company seemed to have learnt the lesson not initially heeded in Virginia: that it was the calibre of colonists which was all-important. They should not be people who had fled abroad in order to escape 'debt, or any scandal at home'. They should certainly not be what Richard Hakluyt had called the 'offals of our people', shipped gladly from England because of their want of industry rather than for their religious opinions. And nor should they be men who hoped to become instantly rich. The personal failings of such people would simply be exported to the colony.

Smith had bitter personal experience. He, of course, had seen what had happened at first in Virginia. 'So doting', he wrote, had the company been in its search for 'mines of gold, and the South Sea', that nobody could have devised a better way of bringing 'us to ruin than they did themselves'. For such colonial projects, he argued, people were needed who were less set upon their own material aggrandisement: for whom 'riches were their servants, not their masters'. They should be 'men of good means, or arts, occupations, and qualities'. They should not, he urged, be 'silvered idle golden Pharisees, but industrious iron-steeled Publicans'.[55] Colonists should have useful skills and they should be willing to work – makers of pots, bricks or furniture, blacksmiths, furriers, farmers, whether of food or of tobacco.

Smith could, he knew, like others in Virginia, make hollow promises about precious metals which just waited in the soil to be found. But he refused, convinced that steady accumulation and industry offered a slow but much more reliable route to power and riches. 'Though I can promise', he wrote, 'no mines of gold', he invited his readers to look at what the Dutch had achieved by fishing – or what, he might have added a few decades later, Virginia garnered through the cultivation of tobacco. (Had he lived long enough to see the slave trade become established in Virginia, he would not, having been a captured slave in southern Europe himself until his escape, have harboured any illusions about this form of labour.)

It was the hard work of truly dedicated subjects – perhaps those who felt themselves, as in New England, to be supervised from above – which could not ultimately be 'suppressed by all the king of Spain's golden powers'. And here the King of England, Smith felt, was in a profoundly powerful position, because 'industrious subjects are more available to a king [at least to an English king] than gold'.[56]

# III

# EQUALITY BEFORE GOD

From his teenage years an earnest and puzzling boy called Robert Cushman lived and worked in Canterbury, the small but largely brick-built city on the ancient road which ran from London through Kent to the port of Dover.

Born in a village to the south, Cushman was a second son, who was expected to make his own way in the world. In any case, his family was not affluent and his parents could not afford to spare him for formal education, even at a young age. Never mind Latin: he had never learnt literacy in English, he wrote later, 'in any school whatsoever', though his family did deeply instil in him the value of learning. Fervent and strong-minded, he taught himself to write well enough that he later published his own religious text, and he gave sermons, as a layman, to the congregation of which he was part, even if he still felt a profound inferiority to those who had had such things fed to them from an early age. Nevertheless, he argued later that expounding the Gospel 'in plain and flat English' to 'a company of plain Englishmen (as we are)' was the best type of teaching.[1]

As soon as he could, Cushman left home, and was no doubt encouraged to do so. Growing up, he had become familiar with the preparation of wool for weaving – an industry which was pre-eminent in the region – but in Canterbury itself lived a large number who were brought up in this line of work, since numerous Protestants from Europe, French or Flemish, who often were weavers by trade, had sought refuge from persecution abroad towards the end of the sixteenth century. Faced with intense competition in his family occupation, the young Cushman decided instead to accept an apprenticeship with a grocer in the walled city, and he lived there for many years, between the cattle market and the 'shambles', the city slaughterhouse.

The location of his new urban home was scarcely congenial. Not only would blood and entrails perfume the air and begrime the streets – food for the wild dogs and vermin which scuttled and skulked and multiplied in the vicinity – but each day the butchers of Canterbury would wheel creaking barrows of tallow (animal fat), still warm, to his door. After the lard was dumped in a stinking, quivering heap, Cushman would work for hours, fashioning this fat into primitive candles which hardened as they cooled, then burnt throughout the city, liquefying and guttering, once darkness fell – a local monopoly which was enjoyed by Cushman's master.

For Cushman, though, the passage of time in Canterbury was marked not just by the progress of the sun across the sky and the arrival of dusk – not just by the descent of a deep darkness which cloaked the land, and which created the demand for his candles – but also by the regular tolling of great bells. And whereas one might imagine now that it was the screams and bellows of terrified cattle or pigs awaiting slaughter which sounded hellish, in fact it was not the noise of animal suffering by which he was pained.

This, after all, was perfectly in accord with the Holy Book: God had put His creation at the service of mankind. On the other hand, the great cathedral which rose over its ramshackle surroundings, towering above him as he paced through the narrow streets, symbolised what Cushman had come to despise about the English Church in the final years of Queen Elizabeth.

Since the earliest days of its religious primacy in the seventh century, Canterbury had enjoyed close links with Rome. And even now, in a supposedly Protestant country, though the city's monasteries and friaries had been abolished, the cathedral retained its monastic framework of administration: its deans and its canons.

Technically, it reverted, after the dissolution, to the status of a 'college of secular canons'. But it remained the pinnacle of a hierarchical system of Church government – the seat of the country's most eminent archbishop, whose 'throne' sat within the cathedral. Nowhere, insofar as radical Protestants like Cushman were concerned, better illustrated the grimy compromises made by England's established Church than this place, with its vast Gothic towers, its stained-glass windows, its elaborate buttresses and its ornate, mystical decoration.

Clearly, felt Cushman and those who thought like him, the Church had not rooted out the old traditions of Roman Catholicism, the accretion and aggrandisement. It had not returned to the simplicity of the early Church. It had not *purified* itself. It is true that Puritanism – a movement for reform rather than a distinct Church – lacked a clear or universal statement of beliefs: that it contained many strands, many varieties. Often it was about a manner of thinking, and about its *vehemence* rather than its content.

King Henry VIII, who drove and oversaw the initial break with Rome, had been a man of conservative religious instincts. His 'reformation' had owed more to marital necessity than it did to genuine conviction. Only under his son Edward did ideologues wishing to press much further rise to positions of authority. Subsequently, during the second half of the sixteenth century, the long reign of Henry's daughter Elizabeth (after the brief Catholic interlude presided over by her half-sister Mary) *had* seen Protestantism become firmly embedded in England.

Internationally, it was true, she adhered to a strong position. In her conflict with Europe's pre-eminent Catholic powers, she was revered at home as a 'Protestant Deborah' – the martial Hebrew judge and prophetess. Internally, though, the approach to which she inclined was cautious and moderate. She did not share the passionate feelings of many of her subjects regarding issues of doctrine or observance. ('There is only one Christ, Jesus, one faith', she had declared: 'all else is a dispute over trifles.') She preferred not to cast out old ceremonies, or clothing, or church ornament, and she warmed to traditionalist clergy who read standard, prescribed 'homilies' during services rather than to those who preached in a free and impromptu fashion.

In the course of her reign, though, radicals grew in number and became more outspoken. The centrality of scripture was something in which they believed ardently. And they urged the importance of literacy, and of the Holy Book's availability, translated into the native tongue, such that all of the country's population had independent access to it. They believed less than did the Catholic Church in the importance of the clergy as mediators between God and His people. The central role of clerics, it seemed to them, was to *preach*: to interpret, and to provoke thought and worship. There could, in fact, be 'no salvation without preaching'.[2] They railed in particular against those who seemed venal, who seemed corrupted by the wealth which was displayed by the Church all too ostentatiously.

For the final decades of Elizabeth's reign, the archbishop who presided in Canterbury – John Whitgift – was a man of conspicuous ostentation and High Church views. He loathed 'Puritans' and perse-cuted them. (The 'Puritan' label, having begun as a term of abuse, had then been proudly adopted by those to whom it was applied.) To them, in a society in which many clothed themselves in rags, the richness of Whitgift's appearance seemed diabolical. Clergy, they believed, should wear only simple, black gowns. They shook their heads and deplored the manner in which those of Whitgift's stamp would 'feast and laugh and domineer in their purple, scarlet and fleshly wantonness', while many of those whom they called 'God's dear children' were left in the dirt, to 'weep and mourn in secret before the Lord'.

When Whitgift arrived in Canterbury, it was with a vast and flamboyant retinue. The stamping, whinnying and manuring of many hundreds of horses was all too obvious to those who lived nearby. Men and women like Cushman – 'hotter' Protestants, as those of a rad-ical bent were known – rolled their eyes skyward, or cast them down towards hell, and lamented how much more 'state and glory' was used now 'for the gathering and governing of the Church, than ever Christ or his Apostles appointed'. How, they asked themselves and each other, could one abide this 'Papist's pomp' in comparison with 'the Apostle's plainness'? How could one not damn outright what seemed 'the vain ostentation' of the age?

Puritans denounced Whitgift as a 'dunce'. And in his broader Church, meanwhile, regalia deemed by radicals to be over-elaborate and ceremonies which were 'superstitious' persisted. Priests wore the white over-gown known as a surplice (that 'popish rag'). The sign of the cross was traced over infant brows as they were baptised. Worshippers knelt to receive Communion – evidence, surely, that they believed in the *real* presence of Christ in the bread and wine. And rings were exchanged during the marriage service. None of this, Puritans fulminated, had any biblical sanction. The Church of England, insofar as radical Protestants were concerned, consisted of 'half protestants, half papists'. The Reformation had been left only half-complete. The job needed to be finished.

Cushman was extreme in his views, but he certainly didn't lack in Canterbury for others who thought along similar lines, who looked at its cathedral with the same disgust that he did. As a county, Kent had long been a centre of radical belief – first of Lollards, then of Protestants prepared even to burn at the stake under Queen Mary's Catholic rule. And living in the city now, alongside home-grown religious enthusiasts, were those many committed radicals who had fled persecution in northern Europe: 'Huguenots', as French-speaking Calvinists were known, 'learned fellows', as one English Protestant called them approvingly, who could assuredly 'set our scholars to school'. Again, these men and women did not necessarily differ from more moderate Protestants on substantial points of doctrine. But the vehemence of their belief was greater, while the words and stories of the Bible suffused their speech and almost their every thought.[3]

Few, in the England of Queen Elizabeth I, were yet separatists in the strict sense. It was only in the final years of her reign that there were enough of them for Parliament to start recognising the refusal to attend regular church services a crime. Despite this the phenomenon began in earnest under her successor, King James. Cushman continued to worship at his parish church of St George the Martyr, even though the general education of the clergy, and the standard of preaching, was well below what he and other radicals believed that it should be. One radical from Kent complained that he might as well sit in the alehouse as be at church, 'to hear a minister read the service which is not a preacher'. (And from the Lincolnshire village from which many of the 'Pilgrims' – the early religious emigrants to America – would come, one churchgoer bitterly complained that 'one of his horses could preach as well as the curate'.) What Puritans yearned for, and what some others did too who were not particularly extreme in their views, was a dramatic improvement in the calibre of clerics: for what they called a 'godly, learned, preaching ministry'.[4]

Unlike strict Calvinists, for whom the elect were appointed at birth – a divine decision which was irreversible, whether or not it was distasteful – Cushman and his companions continued for a time to believe that a small number of turbulent souls might be redeemed by hearing God's message, so that it was worth the trouble of preaching to them. But they found it hard not to look at the squabbling, fighting, unholy congregation around them, and to despair. Among this rabble, those who were the chosen ones – 'God's people' – must, Cushman felt compelled to believe, be few.

The majority, all too obviously, were merely 'common swearers, liars, drunkards, quarrellers, wantons, atheists': 'children of hell', who only attended church at all because the law required them to do so, before slinking back 'to their old vomit'. To radicals it was painfully evident that in spite of decades of Protestant teaching, most of the Church of England still served 'not the Lord but Satan' as well as 'their own lusts'.

As a result, when in Canterbury Cushman walked out of the weekly Sunday service, he felt not fulfilled, not infused with divine spirit, but polluted and defiled.

He yearned for further, *good* preaching. He thirsted for religious discussion which was edifying. And he longed to teach and admonish himself, and to celebrate his faith, 'in psalms and hymns and spiritual songs', in company with like-minded, serious men and women, away from what he called the 'carnal multitudes'.

So, in the evenings, or on Sabbath afternoons, he attended what were known as 'conventicles' – gatherings in private houses of small groups of believers who shared his distaste for the more florid aspects of the established Church, as well as for the less than sincere faith of some of its congregation: those tightly knit groups of the intensely religious which have been called 'holy huddles'.[5] What harm did they do, he wanted to know? Few of them were genuinely radical or separatist in their ideas. These meetings were held in addition to their weekly service, not instead of it. What godly person would not prefer to converse with other faithful Christians?

For a number of years attendance at these 'conventicles' fed Cushman's need for edification. But increasingly, men and women like him were pushed, partly by unwise and indiscriminate persecution and partly by the logic of their beliefs, towards a more extreme position. For one thing, it became gradually harder for Puritans to believe that any general reformation of the English Church was likely. Wasn't Queen Elizabeth's motto, which her successor likewise professed to admire,

'*Semper Eadem*': Always the Same? The well-off in English society, it was lamented, lived 'more like princes than apostles'. Barely one in a hundred of the general congregation, Cushman reckoned, were true believers, if outward appearances were any reliable judge.

On both sides of the debate 'broil and contention' increased. Generic 'disorders' became more common, as a growing number refused to take part in, or even audibly barracked, the ceremonies or 'superstitions' to which they objected. A proclamation issued by King James soon after he inherited the throne complained of the 'tumult, sedition and violence' to which Puritan unrest had given rise. Every weekend a growing number of the 'godly' trudged, for miles if need be, to neighbouring parishes, where they could hear what they considered to be good preaching. So widespread did the practice become, in fact, that a particular term for it was coined: 'sermon gadding'. The phenomenon of attending 'conventicles', at first simply about additional edification, came to represent outright dissent and nonconformity. More worshippers who attended them insisted on the general corruption of the established Church. And more refused to attend it altogether.

King James was immediately aware of the growing rift. Soon after his succession in 1603 he convened a conference at Hampton Court to attempt to heal it by discussion. What Puritans dearly hoped was that the country's new ruler would shift services in a Calvinist direction, something his predecessor, lamentably, had refused to do. Such was their anxiety that no sooner had he crossed the border between Scotland and England after Elizabeth's death, making his way south to London, than they presented him with a detailed petition of requests, referring to him hopefully as 'our physician to heal these diseases'.[6]

At first the new king did hold out hope to all sides. Despite having called Puritans 'pests' worse than cattle-thieves (having had more than enough experience of radicalism in Scotland), he had only been referring, he promised, to hardliners. But though the king himself took part in the discussions, along with leading bishops and representatives of Puritan beliefs, and although some middle ground was found, extremists were not placated, as indeed they hardly could be. James himself clung to a moderate position. He remained firmly attached to the hierarchical structure of the Church, which he believed lent support to that of society in general. 'No bishop', as he famously put it during the conference, 'no king.'

James knew well enough, of course, that religious radicals would never be happy with what might realistically be offered to them. He had referred to the 'troublesome spirits of some persons who never receive contentment', and had bemoaned those he called 'brainsick and heady preachers', while praising the moderate 'learned and grave men of both sides'.[7] Though he had lived with Puritans in Scotland since he was ten, he remarked, he had never sympathised with or understood them: he had never been 'of them'. And when the divisive Archbishop John Whitgift died soon afterwards, he was replaced at the See of Canterbury by another man, Richard Bancroft, who shared Whitgift's firm anti-Puritan stance.

New 'Canons' published that same year, in 1604, imposed excommunication for any who claimed that either the Prayer Book or episcopal government ran contrary to the word of God. But these measures, and the disappointment felt by radicals like Cushman, only drove them to greater extremism.

Late one night, early in James's reign, Cushman strode through Canterbury's quiet, dark streets carrying sheets of parchment, a hammer and some nails.

Whenever he came to a city church he paused and banged noisily as he fixed one of the sheets to its arched wooden door, before hurrying on past faces peering at windows through the gloom. On each sheet he had written, in large letters, 'Lord Have Mercy Upon Us', a message from the Psalms which was often displayed on houses sheltering a case of the plague. In this case the phrase was intended to proclaim the 'contempt' towards God acted out within these churches during each service, which was indeed a plague so far as Cushman was concerned. It invited divine mercy for such sins.

Subsequently, when he was summoned before religious authorities to explain himself, Cushman was unapologetic. He refused to deny the offence. And he was briefly committed to a local prison, describing its awful conditions. At around the same time he began to boycott the weekly services at his parish church altogether – just as did other Puritans, across the country – claiming that he could not be edified at them in any way.[8] For the godly, Cushman had now concluded, a more extreme separation was needed.

One radical, when earlier persuaded to recant, had begrudgingly disowned what he called 'the stinking flower of separation or segregation from others, as from wicked and damned men': but it is notable that such a course was still envisaged as a flower, hardly the most abominable of images, and one whose odour, of course, is rarely held to 'stink'. Cushman himself, who had been willing to attend his parish church as a young man, had found his hope for genuine change too often disappointed. It was, he came to suspect, only 'a sequestration' and 'not a reformation that will heal us'. He was prosecuted again. And as a result, at the start of 1604, he was excommunicated.

At first he was absolved, and the sentence lifted. He was not yet willing to take the radical step of uprooting himself and his family. He was able to complete his apprenticeship, and he qualified formally as a grocer and as a 'freeman' of the city. He opened his own shop. But always he drew strength from the support and friendship of fellow Puritans in Canterbury, who formed a 'holy huddle' – and who often included multiple members of the same family. The local woman who had become his first wife came from the same group. When in 1606 one of them was prosecuted for harbouring 'devilish' opinions about predestination which were damned as 'repugnant to the word of God' – that He chose His people at birth, and that men and women were consigned, therefore, to their fate, without free will – it was pointed out that Cushman himself held precisely the same views, which were those of mainstream Calvinism. It was a clear sign that he no longer saw any point in preaching to the masses: that he had become, in other words, a separatist.

For a while longer Puritans like Cushman continued to live in Canterbury, and in England more generally, worshipping together at private gatherings, abstaining from regular church services and deploring the evidence of Antichrist that they saw all around them. But King James, it turned out, was anything but more congenial to religious radicals than Elizabeth had been. On the contrary, he grew increasingly weary and intolerant of them. 'Daily', he confessed to Robert Cecil, his diminutive chief minister, he had 'more and more cause to hate and abhor all that sect', who were 'enemies to all kings'.

This first of the Stuart line no longer wished to be tolerant. Those who held their own private services or gatherings, and who refused to attend their parish churches, he thundered, should be 'committed to prison'. (In private, no doubt, his language was a good deal more colourful, as it was often prone to be.) The Privy Council continued to be pleased to see the back of those tormented souls 'whose minds are continually in an ecclesiastical ferment' and who saw fit to abandon their homeland.[9] They should leave, and not come back unless they were willing to conform. Puritans should face a simple choice, James proclaimed: unless they offered quiet obedience to the established religion, he would 'harry them out of the land'.

And so, during the few years that followed, radicals like Cushman anxiously talked, studied scripture and prayed, hoping for a sign from heaven. What was it that God wished them to do? They pored over the words He had spoken to Abraham in the Book of Genesis: 'Get thee out of thy country, and from thy kindred, and from thy father's house unto the land that I will show thee.'[10] It was felt to be true that God no longer spoke in dreams, or visions, or clear messages as He had done in ancient times, because now He had given men His word, written down in a Holy Book. But of course it still needed to be 'rightly understood and applied'.

Were they to leave, there was no doubt that the loss of friends and family who stayed behind would be 'grievous'. Nothing, Cushman admitted, could be more difficult than the abandonment, on earth, of 'the sweet fellowship of friends'. But even Abraham and Lot had parted, radicals reassured each other. And the decision, surely, had been taken out of their hands: they too were obliged to avoid what were the 'greater inconveniences' of not parting.[11] The more they dwelt on the matter, the more the conclusion they came to was that inertia was simply a sign of sloth, and of a lack of divine spirit. To be chosen was to yearn to go. Most men and women, Cushman declared with disapproval, would 'rather with all their friends beg, yea, starve' in the country of their birth than 'undergo a little difficulty in seeking abroad'.

So increasingly those, like him, who were extreme Protestants actively yearned to be expelled from the English Church as a clear mark of their own chosen status. 'They weigh it not', it was said of excommunication.

In fact they made 'a mockery and rejoice at it'. They were glad to be ejected from a Church for which they had 'never had any zeal'. And what lasting expulsion from the English Church meant, at the time, was expulsion from England. The national Church was for the whole nation. One could not be part of one without also being part of the other.

It wasn't that there was, then, a 'promised land' on the lines of biblical example. No country now, Cushman confirmed, could be 'of that sanctimony'. None was given by God to a chosen nation, as Canaan once had been. True believers were 'in all places strangers and pilgrims, travellers and sojourners'. Their home could only be in heaven. Modern England wasn't it.

'We do not forsake [our country]', wrote the man who would lead the Church with which Cushman soon became associated, 'but are by it forsaken.' In effect they had been expelled: by 'most extreme laws' and by 'violent proscriptions'.[12] Emigration, they concluded, offered the only solution.

Since late in the previous century those who had come to espouse complete separation, who no longer felt they could live as members of a Church which seemed polluted in every corner by the ghastly odour of Roman Catholicism, had packed their important possessions into a cart, given up their homes and left.

Along small roads or tracks, with wives and often with small children, wrapped against the elements – because those who emigrated then, for religious reasons, were much more likely to travel in family groups than the single men and women who had gone before – they had trudged towards the country's east coast and the sea. Secret agreements had been made with English, or Dutch, boat-owners to collect them from secluded bays, far from any town. Nevertheless, it was not legal to abandon the country, and armed patrols caught and arrested groups of Puritans as they attempted to leave.

The first time that the Lincolnshire community which Cushman was to join on the Continent walked to the coast, they were betrayed by a captain who had promised to ship them. They were searched for money – immodestly, even the women – then carted to the nearby town of Boston, where they were made 'a spectacle in front of the multitude that came flocking on all sides'. When, the following year, they tried once more, the women and children who had travelled to the coast by barge found themselves stranded in an estuary at low tide and arrested again, as their husbands and fathers watched helplessly from a boat at sea. Only later, with the authorities forced to admit that they didn't know what to do with them, were they able to rejoin their families abroad.

Often the destination for which these people made was to the east, across the North Sea, in Holland. There was a reason why, as it was said, 'many notable sects and heresies' had recourse 'unto the town of Amsterdam' – the walled city in the waterlogged lowlands of the 'Low Countries', packed, and bursting now, beyond the canal boundaries which had long contained it. For there, almost uniquely in Europe at the end of Elizabeth's reign and at the start of James's, congregations were able to practise their religion freely without being bothered.

Certainly the Habsburg imperial government had tried to eradicate the seemingly diabolical heresies of the Reformation from their Dutch territories, as they had tried, brutally, to impose their authority. Anyone convicted of Protestant beliefs, the courts had been instructed, should be burnt, beheaded or buried alive. This was not a time for pussy-footing around. No mercy should be shown. A branch of the Inquisition was established to root out and to punish the appearance of any such monstrous doctrine in the region. The city of Antwerp had been sacked, cleansed like an Augean stable. Few believed in the unique right or responsibility of individuals for their own beliefs, thinking instead that the toleration of heresy would be punished by God just as surely as would the heresy itself.

But this hardline policy had failed. And decades of warfare had seen the northern provinces in particular claim de facto independence from Habsburg rule. Here, secular rulers denied the right of Protestant clerics to limit immigration according to faith, too conscious of the economic benefits that refugees of different Christian persuasions – and even Jews – could bring. In fact there was principle too. During the last decades of the sixteenth century the 'States-General', as the federal body oversee-ing all of the largely independent states was known, decreed that both Roman Catholicism and the 'Reformed' religion should be tolerated.

The wisest course, observed one chief official in Amsterdam, would be 'to disturb no man on account of his conscience'.

As a direct result, from early in the seventeenth century, Amsterdam in particular expanded at an extraordinary rate, with planners embarking upon schemes for an enlarged city. Refugees flooded in, both from elsewhere in the region, particularly from the south, and from neighbouring countries like England, where such freedom for dissenters did not exist. King James spoke in disgust of the 'innumerable Sects of new Heresies, that now swarm in Amsterdam', for which hell seemed the only just reward. This city, one Englishman wrote later, was 'the fair of all the sects', where 'all the pedlars of religion have leave to vend their toys'. Here, an English churchman had noted with similar contempt, in the 'common harbour of all opinions', the air itself stank grimly of 'that odious composition of Judaism, Arianism, Anabaptism'. Whatever objections one might have to it, the Church in England seemed like heaven in comparison with Amsterdam.[13]

Distinct areas within the city became known, and visibly marked, by the culture of a certain variety of immigrant who tended, naturally enough, to cluster together. While new streets were hastily planned and houses built, newcomers threw up temporary encampments where they could, dotted within the flooded fields and marshlands adjacent to the city walls. People lived in cramped and claustrophobic conditions, and they struggled to find work in trades which they knew: often, for the English, in the manufacture of textiles.

It was Amsterdam, at first, that the group Cushman and his brethren would join first inhabited. Life was not easy. Some, it was said, would prefer prison in England to freedom in Holland.

Such was the 'hardness of the place and country', wrote one of the congregation, that few would come to them at all, while fewer 'would bide it out and continue with them', unable to 'endure that great labour and hard fare'. If only, they felt, there was some 'better and easier place of living'. Many then in England would be drawn away who resisted the 'discouragements' which here were evident enough.[14] Amsterdam was cramped, more so as the city's population expanded. As 'flames of contention' flared, it was thought better to avoid them by moving again.

English congregations in exile fought ferociously with each other, as exiles – sufficiently strong-minded to leave home in the first place – are prone to do. When the possibility arose of moving on in unison with another group, Cushman commented that the rigour practised by these others made them about as welcome, as partners, as the Spanish Inquisition, while he knew that they in turn inspired the affection reserved for rat poison. For all the divergence of opinion, certainty, in Holland, was not a commodity in short supply.[15]

At first the congregation walked only a short distance to Leiden, wheeling their possessions in carts along sandy roads built up above the flooded channels and fields which characterised the area – to that 'fair and beautiful city', second in size in the region only to their former home with its canals, its textiles, its new Calvinist university and its 'sweet situation' (even if the water standing in channels all around was, as one less reverent observer put it, 'subject to stinking'). It was not the teeming, international marketplace which Amsterdam had been, and trade did suffer: Leiden, it was later admitted, was 'not so beneficial' for 'their outward means of living and estate'. But there was less squabbling among émigré groups. It was a calmer, less antagonistic environment.[16]

Even so, like Amsterdam Leiden was expanding too fast for its buildings and infrastructure to cope. Refugees did flood to the city. And these English men, women and children would hardly have been noticed, for all that formal permission to settle there was sought. They promised the city government in advance that they would never be 'a burden in the least to any one'. Leiden, the city elders decreed in approving the move, refused 'no honest people free entry to come live in the city'. They welcomed its growth, well understanding that its economic and physical expansion were linked. Anyone who behaved in an open and upright manner, and who obeyed its laws and ordinances, they said, would be 'pleasing and welcome'.

When, subsequently, the English government sought further information about these exiles, attempting to discourage such emigration, they were fobbed off.[17] Leiden's city walls were expanded, to create room for all of the newcomers. And it was here, we know, that Robert Cushman joined the congregation, after sailing from somewhere on the Kent coast. A record in Canterbury records the birth of his son. But by 1611 he was living in Leiden with his family, close to the university.

For some years this group lived as a congregation, keeping themselves to themselves: no burden, just as they had promised. They found work where they could. Many – at least half their number – toiled in the small textile mills or factories which proliferated in the city, the manufacture of cloth comprising its foremost industry. Cushman himself must have returned to a family occupation with which he was familiar, and which offered more chance of gainful work, since he mentioned going back to his combs: that is, his wool combs.

And the university, meanwhile, offered a forum for fevered arguments on matters of theology. Daily there were 'hot disputes in the schools', commented one of the group's leading individuals, where the teachers as well as those they taught differed fundamentally.[18] In the evenings men, at least, escaped from their tiny, cramped houses where children slept and where light was minimal, to gather in smoky local taverns, to discuss and argue about plans and ideas, and to 'drink' the tobacco which they pushed into clay pipes then lit from the hot coals provided for each table. By the early seventeenth century the use of tobacco had become widespread in Europe, but the Dutch, even so, had a particular reputation as 'obstinate and incessant smokers'.

For all that Amsterdam might have made more commercial sense, in general 'peace' and 'spiritual comfort', it was said, were valued here 'above any other riches'.[19] It was a time of truce with Spain, which lasted throughout the decade of the 1610s, when the approach of destructive armies was at least not feared. The community continued to expand as word of their existence prompted others to join them, from the 100 or so who had moved to Leiden initially to some 500 in all. 'Many came unto them', it was said, 'from diverse parts of England': particularly, just as Robert Cushman had done, from Kent and the south-east, or from London.


Life in Leiden for Cushman and his fellow Puritans was certainly easier in some respects than it had been in England.

There wasn't the constant harassment by religious authorities. Members of the community who had worked in the printing trade slept in the loft, in the steep-sloping roof, of a house which belonged to one of the congregation's 'elders': down a gloomy backstreet, known as a 'stinck steeg' because of its unwholesome smell, fostered by polluted, stagnant canals. They worked, amid a clutter of clandestine typesetting equipment, in their cramped bedroom, to publish religious books which had been banned, or were likely to be banned, in England. But the press of people, and the competition for resources, were worse in fact than they had been. And meanwhile, the threat of war had become only more urgent.

Even when England had been threatened with invasion at the time of the Spanish Armada, the sea, for most of the population, had prevented the prospect becoming very real or very critical. Here, of course, there was no such protection. And this was no purely human conflict, or didn't seem like one. Satan's armies were marching nearby. The dark shadow of Catholic Spain was now much closer at hand, and here there was no large expanse of water to form a barrier.

For months, only decades earlier, these troops had besieged the city, and the memory of the savage violence inflicted then on townsmen, women and children nearby remained strong. Now the end of the truce that Spain had agreed with the Dutch drew near, as all were aware. The twelve years of peace, signed in 1609, were due to expire in 1621. Nothing now was audible, one leader of the community wrote, but the 'beating of drums and preparing for war'.[20]

It wasn't a situation which was understood by the pilgrim community in a terrestrial context. Cushman and his congregation worried constantly about how to read events in the real world in terms of God's overarching plan, for the earth and for mankind. They exchanged anxious interpretations. They pored over their Bibles. And they prayed to God to show them a sign. At any point the liberty which the congregation had enjoyed in Holland might be withdrawn, and indeed it looked likely to be. Here, after all, they lived as people in exile. They were 'in a poor condition'. And things looked more likely to get worse than better. It was a situation which to them only made sense in eschatological terms. 'I cannot think', Cushman wrote, 'but that there is some judgement not far off.'

Practically, there were many difficulties. Disagreements proved intractable, and prompted expulsion as an occasional last resort, even if most arguments were overcome. Robert Cushman, furthermore, had a young child, a son, who grew up with his parents in Holland – just as did many of the congregation. (Sara, Robert's first wife, died in Leiden in 1616, when their son was about eight, though he married a second time the following year.) Would the next generation continue to feel the same separation as was felt by the original emigrants from the world around them? They surely would not. This fear, of 'how like we were to lose our language, and our name of English', was to many a source of grave concern.[21]

Already, Cushman and those like him could see their children forming playful relationships with local children and learning to speak the native language – in spite of attempts to prevent this from happening. For all that they had more freedom to worship as they chose, the congregation felt no more enthusiastic than they had in England about the people around them, who did not even observe the Sabbath with due reverence. But in all likelihood Cushman and his brethren reflected, as their children grew up, they would feel not separate and divinely chosen, not 'strangers and pilgrims', but simply Dutch.[22]

Conditions in the cheap districts in which the pilgrims could afford to live, moreover, were grim. The atmosphere was fetid, literally. And it was feared that not only would a younger generation grow up speaking Dutch – perhaps even feeling Dutch – but that they might follow many downtrodden locals into a life of crime if they did not flee on a Dutch ship bound for the East Indies, never (very likely) to be seen again.

What course were they then to take? Anxious discussions and meetings were held. Together the congregation prayed and fasted, seeking guidance from God. Increasingly, some of them felt their hearts moved towards a further removal. In due course it was decided that a segment of them, the 'youngest and strongest part' initially, might emigrate, as a community, once again – to find 'some place of better advantage and less danger, if any such could be found'.[23] The widening horizons of the world had combined, naturally, with eschatological ideas – ideas about heaven's plans for mankind. And the result added impetus to the push to emigrate. In the western parts of the world, some among the Puritans believed, God's favour would 'fall in this last age'.

Not all went. Not even a majority. But many of them – good, honest Christians as they were – vowed to leave behind all these troubled lands, which had suffered such 'bitter contention' and which laboured and groaned 'under so many close-fisted and unmerciful men'. For if too many lived in England, and too many in Europe, God had now shown them another way. 'There is a spacious land', Cushman wrote, 'the way to which is through the sea.' In America, urged another leading Puritan, there were 'vast and unpeopled countries' that were 'fruitful and fit for habitation'.[24]

Were they not right to think that they could go? Cushman argued that they were. Those who had lived there of late – the 'Savages', who wore skins and who crept 'in woods and holes', had declined dramatically in number, a fact which to Cushman and his congregation suggested clear heavenly guidance and intervention: the creation, by God, of room for His people. These – the 'Indians' – were not 'civil inhabitants', one of Cushman's elders argued. They were only 'savage and brutish men which range up and down'. They were animals, of no consequence.[25] In America a new life was possible: one of 'easiness, plainness and plentifulness'. There, surely, Cushman thought, they could 'end this difference in a day'.

Some feared that many of the congregation, more than a decade after they had left England initially, were getting a bit long in the tooth for this sort of upheaval. Many, even in this godly community, were daunted and opposed to the move. There were 'fears and doubts'. Objections were made, and diversions attempted. If life had been hard in Holland – as it certainly had been – how much harder would this undertaking prove?

It was true, of course, that others before them had crossed from Europe to America, attempting to start life afresh. But it was not hard for pessimists to find what they described as 'precedents of ill success and lamentable miseries'.[26] To undertake the move at all seemed either praiseworthy or rash, depending on one's point of view, because it was no easy thing for people to transplant themselves 'out of a thronged place into a wide wilderness', risking 'so long and dangerous a journey' across the sea, heading into a world which was little known and bringing, in the process, the Gospel to native Americans who were ignorant of it: to a 'brutish heathen', 'furious in their rage'.

Generally the true motivation of earlier emigrants had been different, and as a result their fates did not seem any reliable indicator of the risks involved. Many of those who had gone to Virginia before, it seemed now to Cushman and his fellow Puritans, had done so out of greed or vanity – for 'carnal' reasons. (And in the case of many of these, certainly, it is hard to disagree.) Most English men and women were mired in what they called 'fleshy wantonness'. No dainties were too good for them. And this, they could not but think, was what explained the failings which that settlement had experienced. Want, and the sight of some of their companions enjoying private plenty while others starved, had made men 'brazen-faced, bold, brutish, tumultuous'. But all the time God, of course, knew the truth.

Cushman recognised for what they were the 'scratchers and scrapers, and gatherers of riches' – those who in truth were mercenary, for whom 'gold is their hope'. Even 'hogs, dogs, and brute beasts', he protested, 'know their own ease, and can seek that which is good for themselves' – and what was it that the 'shifting, progging, and fat feeding' of some men resembled but 'the fashion of hogs'? The 'honest thrifty Christian', by contrast, would only think to accumulate wealth when his neighbours and brethren were not hungry. The praise of fellow men he would treat as what it was: mere 'froth and vanity'.

The fact that the pilgrims were true and faithful Christians made all the difference. 'We verily believe and trust', their leaders wrote, that 'the Lord is with us.' He, they felt assured, would 'graciously prosper our endeavours according to the simplicity of our hearts'.[27]

Once the decision had been reached for a proportion of them to leave initially, with others to follow, all being well, at a later date, Robert Cushman was nominated as an agent, and he returned to England to negotiate with the relevant authorities: to seek funding and support for the move, and to make arrangements, including the securing of ships on which the community could travel. He, it is believed, arranged for one, the *Mayflower*, in which many of the congregation could sail, along with another called the *Speedwell*.

Cushman negotiated with leading officials of King James who sympathised with their cause. The part of the congregation due to leave felt that they would not be alone on board (or in America), since God would be 'going along with them'. And the king himself, of course, was more than happy for the community to move further from England and its affairs, however little he truly felt that their relocation would assist their country's cause. Out of sight, out of mind. Famously, he joked that earning their keep by fishing, as Cushman assured him that the community planned to do in the northern part of what was then Virginia, had been the apostles' calling: an 'honest trade'.

Where exactly did Cushman and his brethren think that they were going? Ideas still fluctuated. As recently as 1616 John Smith had published his *Description of New England*, in which he talked of a coast effectively 'unknown and undiscovered', complaining of the substantial differences between existing maps of the area which made them as useful, he said, as 'so much waste paper'. To many, New England did not seem then – as it is now known to be – simply a more northerly hinterland of the same continental shoreline as Florida or Virginia.

One early sailor and writer had described a broken archipelago in the Atlantic. He had spoken of 'Elizabeth's Isles'.[28] It was an understandable assumption, since sailors to America from Europe tended to approach either from the north, past the island of Newfoundland, or from the south, past the assorted islands of the West Indies. And map-makers reflected this. 'So far as we can yet find', wrote Cushman after he had lived in New England for some time, 'it is an island.' While it was true that John Smith had not implied that it was, the traditional belief, with which Cushman and his group evidently travelled, remained strong.[29] The name given to it by its English colonists was certainly in part a claim of ownership, like 'New France', 'New Spain' or 'New Netherland'. But it also indicated the similarity these men found in it to their home country.

In size – and in its purported island status – it was similar, 'being cut out from the mainland in America, as England is from the main of Europe, by a great arm of the sea'. There were not high mountains, but there were dales and meadows, and a great many rivers and springs. The earth, Cushman reported – comparing it, naturally, to what he knew – was 'somewhat like the soil in Kent and Essex'. The climate was close to England's: moderate, if colder in the winter. (Englishmen reported it comfortable, invigorating and conducive to good health – as evidently it was, to judge by its rate of expansion and the low incidence of mortality.) And while there were clear signs of the age of human civilisation in Europe, where terrible wars and religious clashes seemed to presage a final struggle – when God would punish his people for 'contention' and for 'wanton abuse of the Gospel', by 'Turkish slavery' or by 'popish tyranny' – in America the divine plan seemed to be at an altogether earlier stage.

Here, Cushman wrote, it was 'yet but the first days'. Here those who came from England could be present at 'the dawning of this new world'. And here there was plenty of space. A way was 'opened for such as have wings to fly into this wilderness'.

The departure from England was beset by delays. Robert Cushman had boarded the *Mayflower*'s companion ship, the *Speedwell*. But seawater gushed in through the hull while she was still in the Channel and she proved, as Cushman put it, as 'leaky as a sieve'. After an attempt to fix her proved unavailing, she was prevented from attempting the Atlantic crossing. Lack of wind caused further delays. Supplies were consumed. And some passengers had second thoughts, persuading themselves, probably, that these difficulties scarcely suggested divine approval. But the captain angrily refused to allow them to disembark.

Cushman himself fell dreadfully ill. All the stress caused him to suffer severe chest pains. It felt, as he put it, like 'a bundle of lead' was 'crushing my heart'. Death seemed close, leaving him, he feared, only to become 'meat for the fishes'. While he and his family, as leading pilgrims, were granted a pre-eminent position on the *Mayflower*, reluctantly he decided that they should stay behind, in spite of the fact that he 'much desired' to join the emigrating congregation, and did 'shortly hope' to do so.

The *Mayflower* herself, meanwhile, having already departed from Southampton, was obliged by these problems to tarry in Plymouth harbour. Although for her day she was a good-sized merchant ship – perhaps 100 feet long and 25 feet wide – the pressing on board of most of the *Speedwell*'s passengers had made her exceptionally cramped. And the voyage, when she did finally set out, later in the year than planned, was in any case rough and uncomfortable.

Towering waves crashed across the deck. Damage that they did forced the ship's carpenter to undertake urgent repairs, using equipment that was intended for the building of a settlement. There was a great deal of what one leading colonist referred to as 'trouble and danger' before, at last, they made their way into the Bay of Cape Cod, amazed, though they had certainly heard and read about it, by the abundance of life both in the water and over it. There were more waterbirds, it was said, than 'ever we saw'. And the number of large, dark 'pilot' whales, meanwhile, was astonishing. They would have tried to catch them had they had the right equipment. In America they were forced to wade ashore, thigh-deep through what seemed an interminable (and unhealthy) stretch of cold water, much too shallow for their ships.[30]

After all the problems, it was already November when they arrived. Supplies were now running very low. The weather in New England was significantly more extreme than that to which they were used – 'freezing cold' – and it got worse. For months on end snow and ice lay, inches thick, on the ground. Where they landed at first there was a lack of fresh water, which drained quickly away in the sandy soil. Settlers were obliged to continue living on the ship. And more than forty of them (from a compliment of just over one hundred) died in the course of that first winter, along with a similar proportion of the crew.

They knew already that the land was inhabited, having read accounts by men like John Smith who had paid several exploratory visits. But even so, numerous graves, as well as cultivated fields, along with fires which could be seen at night glimmering far off in the darkness, provided clear evidence – for all that recent epidemics, the source of much of the mortality, had slashed the density of native populations. Even if there had been some prior contact, moreover, the consistent, sustained relationship that the pilgrims had with these 'tall and proper men' – the natives of this part of America – was quite new.

Aware that the great hook of the bay where they had landed initially was imperfect as a place to settle – both lacking fresh water and too exposed, on a coast that was, as one earlier French explorer had commented, 'very low', 'very conspicuous from the sea' – explorations were launched.[31] And in December a site which seemed more suitable was found across the bay, on its inland side, at a place they called 'New Plymouth', having departed from the old one. (The general name for the region – New England – had been bequeathed already, and it appears as such on a map drawn by John Smith.)

Woods and hills formed a backdrop. Trees of all kinds grew thickly: oaks, pines, juniper, sassafras, birch, holly, as well as others the English did not recognise. The place was described as being 'wooded to the brink of the sea'. The meaning of the name 'Massachusetts', meanwhile, adopted from local tribes, was 'the place by the great hills'.

Work was put in, when the weather allowed, on this new town, and after a common shelter was finished it was decided that 'every man should build his own house' – the thinking being that this would prompt greater speed than if all worked together. But the harsh winter conditions did significantly slow progress. 'Frost and foul weather', it was written, 'hindered us much' and 'this time of the year seldom could we work half the week.'

Since the party comprised both the pilgrims of Cushman's congregation and other men, women and children enlisted in England by the company, who were known by the Puritans as 'strangers', and since they had landed further north than intended, beyond the territory controlled by the patent of the Virginia Company, a different legal document was improvised, and signed. 'It was thought good', noted a preamble of what became known as the 'Mayflower Compact', that 'there should be an association and agreement, that we should combine together in one body, and to submit to such government and governors as we should by common consent agree to make and choose.'

In some respects it adhered to the presumptions of its time. It gave a voice only to the 'free': not to servants, even if they were a minority. When it said by 'common consent', it meant by *male* common consent. Women were chattel. But even so, it was a remarkable document. Perhaps only radical Puritans who prioritised God's division of humanity into chosen and un-chosen, over any separation based upon social class, might have produced it. The great majority of men who sailed on the *Mayflower* signed it. Signatures included those of men who were 'merely' labourers.

Self-government – the right to consent to taxation or other measures – was proclaimed. Without doubt this was a radical departure from the class-based hierarchy, from the exclusion of the majority from any sort of political involvement, to which the settlers would have been used in England. Its significance was plainly recognised. It remained, as it was described sixteen years later (by which time it might well have become redundant), 'a solemn and binding combination'.

Robert Cushman himself put the needs of the colony first, continuing to serve as its agent – its 'right hand' – in England. He visited it briefly in 1621, but was able to stay for only a few weeks before he was obliged to return. He advocated the publication of accounts of the colony which would raise awareness of the pilgrim plantation. Sadly for him, though, he was in London long enough to catch the plague in the spring of 1625 – a plague in Europe, as he had foreseen – and he died there that year.

Anne Bradstreet was born in Northampton, a little later than Cushman, though they had much in common. She too was from a Puritan, profoundly Protestant background. She too lamented the irreligion she saw around her in England. She was thoughtful, and highly educated – more so than Cushman – but largely, as a woman, at home by her father, or by her own volition, fortunate perhaps to catch the end of a tradition, strong among Puritans, of feminine education. In her we see, uncommon even within her Puritan congregation – and astonishingly ahead of her time – a profound commitment to gender equality.

While emotional and affectionate, she was also strong-minded, independent and determined. At first she paid lip-service to a patriarchal, male-dominated culture ('men can do best', she wrote while young, 'and women know it well'), but in truth this general, invariable presumption deeply riled her. And it seemed unfounded. She was fascinated by the recent reign of Queen Elizabeth, whose prowess – and the reverence in which she was held – seemed to disprove any notion that women were inferior. 'She has wip'd off th' aspersion of her sex', she proclaimed, 'that women wisdom lack to play the rex.'

Anne had clear memories of growing up in England during the 1620s: a terrible time for the country, vividly recalled by almost all who lived through it. As that difficult decade opened, as Robert Cushman's congregation prepared to set sail for this new land across the Atlantic, she was about seven years old, and her family had recently moved to Sempringham, a small hamlet in the flat fenland of Lincolnshire, not far from England's east coast – an area shaped, just as Holland was, by myriad channels of standing water. London was distant, relatively speaking.

The Earl of Lincoln, whose principal residence was there, had appointed Anne's father as steward, putting him in overall charge of the running of the household. And it was no coincidence that both men (as well as Anne's mother) were devout 'Puritan' Protestants, who believed fervently in the need for more sweeping reformation in England. It seems ironic with hindsight that the mansion in which the Earls of Lincoln lived had been built from the rubble of a razed priory, to which Catholic pilgrims had once made their way in large numbers. Under the 4th Earl, Sempringham became a focal point instead for the Puritan movement. For those who travelled and worked there now, the ideals of the place's, or its bricks', former inhabitants were anathema.

Anne was a serious, sensitive child, alive to morality and to the bidding of her own conscience. She dwelt on things. If she ever felt that she had sinned, she wrote later, the matter played upon her mind: she worried about it unceasingly until 'by prayer I had confessed it unto God'. She took enormous pleasure in books, and was inspired by her father's love of history and learning. (Her father was later described as being a 'devourer of books' and Anne too, no doubt, read for hours in the well-stocked library at Sempringham.) As a young girl, though, inevitably, she remained apart from the adult world around her, clinging to her own narrow horizons. She found, as she later admitted, 'much comfort in reading the Scriptures', a consolation which grew as she did.[32]

During the 1620s, as Anne grew up, just after the *Mayflower* had sailed for America, trade in England was severely depressed and corruption was rife, while famine and sickness spread. Exports slumped. Bullion left the country, and was missed more than the *Mayflower* emigrants. The king, James I, asked experts to explain what he assumed must be 'abuse'.[33] Unable to resolve the crippling financial problems he had inherited, he saw them in fact grow only worse. Foreign policy seemed almost unbelievably disastrous, as enemies were made simultaneously of the two major European powers, France and Spain. For decades after 1618 terrible warfare enveloped the Continent, and resulted in successes for Catholic forces which terrified Protestants. What could this all mean? What did God, who surely favoured the Protestant cause, intend?

Neglected English forces, starved of money, were in a deplorable state, while their limited interventions proved invariably disastrous. King James himself, who much preferred to make peace, bemoaned what he called 'a miserable spectacle' in Europe that was apt to make any man cry.[34] Certainly English Protestants of the time could scarcely any longer see the mainland as a desirable place of refuge. Holland was not the haven it had seemed while the Spanish truce stood. Exiled English communities who were there, if they hadn't left already, began to think about escaping to a new world over the ocean, fleeing countries which seemed to have become – literally, in their eyes – the cockpit for the first stages of Armageddon, while God's plans for the world moved west.

In England itself bitter arguments – 'the spirit of contention' – reigned. Puritans like Anne's parents wrung their hands in despair at what seemed a lavish and decadent, faithless court – one which, as Sir Walter Raleigh had memorably written, shined 'like rotten wood'. To many, true religion seemed 'in danger'.[35] James's policy of balancing extreme Catholic and Protestant factions, at home and on the Continent, collapsed in both arenas. An atmosphere of crisis persisted. And the young Anne must have picked up signs, in anguished, muttered adult conversations, of which she became increasingly aware as the years passed.

She, like Robert Cushman, was a second child, although her prospects, as a girl, were if anything more limited still. But one thing her parents' beliefs did entail was that she was always encouraged to learn; was never held back intellectually by her gender. All her life she would decry those who scorned women's rights or abilities, having been led to believe that she could rival anyone. Her relatively well-to-do background allowed her the freedom to apply herself in areas from which very many (and women in particular) were excluded, and in these she quickly excelled.

Midway through the decade Anne's family moved for a time from Sempringham to the town of Boston ('Botolph's Town', St Botolph being the seventh-century founder) nearby on the Lincolnshire coast, a hub of immigration now as it was of emigration then.

Here a scholarly but vigorous man called John Cotton had become well known as a preacher and a Puritan leader – a man who, like Robert Cushman, had pored over the writings of Calvin and who had even identified those who were the 'elect' members within his own congregation, granting them special services, purified of any offensive elements.

Anne's family must certainly have been among them. Puritans who did believe that they had been divinely chosen referred to this conviction as 'God's caress'. (How those deemed non-elect reacted to this decision is not recorded.) In Boston Anne and her family remained, in other words, among a close-knit community of godly Protestants – like-minded men and women, referred to later as 'a peculiar people, separated from the world'.[36]

It was at around the same time, in 1625, midway through the decade, that King James died of a stroke, and was replaced on the throne by his son Charles. The new king was short – stunted by rickets – and had battled a speech impediment all his life: characteristics which could make him seem shy and lacking in confidence. But some observers were hopeful all the same. He was 'temperate' and 'moderate', wrote the Venetian ambassador; and 'all the prodigality of the past', with which James' regime had been synonymous, Charles would surely exchange 'for order and profit'.[37]

Certainly, Charles was fiercely moral in a way that his father had not been. The colourful invective which had poured from James's lips never passed his son's. Charles's ears, it was said, abhorred 'the least sordid word'.[38] What he craved, by contrast, was order, beauty, correctness. He was private, having new and complicated locks installed on the doors to his personal rooms. And he was self-righteous. He could never have been a lawyer, he once observed, and been obliged to defend a bad cause or yield in a good one, because if he felt that a cause was good – that *God willed it* – he would not for anything give it up while he had the choice.

Whatever their differences, though, Charles wholeheartedly endorsed his father's view that a king ruled on God's behalf, interpreted God's will, and so should brook no disagreement; though the fact that during the first year of his rule the capital was struck by a terrible attack of the plague, forty or fifty corpses being heaved into each fly-ridden pit for ease of burial, scarcely confirmed the idea that heaven had blessed his rule. On the contrary, thundered the Puritan preachers: what this ghastly swathe of death clearly represented was punishment for a country that was mired in popishness and impiety. Perhaps, subconsciously, or even consciously, these Puritan critics yearned to see chaos around them, confident as they were in being among God's chosen few when

He gathered His saints to His side. In any case, chaos was what they saw. When they met together they 'discoursed', with an almost ghoulish pleasure, on 'the badness of the times'.

At first – at least publicly – Charles showed a liking for meetings of Parliament. 'I love parliaments', he declared. 'I shall rejoice to meet with my people often.' But as tempers in the Chamber raged he soon changed his mind, and determined to do without them altogether. While most Members might have the right intentions, he said, from a few noisy 'vipers' – drowning out the rest – he could hear nothing but 'malice and disaffection to the State'. As the session neared its end in 1629, the Speaker in the House of Commons was forcibly pinned to his chair by Puritan Members anxious that measures be passed before Parliament was prorogued. And when it was (determined not to summon this chaotic and turbulent institution again), Charles relied instead, in an effort to raise money, on any financial loophole he could discover: on any measure which had fallen into disuse.

Fines were dished out for the failure to report for knighthood at Charles's coronation. The old charge of 'ship money' – to uphold the navy and England's defence by sea – was extended to inland as well as coastal towns, well after any war or obvious international danger to the country persisted. Monopolies were sold, including one for the import of tobacco from America – a commodity freely exploited for gain by the son of the author of the angry 'Counterblast' (one subject on which King James certainly *had* vented moral outrage). Rumours spread in the aftermath of imaginary new imposts: that women wearing a green apron, for instance, would be subject to a tax.[39] That these were untrue scarcely mattered. People believed them. And what they indicated was an atmosphere of profound unease and suspicion.

In addition, there was much that was real enough in the English Church for 'hotter' Protestants to lament. Church buildings were embellished and beautified: altars, wall decorations, windows. Services likewise, with an increased emphasis on ecclesiastical vestments and on music. The imposition of fast and 'fish days' seemed, to Puritans, reminiscent of the ecclesiastical calendar before the Reformation. And Charles's marriage to Henrietta, a French princess, not only meant a Catholic queen but also the decampment of her large Catholic entourage to London: a source of suspicion and hatred for many extreme

Protestants who believed that the country was in the grip of a 'Romish' conspiracy. The building of a magnificent new Catholic chapel for the queen at Somerset House seemed only to confirm this fear, while Henrietta didn't even have the decency to be shy about it.[40]

In the House of Commons, meanwhile, sedition and unrest hung in the air. Members spoke of a 'general fear' among the people that hidden forces were working 'to introduce into this kingdom innovation and change of our holy religion'. Men and women decried what they saw as 'a plain and popish plot to overthrow the whole church of God'.[41] Meanwhile, the devastation caused by the plague seemed only to confirm what it was that He thought about the matter.

Late in the 1620s, already over fifty, the short, red-faced, earnest figure of William Laud emerged onto the national scene. He was donnish, pedantic and quick to take offence. He was priggish, and – like Charles – profoundly self-righteous. The king liked his style. Both men cherished order and beauty, and they disliked the same things and the same people. Charles chose Laud to preach to the Parliaments that he summoned early in his reign, and he continued to promote him. Laud became Bishop of London. He became a member of the Privy Council. And then he became a successor to John Whitgift as Archbishop of Canterbury.

Here was a man who preached that respect for the Church and respect for the king went arm in arm: that Church authority and Church ritual, royal authority and royal ritual, were inseparable ingredients of the divine order. The king was 'the sun'. His power *was* 'God's power'. Were any attack on the Church to succeed, he wrote, 'we cannot but fear what may next be struck at'. At a time of increasing division, Laud was a deeply impassioned and divisive figure who aroused both fevered support and fevered hatred.

Ceremony, and conformity, lay at the heart of what he believed, and at the heart of what his opponents rejected. For him religion was not a personal matter. The structures, the offices, the sacraments of the Church were critically important. There must be bishops. Clerics must wear appropriate clothing, like the surplice. There must be beautiful Church buildings, with stained-glass windows and ornate altar tables railed off to preserve their sacred status. Towards those who disagreed he could not disguise his anger. One who was examined by him remembered him turning white with rage, and shaking 'as if he had been haunted with an ague fit'.[42] All his career he had worked, he later insisted, to uphold 'the external worship of God', and he failed to understand why this had made him so unpopular. He had a knack for making enemies, which puzzled him more than it does historians.

'They that hate me without a cause', he observed, 'are more than the hairs of my head.' And he wasn't bald. It seemed almost heresy, he commented, to be seen in his company.

As this was going on – as the fires of religious anger in the nation at large were stoked – early in her adolescence, when she was fourteen or fifteen, Anne went through a crisis of faith.

'I found', she wrote, 'the follies of youth take hold of me.'[43] King Charles had not been long on the throne, and she herself, she recalled, grew 'more carnal' – a word which, however apt its modern use might seem, was used to mean not *sexual* but simply 'of the flesh' in the sense of temporal and earthly, irreligious. She sat, as she later described it, 'loose from God'. Doubts plagued her, and she did not study the Bible with the same intensity. Her devout parents (not the first or the last to wonder what had happened to a teenage child) must have noticed her becoming more distant, been disturbed by it, and perhaps grew alarmed.

It was not long afterwards that the family moved from Boston back to Sempringham, back into the service of the Earl of Lincoln. And it was also not long after this that Anne began to feel seriously ill: feverish and faint, with back pain, headaches and an outbreak of scabrous, pus-filled lesions across her face and body. She was now sixteen. 'The Lord', she said, 'laid His hand sore upon me and smote me with the smallpox.' It was a malady which spread markedly during the seventeenth century, and which afflicted children and young people in particular: a 'cruel and impartial sickness' which paid no respect to class boundaries.[44] This, of course, was just a new – just another – contributor to the regular tolling of the 'passing bell' which rang to record a local death: nine chimes for a man, six for a woman and three for a child (an indication of the priorities which were then given to each), prior to a chime for each year of his or her life. Death, of course, was ever present. About a third of those infected with smallpox died from it.

Perhaps, like many who were able financially to indulge the belief, Anne's red, inflamed body, covered in sores, bumps and rashes, was dressed in red, or wrapped in a red blanket – just as that of her heroine Queen Elizabeth had been. She probably escaped the sort of severe and permanent scarring which led some not to show their face in public again, though she wrote in a poem, at one remove, of 'the loathsome pox' which 'my face be-mars, with ugly marks of his eternal scars'.[45] A metaphorical reference made by her brother-in-law to the fact that there was 'no painting to that comely face' suggests any disfigurement was not substantial (unless he was decidedly lacking in tact). In any case, Anne did recover. And the experience for her was a formative one, restoring and deepening her faith. She did not cease, after this, to thank God for sparing her: for, as she saw it, *correcting* her. She returned, with added purpose – and to the relief of her parents – to a godly, ordered life. But this revived intensity of Puritan feeling made her more strongly conscious than ever, along with other 'hotter' Protestants, of the iniquities in English life.

While her family was in Sempringham, she spent time regularly with a young man who was also living as part of the Earl of Lincoln's household, and who was to succeed her own father as the Earl's steward. Like Anne, Simon Bradstreet came from an impeccably Puritan background: his father was a local vicar of decidedly reformist inclinations, until the passing bell rang for him in 1621. And Simon himself had been educated for two years, between the ages of sixteen and eighteen, at Emmanuel College, Cambridge, with which his father had been connected and which had become renowned as a Puritan establishment. (Rather as in Sempringham, Bradstreet had dined, and worshipped, there in a distinctly Protestant fashion, in buildings which had formed part of the Catholic friary that once had stood on the site.)

A mutually satisfactory arrangement was reached, and Anne and Simon were married towards the end of the 1620s, while Anne was still in her mid-teens. It proved a partnership of considerable love and tenderness. 'If ever two were one', Anne would write later, 'then surely we.'

Soon afterwards the Earl of Lincoln convened a meeting at Sempringham for a number of leading Puritans who had talked about the possibility of emigrating from England together.

To many evangelical Protestants, like Anne and her parents, the country seemed beset by evil. They saw it every day, everywhere they looked, and it made them profoundly uncomfortable. What did it mean? What were God's plans for England, and for His chosen people? The place seemed, as one prominent Puritan observed, 'brought to desolation'.[46] True religion came daily under assault. Further punishment seemed near: God was bound to 'bring some heavy affliction upon this land and that speedily'. 'Evil times', declared one document which Puritans studied anxiously and closely, were 'coming upon us'.

It seemed plain to Anne's father, and to all of those who convened at Sempringham, that England was 'weary of her inhabitants', and they agreed (as not all religious radicals did) that no loyalty was owed to the country. 'Since Christ's time', wrote one prominent Puritan who attended the meeting, the Church was to be considered 'universal and without distinction of countries'. It made no sense to think that the godly should sit still, in spite of an impending disaster. Was it not 'more wisdom to avoid the plague when it is foreseen'? Puritans leafed through their well-thumbed Bibles to the Book of Proverbs, where they read how 'a prudent man seeth the plague, and hideth himself', while only 'the foolish go on still, and are punished'.[47]

Where they were, Puritans like Anne and her family felt separate from the world around them. They felt a people apart. They were 'despised', 'pointed at', 'hated of the world'.[48] Emigration seemed the right course. At first, though, they had not known where they might go. 'Where we shall spend the rest of our short time', confessed one man who attended the meeting to his wife, 'I know not.' She did not, of course, have much say in the matter: for he – unlike Anne – held what were conventional attitudes regarding a husband's dominant position in a marriage.

Crossing the North Sea to the United Provinces, as Robert Cushman and his brethren had done at first, no longer seemed a viable option now that warfare ravaged the Continent. Another possibility was emigration to Ireland, though they would still there of course be relatively close at hand. Towards the end of the 1620s, Anne and her family began to think deeply, instead, about the possibility of sailing much further west, across the Atlantic, with a crowd of like-minded believers: about flying 'into the wilderness', to a place that God had provided.

There they would be much further from the interference of hellish, ungodly European governments. This place might truly be 'a refuge for many' whom God meant 'to save out of the general calamity'.[49] Here, it was hoped, God would 'provide a shelter & a hiding place for us and others'. Here, it seemed, He had 'great work in hand'. A meeting had been held shortly beforehand in Cambridge, the university town which was sixty miles to the south of Sempringham; and here (with Anne's father in attendance) a formal agreement had been signed to establish a colony in New England.

We don't know for sure who within Anne's own family was the leading advocate of emigration. Perhaps it was her father. It was the presumption of the time, of course, that husbands or fathers were in charge, and that wives and daughters followed the lead that they were given. But life – human nature – wasn't like that then, as it isn't now. And the fact that women like Anne in radical Protestant circles tended to be well educated gave them all the tools that they needed to press their own beliefs. (For either gender it was what God wanted, of course, that truly mattered; it was purely a question of who had the authority to interpret His desire.) One leading Puritan divine who knew Anne's family well, however, wrote later that it had been Anne herself who had pushed most strongly for the family to leave their home and to relocate. And it certainly seems plausible, given what we can surmise about personalities, that she possessed this natural authority.[50]

When the meeting was held at Sempringham, we do not know whether Anne was personally present, alongside her father, her husband and other leading members of the 'Massachusetts' Company' (like the man who would lead the enterprise, John Winthrop). But she certainly heard at length about the subjects which were discussed. Anxious debates were held about the need to build, in a barren land, new towns, new villages, a new civilisation. The dangers and deprivations that they would face were talked about. But when, those assembled asked, had the Lord ever treated His followers otherwise? Challenges were to be expected. When had they not been 'beset with potent and bitter enemies round about'?

In any case, doubters should remember that those who lived in all the sea towns in England faced precisely the same prospect of attack by a foreign enemy. A lack of comforts in emigration, while it might be awkward and unsettling, would scarcely be harmful. On the contrary:

it would oblige men and women to repent of their former intemperance. This was a burden that the godly, of all people, could bear. (There was – as they well knew, and often read – a biblical precedent: 'so', it was recalled, had God 'carried the Israelites into the wilderness and made them forget the fleshpots of Egypt'.) They talked, furthermore, in hushed, reverent, yearning tones about the chance that the natives who already lived in America might be converted to the Christian religion. God surely intended the spread of right, Protestant religion in America, and this, in all likelihood, would form part of His plan. Besides, they noted: many of the natives had been 'consumed' already by a 'great plague', which had left a swathe of country empty and untended. This seemed a clear sign that the land had been deliberately cleared by heaven for more godly inhabitants.

Were the failures experienced by Europeans in Virginia and elsewhere significant? No, argued Puritans who considered the matter at length. (All matters, invariably, were considered *at length*.) Because the motivation for emigrants then had too often been self-interested: 'carnal'. Far from being God's elect, those who had gone had been 'a multitude of rude and misgoverned persons, the very scum of the land'. The government they had established had been untrue to God's teaching. (John Smith, for one, would hardly have disagreed.) So what would one expect? This time, unlike in Virginia, things would be done properly.

This idea of departure was spoken about and spread much more widely than it had been before. One diarist in the summer of 1630 wrote of seeing what he called 'Books of Encouragement' scattered across various parts of England, intended to recruit would-be emigrants.[51] Radicals who pored over their English Bibles read, and reread, passages about God's people leaving their homes for a 'promised land', where they were free from persecution and where they were able to live happily in their faith.

'Get thee out of thy country', the Lord had said to Abraham, 'and from thy kindred, and from thy father's house unto the land that I will show thee.'[52]

And so, early in 1630, when she was just eighteen years old (though a married woman), Anne Bradstreet packed a few warm clothes into a cart, with her Bible – the English version, produced by exiles in Geneva and favoured by Puritans – and set out with her husband and her parents south from Lincolnshire towards the capital, then on to the port of Southampton. There, they knew, in the same old port city from which Robert Cushman and the *Mayflower* had departed a decade earlier, a large group of men, women and children – hundreds-strong – would be congregating.[53]

In an unknown location close to the docks, the crowd gathered expectantly, in quiet anticipation. Children were shushed. The hubbub stilled. They waited, and craned their ears to hear the words spoken by John Cotton, the trusted Puritan preacher. By then, of course, the decision to leave had been taken. But still Puritans dwelt upon it anxiously, worried about it, and searched the material world for signs that this was indeed what God intended for them to do. And so Cotton took as a basis for his sermon words which seemed highly appropriate, drawn from the Book of Samuel, and which were extremely familiar to his listeners: 'I will appoint a place for my people Israel, and will plant them, that they may dwell in a place of their own, and move no more; neither shall the children of wickedness afflict them any more, as beforetime.'[54]

Cotton referred also to a passage in Exodus, which again was so well known by the congregation that lips moved in silence to form the words as Cotton intoned them: words which showed beyond doubt that God would carry His people safely, 'high above them all, like an Eagle, flying over seas and rocks, and all hindrances', to the place that Cotton himself would later call 'a little sanctuary'.[55] He would plant them securely, Cotton reassured his listeners, having selected those who were 'good people, a choice generation' – 'trees of righteousness' (a phrase which must have drawn a murmur of satisfaction). The questions to which he returned were paramount, and few congregations, however godly, ever hung on or deliberated their pastor's every word like this one. How were they to be sure that what they were doing, in leaving, was what God wanted them to do? And how were they to know that the place where they were heading was the one He had appointed for them? God no longer spoke directly, in dreams or clear indications, as He had in ancient times. It was a question therefore of interpreting His signs.

Had He cleared space for them? He surely had. (The devastation wrought by European diseases upon the native population of New England had done that.) Were there evils to be avoided at home:

'grievous sins' which pervaded the country and threatened desolation, or which burdened men 'with debts and miseries'? Again, in England in 1630, the answer seemed undeniably to be 'yes'. And the problems inflicted by over-population created their own justification, and made it unquestionably right to leave this troubled land. Nature taught to bees, Cotton noted, a similar lesson – and the complex society of the hive provided a regular parallel for those who studied humankind. When the hive was too full, he observed, bees 'seek abroad for new dwellings'. And so, accordingly, 'when the hive of the Commonwealth is so full, that tradesmen cannot live one by another, but eat up one another, in this case it is lawful to remove'.

Most of all, would-be emigrants should listen to the bidding of their own consciences, which would pull them as the sea was pulled, daily, in tides, by the moon; because 'as the beams of the moon darting into the sea, leads it to and fro [Isaac Newton had not, then, advanced his strange idea of an unseen force called 'gravity']: so doth a secret inclination darted by God into our hearts, lead and bow as a bias our whole course'. They felt it to be true. And, fortified by Cotton's message, the faithful climbed on board their respective ships to cast off, for good, from their homeland. If there was any ongoing sense of regret, this was muted by the certainty that they were fulfilling a divine command.

Cotton himself came a few years afterwards, remaining in England just long enough to be punished for his temerity by being temporarily denied the right to preach.

An advance flotilla of five ships had sailed for New England the previous year, in 1629, spurred on by King Charles's angry closure of Parliament and by the arrest of MPs who had criticised royal policy. The die was now cast. The charter of the Massachusetts Company was signed in the same month that Parliament was dissolved, prior to eleven years of 'Personal Rule' with no meetings of Parliament in England. And, unusually, the charter itself, along with the company hub and hierarchy, was taken too. This was a company which truly was based in America. William Laud complained of the large-scale departure: of the clatter of emigrating souls. 'We hear such loud noise', he said, 'of transporting whole households into New England.'[56]

All winter John Winthrop, Anne's father, Anne herself and all of the leading Puritans had worked to recruit Puritan families who possessed useful skills as well as an appropriate desire to emigrate. Many, given the moral climate in England, were keen to join the exodus. Then, in the spring of 1630, eleven more ships sailed: four initially, on which Anne herself embarked with her family, followed by the rest two or three weeks later. Seven hundred people, it was reckoned, would be travelling with Anne that year, along with 240 cows and 60 horses (the latter animal, unlike humans of course, unknown in the New World). They have become known as the 'Winthrop Fleet', after John, the group's leading personality. When they left England's shores it was in company with some smaller ships which were also bound for America, for Newfoundland.

As they departed – or on board, shortly afterwards – Anne listened also to a sermon given by John Winthrop. (Puritans could not have enough sermons.) It urged those who listened to heed each other's wants and needs as strongly as they did their own, needs which were no less strong in 'extraordinary times' like those in which they lived. What they accomplished together in America, Anne was told, would be closely watched. The colony that they established would be like 'a city on a hill', with all eyes upon it. And it would only be with God's blessing that they could create – in the 'good land' over 'this vast sea' – something valuable and enduring.

It was a thought, and an image, which would encourage many others to follow. The actual voyage of Anne and her family, meanwhile, was relatively straightforward, with children seeking solace from boredom in simple games, as the ships rose and fell beneath a changeless horizon.

Those who went did not find life in New England easy. Settlements were carved from a barren wilderness. Sickness and suffering were widespread. Many died. There was not a house, not a family, wrote Anne's father after he had spent a year there, from which at least one person hadn't been lost. And often it was more.

At first the family settled in Salem. But it was not the place they might have imagined. 'We found the colony', he wrote, 'in a sad and unexpected condition.' Many who preceded them had already died, and a large number of those still alive were 'weak and sick'. Indian attacks were a constant source of anxiety. The heat and the cold of the seasons were more extreme than in England. Diet, for those who had been relatively well-off in Europe, was poor. They did not have much food: 'all the corn and bread amongst them all', he said, was 'hardly sufficient to feed them a fortnight'. The 'first brunts' of an empty, unwelcoming land needed to be borne.[57]

Emigrants need not expect, he cautioned, the taverns, the butchers' shops, the grocers' or the apothecaries' to help with 'what things you need'. Houses were not waiting. They had to be built. Many died in their first year, he wrote, because of 'the want of warm lodging'. At first Anne lived through the bitter New England winter with her family – her husband, her parents – in a single room of a single house, where at least there was a fireplace, without so much as a table. By all means let those confident that they were divinely chosen come over to join the colonists, her father said. But for others, for those more ordinary English men and women, he was cautious: 'I conceive they are not yet fitted for this business.'[58]

Still, for the genuinely godly, as Anne herself later testified, the hardship was not a bad thing. It was 'adversity', not 'downy beds', she said, which made them think. Her own periodic bouts of sickness – the smallpox she had suffered as a teenager, for instance – had reminded her, in her own life, of the incalculable value of what she thought of as divine 'correction'. The good times seemed, as a result, much more joyous. It was all relative. 'If we had no winter', as she put it, 'the spring would not be so pleasant.'[59]

Anne and her family kept moving between the new settlements. From Salem they went to Charlestown, then to Boston (the 'city on a hill' named after the port known well to Anne as well as to many of the others in Lincolnshire), and then to the place called 'New Town' which later would be renamed Cambridge, after another English city with which many Puritans – particularly strong in the east of the country – were familiar. A bout of the recurrent illness to which she was prone left her lame and hobbling. It is appropriate that her earliest surviving poem (from early in 1632, very soon afterwards) was written then in Newtown, when she was 'twice ten years old', and was titled 'Upon a Fit of Sickness'. In it she fretted about the things which Puritans often did fret about: the brevity of life, the ever-present certainty of death – 'All men must die, and so must I' – and the promise of eternal salvation. Life, she wrote, was like a bubble: 'No sooner blown, but dead and gone.'

She did not easily conceive the child that she expected, and for which she yearned: a lack, she recalled, which cost her 'many prayers and tears' (though the eight children who followed seemed a fulsome answer to these entreaties). Her father and John Winthrop, both leading lights in New England, disagreed about much. And more generally, in this new land, she wrote, things were different, and people behaved differently. She found 'new manners'. And in protest her heart 'rose'.

Anne did soon become convinced, however, that this was indeed what God intended, that this – moving from Europe across the Atlantic – was 'the way of God'. And so, as a result, she 'submitted'. She became established in America, agreeing with John Winthrop's mother who wrote of her certainty that this was 'the place wherein God will have us to settle', and who proclaimed what she (and others) called the 'good news from New England'.[60] For all its very early struggles, the colony survived, and even burgeoned, as more and more people travelled to it from the old country during the 1630s: families, with wives and children, grandparents and servants, rather than the preponderance of single men which had been seen elsewhere in America. Among Puritans, great moral pressure was exerted on individuals to bring their families with them – to make the transplantation outlive the present generation. The 1630s was a decade in which the emigration of evangelical Protestants from England was extraordinarily high: when people went not to get rich in this life, but to save their souls.

From his seat in Canterbury, once he had been promoted, Archbishop Laud sought to impose uniformity in the Church by conducting visitations of twenty dioceses, anxious to impose ceremonial worship wherever it was neglected, demanding those 'strange innovations' which angered and unsettled more radical Protestants.[61]

He shared King Charles's dislike of Parliament: that body which had proved so tempestuous and unmanageable, so full, he thought, of 'factious spirits'. And he agreed that it would need to be avoided if the spiritual reformation was to be achieved which he felt was needed. By the end of the decade, when Parliament did eventually have to be called, angry Members (like the well-named Puritan Harbottle Grimston, a friend and ally of John Winthrop's) charged Laud with being 'the root and ground of all our miseries and calamities', 'the sty of all pestilential filth that hath infected the State and Government'. For Puritans in general he was the 'fountain of all wickedness'.[62] They loathed him, just as he loathed them. It was no coincidence that from its outset the 1630s saw an exodus without parallel, 'unique', as it has been called, 'in the annals of migration'.

As the colony expanded, letters home, which inspired friends and family members – further emigrants – extolled the location's virtues. 'I know no other place on the whole globe of the earth', wrote one, 'which I would rather be than here: we say to our friends that doubt this come and see and taste.' And meanwhile sermons in England, given by nonconformist, Puritan preachers from temporary stages set up at market or on lecture days, argued similarly that escape to a new land could offer lavish spiritual rewards. 'England hath seen her best days, and now evil days are befalling us', they lamented loudly, to nodding heads and haunted looks: 'God is packing up his Gospel [a metaphor which alluded plainly to a trader at a market], because nobody will buy his wares...'

Many ministers went themselves, ensuring that levels of education among those who sailed were unusually high. Some, like John Cotton, took the godly among their congregations with them. A proportion of those who went, to be sure, were moved first and foremost by economic woes and uncertainties, even if they were happy to sail under religion's flag as a way of concealing their more materialistic motivations. But the Laudian reforms did create a genuine sense of unease, and a yearning for a 'pure and undefiled religion', practised in a cleaner air. Many Puritans admitted that they hadn't heard of New England until word reached them of this mass exodus of the godly. But now, word did reach them. Perhaps 4,000 families, it was suggested, went over the course of twelve years. One radical clergyman estimated in 1641 that about 50,000 English now lived in America, and that about 40,000 of these were in New England, a figure which may not be too excessive when one considers the large growth and general good health within the population itself.[63]

In busy years, during the 1630s, thousands, certainly, rather than hundreds, went. And they left behind parishes all over England, even if heartlands like East Anglia and London provided the highest percentage. Unlike the emigrants to Virginia, say, or to Newfoundland, in New England heads of household tended to be older, and more committed to creating a permanent society. (Few thought of getting rich quickly and then returning.) The presence of children and of the elderly, furthermore, meant that here there was a much wider age range than elsewhere. And meanwhile Anglicans – those who continued to attend church to learn 'the old way to heaven' – bemoaned the 'confusion and disorder' created in England at the time by what they called this 'promiscuous and disorderly parting'. A 'generation of vipers' seemed to be 'eating out the bowels of their mother church and country'.[64]

In any case, American colonies were mutually reinforcing, for all their differences. The ships which took Puritan emigrants to New England returned, often, via Newfoundland, where they packed air-dried fish into now empty holds, for sale in southern Europe where it could then be exchanged again, this time for wine, oil and the products of the sun. Religion and trade could happily coexist. Other ships, which dropped emigrants in the West Indian islands or in Virginia, then took tobacco or salt, or later slaves, to settlements which wanted them in North America. It was only, as regards the great migration to New England, with the recalling in England of Parliament in 1640 – with resulting greater Puritan optimism, followed by the crises of the descent into civil war – that the tide dwindled. Seven ships authorised to depart early that year proved to be the end of the flood. To the Puritan faithful, growing unrest was to be welcomed.

Among believers, hope burgeoned that the dramatic changes taking place in old England brought with them the 'expectation of a new world', without need of travel.[65]

For Anne, England was where she was born, while America was her adopted country, to which God had led her across the sea. For her children, by contrast, it was England which was the 'country strange', of which stories – about a distant land they had not actually seen – were told in flickering light by the hearth, and which required a long voyage to visit. It was America, Anne wrote, which for her son was the 'land of his nativity'.

From Newtown, Anne moved with her family again, first to a

settlement that was called Ipswich, then to another called Andover: English names, for English people. For years she devoted herself to bringing up her eight children, in the sight of God, as she understood it. But she thought much, as was the nature of her inquiring mind, and often she was plagued by religious doubts that at times are quite startling. 'Thousands of times', she reckoned. Doubts which sound remarkably familiar to a modern ear, and which are not heard often from the seventeenth century.

How could one be certain that the beliefs of Puritan, Protestant Christianity were right? It wasn't as if she had seen any purported miracles herself. And how could one even be sure that there was a God, much as the wonders of creation might seem to confirm His presence? 'Many times', she admitted, 'hath Satan troubled me concerning the verity of the Scriptures, many times by atheism how I could know whether there was a God.' 'I have often been perplexed', she admitted at the end of her life, 'that I have not found that constant joy in my pilgrimage' which 'I supposed most of the servants of God have.'

Even on the assumption that He existed, what was He? 'How should I know', she asked, that 'He is such a God as I worship in Trinity, and such a Saviour as I rely upon?' In Europe alone, in the first half of the seventeenth century, there was an explosion of conflicting creeds, all of which proclaimed the correctness of their own religious vision. It was a radical thought for a Protestant Englishwoman, but why, she asked, shouldn't 'the Popish religion be the right?'. After all, Catholics had 'the same God, the same Christ, the same word'. At the end of the day, they 'only interpret it one way, we another'. (The rest, as Queen Elizabeth had famously remarked, was an argument over trifles, although Anne could certainly not have gone this far.) And anyway, this was hardly an end to the matter. Anne might ultimately have no truck with what she called Rome's 'lying miracles and cruel persecutions of the saints', or with its 'vain fooleries', but then what? 'Some new troubles I have had', she confessed, 'since the world has been filled with blasphemy and sectaries.' Sometimes, she found, she had 'not known what to think'.

For Anne, the natural expression of her doubts, and of her ultimate certainties, was in poetry. But she understood that the prevailing view – however wrong, and clearly she did feel that it was wrong – was that a woman should perform her domestic tasks, not spend her time penning verses. As a result she meant these works to be private: for herself, her friends and her family. But one friend who saw them passed them to a publisher in England, with revealing assurances that the author was a virtuous woman who did not neglect her family, for all that she also wrote poetry. (She was 'honoured and esteemed where she lives'.) And before long their renown spread.

These poems, the blurb proclaimed, were written 'by a gentlewoman in those parts' – a 'Tenth Muse lately sprung up in America'. And still today they captivate and move. Her early works tend to be more constrained and formulaic, to ape convention. Now they seem stilted. But increasingly she developed the confidence to display her personal, metaphysical musing, and to give profound testimony of her feelings and affections, and these works – most of which she wrote in later life, in Andover – now seem far more enduring. And Anne, of course, was not just the first colonial poet in America to be published in Europe. She was also a woman, at a time when this made her very unusual among published writers.

Some of her neighbours in America were incredulous, in spite of the fact that poetry was something many, or many *men*, attempted. (Her own father, Thomas Dudley, was found to have two of his own odes, in manuscript form, stuffed into his pockets when he died.) But Anne herself was scornful, as well as conscious, of this misogynistic presumption. 'I am obnoxious', she admitted in one of her works, 'to each carping tongue / Who says my hand a needle better fits'. She was aware of the grumbling. Aspersions, she knew, were cast upon 'female wits'. If any liked what she had written, she noted wryly, 'they'll say it's stol'n, or else it was by chance'.

But of course she has had the last laugh: not a great poet, perhaps, but a good one – vastly better than many others who claimed the mantle, with fewer barriers and more self-confidence – and one whose writing will endure for itself as well as for the fact that it was written when it was, and that it offers a fascinating, heartfelt insight into the mind of a Puritan emigrant to America of the seventeenth century.

From far away over the Atlantic in New England, in the course of the 1640s Anne watched the torments that swelled, then exploded in savage warfare, in the country of her birth. She was greatly moved. In a poem marking the outbreak of the conflict in 1642, a poem that she called 'A Dialogue between Old England and New', she wrote of what she called these 'sad alarms', and of the 'tatter'd state' of a 'groaning land', where 'thousands lay on heaps'.

She was deeply torn. On the one hand she sympathised, of course, with the Puritan disgust at the direction that England had taken under the ghastly stewardship of Charles and Archbishop Laud. This, after all, was what had driven her family to leave the country in the first place. Sacred laws had been breached. 'The Gospel', she lamented, 'is trod down.' Worthless adornments had been restored: 'copes, rochets, croziers, and such trash'. As the defilements of Catholicism seeped back, the pope, she feared, might with reason hope 'to find *Rome* here again'. It was no wonder that sermons had 'cried destruction' to what had become a 'wicked land'.

Puritans, like those in her own community, had actively desired the bloody conflict which might put an end to all this. It would surely be false, now, she admitted, 'to weep' for that which they had 'pray'd for long'. No. Let jails be filled. Let the gallows at Tyburn be 'loaded till it crack'. And after misery – 'after dark popery' – *then* the sun could shine: 'Out of all mists such glorious days will bring / That dazzled eyes . . .' After the war, and the chaos which would surely follow, came her promise from New England: 'days of happiness and rest'.

On the other hand, though, she could not help but deeply mourn the 'sad perturbation' of tormented England, her birthplace. She genuinely loved it, and she was profoundly distressed by the upheaval: by the massacres, the destruction, the plundering, the women raped, the 'young men slain'. In fact, of course, it got worse before it got better. (The poem was dated 1642, although the collection of which it formed a part was published only after the war, in 1650.) For all that she was profoundly immersed in Puritan thought – thought that focused more upon the afterlife than it did upon this one – Anne found it impossible not to dwell upon what happened on earth. On her own thoughts and feelings. On her human attachments: to her husband, her children (those 'eight birds hatched in one nest'), her parents and her wider family. And of course she could sympathise with the many others, seemingly blameless, who lost loved ones as a direct result of the Civil Wars.

All her life she felt profoundly the loss of children or grandchildren of her own, and while she bowed to a divine plan beyond her understanding, she did rail against suffering that seemed unjust. 'I knew she was but as a withering flower / that's here today, perhaps gone in an hour', she wrote later of one beloved granddaughter who died while small. Without such pain, without the undeniable fact of premature death and general decay, the need for religion, she argued, would be removed: 'for were earthly comforts permanent, who would look for heavenly?'

Some years later, when her house in America burnt down, she mourned its destruction but sadly accepted its loss, and the loss of the things, and the memories, that it had contained. 'My pleasant things in ashes lie, / And them behold no more shall I.' The Lord was right to reclaim what was His, just as He did the dear grandchild who – she could not but think – would no longer 'come to me'.

These, she told herself, buildings and humans too, were transient things. 'The world no longer let me love', she concluded, 'my hope and treasure lie above.' She certainly wanted to believe it. She did, perhaps, some of the time. But whether or not she truly did, all of the time, is hard to say.

# IV

# KING

With a group of nineteen passengers – some sick and suffering, all hungry and desperately thirsty – a tall and thick-set man, with dark black hair, rowed on his ship's boat through water that was finally calm towards a wooded shore.

Henry Norwood's wide, flattish face was badly scarred, violent splashes of red mixing with specks of dark, unexploded gunpowder beneath his skin. For miles he pulled at the oars, the land not so close as it looked, fortified by the thought of finding fresh water at last. They made towards what (as it later became apparent) was an island among the shifting, wind-blown and tide-shaped sand and marsh which formed a thin, spit-like barrier at the eastern edge of the North American mainland.

A screaming storm – the 'merciless sea' – had left their main ship terribly damaged. Masts and forecastle had been ripped off by the wind, crashing overboard into the waves. Without rigging, the vessel had been helpless, tossed about for days by a 'raging sea'. The hold had filled with water, requiring it to be constantly pumped. (Norwood thought that the hours he had spent doing this had put him in good shape for rowing.) Seamen were hurled regularly into the angry, frothing, seething foam. The noise was deafening. After 'many sorrowful days and nights', he wrote, the crew were 'almost worn out' – through toil and lack of sleep – while passengers were 'overcharged' with fear.

Even after the worst of the storm had subsided, supplies were desperately short, while the means to cook them, which had been in the castle, had been lost. Famine grew 'sharp upon us'. Only the rats grew fat, and were caught and sold, for soaring prices, for their meat. 'Many sorrowful days and nights we spun out in this manner', he recalled; 'my greatest impatience was of thirst, and my dreams were all of cellars, and taps running down my throat.' 'All things', Norwood remembered, 'were in miserable disorder', while 'all hopes of safety' were 'laid aside'.

When at length a wooded shoreline had become visible, a group of those who survived made for what they hoped might be safety on the ship's boat. 'Cruelly' abandoned, though, by the main ship, Norwood and the others were left in America, cursing the captain but giving thanks, nevertheless, to what they called (and Royalists were no less quick than Puritans to do so) the 'miraculous mercy of God' – hardly believing that they were still 'what they seemed to be, men of flesh and blood'. And this was a man of sound good sense, reluctant, for instance, to follow mariners in crediting a preponderance of porpoises with foretelling a storm which in fact had blown up already.

Having seen so little of the sun, and a sighting being near-impossible in any case on the deck of a lifting, plunging, storm-tossed ship, they had lost all sense of their location, though Norwood guessed, rightly as it turned out, that they must be a little to the north of Chesapeake Bay. Through a freezing winter, the party had the great good fortune to be assisted by friendly Native Americans – 'Kickotank' Algonquians – just as the 'dreadful circumstances of a lingering death' seemed assured. At first these visitors seemed a mirage. But they proved very real. They appeared in canoes, hollowed out from the solid trunks of trees, and carried the English over a thin channel of water to the mainland.

Chosen as leader, in part – naturally – for his good birth, but also because he was decisive and strong-minded, Norwood enjoyed the somewhat regal advantage of a 'camblet coat glittering with galoon lace of gold and silver'. In vain he attempted to communicate with these Native Americans who nurtured them. He was good at such diplomacy. In general, it was said by those who knew him, he 'exceeds in courteous carriage and speech most men'.[1] But politeness did not go far when they had no language in common. 'Neither of us', Norwood admitted, ended the exchange 'one jot the wiser', though their kindness and good nature were entirely evident.

Any of the English physically ill or frail after their ordeal was tended. One woman who was able to survive against the odds lived subsequently to be married and 'to bear children'. No more about her, or her progeny, is known, but thus – unseen to history – was America peopled thickly by the English. As for those who were there already, the conduct of these 'Indians' was surely, Norwood wrote, a 'just reproach to Christians', who rarely, he admitted, displayed such mercy to the victims of shipwreck on their own coasts.

Taken to their leader, Norwood later spent time as the guest of a 'poor fisherman' whose kindness and lack of material greed astonished him. 'I can never', he declared, 'sufficiently applaud the humanity of this Indian.' And in general the community, from leaders downwards, showed extraordinary 'charity and generosity to us poor starved weather-beaten creatures'. More than most, he had reason to believe in the notion of Native Americans as pure, untainted, 'noble' savages: to agree with that earlier European verdict of them as an unfallen, Edenic people 'void of all covetousness', 'free from all care' – the care that preoccupied Europeans – 'of heaping up riches for their posterity'.[2] But he knew (and his description makes this clear) that this characterisation did not apply to *all* of these people.

Norwood was not under the illusion which affected previous generations that here, across the Atlantic, was an idyllic land: a Garden of Eden, Arcadia. By then bitter acquaintance had disabused the English of this early, naïve picture of peoples who were, in reality, fractured (just as Europeans were) by political and geographical conditions, into all manner of cultures and traditions.[3] But America had the edge nevertheless on tormented, ravaged, regicide England. Just like the religious emigrants of ten to twenty years previously, Norwood felt that he had left a place which heaven had abandoned.

Furthermore, those Native Americans who lived along the coastal strip, close to where Norwood's party had landed, do seem to have been uncommonly welcoming and kind to the English strangers. In general, it seems, the natives who lived on the 'Eastern Shore' were less aggressive towards the English than those in the vicinity of Jamestown had been – less warlike in general, sheltered as they were from attack by their secluded position (and indeed it had been the refusal of one such group, presided over by a man called the 'Laughing King', to be a party to the bloody attacks of 1622 that had allowed the English then to survive).

Eventually – when 'fair weather and full stomachs made us willing to be gone' – Norwood, with the rest of his party, was helped to travel to the English colony of Virginia, which was only, they learnt, about fifty miles distant. On departing, Norwood presented his camblet coat to the 'good old king', who seemed to desire it as a pledge of affection, and who promised to wear it as long as he lived. He, Norwood joked (a man who was favourably inclined towards royalty and who was warm and witty, for all that he was a tough soldier), was 'the first king I could call to mind that had ever showed any inclinations to wear my old clothes'. And thus did his party arrive, at 'English ground in America', after 'all the storms and fatigues, perils and necessities to which we had been exposed by sea and land for almost the space of four months'. Thanks were due, he wrote, to a gracious God: a God who 'causeth his angels to pitch tents round about them that trust in him'.

When the English group departed they walked along tracks through the thick, ubiquitous woods – through cedars, cypresses, pines – which had seen Virginia portrayed as a forested idyll in early English scenes. Before long, at a place the Native Americans called 'Achomat', on the strip of land which constituted the eastern shore of Chesapeake Bay and which the English now labelled with the more familiar name Northampton County, they entered what they called 'our king's dominions' (royal territory of which Republican England itself would have denied being a part), where, according to one promoter, about 1,000 English now lived. Norwood and his small group were assisted by a Native American guide, who performed so admirably, using the moss which grew on the north-western flanks of trees exposed to the sunshine as a means of finding direction, that subsequently Norwood employed him. The man was, he said, 'a most incomparable guide in the woods we were to pass', and afterwards, he wrote, this Native American 'lived and died my servant'. It was cold, particularly in the deep shade of the forest, though if he missed the coat that he had given away he was too dignified to say so.[4]

In the middle of February 1650, having reached the scattered outposts of the English colony, Norwood took himself to various residences in 'those foreign parts'. His familial connection to William Berkeley, the man who then was still governor, for all his allegiance to a king who had by this time been executed in England, saw greater hospitality extended to him than was even generally the case in a region known for the welcome it gave to visitors. He was, he later wrote, 'welcomed and feasted', not only by those who took him in but 'by many neighbours that were not too remote'. He was 'received, caressed more like a domestic, and near relation, than a man in misery, and a stranger'.[5]

On one visit he paid to a captain who was a member of His Majesty's Council in Virginia, Norwood passed a pleasant evening in the company of like-minded exiles: 'the royal party, who made that colony their refuge', many of whom had 'lately come from England'. The captain had made a point of welcoming Royalist émigrés as 'guests in his house' on the York River. There was 'feasting and carousing'. And numerous toasts were drunk, no doubt, by candlelight to the health and prospects of the man they thought of now as King Charles II.[6]

Another house in which Norwood was welcomed was that of the governor himself, and here he stayed for some time. Berkeley evidently advised Norwood as to how he could secure a post in Virginia which would safeguard his future in the colony. Subsequently, with Berkeley's encouragement, Norwood sailed back across the Atlantic, to Holland – an easier voyage, one assumes – in order to try to obtain from Charles the post of Virginia's Treasurer. Charles duly granted it to him, praising Norwood as his 'deserving servant'. And a devoted servant he certainly was.[7]

Not a great deal is known about Henry Norwood's early life. He was a second child, a second son. He was born around 1614. His father died when he was too small to remember him, just as his paternal grandfather had done in his own father's case, and he grew up with his mother, Elizabeth, in a large manor house at the foot of the Cotswold Hills, near Gloucester. Then, late in the 1630s, not standing to inherit the family property, he moved to London to pursue a legal career, as his father had done. The record exists of his entrance to Inner Temple, one of the city's four, expanding Inns of Court, in 1637.

Many, of course, experienced the profound culture shock of moving from the country to England's biggest city. As well as London's sheer size and population was the barrage of opinions to which one was exposed – something that was particularly true late in the 1630s, when the capital was a deeply divided place. Tensions were barely suppressed by a benign economic climate, and by restraint from Continental warfare which did help to bring government costs, and debts, down. With official policy increasing animosity and polarisation, the decade saw the large-scale emigration of religious radicals, like Anne Bradstreet and her family, who felt unable to continue living in a country that they felt to be damned.

Efforts by Archbishop Laud to impose ceremonial reforms in the Church had angered London's many Puritans, who feared that Charles was deliberately pushing England back towards Rome. Hadn't he married a Catholic? Wasn't his wife, Henrietta Maria – to whom he was increasingly, visibly close – surrounded by a substantial, flagrantly Catholic entourage? Weren't Catholics in the country as a whole increasingly numerous, and able to practise their faith almost openly? And, at the same time, didn't royal government more broadly rely, to a growing extent, upon arbitrary prerogative power? It was years now since Charles had called a Parliament, after the profound problems these bodies had given him late in the 1620s. As a result problems festered, without any redress. No escape valve existed for the anger provoked by particular policies.

In the middle of 1637 – the year that Norwood came to London – one fierce and prominent Puritan named William Prynne had his ears hacked off, his cheeks branded and was clamped in stocks to invite public ridicule. Nor was this an isolated case. The absence of Parliaments, as well as years of inflation, had left the royal government in desperate need of other means by which to raise money. So it demanded unpopular 'forced' loans: not voluntary and highly unlikely ever to be repaid – not 'loans' at all. It also unearthed forgotten feudal dues and fines to slap upon unsuspecting subjects. Later that year an MP called John Hampden (an MP when Parliament actually met, that is) was brought to trial in London for refusing to pay part of what he owed according to the ancient 'ship money' charge, now controversially extended to inland as well as to coastal counties. It was seen as a test case and was widely and keenly followed by both sides. And the courtroom was packed.

In the Inns of Court, where Norwood was, little else was spoken about. Norwood probably found himself in a minority, albeit a powerful one, in sympathising with the defence that was mounted of the king, 'the first mover among these orbs of ours [...] whose proper act is to command'.[8] Though Hampden ultimately lost, the very narrowness of his defeat, in clear opposition to the royal interest, ensured that popular resistance to the charge only grew. And Hampden himself was transformed overnight into a national hero. The fact that (unlike Prynne) he was moderate in his opinions, and had a reputation for honesty, made his determined opposition to the regime all the more potent.

It was also early in 1637 – not that this would have been immediately obvious in London – that Charles and Laud imposed a new Anglican-style Prayer Book on the Scots which provoked riotous rejection. Charles, as was his way, confronted opponents not with tact but with fierce denunciation. Opposition, to him – any opposition to him – was rebellion. And even though Charles's father James had moved down from Scotland, neither he nor his son had spent much time there since. In spite of sharing a king, England and Scotland remained separate nations. When the Scots refused the religious demands made of them, Charles was determined to impose his will by force. And war broke out.

In a resulting desperate bid for funds, Charles had no option but to recall Parliament. While he hoped that the climate of crisis would rally unstinting support, he found himself obliged – having made enemies even of many natural supporters – to accept the torrent of petitions and grievances which tended to preface any financial grant. They made him furious, and he angrily terminated this, the 'Short Parliament', after only three weeks, with little achieved beyond a markedly raised temperature. Before long he was compelled to call another. Meanwhile a Scottish army – more disciplined and effective than expected – had swept into northern England, occupying Newcastle, a vital source of London's coal. The new body in Westminster was known as the 'Long Parliament', precisely because it endured for years, and even outlived the king himself.

Members promptly devoted themselves to an astonishing series of reforms. They tried the king's hated favourite, the Duke of Wentworth – first by impeachment, then by a bill of attainder, which had a lower burden of legal proof. (Standing by the scaffold, Wentworth asked rather persuasively how likely it was that the beginning of the people's happiness would 'be written in letters of blood'.) They hurled Arch-bishop Laud into the Tower, from which he came out, years later, only for his trial and execution. Prerogative courts – of Star Chamber, and High Commission – were abolished. Parliament itself was safeguarded: the king no longer able to adjourn and rule without it as he had done throughout the 1630s.

Increasingly – in this atmosphere of general crisis – it was impossible for someone like Norwood, living in London, to focus on narrow legal studies, however much of a 'scholar' he might by nature have been.[9] Everywhere in the capital there was chaos and clamour and hysteria. Waves of panic crashed through the streets. Mobs surged and shouted. Violent demonstrations paraded through the city and through neighbouring Westminster. Shops were boarded up. Presses churned out inflammatory material, showing little regard for censorship. People spoke darkly of imminent invasion by Scots, by Irish, or by unspecified 'papists', even if few still suspected the Civil Wars which would shortly ensue. It was true that strict Puritans did anticipate an unspecified divine judgement upon England, while many others shared a sense of fear and impending doom. But few expected that soon they would fight not an invader but *each other*. Royalists – men like Norwood – were quick to develop a nostalgic memory of the 1630s as a halcyon period of wealth and calm.

A peace with the Scots in September 1641 was followed by an all too brief period of quiet and optimism, before word came, a month later, of Catholic rebellion in Ireland and its grim (if often exaggerated) consequences for God-fearing Protestants. As brutal rumours circled and spread, fear, uncertainty and alarm swelled. Wood-cutters and printers capitalised on the appetite for scaremongering literature, churning out imagined, terrifying, gut-wrenching images. In Parliament, objections to the king's non-parliamentary rule were laid out in a formal document known to posterity as the 'Grand Remonstrance'. Early the following year, when Charles tried – and failed – to arrest five Members whom he deemed principal offenders, he and his family fled the capital. Soon afterwards, it seems reasonable to suppose, Henry Norwood went too, though Royalists whose home was in London, including some of the city's wealthy merchants, did for a time remain. They proclaimed their Royalism by wearing red ribbons in their hats. And there were enough of them, for a time, to fight off Puritan mobs who planned to desecrate some of the city's great churches.[10]

As Parliament took upon itself by a Militia Ordinance the right to raise troops in England as well as to suppress the rebellion in Ireland, the king responded. A turbulent and fearful nation resolved into armed camps. Panic and paranoia grew. In August, Charles raised his standard, unfurling it from the highest tower of Nottingham Castle. A legend on the banner read: 'Give Unto Caesar His Due'. That evening, as the sun fell, the wind shrieked, a storm picked up and the gusts were so strong that the flag was blown over.

This was not like other, international wars, where patriotism decked each confrontation in a clear 'us-and-them' strip, removing any question of whom to support. Now, often enough, family members found themselves in opposing camps: sometimes deliberately, to ensure that representatives would be on the winning side, sometimes as a matter of passionate ideology: a division felt with a visceral, lasting and tragic bitterness.

As the months passed, without any swift resolution, the state of conflict became normalised. The expected sharp, short downpour set in, for all that most just wanted this deeply disruptive war over, preferring 'their pudding at home' to 'musket and pike abroad', and yearning for peace without caring 'what side had the better'. One prayer years later reflected that the Lord had 'given us / now more war than we expected'. Polarisation increased, and fewer were able to balance on the fence. 'No neutrality', it was complained, 'is admitted.' 'Both parties resolve that those who are not with them are against them.'[11]

Although Henry Norwood had moved to London to study late in the 1630s, the West Country was his home. This is where he had grown up, and was where his surviving family lived. It was here, in this time of upheaval, that he returned. And here – not coincidentally, given his own stance – Royalism was strong. He was not in a minority, as he had been in the capital. He was related to the Berkeleys, a prominent local family who owned Berkeley Castle and who were important in the Royalist cause. John Berkeley was one of Charles's chief commanders in the west. And his brother William, of course, had already sailed overseas to become, in 1641, the Governor of Virginia.

Once Charles too had made a fateful decision to abandon London, a rough line came to separate the north and west of the country, where he was strong, from the south and the east – richer, and more populated – which were controlled by Parliament. Instead Charles made his new capital in Oxford, failing to recapture London, though he did hope that in due course the strong Royalist armies in the north and west would sweep south and east towards the Thames below the capital, clamping shut the city's vital artery and starving it into submission.

Norwood became a 'dragoon' – an infantry soldier who travelled between engagements on horseback – in Charles's 'Oxford Army', tasked with assaulting those major settlements in the west which held out for Parliament. In the summer of 1643 he was part of the Royalist seizure of Bristol, a place second only to London as the largest conurbation in England (noted for its ships which took emigrants over the Atlantic to America). The fighting was ferocious. 'Gallant men', it was recalled, 'lay upon the ground like rotten sheep.' Under fire, though, Norwood was in a group which broke through. Having charged in among the defenders, it was recalled, Captain Henry Norwood 'was shot in the face with powder by the enemy's captain, whom in recompense he killed upon the place'.[12] The Parliamentarian governor surrendered. And the action, with hindsight, seemed a great Royalist victory.

The action seemed too, though, with a little more hindsight, to mark a high point of Royalist fortunes. No truly decisive blow was struck that year. In spite of their victory at Bristol, Royalist losses were heavy, and discouraged Charles and his Council from another direct assault. Bitter squabbling and jostling for position continued to undermine the Royalist high command. Early in the autumn, when Royalist and Parliamentarian armies clashed by the waterlogged meadows of Newbury (the weather, all decade, being terrible), the Royalists confidently expected to triumph.[13] Norwood, again, was present. But there was no conclusive outcome. Stronger in cavalry, the Royalists were fatally short of hardware – as they often were – and had to stop fighting. Ultimately this very lack of a decisive 'result', on repeated occasions early in the war when one did seem within the king's grasp, played into his opponents' hands. For time, in the end, was not on Charles's side.

A restructured Parliamentarian army began to gain the upper hand, aided by entry into the war on its side of a large Scottish army, while control of London and more affluent, populated areas of the country gave it a significant numerical advantage. Near the village of Naseby, not far from Leicester, a huge battle in 1645 ultimately decided the war. And meanwhile Royalists like Norwood bemoaned the radical measures taken by the Puritan government: 'England itself', one declared – 'the paradise of the world' – had become 'our Babylon.'[14] The thoughts of more and more in the Royalist camp turned towards escape.

With the Royalist command in the west riven by 'jealousies and bickerings', the city of Bristol, so expensively won, was abandoned without a struggle. The region was beset by a 'fearful visitation' of plague. And with other dragoons (their horses commandeered by Royalist armies in the north), Norwood moved first to the border with Wales, and then to the 'faithful city' of Worcester, which was loyal to King Charles to the end, even after the surrender of Oxford in the spring of 1646 – when Charles himself fled in disguise, his hair roughly chopped and referred to as 'Harry'.[15]

Everywhere, the Royalist cause collapsed. And finally, early one morning late in July 1646, leading Royalists in Worcester held a final, Anglican service in the cathedral, presided over by a bishop, before episcopacy itself was abolished shortly afterwards (no bishop was to preach again in Worcester Cathedral for fourteen years). The city surrendered. And the departing Royalist garrison – Norwood among them – was marched up a nearby hill.

There they were handed the text of an oath to declaim in return for their freedom. Never again, they promised, would they take up arms against Parliament, although this was not an oath that Norwood was to keep. Then passes were provided, valid for two months, permitting any who could not accept a quiet retirement in England to travel 'beyond the seas'.[16]

Nothing is known directly about Norwood's movements for the next couple of years. He turns up next, though, in Holland, and his connections – through the Berkeleys – to Prince Charles (and the letter which he obtained in due course from the younger Charles himself) suggest that he might have followed him into exile, as did a number of committed Royalists.

This would certainly be likely. The end of the 'First Civil War', with hopes of a resounding Royalist victory shattered, saw the peak of emigration from England by despairing Cavaliers. Hundreds of Royalists went, with their households in tow, with 'wives and children, chambermaids and chaplains, secretaries and servants', though some did stay to await the outcome of negotiations, only for further disappointment, further defeat and the ultimate execution to prompt more to go.[17] With differing degrees of secrecy, they left from port towns and villages all around the coast of England and Wales.

Back in the spring of 1645 the young prince, who only turned fifteen in May that year, had been sent by his father to act as a figurehead for the Royalist war in the west: a course his parent thought would 'unboy him, by putting him into some action'.[18] As a youth the prince was tall, rangy and handsome, the face 'very lovely' that would later become jowly and severe. He was sociable and generous, though he lacked his father's religious conviction, or indeed any great conviction, but he did share the Stuart belief in the divine right of kings. By then, though, the Royalist cause in England was deeply troubled. Optimistic supporters might proclaim that here, in the west, 'truly great things may be done', but the truth, as one letter admitted in cipher, was that the enemy was powerful, senior Royalists were bitterly divided and that little good was to be expected. For those with the prince, news of the catastrophic defeat suffered that summer at Naseby was encountered first in the noisy celebrations of nearby rebels. It was after this that the king became willing to listen to advice that his son, for his own safety, should leave the kingdom.

As things deteriorated, indeed, Charles I became frantic. Not only did Bristol fall back into Parliamentary hands, but other western towns and cities followed. As the Royalist west subsided into the control of Parliament, it became, the king wrote, a matter of 'absolute necessity' that his son be transported out of England, 'to France, Holland or any other country'. As Parliamentary armies advanced, Prince Charles retreated. Though the young prince himself was reluctant, his father was adamant. 'If I mistake not the present condition of the west', he wrote at Christmas, 'you ought not to defer your journey one hour.' 'Your going beyond sea', he insisted, 'is absolutely necessary for me.'

In the depths of a difficult winter, while Norwood was ensconced further north at Worcester, Prince Charles trudged with his troops to Bodmin, high in central Cornwall, on the edge of the moor. Conditions were terrible. The ground, as men described it, was 'all covered with snow, the ways so slippery, and the weather so bitter cold'. Provisioning a ship in secret for a fairly long voyage to Denmark – the king's favoured destination – was thought to be too difficult. Royalists worried about opposition, from within their own ranks as well as in the country at large, to the prince going to stay with his mother in Catholic France. Better, some felt, that he be 'in the hand of the rebels than in that kingdom'. But with further military defeat leading to rumours of an imminent end to the royal cause, as well as of a Parliamentarian attempt to seize the prince, the young Charles moved on. Parliament's army gave chase. And 'the hour of pressing danger, so long expected', it was said, was 'at hand'.

Reluctantly, early in March, the prince saw no choice but to embark. The Isles of Scilly – part of Cornwall – seemed an uncontroversial destination, from where further escape could be made as required. At St Mary's, though, the largest island of the chain, provisions were short, and suitable accommodation did not exist for such a large and proud party, unimpressed at having to share their sleeping quarters with drying fish or incoming seawater, regardless of the extremity in which they found themselves.[19] Narrow escape from a Parliamentarian fleet, though, obliged the prince to move on to 'a place of greater safety', and in mid-April he reached the isle of Jersey, that 'loyal little island' – loyal, that is, to the king – close to France. No celebration marked their arrival, which served, as all knew, to illustrate just how badly the royal cause fared.

It did, though, have comfortable town houses for Charles's entourage, and was close to France. Charles played the resident royal with gusto, dancing, learning to sail and racking up (and failing to settle) local debts. Still, though, his party constituted a bedraggled, 'forlorn community'.[20] The prince was persuaded to move on, to stay with his mother in or near Paris – at the Louvre, or the palace of St Germain-en-Laye – at what became, for the next couple of years, the most important meeting point for Royalist exiles.

His court was richly honoured by the French. This, for a royal, was *real* life. He dined at feasts, attended hunts and sat prominently at the theatre. The truth of his situation, though, kept recurring. His mother fumed, and suffered toothache. And infighting made the atmosphere tumultuous. Skulking with a Catholic enemy (even his mother) was not considered a popular move, though his popularity at home – other than with Puritan extremists – did in fact remain high. And from Paris, in the summer of 1648, after almost two years, his group moved on to Holland, and here, if he had not done so already, Norwood joined the party.

It was at a tavern in Rotterdam, in the autumn of 1648, that he met up with two like-minded friends and cohorts. They discussed what to them was the sad situation. And the options available. Military defeat, combined with some kind of humiliation for the king, had become inevitable. Norwood loathed the Parliamentarian regime, and he could not face life in England. Some further escape therefore seemed the only answer. 'When we meet', wrote another Royalist (who many years later, after the monarchy's restoration, would become Archbishop of Canterbury), 'it is but to consult to what foreign plantation we shall fly.' Until vows could safely be made to the rightful Stuart king in England, he confided, 'there are caves and dens of the earth, and upper rooms and secret chambers, for a church in persecution to flee to'.[21]

Norwood and his fellow Royalists expressed themselves profoundly dispirited by the weakness of their cause, and by the imprisonment of their king. Already 'our spirits were somewhat depressed', he later wrote, by the fate of 'Royalism' and by what he called Charles's 'barbarous restraint' on the Isle of Wight – the king having attempted to escape but mistakenly put his trust in a Parliamentary governor who was less sympathetic than Charles had been led to believe. The defeat of the Scottish army, in which Royalists had placed such hope, at Preston and the consequent flood of further exiles to the Netherlands had been a further blow. Norwood suggested travelling much further. He had a family connection, he said, with the Berkeleys, which gave him an introduction in Virginia. (In addition to this link, his maternal grandfather had been a founder member of the Virginia Company, so the settlement was one with which he had grown up entirely familiar.) The men agreed, resolving to meet the following spring in London, with a view to crossing the Atlantic. All resolved, Norwood wrote later, 'to seek our fortunes in Virginia', now that the Royalist cause in England seemed – at least in the short term – so hopeless.

'Surely', wrote another Royalist with whom Norwood would have agreed, 'God Almighty is angry with England.' How else to account for all the warfare and suffering? The trio were among the many who decided to emigrate – who 'left England in that unhappy time' – some for a short period, some for many years, others for good, when continuing to live in the country of their birth seemed 'worse than banishment'. Some perhaps feared (what was in fact ruled out) a reign of terror, a 'general massacre of the royal party'. Others felt simply, as one put it, 'unwilling to draw in the air of my own native soil, lest I should be tainted'.[22]

The Second Civil War, which lasted less than a year, from February 1648 ended for the Royalists in swift and decisive defeat, adding impetus to the movement towards exile. Within the army, optimism that the king might be amenable to negotiate dwindled. Instead, determination grew to punish that 'man of blood', to call Charles to account for all the deaths and suffering for which he was held responsible. That winter the Parliamentarian army purged Parliament, excluding any MPs inclined to accept concessions which the king had made from a prison cell on the Isle of Wight. A tribunal was also established to try King Charles for his life.

Frantic diplomacy on the part of his son failed to turn the tide. Early in February, Norwood and his friends learnt – as did Prince Charles himself – that the execution of the king had taken place. Prince Charles was eighteen. Now for many, himself included, he was England's rightful king.

Why Virginia? Royalists dispersed widely, of course. But the man who was governor here, Sir William Berkeley, remained firmly and vociferously loyal to the Stuart monarchy. It was true that he had had his doubts about Charles as a man: had thought him weak, and not to be trusted.[23] But so did other of Charles's future diehard supporters. And neither Berkeley nor they doubted the importance of kingship in general as the lynchpin of society, or the divinely ordained right of the Stuarts to hold the office in Britain. Cromwell, on the other hand – that bloody, dictatorial unseater (and now murderer) of kings – was unquestionably 'the worst of men'.

Berkeley was to note subsequently how the Cromwellian 'tyranny' had propelled 'worthy' families to his colony, and he made, indeed, a quite deliberate effort to capitalise on the opportunity. He had taken over as governor of the colony back in early 1642, before the war had erupted, having been stripped by Parliament of the monopolies and privileges which had underpinned his precarious position. Always mercenary in mindset, his allegiance was plain. Like his brother, he damned the aims of Parliament as 'most wicked' – the design of a few men, 'not of the greatest quality', to assault 'the whole genius of the nation, that had been accustomed, for so many ages, to a monarchical Government'.[24]

One eminent Royalist observed how, in the wake of England's troubles, Berkeley had 'invited many gentlemen and others hither, as to a place of security which he could defend against any attempt, and where they might live plentifully' (a promise which he could not, as it turned out, fulfil). And the invitation had been taken up. 'Many persons of good condition, and good officers in the war, had transported themselves', he recorded, 'with all the estate they had been able to preserve.'[25] By Charles II Virginia became known as his 'old dominion' – as 'cavalier country'.

Norwood was further influenced by the fact that King Charles II, as they soon thought of him, well before he was crowned as such in London, could provide a personal letter of introduction, more effusive and insistent than he anticipated, commending him to Governor Berkeley's 'particular care', meaning certainty of employment and equally certain protection from the affliction of poverty.[26] And here, in America, Berkeley – this clever, curious, ever-experimenting man – aloof from the squabbles and bloodshed in England (perhaps rather aloof in general) hailed a 'glorious and flourishing country'.

By now the colony's early difficulties had been overcome. Since about 1630, Berkeley noted, Virginia had become thriving and productive – even if he disapproved, just as James I had done, of its concentration on what he called 'the vicious ruinous plant of tobacco'. He sought endlessly himself for a viable alternative – rice, silk, sugar – though sadly nothing rivalled the colony's aptitude for supplying a habit which had now spread 'into most parts of the world', becoming a near 'universal vice'.

Here in America younger sons like Norwood – those who had been inclined, given the way English society was organised, to be 'prodigal and riotous', and whose opportunities often were largely military – found instead that they could build a lasting legacy by being provident and industrious. A bright future could be built abroad, as opposed to death, as Berkeley wrote pointedly in the light of what had happened in England, 'forgotten and unrewarded in an unjust war'. He noted the 'tens of thousands of his fellow Britons who were pulling up stakes and migrating to the Western Hemisphere'. The growth of a plantation like Virginia – its numbers doubling every twenty years – had led, he observed, to 'wealth our fathers never knew'.

'In one age more', Berkeley wrote in the 1660s, by when he thought there were some 200,000 English in Virginia (in reality almost 80,000), 'how great will our power, strength, and reputation be in this new Western world?'[27]

Norwood was in the Netherlands when he received news of 'the bloody and bitter stroke of [Charles's] assassination at this place of Whitehall'. To a lawyer and fervent Royalist like him, the word 'execution' would have lent the deed legitimacy. No, this was an assassination – a crime, and a mortal sin. He abhorred what England had done to its king, and loathed what it had become, as a 'republic'.

Many Royalists were resigned to their defeat, and returned to their homeland to lie low. 'Now the king's party are in a manner destroyed in England', wrote one, 'I do not see how I can be of any use or service to his Majesty, and shall therefore take the best course I can to preserve myself and my poor family from starving.'[28] Others, though, were more combative. Works by Royalist writers were rushed to print condemning 'the poisonous asps, king-killing basilisks, weeping hypocrites, and devouring caterpillars' of 'the bloody court' which was responsible for this 'tragedy of all tragedies'.[29]

Royalist exiles, meanwhile, dispersed all over Europe as well as beyond: a scattered crowd of bitter, frustrated, fugitive émigrés. The flow, which had declined during much of the 1640s – when many who had emigrated already felt compelled to return to fight in the wars which would decide England's future – then increased again with the demise of Royalist fortunes in the First Civil War, and intensified once more with the execution. It remained high thereafter, during the decade of the 1650s.[30] While Royalists despaired of immediate redress, Norwood wrote that after the 'unparalleled butchery' of Charles's execution, in the bitter cold of January 1649, 'a very considerable number of nobility, clergy and gentry [. . .] did fly from their native country, as from a place infected with the plague'. There seemed little prospect of the tide turning quickly, and a strident minority of exiled Cavaliers who did not call it a day – who did not return, to 'compound' for their former errors, admitting their former delinquency – thought instead about how they might manage a long absence abroad.

Maintenance was obviously easier for those Royalists of independent

means. And it was partly for this reason that an 'abundance of quality', as one woman wrote, set sail in the autumn of 1649, not long
after Charles's execution, both for mainland Europe and for England's
colonies west of the Atlantic. As she noted, four ships were then on the
point of departure. And few people whom she met, she observed, knew
no one who was planning to emigrate. For Norwood and his brethren,
the yearning to breathe air less fetid and tainted than England's had
become was now only firmer. To what 'horrors and despairs', he wrote,
had the killing of their king reduced them. 'The black act is done',
wrote another Cavalier to his father, 'which all the world wonders at,
and which an age cannot expiate.'[31]

With differing degrees of secrecy, then – some in pomp, some in
disguise – the Royalist emigrants went, from ports all around the
coast of England and Wales.[32] 'Many who had made escapes', it was
written, 'arrived every day in France, Flanders and Holland.' Few went
further since most expected, and certainly hoped, that they would soon
return. And here, on the coast of the Continent, there was 'cheapness',
and easy communication with friends. Back in the late spring of 1648
John Berkeley – William's elder brother – had been made governor to
Prince Charles's younger brother Prince James, and the circle grouped
around him had made its base in the port city of Rotterdam: a centre
for exiled Englishmen now as it had been in earlier decades for the
Puritan English. Here, it was reported in the following spring, were
'many persecuted Cavaliers'.[33]

In general, life in exile was grim, argumentative and expensive. Existence outside England for the Cavalier communities which clustered
around the various other members of the Stuart family was characterised
by what one historian has called 'years of grinding penury, of delusory
plots and frustrating failure, of the tedious triviality of court intrigue,
of the repeated disappointment of ill-founded hopes' – a life, as another
put it, 'of suffering, material and intellectual poverty, frustration and
paralysing unhappiness'.[34]

Increasingly, the Royalist cause, which now lacked a single focus,
was blown into loosely connected fragments. The king's friends, one
elegy observed, were 'scattered in every direction'.[35] Surrounding Charles
I's queen, Henrietta Maria, in Paris, gathered one group. Around his
eldest son, Charles, grouped another. And some clung instead to his

second son, James, who had daringly escaped from Parliament's clutches in England. Many moved to Ireland, where hopes grew of a Royalist revival, and which would act, it was hoped, as a launch pad for the reconquest of England. Others went to Scotland, buoyed by similar expectations. Often the armies to which Royalist hopes became attached had wildly divergent motives, suppressed – some of the time – by virtue of a shared enemy in the forces of the English Parliament, though certain of course to re-emerge should that enemy ever be defeated.

Those who acted as envoys, who carried messages between the different groups, were obliged to adapt. No longer could they conduct themselves openly, or expect recognition and protection as diplomats. Now they were spies. They had to move secretly and shiftily, not with pomp and swagger. Foreign regimes, even if they were sympathetic behind closed doors, and were certainly little inclined to give succour to the idea that a crowned monarch might be deposed and even decapitated, were reluctant to anger a Commonwealth government which held de facto power in England, by seeming to provide support to its enemies. Royalist agents, in other words, could expect only arrest and detention, and must act furtively.

Almost everywhere Charles's execution caused a stunned silence. Few – even those whose sympathies were with the Parliamentary cause – could believe it. They thought that the king should be forced to accept a settlement. They argued that he should be obliged to recognise limitations upon his authority. But to be executed? It was unthinkable. Hadn't he been directly appointed by God? Many, regardless of their sympathies during the Civil Wars, would have agreed with Norwood that this was 'unparalleled butchery'. The climate which resulted, of numb horror and outrage, characterised the Commonwealth's first months. And while most simply recoiled at the act and wished to have no part in it, for passionate Royalists like Norwood the response was a furious desire for revenge – a determination permanently to 'cast away the scabbards of their swords', a desire, as another Royalist wrote, for 'the highest vengeance on this transcendent villainy', an injection of 'new fire of honest rage and fury into us'.[36]

And so, a few who remained deeply wedded to the royal cause looked not to join those armies which hoped to return Charles's son to the English throne, but attempted to further the cause in other, sometimes violent ways – determined, as Charles II proclaimed, 'to be severe avengers of the innocent blood of our dear father'. They would 'chase, pursue, kill, and destroy as traitors and rebels' any who had been plainly involved in Charles I's 'murder'. They felt like the Marquis of Montrose, who promised – addressing himself to the dead king – to 'write thy epitaph with blood and wounds'.[37]

This was the passion which drove Henry Norwood. Yes, he had resolved already to sail for a prolonged exile in America. But this was not to say that he could not act decisively beforehand. In exile in the Netherlands he became involved with a mixed band of others like him, who learnt of the imminent arrival there of one of those who had been directly involved in the hateful 'execution', or murder, at Whitehall.

The donnish ideologue Isaac Dorislaus was a man as extreme and disliked as William Laud had ever been, diametrically opposed to Laud's as his ideas were (in spite of the moustache and long hair which give the lie to the cartoon image of pudding-bowl Puritanism).

He was Dutch in origin – the reason for his mission now – though for many years he had lived in England and had long expressed radical, Republican sympathies, lending his judicial expertise to the Parliamentary cause during the Civil Wars. The biblical Puritanism in which he was raised is hinted at by the fact that he and his two brothers were named Abraham, Isaac and Jacob, and his lectures at Cambridge before the war – packed, in these 'villainous times', with what one opponent called 'dangerous passages' – were terminated as a result of what opponents perceived as his anti-monarchism.[38]

When, ultimately, King Charles I was brought to trial, Dorislaus had acted as a prosecuting counsel. In the spring of 1649 he was then tasked by the Republican regime with negotiating a peace with the 'United Provinces' which would permit commerce between the two powers. He travelled to The Hague and was promptly met by the English envoy there, who hastened to pass him a warning. The city, he said, was swarming with Royalist émigrés – scarcely a safe place for someone like him.[39] Others who were in The Hague and who were sympathetic urged the stubborn Dorislaus at the least to stay in a private residence as opposed to an inn. But he refused to listen, choosing to ignore this well-intentioned advice.

On 1 May there was an unsuccessful attempt on his life. And even this, it seems, did not persuade him to change his plans. Then, at ten in the evening on the following night, he was eating dinner in a private chamber at the Witte Zwaan Inn. As he and his party ate and talked, twelve armed men arrived suddenly. While six of them stood guard by the door, the other six made noisily for the chamber in which Dorislaus sat, impervious to the screams which their presence aroused. Bursting in, they made quickly for their target.

Pistols were pointed threateningly at his companions to keep them quiet. And Dorislaus himself was run through with a sword – having briefly looked for, but failed to find, the entrance to a secret passage about which the innkeeper had told him, having not, in his smug self-assurance, paid much attention. As they left, the murderers shouted in triumph. 'Thus dies', they proclaimed in English, to the bemusement of Dutch passers-by, 'one of the king's judges.' Dorislaus' body was sailed back to London, where a lavish state funeral was conducted in Westminster Abbey, though there is little indication that the public at large was much moved, after all that they had suffered.[40]

That summer one Cavalier from Kent was arrested as he returned from Holland, and sent to the Tower. Another was ordered by the sheriff of that county to pay a bond of £500 in recompense for the part which he had played. His name was taken down: 'Captain Norwood'. There is little doubt about who this was. He had become involved with this curious, rag-tag band of Scots as well as men who – like him – had served in Charles I's Oxford garrison.

An indictment issued by the English Parliament condemned the perpetrators of Dorislaus' murder as 'that party from which all the troubles of this nation have formerly sprung'. Other similar assaults and assassinations followed. Parliamentary envoys expressed fears, on travelling abroad, that they would go the same way. 'This law of taking and killing men is grown thus common in foreign parts', wrote one who feared that he might get the same treatment himself.[41]

Without doubt, these events added impetus to the agreement Norwood had already made with fellow Royalist soldiers, to emigrate – over the Atlantic, to Virginia. In the late summer of 1649 he kept the appointment that the group had made, meeting up at the riverside in London.

Norwood's facial scars might have seemed distinctive, but at the time they scarcely marked him out, when so many people in the city carried visible wounds or amputations after all the years of bitter domestic warfare. The streets resounded to the tap-tap-tap of crutches as old soldiers moved by on one leg. Men and women believed the darkness peopled by ghosts, more likely to haunt the living world when someone had died a violent death and had a cause to avenge.[42]

All three men now were cautious and clandestine in their movements, though from fear not of the supernatural but of the authorities. They looked behind them regularly to check that they weren't being followed. Norwood – after his involvement in, and punishment for, the murder of Dorislaus – did so in particular. He felt, no doubt, as another Royalist declared himself, a 'stranger in my own country'.[43] But there was no sign of danger. In spite of the care they took, they were appropriately military in their timekeeping. 'All parties very punctually appeared', Norwood wrote later, 'at the time and place assigned.'

Together, near the grand if rather dilapidated buildings of the Royal Exchange, as large ships rocked gently at the quay close by, they went to meet one Captain John Locker, whose name and details they had seen on advertisements affixed prominently to posts in the vicinity.[44] Locker was the master of a large ship called the *Virginia Merchant*. In return for a charge of £6 a head, he offered to take them and their servants over the Atlantic to Virginia, just as the name of his ship implied. The men winced as they passed the scar by the Royal Exchange where a statue of Charles I had stood not long before. In recent years it had been pulled down, smashed angrily and replaced by a Latin plaque which read (in translation): 'Exit last of the tyrants'.

Certainly Captain Locker would have been aware that escape from England was something for which there had been a particular demand of late. When Norwood and his friends eagerly committed, Locker told them that, rather than boarding conspicuously in London, they should make their own way east to 'the downs', near the mouth of the Thames (meaning not the hills in southern England but a region of the sea off the Kent coast). There, he said, he would send them a signal to embark.

So they travelled by coach to Deal, the site of a late, doomed attempt by Royalist forces to seize control of the castle, where an offshore sand-bank – shifting and perilous for shipping – provided the shelter of a harbour. And they waited. Assorted boats lingered here, as in general they did, hoping for the elements to change. Eventually they saw Locker's ship, as well as those sailing with his, approaching down the Thames. But even then unfavourable winds pinned the ships at anchor on this protected part of the Kent coast, while Norwood and his friends exhausted their funds on land. Only late in September, finally, did the wind veer to the east, at which great guns fired and echoed over the water, to summon passengers to the ships. In haste small boats rowed passengers back and forth. In total 330 individuals crushed on board the *Virginia Merchant*. And then, at last, they took sail, down the Channel and into the Atlantic, pausing – as the weather grew warmer – to replenish supplies in the Canary Islands.

As gentry, Norwood and his friends enjoyed the use of cabins, and they dined with the captain. They were joined by the leading passengers of another, Portuguese ship which they encountered. Together the captains and their important guests drank 'the health of the two kings', a blast of mutual royalism which was cemented by 'thundering peals of cannon'. For the English, the king in question was no longer Charles senior, Charles I, whose 'health' (post-mortem) was decidedly poor – but his uncrowned heir, Charles II.[45] The son of a Portuguese lady who was present looked, the English agreed, strikingly like their dark, heavy-featured, exiled king. Norwood himself, meanwhile, took the opportunity provided by a warm climate to gorge himself on peaches: 'to satisfy a ravenous appetite nature has too prodigally given me for that species'.

Dreadful weather, though, and the damage which it did to the ship made much of the voyage a torment. Those on board passed 'many sorrowful days and nights', Norwood wrote, before the ship's boat left him and other survivors stranded, but not far from their destination, on the American coast.

For Henry Norwood himself, the move to Virginia was a temporary relocation into which he – along with many others who felt the same way – was forced by the events of the Civil Wars. England, under its rightful Stuart king, was where he wanted to live. But for eleven years after Charles I was executed, this place had ceased to exist.

During the later 1630s and 1640s, as problems and unrest at home mounted, the Virginian governor William Berkeley had spoken of what he called the 'unkind differences now in England'. But in the course of the Civil Wars themselves, attention in Virginia had been seriously distracted by another massive assault, in 1644, by the 'Powhatan' Native Americans – an assault that was motivated in part by the Native Americans' (accurate) presumption that the English colonists were distracted by events back at home. This time, in spite of the natives' intentions, the very survival of the colony was not at stake, as it had been in 1622. By now the English presence was much less small, much less tenuous. Nevertheless, a great many – around a tenth of the colony's population – were killed in the initial attack. And the war which ensued dragged on for years, into 1646. Three forts which were constructed on the frontier were named, significantly, Fort Charles, Fort James and Fort Royal – a sign, were any needed, of the senior colonists' inclinations.

In general, the religious issues which split the English were less divisive in Virginia, where sheer distance from the home country, and a smaller institutional presence, ensured more diverse and more tolerant worship. In any case, allegiance was principally, if not entirely, Royalist. Nevertheless, inevitably perhaps, the Civil Wars among the British did find a way of imposing themselves. 'Parliament', for many, became the bogeyman – took on the role of general, unseen wickedness. In Virginia, its agents were blamed for inciting the conflict between settlers and the 'Powhatan' Native Americans. And Governor Berkeley sought to impose an oath of loyalty to Charles I, while he buttressed his (and the colony's) Royalist reputation by expelling anyone of Puritan persuasion.

When Charles I was executed at the close of the decade, in Virginia his eldest son was promptly recognised by Royalists in exile, like Norwood, as the rightful king. Other English colonies which had backed the Royalist cause did likewise. Of these there were four. And only one of them – Virginia – was in North America. Here Sir William Berkeley, while not personally enamoured of Charles, certainly was enamoured of monarchy in general, and of the right of the House of Stuart to rule in England. In no way was he attracted by a murderous Puritan regime that he despised. And he did make contact with the exiled court of Charles II, encouraging Cavaliers like Henry Norwood to travel to Virginia, which might then be used as a base against the Puritans.

As it happened, furthermore, only Virginia, along with the largest Caribbean colony of Barbados, offered significant, sustained opposition to the English Republican regime. In Virginia, Berkeley's, and his colony's, allegiances were clear-cut. It was the king's views on religious conformity which Berkeley had followed, as opposed to those of Parliament, even when Charles had clearly lost the war in England, though not yet his life, and even when the resulting policy clearly contradicted the line that was taken by Parliament. In the Virginian Assembly, furthermore, laws were subsequently enacted which made punishable both support for the regicide, and any refusal afterwards to proclaim his son as the rightful king.

For substantial Virginian planters this was, no doubt, a matter of self-interest as well as of principle. They had benefited greatly from trading articles like their tobacco crop with the Dutch, and this trade had burgeoned in the wake of dramatically reduced English merchant shipping during the Civil Wars. Virginians had been only too glad to proclaim the 'freedom & liberty' of the Dutch 'to trade within the colony'.[46] It was no wonder that now many of them baulked at the idea, fostered by the Republican regime, that this trade would not be permitted to continue on a free basis.

Powerful personages in Virginia also valued land grants which had been made under the English monarchy, and had no desire to see these threatened. Virginia had grown fast in recent years, and it had at last become prosperous. Its declaration of loyalty to Charles II was clearly in part an attempt to preserve the prosperity and security which the colony had latterly, much of the time at least, enjoyed under his father's (largely negligent) rule. Virginia's elite – most of whom lacked the Puritanical persuasion which was common, for instance, in New England – supported a favourable status quo, and were nervous of any upheaval.

For a time, in any case, Parliamentary armies in England were too busy with matters nearer at hand to respond to a challenge from over the Atlantic. The truly urgent need for them was to suppress elements loyal to the Stuarts in Scotland, in Ireland, as well as in small offshore territories like the Scillies or the Channel Islands. Unable to mount a large-scale military operation, Parliament instead did what it could, and targeted 'delinquent' colonies like Virginia by legislation. An act of 1650, for instance, banned all trade with those there who had 'contrived, abetted, aided or assisted those horrid rebellions' (rebellions against *Parliament*, it meant, of course, as opposed to against the king). And it authorised privateers to assault anyone who did trade with them. But it was understandable that Governor Berkeley urged Virginians to ignore what he called mere 'paper bullets'.

He promised defiance, and he impressed his loyalty to the king upon those beneath him. 'Consider', he urged, 'how happy you are, and have been, how the gates of wealth and honour are shut on no man.' What, he asked, could a significant change possibly offer 'which we have not already?'. The Native Americans were now subdued. It was only London which was still to be feared. After the execution of the king, he cautioned, Parliamentary rule from Westminster could mean a return to 'the same poverty wherein the Dutch found and relieved us'.[47] The preoccupation of England had been nothing but a benefit. It was London, he warned, which could 'take away the liberty of our consciences, and tongues, and our right of giving and selling our goods to whom we please'.

No, he implored: 'we will not so tamely part with our king, and all these blessings we enjoy under him'. 'If they oppose us', he declared, 'do but follow me' – 'I will either lead you to victory, or lose a life which I cannot more gloriously sacrifice than for my loyalty and your security.' Leading colonists responded in kind, refusing to 'yield to whosoever possesses themselves of Westminster Hall', and resolving 'to continue our allegiance to our most gracious King', for whose 'happy restoration' they would, they promised, continue to pray.[48]

In the meantime, though, the English Parliament's military priority – the extinction of significant loyalty to Charles II in and around England itself – was duly accomplished, in particular when a Royalist army was defeated at the Battle of Worcester in the autumn of 1650. The following year's Navigation Act outlawed all colonial trade with the Netherlands. And a large fleet was assembled in England – some fifteen ships – whose purpose was to bring this oldest American colony into line, if necessary by military means: to reduce Virginia 'to the obedience of this Commonwealth'.

On its voyage to Virginia the fleet was hit by a major storm, which caused many of those on board to drown. Only four of the original fifteen ships survived. But those that did duly reached the Chesapeake in January 1652, where they anchored in the lower reaches of the James River. When a message was despatched to Governor Berkeley, calling for his surrender, Berkeley refused to send an answer. Weeks passed. And the situation became increasingly tense. Over 1,000 men of the Virginia militia were summoned to serve, and were positioned around Jamestown, as well as along the approaches to the small capital. Conflict, by early March, looked increasingly likely. But Berkeley, at the last minute, surrendered, and ordered his soldiers to disarm, conscious of 'the great miseries and certain destruction' which warfare would bring.[49]

Although it was now inevitable that Berkeley would be deprived of his post as governor in Virginia – as indeed he duly was in the spring of that year – his refusal to surrender immediately did force concessions and protections for those (like himself) who had Royalist inclinations or were hostile to Puritan ideas about religion. Furthermore, it was formally accepted that Virginia's surrender had been 'a voluntary act', not forced by conquest, and that the colony's General Assembly could impose on those beneath it any kind of taxes, customs or 'impositions whatsoever' without interference from London. Nor might forts be erected, or garrisons maintained, without consent.

A period of a year was granted in which any colonist might decide whether to remain or leave. And Berkeley himself was granted permission to pray for, or to speak well of, the king, for the same period, in the seclusion of his own home. He could hold on to his land and possessions. If he wanted to return to England he might do so. And he could send an agent to report to Charles Stuart (Charles II, for those of Royalist inclination) on the events which had taken place.

Berkeley himself – loyal to his new territory in America – chose not to leave, but retired to his estate, to private life, replaced as governor by one of the few prominent men in the local assembly who was clearly of a Puritan persuasion. In a letter, Berkeley begged Charles's forgiveness, imploring his pardon, 'for delivering up your majesty's colony into the hands of your enemies'. Colonists, he protested, had cried out 'for any accommodation', while the Council had begged him 'to consent to articles of surrender'. In truth, he said, bearing this in mind, he might have 'destroyed the country with those forces I had, but preserve it I could not'.

*

When Parliament imposed its authority in Virginia as well as in the British Isles and deposed Berkeley as governor, Henry Norwood must have felt that even this American sanctuary had been removed. He was anxious, in any case, to work further, in any way that he could, for the Stuart cause, to assist a restoration of the monarchy in England, in spite of the weakness of those who advocated it (and in contempt of his own oath not to act in any way against the Republican government).

Returning to Europe, he was tireless, and quite undaunted by material poverty. He was involved, in 1653, in a scheme to distribute arms to Royalists in his native Worcestershire, as well as in other Midland counties. In 1654 he worked with members of the secret Royalist society the 'Sealed Knot' towards a planned – and utterly unsuccessful – insurrection. Along with hundreds of others whose allegiance was suspect, he was arrested, then freed. He pretended, while in fact supplying arms to Royalist subversives, to be organising shipments for Virginia. Early the following year he was arrested again, and this time he was imprisoned in the Tower, where he was held until being transferred, near the end of the decade, to a prison on the isle of Jersey. The Republican regime took his activities seriously. Even when released he was forbidden to return to the country. And it was reported that he was interrogated by Oliver Cromwell in person.[50]

Only with the restoration of the king a year and a half after Cromwell's death (the latter's son and successor as Lord Protector having conspicuously lacked his father's ability) could he return openly. Then, suddenly, the mood in England seemed to Royalists like Norwood to have transformed. In the spring of that year, 1660, he carried letters to the waiting King Charles II in Brussels. Suddenly, he found, he did not have to move furtively, but could go in state. In March the 'Long Parliament' was finally dissolved, before a new election. Norwood was appointed an 'Esquire of the Body' – an honorary attendant on the king. And it was in that capacity that, in April 1661, he attended Charles's coronation at Westminster – a day whose glory was (according to Samuel Pepys, and doubtless according to Norwood too) 'impossible to relate'.[51]

Under the revived Stuart monarchy Norwood was granted the office of Captain of Sandown Castle, in Deal: the very point on the east

Kent coast, looking out into the North Sea, from which he had left England for America all those years previously. The place must have stirred memories – not entirely happy ones – of his original emigration.

Many Royalists did return to England, with their households, once Charles II was restored to the English throne. The hated Republican experiment was over, and the return of the Stuarts meant the return, too, of some of their most loyal supporters. Now it was the most radical Parliamentarians who either thought it wise, or simply desired, to leave the country. For many who had tasted religious freedom, and the licence to indulge their radical inclinations, a return to the constraints of old – constraints which became only tighter as the decade passed – seemed intolerable.

By no means all Royalists who had left England after Charles I's defeat did return though. Many years had now passed. Some of those who were still alive had become established, in the meantime, in a new life abroad. They had put down roots. They had married; inherited land. And many of them stayed, wherever they were, but certainly here, in this 'new Western world', America.

With Charles restored to the English throne, in Virginia William Berkeley himself stepped out from his potting sheds and his horticultural experiments to be reinstated as 'His Majesty's Governor', and other Royalists, when he did so, were less shy about wielding significant influence. Berkeley himself nakedly promoted those who shared his own Royalist leanings, helping to establish a Royalist, aristocratic elite.[52] For the remainder of the century they and their families proceeded to shape life in the colony.

Most of those who had emigrated did not, naturally, enjoy Berkeley's social prestige, or anything like it: not even that of someone like Henry Norwood. They derived from the 'middling sort' and lived, as their enemy Oliver Cromwell had put it with regard to himself, 'neither in any considerable height nor yet in obscurity'.[53] Their background was in trade. And they sought to establish their importance in colonial society less by pre-existing status than by regular participation in local governance.

As thousands of them arrived, though, the nature of the landscape in the small English colony – largely confined, as it was, to the coastal strip – began to alter. Along the James and York Rivers, and on the eastern shore of Chesapeake Bay, trees were felled as land was cleared for tobacco. Game was hunted and became less numerous. And pigs and cattle proliferated. The substantial land granted on the basis of numbers of dependants favoured the establishment of an aristocratic, planter society, dominated by large estates. Native American societies, unable to co-exist, unable ultimately to resist the tide of incomers, were pushed further afield, after their fierce military campaigns against the English had died out (if random skirmishing continued).

When King Charles II was restored to the English throne – to the noise of trumpets and revelry in Virginia – putting the chaos of the 1640s to bed, ongoing English wars with the Dutch saw the final, protracted demise of the latter as a serious threat to the English in America, particularly once the Dutch colony of New Netherland had been expunged. The rise of other, neighbouring English colonies – Maryland, Carolina – meant that Virginia was no longer a lonely outpost on a hostile continent. Royalist Englishmen in America may have been disappointed to discover that Charles II never had the degree of interest that his exiled supporters might have imagined for him in his colonies across the Atlantic. But Royalism, of course, had always been about the political state which God intended, not about the tendencies of any individual king.

The date of Charles I's execution – 30 January – was declared in Virginia to be a day of annual commemoration, 'solemnized with fasting and prayers': a chance for those colonists who had welcomed 'that execrable power' to 'expiate' their crime and, with their tears, to wash away their guilt. Acts which might recall the colony's 'enforced deviation from His Majesty's obedience' during the Protectorate were repealed.

In general, the emphasis on empire by the Restoration regime added intellectual support to what was already a substantial English emigration to the colony – an emigration which ensured that law, language and culture in Virginia would be forever English in origin, with other foreign arrivals compelled to adapt. It was a culture, moreover, which unlike that in New England was emphatically hierarchical, emphatically unequal, from the lowly subjects – the indentured servants and increasingly the slaves – at the bottom, to the 'better sort' and ultimately, far in the distance, at the top, the king.[54]

# V

# FUR

Midway through the 1630s, on the deck of the *James* – a ship named in memory of the late king – a father hunched with a small, nine-year-old boy, and shivered.

As cold winds blew across the choppy surface of the Atlantic the man and his son pulled tight around them a blanket of rough woollen cloth. Initially water-resistant, it was soon soaked, and offered only limited protection against the elements. The boy was called Daniel. His father, Richard, was a small man in his early thirties who wore a piratical patch clamped over one eye. It failed, though, to mask a demeanour that was impassioned but also kindly.

For weeks on end the grey waves alone reached to the horizon, broken only, perhaps, by one or more of the four other ships. For protection the group attempted to sail together, in a single fleet. In general the voyage was uneventful. Then, as they approached the rocky coast of New England – an area that was prone to storms – the sky darkened, the waves reared and noise made by the wind increased. Fearing the worst, sailors hurried to obey their captain's orders and to take down the sails.

In the face of this gale, though, the fleet quickly became scattered. On the *James* herself, the sails – not removed fast enough – were shredded by the strong wind, 'as if they had been rotten rags'. Anchors would not hold. Three of her companion ships were lost as their ropes snapped like cotton in the water. It seemed hopeless. The ships, their sails, the passengers – all were, or felt, 'torn to pieces' by the extreme weather. The lives of all on board, the helpless captain wrote in his log, 'were given up for lost', as the shoreline with its dreaded 'rocks of death' rapidly approached.

Richard Denton was a deeply religious man. For the past decade he had worked as pastor at a small settlement called Coley, near Halifax in Yorkshire. If diminutive in size, he was dynamic, eloquent and passionate. One close acquaintance later described him as 'an Iliad in a nut-shell', a man who, while he did not tower physically in the pulpit, could 'sway a congregation like he was nine feet tall'. His voice was rich and carried even in the screaming wind. In his 'lesser body', it was said, existed a 'well-accomplished mind' and a 'great soul'.[1]

Now, with his family around him – his wife (if she was alive, though sources make no mention of her), nine-year-old Daniel, Daniel's older sister, as well as his two younger brothers, one seven, the other only four – he looked up to the heavens in prayer. And he must have felt that his invocations had been duly answered. 'In an instant of time', wrote one who was on board, 'God turned the wind about.' And, with no loss of life, when its situation had seemed desperate, the *James* made it safely into Boston harbour, while another ship which sailed with her raced on northward towards Newfoundland.

This – the 1630s – was a time when emigration from England was much more substantial than it had ever been. More than thirty ships are recorded to have taken emigrants to Virginia or to New England that year, not counting others which sailed for the Caribbean and elsewhere. In the wake (literally) of Anne Bradstreet and other Puritans, crowds went, pressed onto the decks and into the holds of ships, as the extraordinary flood which marked the decade of Archbishop Laud's preeminence continued – for all that the movement's founder had urged, rather belatedly, that 'not too many at once' should leave the country.

England seemed damned, its practice of religion satanic. Catholics and Catholicism seemed resurgent. And London itself, with the royal court – to those who depended only on hearsay – appeared 'a nursery of lust and intemperance'. Nowadays we would consider most of these adults who sailed to America young. They were in their twenties, thirties or forties. And, as this age range suggests, many travelled with spouses and small children. They were willing to trust themselves to God, young children, at least, largely oblivious of their intended destination. The latter – like Daniel Denton and his siblings – grew up, many of them, to identify first of all with the environment in which they now found themselves, harbouring only hazy (if indeed any) memories of 'old'

England. Home, for them, was not England: it was this 'new American world'.[2]

At first, like so many others in this 'great migration', the Dentons sailed to Massachusetts. 'By a tempest', wrote the same close acquaintance, Richard was 'hurried into New England.' But however free the primitive churches there were from the railings, the rituals and the beautification of worship in places where William Laud could more easily control it, Richard soon found that this was not – any more than Laud's England – a place tolerant of dissent or dissension.

Denton was an early English Presbyterian. He disapproved of government structures, disapproved of bishops and of hierarchy in the Church. At a time when 'democracy' was still a dirty word in England, as it long would be – and a dirty word in New England too, where a leading Puritan had labelled it 'the meanest and worst of all forms of government' – Denton espoused it. And, perhaps not surprisingly, so did his parishioners.[3]

Together Denton's congregation made the decision to move again. First they went to New Haven, a colony then in its own right (one of four English colonies which had recently joined to form a Confederation of New England).

Afterwards, still unhappy, and feeling no urgent need to live under overarching English rule, they listened to encouraging stories about New Netherland, that 'naturally beautiful and noble province' which separated Virginia from New England on the eastern coast of North America between 40 and 45 degrees of latitude, just to their south. When individuals were sent to investigate, an offer was made by the government of the colony. A community might live, unbothered, on the vast, 'Long' island which stretched east into the Atlantic – a crab's claw pointing, upside down, towards the hook of Cape Cod.

The terrain, on inspection, seemed very promising. Here on Long Island there were 'excellent bays and harbours as well as convenient and fertile lands', in what the Dutch considered (more even than the island of 'Mannados', or 'the Manhattans') to be the 'crown of the province' of New Netherland. Fish-filled rivers bubbled into fountains. Good land for farming lay unclaimed. And a rich variety of fruits flourished in the woods. When the scouts returned and reported, Denton and those with him took a democratic decision – since he and the community believed in democratic decisions – to move as a group once more, to escape friction and quarrels with their English neighbours.[4]

They applied to the local Native American communities to purchase some land: a rectangle which bounded the sea and which, inland, was drawn by 'marked trees', one of which stood 'at the east end of the great plain'. They confirmed their purchase with the Dutch authorities of New Amsterdam, who could find no 'very great objections' (and financial persuasion, indeed, in the form of fees) 'to allow them [the English] for the present to come in in reasonable numbers'.[5] So they walked, and pulled wagons, before clambering into boats to ferry them across to the island.

Around twenty families are known to have moved with Denton, along Indian tracks through the forest noisy with birdsong, and noisy too with the scutter and scamper of animal life. Small children – like Daniel's younger siblings – lurched over bumps in the track alongside possessions. Sentries sat through the night armed with guns, next to fires which cracked and fizzed and sparked amid the deep enveloping darkness. And beneath the trees, by day, the community sat together to sing and to intone its prayers, with Richard Denton leading the impromptu service.

At a place in the centre of the western half of the island – a place deemed 'superior to all the rest', where a brook bore fresh water along-side a vast, open, treeless grassland which reached far and featureless to the horizon – they stopped, and within a hastily erected barricade to provide some protection, they built houses, as well as a larger structure which served both as a church and as a space for public meetings. Properties were marked out, as throughout New Netherland, using landmarks such as 'the beech tree [which] lies across the water', or the territory of 'Peter the Chimney Sweep'. The prairie land was ideal for the pasturing of cattle. 'Very fine grass' grew thickly on the plain. And the lack of sticks and stones meant that horse-racing soon became an established sporting activity. Once a year, wrote Daniel Denton a little later, 'the best horses in the island are brought hither to try their swift-ness', the (human) winner being presented with a silver cup.

In return for an oath of loyalty, scarcely meaningful in practice because it was so little enforced (though perhaps Denton and his companions hoped that it might provide some measure of protection against the threat from Native Americans), this cluster of English migrants was granted rights of self-governance, their own court and liberty of conscience – freedom from any 'molestation or disturbance' on account of what they believed, rights which certainly had significant appeal to a Presbyterian activist like Denton, and which he had been unable to secure under English rule.

The English christened their settlement 'Hempstead', thinking perhaps of 'Hemel Hempstead' in England. Here, in return for an undisclosed fee, the Governor of New Netherland granted Denton permission to establish a town.[6]

The 'rights' to this territory in America, argued over bitterly by powers in Europe, do not now seem very persuasive and did not, in truth, persuade anyone at the time who was not already inclined, by national loyalty, to be persuaded.

England's legal claims were based originally upon the twin patents issued in 1606 which covered all of the territory of eastern North America, between 34 and 45 degrees of north latitude, 100 miles from the coast to the west, or to the east (in the case of offshore islands). The two patents overlapped – one reaching north to 41 degrees, the other commencing at 38 degrees – to make certain that no stretch of this coastline, from the Chesapeake to the St Lawrence, went unclaimed. The land of New Netherland lay on the join, at very close to 41 degrees. But the English claimed, of course, that there was no join: that the territory lay squarely within the northern patent.

The 1606 charters had conceded only that the territory must not be 'now actually possessed by any Christian prince or people', which of course none of it was. Prior possession, by 'Christian' people, in other words, was granted legal power. But it did – or so the lawyers claimed – have to be *prior*. (Dutch settlement which came after 1606 was not deemed to qualify; these people, it was charged, had 'intruded'.) In truth, in any case, such legal arguments exerted little force in an international context, even if they held sway among the English. 'International law' was at an embryonic stage.

Charters to these vast lands, uninhabited by Europeans, could be, and were, very generous. From the point of view of disagreements between the English, the French, the Spanish or the Dutch (or other European powers), what counted in reality was the 'right of discovery', by which was meant of course European, 'Christian' discovery, and de facto ownership – boots on the ground.[7] The surprise, and evident rejection, that King James had expressed when Spanish claims to North America were raised, many hundreds of miles from their colonies further south, may be recalled. And even then, of course, might was right: settlers could be violently evicted, as fledgling colonies like that belonging to the French in Florida certainly had been, if they were not sufficiently powerful.

Where 'discovery' of this particular region of North America was concerned, however, confusion was magnified by the fact that it had been made, initially, by an English navigator who was working in Dutch service, giving both nations, so they alleged, a valid claim. (The fact that the site had previously – almost a century previously – been 'discovered' by an Italian explorer who was working for the French was quietly ignored.) It was in 1609 that Henry Hudson had sailed into the valley of what seemed 'as fine a river as can be found', looking, unsuccessfully, for a passage to the Far East. Subsequently the English gave his name to the river, though he called it the 'River of [submerged] Mountains', because further upstream his boat kept running unexpectedly aground.

Hudson had a crew which, aptly enough, comprised a mutually suspicious mixture of Dutch and English. His mate referred to the Dutch sailors as 'an ugly lot', while another Englishman claimed that their 'fat bellies' showed that they thought 'more highly of eating than of sailing'. (The affection, needless to say, was mutual.) Many of the natives whom Hudson met by the river, meanwhile, were keen to trade. They sold him 'good skins and furs', at what seemed 'a very low price', in exchange merely for 'beads, knives, and hatchets' – though as heathens, of course, they had no right to the land.[8] America, though, was a big place and the English, often literally, had other fish to fry. Certainly it was the Dutch who followed up the 'discovery' first, even if they were not either in any apparent hurry.

Although Dutch merchants did return briefly to the Hudson in subsequent years, to barter with the Native American communities who waved at them from the riverbank – bartering, predominantly, for the rich furs which were available at such a good price – it was only fifteen years later, in 1624, that the first settlers arrived. Then, in the 'wild and uncleared lands' upriver, they established a permanent fur-trading community, at a place they called 'Fort Orange', which is known now as Albany. In return for simple manufactured commodities like cloth, axes, kettles or alcoholic drink, Native American hunters kept the Europeans well supplied with skins.

Two years later one Dutch ship, called the *Arms of Amsterdam*, sailed back to Holland laden with more than 7,000 beaver skins. And the Dutch West India Company felt sufficiently encouraged to send further colonists, bearing further supplies. Meanwhile, at the southern end of a large island near to where the River Hudson emptied into the Atlantic, which acquired the name 'Manhattan' from the local Native Americans, the Dutch established a fort (which grew quickly into a settlement) to protect their fur-trading operations upriver. In 1625 this settlement was designated the capital of the province.

Like metal, alcohol had been unknown to Native Americans. While most resisted, a few of them took to it all too enthusiastically, and many among them were alarmed by the thirsty consumption and altered behaviour of some of their fellows. Their languages, though varied and rich, noted one European observer, lacked any word for 'drunk'. Commodities like furs, one English resident later noted, were bartered for European products, 'but too often for rum, brandy and other strong liquors, of which they are so intemperate lovers'. Another observer reported seeing one Native American community 'all lustily drunk, raving, striking, shouting, jumping, fighting each other'. It is no coincidence that an English term for illicit liquor, 'hooch', is derived from a Native American word: *hoochinoo*.[9]

This Dutch colony, and the town on 'Manhattan Island' – New Amsterdam – in particular, was badly run: a ramshackle frontier territory, known for immorality and heavy drinking. It was divided and disputatious, 'split into factions' and beset by 'schism and contention'. Gallows and stocks stood prominently on the waterside, in a vain attempt to instil caution and to moderate behaviour. Immigrants boasted a wide variety of backgrounds. But all, as one Dutch pastor put it, were 'rough and unrestrained'. The town was edged by the palisade which crossed the island. The street which ran alongside it became known as 'Wall Street'.

The Dutch West India Company controlled the fur trade in New Netherland strictly for its own benefit, objecting to those private traders – 'impertinent fellows' – who attempted to gatecrash, and referring often to what it called the 'company beavers'. But so widespread were mismanagement and corruption that profits were not high. And prophets, meanwhile, looked on gloomily, foreseeing, for all the situation's promise in geographical and mercantile terms, 'the general ruin of the land'.[10]

Since conditions for ordinary colonists in New Amsterdam were not appreciably better than they were for the Dutch in Europe, there was no great incentive for families to embark on the long and dangerous voyage across the Atlantic. And not many did so. While people were plentiful in the Netherlands, the company struggled to persuade emigrants to go in anything like the numbers in which the more desperate and divided English were soon flooding to north-eastern America. These lands, wrote one Dutch emigrant, remained thinly settled. 'Not so much for want of population' in the Netherlands. Because with people, he said, 'our provinces swarm'.

Early in the 1640s, the population of the Dutch colony was only around 500, many of whom were not Dutch. Already almost twenty languages were heard in the settlement, a multiculturalism for which it has remained famous. This was at a time when there were 10,000 English to the north in New England, and over 10,000 more in Virginia to the south. Given that the Dutch in America also continued to depend on the shipment, across the Atlantic, of supplies from Amsterdam, they had good reason to be concerned.[11]

Desperate for the security which only population could provide, company directors were happy to accept colonists of almost any nationality, relying simply upon oaths of loyalty. When a new town sprang up further to the north on Manhattan Island, known as Nieuw Haarlem – known now, of course, simply as Harlem – its first thirty-two male residents included eleven Frenchmen, four Walloons, four Danes, three Swedes, three Germans and seven Dutchmen.[12]

Hempstead, meanwhile, was one of a growing number of English settlements – much more homogenous, ethnically and in terms of their religious and political background – on Long Island, outside the principal site of New Amsterdam, which proliferated during the early 1640s.

*

The English, the Dutch administration reported, requested permission 'to come and settle among us', and short-sightedly, perhaps, this permission was granted. No individual application, of course, ever seemed significant. But taken together they amounted to a sizeable movement of population, and the more the ball picked up speed, the harder it was to stop. Before long the regime was noting with concern 'the great number of English who come daily to reside here under us'.

The Dutch observed how incoming English settlers 'greatly hanker[ed] after' the area, and how they outnumbered their own. While some of the English kept themselves to themselves (and, plainly, those who were at Hempstead fell into this category), elsewhere – it was observed with frustration – they 'greatly troubl[ed] and harass[ed]' their Dutch neighbours. 'Even our villages', company directors back in Holland noted with alarm, 'are mostly inhabited by English people.' Regular references were made in documents to 'the English villages on Long Island'.

Native Americans who lived there were no more able than the Dutch to compete with the English flood. And if this wasn't bad enough, they fell prey, at the same time, to what Daniel Denton called the 'hand of God' – a divine scythe which decreased their number 'strangely', 'removing or cutting off the Indians, either by wars one with the other, or by some raging mortal disease', reducing them in his time, Denton wrote, from six towns to only two small villages. While a number did remain, he observed, before long there were 'but few upon the island'.[13]

At first most of the communities founded by English migrants on Long Island lay in the east, while the Dutch tended to congregate in the west. The two cultures, by and large, remained distinct. And in this respect, Hempstead was untypical. But it was part of a general English expansion westward. With extraordinary speed, by 1650, with the exception of two Dutch villages that were considered 'of little moment' in the west of Long Island – 'Breukelen' (Brooklyn) and 'Amersfoort' (named after the city in the Netherlands) – the English were held by the Dutch to have 'entirely usurped' the place.

The names of the newly founded villages – Southold (an elision of Southwold), Southampton, Gravesend, Hempstead – were all too clearly reminiscent of their settlers' country of origin.

\*

Quickly, it was the fur trade which became what all Europeans did in this region of America, which dominated economic life for all those, like the Dentons, who settled here. From the first – from the time of Hudson's voyage early in the seventeenth century – its potential had been obvious both to explorers and prospective settlers.

While elsewhere European merchants and colonists had focused on fish or on gold, here it was beaver skins which in effect *were* gold, leaving little time to look concertedly for the metallic stuff. With a mere ten pelts buying enough wheat to feed a family for a year, most emigrants soon abandoned their former professions. Beaver skins were used as currency, and an exchange might commonly be priced at 'three beavers' or 'four beavers'. The expression 'to earn a beaver' (which long outlasted its origin, just as most expressions do) became common usage to indicate any form of commerce.[14]

As the town of New Amsterdam established itself, it became the hub of a thriving seasonal fur trade. Native Americans carried beaver and other skins down the spine of Manhattan, to the settlement built at its southern tip. Their communities that lived on Long Island made the strings of whelk and clam shells known as 'wampum' – faster and in greater bulk now that they were shown how to use European tools and techniques. And the colonists assumed that these were the local currency. (The Dutch referred to Long Island as *sewan-hacky* – the 'land of the shells'.) And, having obtained these with European goods, the Dutch then exchanged them for furs. 'Wampum', it was said, was 'the source and the mother of the beaver trade.'[15] In the late summer ships docked from Europe, from Amsterdam, to collect the pelts in tightly bound piles.

Townships grew, upriver, which were devoted to the industry, as well as on nearby lands like Long Island. One Dutch settlement further up the Hudson River that was dominated by fur traders was christened Beverwyck, in honour of the animal on which its foundation and rapid expansion was based. One of the earliest roads in New Amsterdam was called Beaver Street, and it continued into Beaver Path. One of the ships which traded regularly between the Netherlands and New Amsterdam was called the 'Beaver'.

The Broad Way (as its name implies) was widened, to assist natives who were bringing furs into the greedy arms of European traders. A Dutch colonist named Adriaen van der Donck – deeply fascinated by the land, with its hills and thick forests, different Native American tribes, whose cultures, and language he studied, and its dense, diverse wildlife – wrote an enthusiastic 'Description of New Netherland', by which he hoped to encourage further emigration from his homeland. The 'Description' was an admirable work, sane and accurate, uncluttered by the implausible hearsay found in many other European accounts, which told of barley degenerating into oats, or of frogs standing a foot tall on their haunches.

The country, der Donck stated, was 'a very beautiful, pleasant, healthy, and delightful land, where all manner of men can more easily earn a good living and make their way in the world than in the Netherlands or any other part of the globe that I know'. The air, he enthused, was 'marvellously pure', and left one feeling 'as fit as a fiddle'. As well as the otters, deer, bears, wolves, eagles, turkeys, rattlesnakes and even lions (he was thinking of the big cats that we call cougars), he added an entire chapter – no other animal was so honoured – that was devoted to what he called 'the nature, amazing ways, and properties of the beavers'. He talked of the unusually significant role that this mammal had played in the province's history. It was the beaver, he wrote, that was 'the main reason and the source of the means for the initial settlement of this fine country by Europeans'.

It was a subject that der Donck knew very well. In nine years in the colony, he said, he had 'often made a meal of beaver meat', which was much prized by Native Americans, particularly the tail. He had kept the creatures, he said, 'from a young age', and had handled and traded 'many thousands of beaver skins', as did almost all the early settlers in New Netherland. Here, as well as in the immediately neighbouring districts, he wrote, 'some eighty thousand beavers are put down every year'. Even more than the English, it was the beaver trade on which the Dutch concentrated. The trade was, as Daniel Denton would later observe, 'the main thing prosecuted by the Dutch'.[16] But it was not sustainable. Since the animals did not migrate fast from elsewhere to replace those which were trapped, we can see now that it was a cull which could not last, however much the profusion of New World life seemed to early settlers too substantial to staunch.

The English were scarcely less quick than the Dutch to spot the trade's lucrative potential. Early English residents, while the province was still under Dutch rule, became involved in a smuggling trade which deeply disturbed the administration. 'Clandestinely', they moved beaver skins to New England, carrying them 'out of the country by night and at other untimely seasons across *Long Island* and along the *East River* in small boats and canoes'. On perhaps only a half of them, it was reckoned, had the requisite duty been paid.[17] It was no coincidence that the name of the new settlement at which Daniel Denton and his brother came to live during the late 1650s – Jamaica – derived not from the Caribbean island of the same name, but from the word 'Yameco', a corruption of the word used in a local Native American language for 'beaver' (a name which was applied to a pond nearby).

Why was there such a demand for the fur of this animal in particular? There were many other fur-bearing animals, after all. But as der Donck noted, the beaver pelt – brown, with a reddish tinge – is unusual. The creature, he wrote, is 'densely covered all over' with 'very fine fur'. The number of hairs in a square centimetre is uncommonly high. Unusually, the hairs of this thick fur are barbed, which means that they mat easily together. And the process is aided by human sweat, meaning that the most valuable skins, and the most in demand, were not pristine ones but rather those which had been worn by people for some months. Through a lengthy procedure the pelts could then be 'felted'. And the fabric which resulted was not only soft and warm but also waterproof. In the hands of European furriers it made, as der Donck put it, 'the best hats that are worn', named 'beavers', or 'castors', after the raw material used. 'Demi-castors' were a slightly cheaper alternative made, as the name suggests, with beaver along with additional rabbit or some other fur. The application of mercury, with its lasting neurological consequences and the even more lasting colloquial expression 'as mad as a hatter' had yet to be introduced.

If this wasn't bad enough for the unfortunate creatures, the beavers' aquatic habits made them permissible eating, like fish, on Catholic holy days, on the dubious basis that their environment rendered them 'cold', while their oil and their fatty tails were reputed to be an aid to the maintenance of an erection (with what seems now, no pun intended, to be an equal lack of rigour). This was a substance, one un-cloistered English emigrant observed, 'of such masculine virtue' that 'if some of our ladies knew the benefit thereof, they would desire to have ships sent of purpose, to trade for the tail alone'. But, increasingly, it was the fur which came first. And the central importance of the beaver for the colony was recognised by the animal's presence on the seals of both New Amsterdam and New Netherland, as well as on that later adopted by the city.[18]

As fashions in Europe changed, so the desirability of the beaver hat swelled, and the Continent, in the early seventeenth century, witnessed a craze for this wide-brimmed, waterproof headgear. By now, der Donck commented, beaver hats were 'well known throughout Europe'. Sumptuary laws, restricting particular items of luxurious clothing to carefully-defined classes, began to fall into disuse. It ceased to be the case, as it long had been, that the most desirable furs (as well as being highly expensive) were restricted by law to a limited number of the uppermost classes. And the more lowly majority, or those at least with some money to spare, were no longer confined to 'such grave and honest apparel as befits their station'. Now, assuming that they could afford it, they were free to join the queue for a beaver.

In previous centuries Europe had had its own supply of the animals. The last is believed to have been seen in England early in the sixteenth century. Subsequently their pelts were for a long time imported from Russia, where the creatures had been, as one cleric lamented, as 'plentiful as dung'. An English writer of the later sixteenth century noted that beaver hats were 'fetched from beyond the sea' – referring to Russia. But there too, in time, they were hunted to extinction.[19] So when a vast and (surely this time) inexhaustible new supply was discovered across the Atlantic, merchants could barely contain themselves. Native Americans rushed to satisfy this curious demand, just as baffled and discreetly amused by European desires as Europeans were by the Natives' demand for baubles and kettles and similar 'trifles'. Both sides thought, with some reason, that they had much the better of the exchange.

For the Dutch, as for other European merchant companies, furs – this 'handsome and considerable peltry trade' – often took precedence over settlements, at least until in the 1650s an urgent attempt was made to combat this problem.

The English group that was led by Richard Denton was very fortunate in its timing. They had not arrived by the time of the retaliatory Native American attacks in 1643 – that 'year of blood' for those in this part of

North America just as it was for those living back in England as the country fell apart.

Here in New Netherland, surviving European inhabitants bemoaned their fate. They called themselves 'wretched', and 'forlorn' people. They cried that they, with their wives and children, were merely 'prey' to 'these cruel heathens' – 'our enemies'. They complained of 'great injury'. Native populations, though, who had suffered horribly when the Dutch struck first at them, felt, and were entitled to feel, precisely the same way. Blood had been shed, houses and cattle burnt, as some of the Dutch did admit, 'on both sides'.[20]

It was close to the site on which Hempstead would shortly be established that one native village, in the bloody aftermath, was subject to a revenge attack. Over a hundred men, women and children were murdered as they slept. And shortly afterwards, one 'calm and cloud-less night' a small Christian army – Dutch and English laying their differences to one side in the face of the shared crisis – trekked across 'snow-clad plains' and 'rugged hills' to slaughter many hundreds more at a large native camp on the mainland.

When this 'army' returned to New Amsterdam crowds gathered to applaud and cheer. A public service was held to offer thanks to God, for what seemed a grave threat averted and a sign of His loving supervision. Subsequently a treaty of peace was signed between the Europeans and the Native American tribes, out of mutual fear rather than friendship. And the temporary alliance which had been forged among the latter collapsed under the strain. The alliance between the Dutch and English did too, with one Dutch account lamenting the way in which the Eng-lish made use of them 'as a cloak in time of need' before then ignoring and '[making] fools of them'.[21]

If the Dentons were fortunate not to have arrived on Long Island by mid-1643, they did so later that year, seeing signs of the recent destruction. By 1647 'deputies from the village of Hempstead' are referred to in a resolution signed by the Dutch governor, and names of families who travelled with them appear on a census, taken early in the second half of the decade, after the First Civil War in England and before the Second. Throughout these years Dutch company leaders were conscious of the difficulty of settling any disputes with a divided, fractious England. With whom were they to deal? 'At this time', it was written, 'it is impracticable to make an agreement with the English [...] for we cannot discover, that anyone is authorised thereto.' The king was detained and imprisoned. Everything in that country was 'turned bottom upwards', while efforts – it was noted – were apparently being made 'to establish another form of government'.²²

The Dentons' arrival in the mid-1640s coincided, by chance, with that of a new leader for the province. Peter Stuyvesant was thirty-five when he took the helm. He had lost his lower-right leg in a fight with the Spanish in the Caribbean, and used in its place a wooden stump wrapped with metal bands which earned him the nicknames 'Wooden Leg' or 'Old Silver Leg'. He was a fierce Calvinist, intolerant of other faiths – intolerant, for example, of the toleration that the company insisted be granted to Lutherans, or even to Jews – and he inclined, no doubt, to look more favourably upon Denton and his community precisely because of their Presbyterian, 'Reformed' (and Calvinist) faith.

Stuyvesant was autocratic by nature. And hot-tempered – banging his wooden stump repeatedly on the ground when angry. He considered it a general point of principle that colonists should not petition against their magistrates, 'whether there was cause or not'. Anyone who did appeal he promised to make a foot shorter before sending 'the pieces to Holland' ('and let them', he fulminated, 'appeal that way'). 'We derive our authority from God and the company', he proclaimed, 'not from a few ignorant subjects.'²³ Whatever the similarity in their religious views, this was not a man who shared Richard Denton's ideas about democracy.

Nevertheless, unlike some of his predecessors, Stuyvesant was not incompetent. The need for reform, he admitted, was 'as palpable as the sun at clear noon'. On his watch, trade became freer. The company's monopoly was abandoned, such that independent colonists now had something to gain. And government, which should not simply be left, critics complained, 'to a set of hare-brained people, such as the Company flings thither', became more open. Complaints which had been made against an imperious director-general who acted like a 'sovereign tyrant' were heard, and there was in any case a strict practical limit to the interference that he was able to make in the lives of colonists, who overruled him at times when moralising measures seemed 'contrary to the freedoms' of the fatherland, and who cherished ideas of what

Stuyvesant contemptuously called 'an imaginary liberty in a new and, as some pretend, a free country'.[24]

In particular the proliferation of English settlements made active supervision or intervention impossible. And here the regime had learnt its lesson about imposing arbitrary rule. The sheer numbers of the English, as well as their links to neighbouring English colonies, made them impossible to bully. They were, admitted the directors, 'much too powerful for us'. It is 'not advisable', they warned, 'that we should be involved into a war'. In general they instructed their man on the spot to 'govern the people with the utmost caution and leniency': they – the directors – had 'learned by experience', they warned, 'how too much vehemence may draw upon you the hatred of the people'.[25]

In spite of Stuyvesant as this liberalisation may have been, it did manage to secure a rise – at last – in the number of Dutch (and other) colonists living in the province. Belatedly, to the relief of company directors, the population of New Netherland began to increase. 'Inducements' were offered to immigrants. The regime clamped down on company misrule. And they offered more liberty, and more self-government. Colonists harboured ideas of freedom, whatever their governor thought. And the Dutch company which owned the colony admitted that it seemed no longer 'a little colony' but rather a 'rising republic'. Dutch and other settlers saw the appeal, and the company understood the necessity of encouraging immigration by almost any means. It was certainly the case, wrote the company hierarchy, that 'the welfare of the country depends on the population'. As a result of these reforms, the settlement at New Amsterdam did finally begin to flourish. From being a small, precarious, fly-blown town in a wider region which cost the nation – 'dear Fatherland' – 'so much blood, trouble and expense', the place became a busy, bibulous port.

The largely wooden town that Stuyvesant inherited became one predominantly of brick and tiled roofs. The place was 'adorned', he wrote, 'with so many noble buildings' as almost to excel 'any other place in North America'. Commerce was prioritised. Trade, Stuyvesant observed, was 'the soul, the life, the salvation of a place'. Within a few years, he reckoned, 'if it pleased God', the community 'might become a mighty people in this happily situated province'. Tavern-keepers as well as fur-traders proliferated, but while the Calvinist Stuyvesant still bemoaned 'the profuse consumption of strong drink', in fact that 'swinish vice' of drunkenness became somewhat less stultifying for the Dutch, even if they did remain what one later observer called 'obstinate and incessant smokers'. It was left to the English to bemoan the bad habits they saw among their co-nationals: what they called the 'piping, potting, feasting, fashions, and mis-spending of our time'.[26]

Literacy, and the rights of women, were high for a European society in the middle of the seventeenth century. One historian has noted that names were signed on documents, as opposed to having a 'mark' applied, as often in New Netherland as in any of the English communities, either on Long Island or further north. (In Hempstead one such document in 1656 had twenty-three names and eighteen marks, while one in the town of Jamaica in 1661 had eleven names and nine marks; the last popular petition in New Amsterdam, made in 1664, boasted sixty-nine signatures alongside only nine marks.) Immigrants, few of whom came from classes with any sense of entitlement, were men and women 'inured to toil and poverty'. Few in New Netherland, as in the Puritan provinces to its north, were gentlefolk, entitled to the rarefied title (which has lost now its class connotation) of 'Mr'. But while the moralising residue of class remained powerful in New England, where in fact efforts were made to preserve it for fear that its clear and stabilising lines might dissolve or weaken in the New World, it was much less so in New Netherland. While the former continued to frame sumptuary laws well *after* their demise in the old country – continued to express an 'utter detestation and dislike' for people of 'mean condition, educations and callings' aping the 'garb of gentlemen' – never were such regulations considered further south.[27]

Tired of being told that 'the province is only a burden upon our shoulders', and that 'the Company would do better to abandon it', directors in Holland 'rejoiced' at what they saw now as belated 'signs of progress'. Where formerly, they observed gladly, '*New Netherland* was never spoken of' in Europe, it seemed all of a sudden that 'heaven and earth' were 'stirred up by it'. Everyone wanted to be involved. Everyone tried 'to be the first in selecting the best pieces there'. The colony began, finally, to pay its way. 'At last', wrote the directors, 'we can reap the long expected benefits.'[28]

*

For some years Richard Denton's community had been able to live and worship in peace, protected by Dutch numerical weakness as well as by a stockade built around their settlement as a defence against the encroachments both of Dutch and Native Americans.

Nominal Dutch control was loose. And oaths of loyalty taken to New Netherland – and to its 'High Mightinesses' back in Europe – meant little in practice. Whatever the English influx's benefits to the settlement in terms of population, nationality did matter, the Dutch administration realised, just as much as did religious faith. If it came to conflict, the English would fight 'rather against, than for us'. In thinking about the security of New Amsterdam, Stuyvesant resolved 'not to call upon them either for the repairs or for the defence, that we may not ourselves drag the Trojan horse within our walls'.[29]

And so the population at Hempstead kept to themselves. Like other English migrants, they were granted rights of self-governance, their own courts and liberty of conscience – freedom from any 'molestation or disturbance' on account of what they believed. These last were rights which had had significant appeal to a Presbyterian activist like Richard Denton. Dutch company governors worried that the 'plan of self-government' espoused by English settlements set a rather 'dangerous precedent'.[30] Using the meeting house built by the English at Hempstead both for worship and for holding town gatherings, Denton worked to promote his civic along with his religious ideals. For adult males at least, he held both politics and religion to be associated duties. And voting for town officials was made a compulsory requirement.

For a while longer there was calm. Late spring was a wonderful time when, as one observer put it, 'all of nature bursts free, fish dart forth from muddy depths, the trees bud, and the grass sprouts', when 'the cold is gone, and the burning heat is yet to come', when 'the trees are in flower, and sweet scents pervade the forest'. Each year the fields were 'dyed red' in June by thousands of wild strawberries. Armed 'with bottles of wine, cream, and sugar', the inhabitants rushed into the fields on horseback to 'disrobe them'. Rich banks of wild flowers – an 'incredible multitude' – meant that here in America untended nature alone excelled 'many gardens in England'. Birds sang, saluting 'the ears of travellers with an harmonious discord'. Frogs lay in every pond and brook, 'warbling forth their untun'd tunes'. And the English were astonished by the quantity of timber, which was in short supply now back in England: oaks, white and red, chestnut trees, walnut trees.[31]

Each year the intense heat of summer gave way to the rich colours of autumn, and to the harvest of crops. The temperature dropped to a level that was 'seasonable and comfortable'. 'The autumns in New Netherland', wrote one inhabitant, 'are normally as fine, lovely, and pleasant as could be desired anywhere on earth.'[32] And then the snows fell. Fires were lit. And cold winds blew across the open plain. The Dutch love of skating and sledging – *slee* (from which we get the word 'sleigh') was a Dutch word – was something which was adopted by all immigrants to the province. Although Daniel and his brother were living and working a short distance away in the town of Jamaica, he regularly made the journey back to see his father at Hempstead.

Stuyvesant, though, was merely biding his time. Ultimately, he regarded conflict between the English and Dutch communities as inevitable. It was beyond doubt, he thought, that the English would look to seize New Amsterdam as the key to all New Netherland. Already in 1648, it was written, he was 'expecting a war with the English', and he directed his thinking accordingly. Five years later, in 1653, while Richard Denton was still at the centre of Hempstead life, a group of local Native Americans approached his community. They spoke to Denton personally, whom they trusted. They warned that Stuyvesant was planning a radical and violent solution to the problem keenly felt by the Dutch at the growing English presence. With other natives, these men said, the governor had conspired to sponsor a brutal attack on the English Long Island communities, like that at Hempstead, in which all – men, women and children – would be murdered as they slept, their houses burnt and their wells poisoned.[33]

In Europe, not coincidentally, this was a time of war between Holland and Republican England. Armed conflict – 'undesired and unexpected bloody differences' – had broken out a year previously. Although for a time the fighting did not spread to the New World, where many of the English were much closer to the Dutch faith than were their compatriots in Europe, tension did inevitably rise, and Dutch company leaders warned Stuyvesant to put no faith in the English, to 'keep an eye on them' and not to trust what they called their 'sinister machinations'. After what he learnt from the Native American messengers, Denton might have responded that he could say precisely the same about Stuyvesant.

At an urgent meeting it was decided to confront the governor directly. And any immediate trouble, as a result, was averted. English pastors on Long Island – men like Denton – advised their congregations that the closeness of their religious beliefs with those of the Dutch did not justify any conflict. Denton assured Stuyvesant himself that in spite of the war between England and the Netherlands in Europe, his community remained, and would remain, entirely neutral. A little later, Stuyvesant expressed his personal appreciation for the calming role that Denton had played. Dutch ministers who paid a visit to Hempstead a few years later, meanwhile, were full of praise for what they called Denton's 'friendly disposition'. He was devoid of national chauvinism. And plainly, given the tip-off he had received regarding the threat that his congregation faced, local Native American communities also valued his kindness and friendship. He was, the Dutch ministers said, 'beloved by all'.[34]

Richard Denton's son Daniel was by then a young man in his early twenties. Having accompanied his father over the Atlantic, he had lived in America since he was a child. As an adult he worked, part-time, as a town official for the neighbouring English settlement called Jamaica, some ten miles due west from Hempstead, along the spine of Long Island, where his younger brother Nathaniel was also a town clerk. The Denton siblings seem to have been among the place's founders. Daniel was one of those who petitioned Stuyvesant for the original grant of land.[35] Records for a meeting held in the town in February 1656, when Daniel was about thirty (Nathaniel about twenty-eight), mention that Daniel – taking advantage of his literacy and education – had been chosen to enter 'all acts and orders of public concernment' into a town book. It also mentions a public vote (for thus, in Jamaica, as in Hempstead, were things done) by which it was decreed that anyone killing a wolf, or wolves, within the town boundary should be granted fifteen shillings per wolf – an activity encouraged for reasons of the safety of penned farm animals as well as of people.

Late in the 1650s Richard Denton was beset by personal problems. His wife became seriously ill. And he was plagued by financial worries, sinking deeper into debt and unable to resolve it with the small salary that he was paid by the Hempstead community. (He was not the only English minister on Long Island to find it hard to make ends meet: one left for Virginia, being 'not well supported'; another struggled to manage with the 'meagre and irregular payments from his hearers'.) In desperation, Denton likewise travelled overland the hundreds of miles to the south, to Virginia, in search of a more lucrative position, but was forced to return without finding a solution. Every day he prayed, seeking divine guidance for his problems. When subsequently he did receive some extraordinary news it must have seemed to have been sent by God. A friend in England who had died, he was told, had left him a significant legacy of £400. His difficulties would be resolved entirely. The only problem was that either he or his wife would have to attend in person in order to claim the money.

Since his wife was too unwell to manage the trip on her own, or to be left untended, he knew that he would have to go with her. Numerous attempts were made to persuade him to stay. But the legacy was too substantial, and too opportune, to ignore. The heavens seemed to have made their will plain. (Stuyvesant himself promised to do what he could, while visiting Dutch ministers commented that Denton could not 'be induced by us to remain, although we have earnestly tried to do this in various ways'.) With a heavy heart he bade his family, his friends and his parishioners farewell and boarded a ship for the old country that he had left – reluctantly but single-mindedly – more than twenty years previously. The final mention of Richard Denton's name in the Hempstead Town Books comes under 4 March 1658, when his meagre salary was logged and paid. He never returned to America. He settled instead in Essex, some distance south of his native Yorkshire, where he found a clerical post. There he died, a few years later, early in the 1660s.[36]

In New Netherland, meanwhile, tensions mounted. Just as the growing population and success of the colony made the Dutch West India Company value it more highly, mounting English pressure – from within as well as from New England – began to seem irreconcilable, as Stuyvesant had foreseen. (He wrote subsequently of the 'overpowering might' of the English, estimating – something of an exaggeration – that the Dutch were outnumbered by a margin of fifty to one.)[37] The colony's position between Virginia and New England also saw it increasingly desired by England, whose commercial rivalry with the Dutch in particular swelled.

Without control of the Hudson, and the territory around it, as the leaders of the English Republic were aware, England was not able to slow the advance of the French to the north, and neither could it profit from the lucrative trade in furs both there and in New Netherland. Claims were made with regard to the early patents which were alleged to justify England's right to the territory, though the Dutch presence, of course, had not bothered the regime in London while English expansion was at an earlier stage, and while the two countries were allies.

Now the Dutch, it was claimed, were 'monsters and bold usurpers', who had occupied the province only by 'fraud and treachery'.[38]

After the death of the English Republic's presiding genius and 'Lord Protector', Oliver Cromwell, and his son's inability to fill his shoes, 1660 saw – as we have seen – the restoration of the Stuart family to the English throne. Charles Stuart, eldest son of the unfortunate king in whose reign his country had been racked by a ruinous civil war and whose execution had taken place over a decade earlier, was restored to the throne in Westminster as Charles II. Monarchists in England rejoiced.

Initially the Dutch West India Company was hopeful. While England and the Netherlands might both have been republics, the latter had distrusted, even hated, Cromwell's regime. It had heeded the 'distressing rumours of danger' which threatened its colony of New Netherland. And it had loathed the general uncertainty that existed for as long as England was 'very much disturbed' in both political and ecclesiastical government. 'Better things may be expected', they thought, 'from [Charles's] honesty and righteousness than from the former unlawful government.'

The king, surely, would not support the 'unjust claims' that were made by the English colonies, would not encourage them, 'as the preceding government has undoubtedly done'. This optimism, however, soon died and was replaced by further 'flying rumours' of hostile English intentions. The English continued to tussle with their great rivals the Dutch for commercial supremacy. The restoration made little difference. Having fought the English Commonwealth, the Netherlands went to war with the English again under the Stuarts. Near the mouth of the Thames further major sea battles occurred between the two, the noise of the great guns faintly heard from the windows of government departments in London. And meanwhile the rivalry continued to spill across the Atlantic, from Europe into the 'American wilderness'.

If the return of the Stuarts to the English throne did see a shift, it was not one favourable to the Dutch colony. While Stuyvesant and the Dutch longed for the 'quiet possession' of territory which had 'caused and cost here so much labour, anxiety and troubles', the regime in England now was less preoccupied than the Cromwellian Republic had been with security at home.[39] And it was more able, as a result, to focus on imperial matters overseas. Colonial expansion was actively sought. And greedy English eyes continued to fall on New Netherland – ever more longingly now that the place was not only necessary to unify North America, and to combat the French in 'Canada', further north, but was also, increasingly, affluent in its own right. The English were no less conscious than the Dutch that, left to develop, 'in the course of a few years' the settlement 'might become a mighty people'. In its situation, and for trade, wrote one English account in 1663, the city of New Amsterdam was 'very delightsome and convenient'. It was – and the smacking of lips is almost audible – 'the very best part of all that large northern empire'.[40]

Early in the 1660s, when three members of the royal Council for Foreign Plantations were appointed to consider the matter, they included Sir John Berkeley, the one-time Royalist soldier and brother of William, the Governor of Virginia. Detail was demanded from them regarding this 'Dutch intrusion' into North America, as well as regarding the ease and likelihood of the English being able to force them out, in spite of continued Dutch insistence upon their 'indisputable, real and effectual' right to the region. A recent treaty between the two countries which overlooked any such unjust incursion was quietly ignored. The English were looking for a fight. 'All the court', admitted the diarist Samuel Pepys, was 'mad for war.'[41]

On Long Island, meanwhile, Stuyvesant, and the Dutch West India Company in general, continued to struggle against the accumulated weight of English people pouring into the colony. By early in the 1660s thirteen English towns had been founded on the island, compared with only five populated by the Dutch.[42] Unrest mounted, fomented by a long-standing failure to clarify the boundary lines between the English and Dutch colonies.

Early in 1663 the ground itself shook, and the tremors continued for months. Further north, in Canada, a severe earthquake had struck which affected the whole of north-eastern America. Bells rang of their own accord as church towers rocked. Buildings and entire mountains collapsed. Trees and palisade stakes reared and danced, while vast fissures split the earth which shook and plunged like the ocean. A 'prodigious extent of country', it was said, was 'utterly wrecked'.[43] It was an awesome event almost universally interpreted in terms of divine distemper – distemper with Dutch rule, as it suited some to argue.

Later in the year, in Jamaica, Daniel Denton watched as hundreds of Englishmen, some on horseback and well armed – 300, it was claimed, though that estimate was subsequently downgraded – gathered in the town, summoned the magistrates and the inhabitants, and insisted that they defy their colonial authorities. This, they said, was 'the King's territory'. Englishmen present should take an oath of allegiance to King Charles, and not pay taxes to the Dutch. They promised to thrust a rapier 'in the guts of any man who [...] says this is not the king's land'. Among those who listened the armed crowd provoked a 'great hubbub and fury', threatening any who were doubtful with 'loss of their property, if they did not [...] take up arms against the Dutch'.

From the Dutch perspective these attempts to incite the English to 'sedition' were wholly contrary to the 'obliged duty & sworn oath' taken by the Long Island inhabitants. Stuyvesant reported what he called these 'unlawful, not to say decidedly hostile proceedings of the English'. They were made, he said, by 'diverse persons driven with a spirit of mutiny aiming at nothing but to fish in troubled waters'. The Dutch and the English ceased, increasingly, to work together. Many English towns refused to obey or to listen to the instructions emanating from New Amsterdam. And the Dutch authorities barred the 'malevolent' or 'malignant' English from participation in colonial business. The Dutch were, in any case, severely distracted at the time by conflict with a Native American tribe, upriver on the banks of the Hudson, which prevented them from focusing on the problems in Long Island.

Our 'weak military force', Stuyvesant admitted, was powerless:

prevented 'from doing anything against [the English rebels]'. With their attention (and military power) thus occupied, they offered the English towns autonomy. In any case, as Stuyvesant kept reminding his parent company in frustration, even if he could impose his will upon the soldiers now in Long Island, reprisals should be expected from the neighbouring English colonies and these would lead to 'unavoidable poverty, famine and destruction of the Dutch nation'. 'It would be folly on our part, it would be like running with our heads against a wall', he insisted, 'to make a hostile opposition.'[44]

All this time, furthermore, well-informed rumours abounded that Charles's brother James, the Duke of York and Albany – more conscientious than his older brother in his attraction to the Roman Catholic faith, a more conscientious imperialist and an even more conscientious womaniser (an activity in which Charles had set the bar high) – intended to seize New Netherland. The outnumbered Dutch, and their brethren on Manhattan, feared the worst. Though Stuyvesant tried to improve the city's ability to resist – 'to heighten the walls of our fort, strengthen it with gabions and make all arrangements for defence' – he was painfully aware in particular how short he was of military supplies, and if his capital was lost, as he admitted, 'all is lost'.

The colony, the regime wrote to its rulers in Europe at the beginning of 1664, was likely to be 'torn away' by the English. The English colonists were plainly receiving encouragement 'from the King, the Duke of York or some other great men'. The following month the Dutch administration signed a plea to their parent company, insisting to the directors that without their help the province would either be lost or be so diminished – 'so cramped and clipped' – that they would be forced in any case to leave. For all that the population had increased in recent years, still their own strength, they admitted, was so 'feeble and impotent' by comparison with the English that it seemed a miracle they had been granted 'so long a reprieve'. Without doubt, they insisted, England would now seize New Amsterdam, and with it all of New Netherland: all of what they called this 'happily situated province', which was now, as officials admitted, in a 'desolate condition'.[45]

In spite of the threats and the strong-arm tactics, some of the English colonists were torn, and Daniel Denton himself was in this camp. As his father had been, Daniel had been minded to side with the religious radicals of the Republican regime, but he – and many Long Island English like him – found it hard to rally behind the restored monarchy. After all, it had been to escape the injustices and impositions of Stuart rule that his family had emigrated to America in the first place. When a document was written calling upon the regimes in England and the Netherlands to settle their differences – to 'determine the whole difficulty' about Long Island and 'the places adjacent' – it was attested and signed both on behalf of Stuyvesant and the Dutch, and by several leading English personalities, who included Daniel Denton.

The settlement of Hempstead is said to have remained loyal to its Dutch overseers through this crisis, in spite of the demands made by English rebels. Others among the English, meanwhile, found it hard to feel much enthusiasm for the Puritans of New England, even when most of the latter did, somehow, manage to proclaim their loyalty to King Charles. Ethnicity was certainly not the only dividing factor.

In their report the Committee of the Council for Foreign Plantations in London addressed the issue of how much force was necessary to wrest New Netherland from the Dutch. Three ships, they said, carrying 300 soldiers should be enough, given that a significant percentage of the population on Long Island was English, and that Englishmen could also be relied upon – just as the Dutch feared – to come from the other American colonies to assist.

Three armed ships was what had been foretold, for months, by the Dutch authorities, and at the start of 1664 it was confirmed to them by Native Americans (who had heard it from the English) that 'three ships would come from England, to drive out the Dutch'.

Like Henry Norwood, Richard Nicolls had been a lifelong supporter of the Stuart cause. As a 'bold and intrepid youth', only eighteen years old, he had led a Royalist cavalry troop on the outbreak of the Civil Wars. Like Norwood, again, he had followed the Stuarts into exile, fighting with Charles's brother James in France, and cementing a relationship with the prince. He was highly educated, knowing not only Latin and Greek but also French and Dutch. He was tall, with grey eyes and curly hair. He was prone to bouts of impassioned ill-temper. But in general he was kind. 'I am too well natured', he wrote after dealing with some

Englishmen whom he found frustrating, 'to deal harshly' with even 'the worst of men'.[46]

On the Restoration Nicolls had returned to England, taking up a post as one of the Gentlemen of the Bedchamber. When Charles presented to his younger brother 'a patent for Long Island, in the West Indies, and a tract of land between New England and Maryland' – land which, it was somewhat dubiously alleged, had 'always belonged to the crown of England since first discovered, and upon which the Dutch had encroached' (building a town and some forts in order 'to secure the beaver trade for themselves') – it was Nicolls who was chosen by James to lead a naval expedition to enforce it. The expedition's plan was to seize the city of New Amsterdam and its province, although its ostensible purpose, which fooled few either in Amsterdam or in London was to look into 'the state of New England'.

In May 1664 it sailed from Portsmouth: a time, supposedly, of peace between England and the Netherlands. Late in August, from Manhattan Stuyvesant saw the large English ships anchored off Long Island. He demanded to know their intentions, since they had not announced them. The following day Nicolls sent him a response. 'I think it fit to let you know', he declared, 'that his Majesty of Great Britain, whose right and title to these parts of America is unquestionable' (questioned as it certainly was) 'hath commanded me [...] to require a surrender of all such forts, towns, or places of strength, which are now possessed by the Dutch under your command.' He would much prefer to take over the city in peace, he said. His Majesty was 'tender of the effusion of Christian blood', and he, Nicolls, would guarantee to every man his 'estate, life, and liberty' should they readily submit. Otherwise they must expect 'all the miseries of a war, which they bring upon themselves'.

We do not know what precisely Daniel Denton was doing as the small flotilla of English warships sailed into the harbour, then docked at Gravesend on the south-west of Long Island, allowing hundreds of troops to disembark in order to rally the English colonists. (There *were* three substantial naval ships, just as it had been predicted, though they were joined by a fourth, smaller vessel.) As the clerk at Jamaica, though, Denton must certainly have followed the events closely. It was 27 August 1664 – a hot, humid day in midsummer. As the troops marched north at the western end of the island towards the Manhattan ferry, men went in advance to distribute handbills (printed in English as well as Dutch) which promised fair treatment for any who surrendered, but which also threatened violence were the place and its inhabitants to resist. If the handover 'could not be done in an amicable way', wrote one Dutch clergyman, 'they were to attack the place' – 'everything was to be thrown open for the English soldiers to plunder, rob and pillage', as many of them plainly hoped.

'I have employed these gentlemen', Nicolls said of his recruiting sergeants who went ahead, 'to raise what men they can.' They should have 'free liberty', he proclaimed, 'to beat their drums for that end' in any town here in the west of Long Island. Again, no doubt, Denton was torn. On the one hand these troops were Englishmen, come to impose the rule of their king and countrymen upon the Dutch. The English, as he commented, had a 'general dislike' of 'living under another government'.[47] But on the other hand the soldiers represented a monarchy from which he and his father had long ago fled.

Nicolls sent to Stuyvesant a letter which formally demanded the colony's surrender. It promised that all the residents of New Netherland might continue to live 'peaceably', to enjoy the fruits of 'God's blessing' and of 'their own honest industry'. Stuyvesant, though, was inclined to resist, whatever the cost. Angrily, he ripped up the letter. For days the impasse continued. The Dutch requested that the matter be passed to Europe, for the Dutch and English governments to resolve. But Nicolls refused. He ordered his ships to sail past Manhattan with their guns trained on the city, signalling their intent to fire a broadside on the place and to take it by storm at the first sign of any resistance.

At the same time, it was made painfully clear to Stuyvesant how impossible it would be to defend New Amsterdam. In spite of efforts that had been made, the city was not properly fortified. He claimed – though this may well have been an excuse concocted in the aftermath, to mitigate his own action – that the fort was 'crumbling'. And even if the defences were adequate, there were not sufficient men, or gunpowder, to undertake the job. If he started firing in the morning, the gunner complained, he would run out of powder by noon.[48] Provisions were wholly inadequate. 'No relief or assistance could be expected', as one Dutchman reported. And meanwhile the numbers of opposing English mounted, and more no doubt would follow. 'Daily', wrote the same witness, 'great numbers on foot and on horseback, from New England, joined the English, hotly bent upon plundering the place.'

When word of the terms that he had been offered leaked out, Stuyvesant was obliged to collect the pieces of the letter, reassemble them and report its contents in detail to his subordinates. While Stuyvesant himself wanted to hold out, in the broader community there was no stomach for a fight, given the favourable terms on offer and the seeming inevitability of the English conquest. Already there had been 'popular murmurs and disaffections' in the town. 'A general discontent and unwillingness to assist in defending the place', reported Stuyvesant, 'became manifest among the people.'[49]

Nicolls gave his word that residents would not be affected by the change in rule. And colonists of all nationalities preferred, not surprisingly, to continue life uninterrupted under English rule rather than to undergo 'pillage, bloodshed and general ruin'. Residents could continue in their trades. Public houses would remain open. The population would enjoy complete liberty of conscience, which was an important factor not only for the Dutch but for the highly mixed (by faith as well as ethnicity) resident community. And they would never, in the likely event that England and the Netherlands went to war again, be expected to fight against their own country. A letter addressed to Stuyvesant by prominent men of New Amsterdam, a group which included Stuyvesant's own teenage son, pleaded with him not to hold out against 'so generous a foe'. One Dutchman was sanguine about the likely change of government. 'It has pleased the Lord', he said, 'that we must learn English.'[50]

The garrison in Fort Amsterdam, on the tip of Manhattan Island – a fort considered by Denton, whatever the general manning of the colony, as 'one of the best pieces of defence in the north-parts of America' – would be permitted to leave in honour, with 'drums beating and colours flying'. Faced with such united desire to submit, Stuyvesant had little option but to accept. Only those English troops who looked forward to 'pillage, plunder and bloodshed' were sullen at the prospect of a peaceful surrender, reacting with 'cursing' whenever 'mention was made of a capitulation'.

And so, early in September, Stuyvesant surrendered formally, swearing allegiance on behalf of New Amsterdam to the English crown. He resigned his office as governor of the colony and, after sailing home to report on what he called this 'unfortunate loss and reduction', which (as he was desperate to point out) 'could not be avoided by human means', returned to retire on his farm in the province that he had ruled for sixteen years.[51]

Nicolls took over, formally as 'deputy-governor' on behalf of the Duke of York, though in reality as the colony's governor. His good nature and fair-minded temperament endeared him to all communities – even to Stuyvesant himself. He gained no benefit from his position, he promised, nor sought any apart from a good name. He was, he declared, very unwilling to act 'with severity' whenever he could 'possibly avoid it', a consequence of what he said was his 'patient temper' while that of others was 'hot and fiery'. 'I am very tender in giving credit to the reports on one part', he told one side of a dispute, 'till the other is heard.'

He disliked oppression much more than he valued nationality or class or hierarchy, being never unwilling, he said, 'to manifest the openness both of my ears and heart, to the meanest man in the world, who can object to me the least oppression upon him'. He took little financial reward for his pains, happy to justify himself and his actions, he proclaimed, 'before God and the world'. While the fur trade became gradually less central in its importance, meanwhile, it did remain a primary industry, and Nicolls was quick to approve, for instance, one English request from Long Island to 'trade with the Indians [...] for peltry'.

The price paid by the Duke of York to his brother – an annual rent for the province, to recognise that he held it from the king – was forty beaver skins.[52] The place was renamed in honour of the absent duke. One new name that Richard Nicolls considered was 'Albania', since James was the Duke of York *and Albany*. Instead, though, he plumped for what had already been agreed. And it still possesses that name today: New York.

Soon after he took over, Nicolls promised to convene a gathering of representatives of all the major communities who lived in the state, in these 'remote parts' of King Charles's dominions.

Legal matters and any disputes might be aired. Relief could be provided, he guaranteed, for any 'grievous inconveniences' felt by the settlers – for the 'private dissensions and animosities' which too often had 'prevailed against neighbourly love, and Christian charity'. He was reluctant for the meeting to take place during winter, Nicolls thoughtfully said, because he did not want delegates to be expected to make a difficult journey through the snow. Instead, it would happen as soon as the weather eased, early in 1665, in the town of Hempstead on Long Island, in the building which Richard Denton had overseen and had used so often both as a church and a meeting house.

Each community (or the adult male part of that community) was to elect representatives, and Nicolls recommended that choice be made of 'the most sober, able and discreet persons' – those free from 'partiality or faction' – who might contribute to 'a full and perfect settlement and composure of all controversies', and to 'the propagation of true religion amongst us'. In Jamaica, Daniel Denton was one of those who was elected to attend: a shorter journey for him than for most. Nicolls went with a text which he had drawn up after consulting the laws of other English colonies in America, although in important ways he modified their severity, insisting upon a greater degree of religious tolerance and removing, for instance, any penalty for witchcraft – that crime which worried an increasing number of people at the time. In the two witchcraft trials which he did oversee, in which the charge was altered to some other crime that we would recognise, Nicolls refused to convict.[53]

The conference was less a forum for negotiation than some delegates anticipated. Rather, Nicolls simply informed representatives that a governor and the Council would henceforth rule the colony with the aid of sheriffs and justices of the peace appointed by the governor, while the Council would sit too as the court of assize – the colony's highest court. Nicolls imposed a code of laws, known as the Duke's Laws. And a new county was created, within which the English communities on Long Island would subsist, known (again after James Stuart) as Yorkshire. For the time being the Dutch were permitted to maintain their own institutions, but gradually, over a period of months, English government forms were extended. Within New York itself Dutch local government was replaced by a new city council: with aldermen and an appointed mayor. Nicolls – a Royalist, who lamented 'the late rebellion in England, with all ye ill consequences thereof' – admitted, though he was not sorry, that the imposed system might be 'grievous to some Republicans'.

The following year, now that a state of warfare did exist between the English and the Dutch, and reprisals were anticipated in New York, Nicolls addressed a cautionary letter to several of the JPs whom he trusted on Long Island, one of them being 'Mr Denton'. Nicolls only remained in New York until 1668, finding his personal financial outlay crippling, though even the Dutch now confessed their sorrow in losing a man whom they considered a 'wise and intelligent governor'. He returned to the side of Prince James, the Duke of York and Albany and England's Lord Admiral.

Not long afterwards, in 1672, he was killed by a cannonball while standing on deck at James's side in another naval battle with the Dutch which took place off the East Anglian coast.[54]

New York, under English rule, remained a cosmopolitan place. Many Dutch immigrants, as well as a wide mixture of other nationalities, lived within the city itself, while neighbouring places like Long Island remained predominantly English.[55]

In 1670, six years after England seized the colony, Daniel Denton was obliged to return to England. And he was encouraged, while he was there, to write an account of the province for publication, as a means to encourage other English settlers to follow him across the Atlantic. He did certainly lay it on. But his enthusiasm was sincere. So 'fragrant' was the air, he promised, that passengers from Europe would smell it across the water before they landed (a claim that was true, and was often repeated). The place was healthy. He claimed that people could reside there for twenty years without knowing what sickness was (which seems improbable).

The climate had 'such an affinity with that of England', he promised – though in fact of course it was significantly hotter in summer and colder in winter – that no 'seasoning' (no period of adjustment during which sickness and mortality were high) was known. 'If there be any terrestrial Canaan', he wrote, ''tis surely here, where the land floweth with milk and honey.' He denied exaggeration. 'If I have erred', he said, 'it is principally in not giving [the region] its due commendation.' Moreover this new world was devoid, or largely so, of the class hierarchies which characterised society in old Europe – it was free, he promised, 'from the pride and oppression', ignorant 'of that pomp and bravery'. Here 'a wagon or cart gives as good content as a coach'; here 'home-made cloth' was 'better than the finest lawns or richest silks'; here, he might have said, more lowly clothing was counted as good as the most carefully made beaver, though the latter, of course, was considerably more affordable for the well-connected in the New World. America's pride in its simple, homely, ungentrified origins began early.

The city of New York was now, he wrote, mostly 'brick and stone', 'covered with red and black tile'. Beehives abounded on the sunny side of houses. Gradually the population was managing to diversify. From being largely devoted under the Dutch to the trade in fur, and beaver fur in particular, the colony had become less dependent on this one commodity, though the trade did remain of great importance. (Denton spoke of 'those great number of furs that have been lately transported from thence into Holland', but also observed the current inhabitants' 'considerable' ongoing 'trade with the Indians', mentioning skins, and those of the beaver, in particular; by the eighteenth century beaver hats still constituted a very significant part of England's fur exports.)

All manner of tradesmen, though, now did well in New York: 'carpenters, blacksmiths, masons, tailors, weavers, shoemakers, tanners, brick-makers, and so any other trade', while 'them that have no trade betake themselves to husbandry, get land of their own, and live exceeding well'. There were none, he promised, not entirely plausibly, 'but live happily here'.

Subsequently, he may in fact have been unhappy there himself, though this had nothing to do with deprivation or ill-health. While he was in England his wife, who had remained behind in America, was unfaithful to him. On his return over the Atlantic he found out, and took what was then the extreme step of divorcing her. (Unlike Native American communities, the English did not simply accept marital infidelity as the natural order of things – particularly, of course, if it was the woman who had been unfaithful.)

Life in New York, meanwhile, continued largely undisturbed, with the exception of a brief period – fifteen months – during the early 1670s when the province, and the city, was taken forcibly back into Dutch control. It continued to be a decidedly mixed settlement. For some time the city itself remained more Dutch than English, though in the province at large, on Long Island for instance, immigrants *were* often English. They came, as Denton wrote, from other parts of America as much as they did from across the ocean. But come they did. 'Every day', he said, 'more and more' arrived. It was a movement he could well understand, because this, of course, was what his own community had done, looking 'to view and settle', under his father's guidance, while he himself was a boy.

Still, he promised – and history has tended to concur with him – that the country was capable of supporting many more than were there in his time. 'So great a number of inhabitants' could exist here, he said. The land could provide for 'many thousand'. And they could live, he assured readers, 'as happily as any people in the world'. A vast amount of good land was available: good land which back in England seemed now in decidedly short supply as the population expanded. A settler in New York could easily 'weary himself', Denton said, 'with walking over his fields of corn and all sorts of grain', as his stocks of cattle increased by the year. There was no fear of a want either of pasture in the summer or of fodder in the winter, when the woods would afford sufficient supply.

A man or woman could travel on this American continent for many hundreds of miles, he said, without hearing the least complaint of want. To be sure, not all emigrants would have seconded his praise: certainly not those who suffered from the assaults by native communities (and not, of course, those who lived within these communities themselves, devastated by European, particularly English, competition, as well as by a seemingly callous 'hand of God'). But to be fair, Denton and his father had done so themselves, had travelled far by foot on this eastern American coast, on which the European colonies still perched.

As the settlement of New York became established – the days of New Amsterdam drifting into history (with the exception of the city's brief, year-long return to Dutch control) – the fur of the beaver ceased to be the central commodity in the colony's commercial life that it had once been. Trapping the animal remained a pursuit over which Native American hunters took 'great pains and pleasure'. They knew that demand among European merchants remained high. And the creature's pelt continued to constitute an alternate currency, though not now an exclusive one (one English observer who lived there late in the 1670s referring to one cost as being 'six beavers or an equivalent in money'). But in New York the fur trade in general by that time had declined dramatically in relative importance, falling to only one-fifth of what it had been at its height during the 1650s, shortly prior to the initial English capture.[56]

While demand remained high, and indeed climbed during the first half of the subsequent century as the vogue in Europe for beaver hats reached its zenith, the central region in America for export shifted towards the Canadian lands around Hudson's Bay, and the early history of New York as a ramshackle, disordered, disputatious centre of the beaver trade was largely forgotten.

# VI

# LIBERTY

At the end of August 1682, the carts laden with dark wooden fur-niture, blankets and heavy chests finally ceased rolling across the harbourside at Deal towards a ship named the *Welcome*. She was just over 100 feet long, with three square-rigged masts (although at 300 tons she was only a modest size, by the latter half of the century, for a transatlantic vessel). The chests, piled into the hold, were tightly packed with clothes, since many passengers took with them a lifetime's supply – on an optimistic estimation of how long that lifetime might last.

Here, on the Kent coast, in the place in which Henry Norwood had waited thirty years earlier, the wind moved obligingly until it blew from the north-northeast, allowing quick progress along the Channel and out – past Cornwall, past Ireland – into the Atlantic. Around thirty merchant ships then were moored at Deal, and as the weathervanes swung many quickly prepared to depart. At least two or three of these ships, including the *Welcome*, were bound for Pennsylvania. As soon as he was told about the wind, the captain of the *Welcome* ordered that all of just over a hundred passengers be hastily summoned on board. Most of them were English Quakers, many from Sussex, though one family had travelled from Ireland and two came from Wales. There were children too, and a few servants – neither group considered to merit independent inclusion on the passenger list. At least one among the crew or passengers also brought on board, along with his or her luggage, an unseen infection.

The thirty-seven-year old William Penn – plainly dressed, kind and softly spoken, if somewhat other-worldly – felt deeply torn. On the one hand he was elated. At last, having dreamt for many years about the venture and planned it at great length, he was doing God's work. He was leading many hundreds of Quakers away from persecution in

England, to their very own colony in America: to a place where they and others would be free to worship as they chose. On the other hand he experienced a profound personal sadness. His beloved family came with him, but only as far as the road to the English coast. At Canterbury they bid him farewell. He gave to them separate letters, as well as a joint one. As he wrote – 'to one a husband', he said, 'and to the rest a father' – he could not know 'whether I shall ever see thee more in this world'. The fact that he did owed much to his having been seriously ill as a child.

It was normal for those undertaking an ocean voyage in the seventeenth century to dwell upon the danger of shipwreck, and to bid farewell to those they left behind. At a time when death often came randomly and suddenly, voyages seemed especially dangerous – rather more so, perhaps, than the numbers would seem to justify. But very few, it should be remembered, had ever stood on the deck of a rearing, plunging ship before. Many could not swim, and were profoundly frightened – understandably so – of the sea. In the case of those crammed on board the *Welcome*, it was in any case not the elements which were unkind. For around a fortnight after infection, whichever passenger or crew member was incubating smallpox would have felt fine. Then he or she would have begun to feel feverish and unwell.

Often the virus, widespread as it was, was simply labelled 'the pox'. The prefix 'small' differentiated it from the 'great' pox, which was syphilis, but certainly did not deem it trivial. Rates, both of death and disfigurement, were high – increasingly so, in fact, because the contagion mutated during the century and became more serious. The disease, noted a seventeenth-century physician, was 'epidemical and contagious, and kills very many'. It was also undiscerning as to class. Soon after his restoration both the brother and the sister of Charles II died of what was called this 'cruel and impartial sickness', as Queen Mary II (Charles's niece) also did a little later, while in her early thirties. At first, wrote another contemporary physician, an infected patient felt shivery and cold, then excessively hot, with 'a violent pain in the head and back', vomiting, and 'a great propensity to sweat'. A few days after feeling ill, the tell-tale flat red spots appeared and spread across the face, limbs and trunk, blistering and filling with pus, before forming scabs and leaving ugly scars. The person turned 'a very florid colour' – 'not unlike a damask rose'. Not for nothing was the disease also known as the 'red plague'.[1]

Within the close confines of a ship, on which almost all the passengers were pressed tightly onto the deck of the vessel – sleeping, as best they could, upon the wooden planks – containing an infectious disease was impossible, even had the means of its transmission been understood. William Penn's advice for preserving health on board was to keep rosemary, among other sweet-smelling herbs, close by, while also burning pitch and sprinkling vinegar. More usefully, he recommended that it was healthier to 'keep as much upon deck as may be' for 'the air helps against the offensive smells of a crowd', and in terms of infection, of course, he was right. He recommended regular cleaning of the cabins, including under the beds, stressing that he spoke from experience. But the disease did duly spread all the same, until most of those on board had become ill.

Only a few, and Penn was one of them, did not. Although the mechanism was not understood, it had been observed that those who had survived the illness once were unlikely to get it a second time. (One seventeenth-century physician noted that the ailment infected 'whole families', 'sparing none', 'if they have not had this disease already'.) Quakers, in any case – and most on board adhered to the creed – had earned praise for their willingness to put themselves in harm's way, tending victims of the great bubonic plague in 1665, while many of those who could afford to do so fled, as well as those who were left homeless by the fire which devastated London a year later.[2]

One fellow passenger recalled the energy and devotion with which Penn nursed those who were ill, paying tribute to his 'singular care' of those 'many who were sick on board of small-pox'. He liberally distributed his personal stores. But these of course were only an aid to comfort, and ultimately those infected could do little other than to pray for their recovery. For more than thirty – a quarter of those on board – prayer was not enough. John Barber, Mary Fitzwater, Thomas Heriott, Grace and Mary – two daughters of Dennis Rochford – were among the passengers who never made it across the Atlantic. Their bodies were cast into the waves, 'to be turned into corruption', as it was put in the 1662 Book of Common Prayer, 'looking for the resurrection of the body, (when the sea shall give up her dead), and the life of the world to come, through our Lord Jesus Christ'. For passengers who remained alive and sufficiently conscious it must have seemed, as it did for one earlier emigrant, that days were filled merely with 'throwing folks over board'. Meanwhile, in the midst of all this suffering, at least one person saw America, having never seen England, being born during the crossing.[3]

The wind, at least, was reasonably kind, and the voyage to America was completed in under two months. The surviving passengers, wasted and weary, were even more glad than most to spot, then approach, a green, thickly forested land. Their ship sailed up the Delaware River, to a settlement which Penn renamed Chester, in recollection of the English city. First impressions of the territory were favourable. It seemed, just as Penn had been told, 'a very fine country', well suited to the 'country life' that he liked.

He also inspected the site on which he planned the building of a new city – a city which would be full, as was not then normal, of trees, and gardens. A place that he christened Philadelphia.

Three decades previously, early each midsummer morning, through woods and meadows, marsh and scrubland, alongside the River Roding, a young boy ran alone.

It was before six o'clock. The air was cold in the countryside north-east of London, in spite of low, hazy sunshine which bounced off dewdrops arrayed in geometric patterns on the webs of spiders, or aligned upon leaves or blades of grass. He was not badly scarred from the smallpox through which his mother had nursed him (and to have survived at all was good fortune – a divine blessing, he would have called it – given that more than half of the children then infected did not). His hair afterwards was patchy and thin. Later, under the stress of imprisonment, it would fall out in clumps, forcing him to shave it entirely and wear a wig.

William ran now simply because he enjoyed running, long before jogging was a popular pursuit. He found it a great pleasure, a pleasure for which he was grateful to God. He was athletic and fidgety – 'mighty lively', as one contemporary put it. Later in life he had to force himself to sit still while he was writing. From America he wrote to an old friend, remembering time that they had shared decades ago, and hinting at how they had spent it: 'a time', as he described it, 'of twenty years' standing, or running rather'.[4]

From his home in the village of Wanstead he covered the three or four miles northward to his school in Chigwell, before later, as the sun descended, running home. England then was a Commonwealth, having executed its king – an event that Penn had been too small to remember, though adults, as he grew up, talked often about what was a defining event. From time to time a rabbit, a fox or a deer retreated hastily into the undergrowth, surprised by his sudden approach, scuttling, pausing, frozen, then vanishing. William was fascinated by the natural world. Regularly he stopped to admire a butterfly or a bee, a meadow buttercup, a primrose or a cowslip. 'All along, since his childhood', one admirer wrote later to his father, he had 'sought to understand' the Lord's design for the world.[5] He confessed later to having been, while growing up, 'a child alone' – 'a child given to musing'. Certainly he had time enough, during this daily commute, to muse in the midst of God's creation.

While his headmaster was tasked with restraining his charges from hot-headed, boisterous behaviour – from ribaldry, swearing, wrangling, fighting or from carrying daggers and other weapons – it seems unlikely that, even as a boy, William was guilty of such riotous disorder, more inclined as he was by nature towards quiet contemplation. 'Very early', wrote one contemporary, he 'delighted in retirement', 'much given to reading and meditating of the scriptures'.[6] It was in the course of one day at Chigwell School that he first felt a divine presence. In a solitary moment, beneath its dark, beamed roof and within its panelled walls, dimly lit even when the sun did manage to penetrate the small casement windows, a strong sense of inner peace enveloped him. And the gloomy room, it seemed, brightened.

Soon afterwards, when William was almost eleven, he was summoned unexpectedly home before the end of the school day. With his young sister he was taken immediately by his mother to London, where his father – famous for his naval heroics, and a fleeting, sweeping, awe-inspiring presence in the boy's early life, marching noisily and sporadically into the house in his wide-topped boots and with a brightly coloured plume in his hat – had been slung into the Tower. Although he was soon released and granted a fulsome apology, he was even less enamoured now of the Cromwellian regime (having always been a monarchist by inclination), and decided to move – 'with his lady and family' – to the relative peace of estates he had been granted in the south-west of Ireland.

Here the country as a whole had recently suffered appalling starvation and torment, having been battered grimly into submission by Cromwell's fevered, fervent, hate-fuelled armies. While serving for the Parliamentary navy, in fact, William's father had himself scoured Ireland's western coast, landing with his troops and burning 'all the villages and houses' that he could see. But now, a decade later, William – living in the castle near Cork which his father had been granted by the Parliamentary regime, together with his mother, baby brother and four-year-old sister – was able to lead a quiet, thoughtful, rural life in emigration. He remained there for four formative years.

For the first time his father was a daily presence, and he came to value and love his parental influence, for all their differences. 'I never knew what a father was', he wrote to him later, when the latter was again away fighting at sea, 'till I had wisdom enough to prize him.' He bid him 'refreshment from your continual toils', and paid homage to a man who was both 'a father and a friend'.[7] His father did still hope, though, that his son might be coaxed away from his strange, spiritual ruminations into a lucrative career at court.

During their time together in Ireland William Penn senior taught his son how to carry himself like a courtier and how to handle a sword. When they came back to England upon the Restoration, father and son together attended the great festivities in London which marked Charles II's resumption of the throne, delighted when the returning king saw and gestured to them. But young William spurned what his father regarded as chance upon chance. He was expelled from the university at Oxford. He was sent travelling in France, given access to the French court of Louis XIV and, though granted always the 'thorough indulgence to keep pace with the best sort of company', found the study of theology at Saumur more captivating. He failed to stick at the legal studies which might act as a prelude to government service. When he committed wholeheartedly instead to the ideas of the Quakers his father wept with frustration and for a time barred him from his home, threatening to disinherit his eldest son, being 'at that time', as William admitted, 'in high wrath against me, because of my separation from the world'.[8]

William's father had, however, something of his son's receptiveness to novel ideas, and even his tolerant disposition (in spite of his successful military career). While his son was in Ireland settling his father's lands there, the older man wrote to the younger stating that his only desire was for 'peace with all men'.[9] When the family had been living in Ireland during the 1650s, William a teenage boy, it was his father who had invited into their home a travelling Quaker preacher because he was interested in what the man had to say – barely a decade after the movement had been founded which focused on people's direct experience of God, without the intercession of a priesthood, and rather less than a decade since one judge had given its adherents the mocking but, as it turned out, enduring nickname 'Quakers' because they were bid to 'tremble at the word of the Lord'.

Young William was fascinated, and listened in wonderment. 'The Lord visited me', he wrote of the occasion later, 'and gave me divine impressions of Himself', even if it was another decade before he converted to the movement wholeheartedly and began to campaign. He argued too, critically, for the freedom to form his own judgements on such matters, and reminded his father that he had himself once advocated such a right. 'It is not long', the son admonished his father, 'since you were a very good solicitor for that liberty I now crave.'

The notion that people might be forced to alter their beliefs, that men might 'form their faith in God, & things proper to another world by the prescriptions of mortal men', seemed to him 'both ridiculous & dangerous'. Prisons should be emptied of harmless 'conscientious persons'. And certainly, when incarcerated himself, he sent word to his father – it was scarcely reassurance – that 'my prison shall be my grave before I will budge a jot, for I owe my conscience', he proclaimed, 'to no mortal man'. Not 'all the powers on earth', Quakers insisted, would divert them 'from reverencing and adoring our God, who made us'.

Hadn't his father seen, in the course of his travels, his son asked, that diversity both of faith and of worship caused no public disturbance? In any case, it was no more feasible to expect 'uniformity of mind' than that people should look identical. The explosion of sects in Cromwell's time, and indeed the tense, simmering unrest which preceded it, had shown as much. No one, as a matter of principle, should be deprived of 'so eminent a right as liberty'. He quoted with approval the Roman author Tacitus, who had written long ago of 'the rare happiness of the times when you may feel what you wish and say what you feel'.

As he well knew, though, in England under Charles II this was impossible. The relative freedom – some would have said chaos – of the Commonwealth had been terminated. Early in the 1660s, soon after the Restoration, laws targeted all who refused to conform with the Church of England. They banned gatherings known as 'conventicles', hoping to contain what this law's preamble called 'the growing and dangerous practices of seditious sectaries'. They effectively barred from public office any who dissented. And they forbade ministers from living within five miles of any town from which they had once been expelled. In particular, the Quakers, as a rapidly expanding group with some 40,000 members, experienced significant persecution, for all that Roman Catholicism might have been regarded as an even greater threat. One Quaker from Bristol wrote in 1670 of 'our seventh persecution in Bristol, since King Charles II returned'.[10]

Contrary to their subsequent reputation for unthreatening conduct, the Quakers were perceived as profound threats to the social fabric because they rejected any kind of social hierarchy. Not only did they refuse to swear oaths (which they felt called into question their original honesty, and following Jesus's command to 'swear not at all'), but also to doff their hats to those deemed their superiors and to address them with the polite, then plural form, 'you' as opposed to the familiar 'thee' and 'thou'. They were considered 'persons of very dangerous principles', 'monsters of men' – liable, 'should it lie in their power', to 'kick up the heel' against the king's 'sovereign authority'.[11]

This was a time when a class system was considered part of the divine natural order – when Lincoln's Inn thought it a sensible reaction to the plague of 1665 to admit 'none but persons of quality'. But God, the Quakers insisted, was 'no respecter of persons'. They scorned the clergy likewise, as 'hirelings'. Instead religious meetings awaited a member of the congregation – any member – to be moved (by God, it was assumed) to speak, or to lead a prayer. Where Puritans like Anne Bradstreet considered that the biblical days of direct divine command had now passed, Quakers were convinced that God still spoke to them, through what they called an 'inner voice'. Moreover He certainly did not, contrary to the Calvinist worldview, separate at birth the saved from the damned. In 1662 an act of Parliament known as the 'Quaker Act' had forbidden more than five such people from gathering, as it put it, 'under pretence of religion', since large assemblies were held to endanger the public peace and to cause 'the terror of the people'. People were profoundly alarmed at what they called these people's 'frantic doctrines'.

Quakers, and other dissenters, were placed in stocks. They were flung into prisons in growing numbers. They were tortured, assaulted and publicly ridiculed. 'Oh, the rage and scorn, the heat and fury that arose!', wrote George Fox, the movement's founder – 'Oh, the blows, punchings, beatings and imprisonments that we underwent for not putting off our hats to men!' It was, he said, a 'cruel bloody persecuting time'. William agreed. 'The storms of persecution beat', he wrote, and the 'sea of raging malice foam[ed]', while he and fellow Friends persisted, 'through travels, trials, perils, temptations, afflictions, cruel mockings', to uphold what he called 'our so much condemned principles'.

It was no coincidence that when a regular Quaker meeting was set up shortly afterwards to protest against this persecution it was called the 'Meeting for Sufferings' (as a formal protest to Parliament was made in three 'Books of Sufferings'). The social connections which Penn enjoyed through his father gave him access that was denied to his fellows, and he discussed with the Duke of Buckingham – though to little effect – the 'stocks, whips, gaols, dungeons, praemunires, fines, sequestrations, and banishments' which were suffered by Quakers as a result of 'their peaceable dissent in matters relative to faith and worship'.[12]

Meanwhile, the mid-1660s saw dreadful afflictions hit the people of London, and England more broadly. In 1665 the Great Plague struck. Pits were dug into which many thousands of dead were slung. Signs on doors pleaded for God's mercy. While Quakers stayed to minister to the sick, most of the upper classes, and certainly the royal family, fled to the country. Death was everywhere around. 'Little noise heard day or night', noted Samuel Pepys in his diary, 'but tolling of bells'. 'Lord!', he wrote, 'how empty the streets are and melancholy, so many poor sick people in the streets full of sores; and so many sad stories overheard as I walk.'

For Penn, the devastation wrought by an epidemic which killed in the region of 100,000 people in London – or around one-quarter of the population – only solidified what he called 'a deep sense of the vanity of this world'. He was appalled, and deeply distressed, by the carnage. And then, the following year, while William spent time tending to his father's affairs in Ireland, the capital was laid waste once again – its buildings this time, rather than its inhabitants – by the Great Fire, blown west through the city by high winds: the 'most destructive accidental fire' in the history of western Europe.[13] Thousands of survivors were forced to sleep in open fields outside the capital, since their homes had been destroyed. Much of the city afterwards was a charred, smoking, unpopulated ruin. It was no wonder that William, on his return, thought England divinely afflicted.

William's life back in England resumed its pattern of preaching and imprisonment. In 1670 he and another Quaker found themselves defendants in a landmark case, when a jury refused to obey the judge's instructions to find them guilty of causing sedition and insurrection while preaching. 'You shall not be dismissed', the court recorder instructed the jury members, 'till we have a verdict that the court will accept.' Until then, he thundered, all of them could 'starve for it'. It was in vain that William protested that the jury ought not to be 'thus menaced', that their verdict ought to be 'free, and not compelled'. 'What hope is there of ever having justice done', he demanded, 'when juries are threatened, and their verdicts rejected?' The twelve good men and true found themselves fined. And those who refused to pay (Edward Bushel, John Hammond, Charles Milsson and John Bailey) were promptly carted off to Newgate Prison with Penn himself, while the case went higher. Eventually the House of Commons ruled, in what was a defining judgement, that jurors ought not to be punished for their verdicts.[14]

Unfortunately, William wrote to his ailing father, with whom he had now been reconciled, those who lived 'godly in Christ Jesus' were bound to 'suffer persecution', while liberty, 'which is next to life itself', was denied. Do not be tempted on any account, he implored his parent, to purchase his freedom. But the father had learnt his lesson at the hands of his son. 'Let nothing in this world', he advised him, redundantly, 'tempt you to wrong your conscience.'[15] It wasn't long before William was back behind bars, in the 'common stinking jail'. This time, unable to preach, he passed the hours penning a tract – a tract which he later entitled 'The Great Case of Liberty of Conscience'.

In it he lamented the 'cruel sufferings' to which Quakers had been subjected, 'for only worshipping our God in a differing way, from that which is more generally professed and established'. He bemoaned 'the unspeakable pressure of nasty prisons, and daily confiscation of our goods' – 'the ruin', even, 'of entire families'. Not only was such persecution unchristian, he asserted. It was futile. And actually counter-productive: 'destructive of all civil government'.

Coercion, he insisted, could not 'convince the understanding of the poorest idiot'. 'Fines and prisons' were not appropriate penalties 'for faults purely intellectual'. And by liberty of conscience, he was clear, he meant not only the freedom to think what one wanted, but the right also to worship outwardly as seemed fit. The Church hierarchy should not be aggressive and judgemental. A bishop ought to be 'gentle unto all men, patient, in meekness instructing (not persecuting) those that oppose themselves'. He attacked what he called 'the truly anti-christian path' of 'persecuting honest and virtuous Englishmen, for only worship-ping the God that made them, in the way they judge most acceptable'.

The notion – advanced by leading Puritans like John Winthrop, as well as by many others – that class could be taken as an outward sign that God had sanctioned anyone's earthly rule was one he deplored. 'Let no man', he warned, 'think himself too big to be admonish'd.' 'It will become him better', he urged, 'to reflect upon his own mortality, and not forget his breath is in his nostrils.'

Invoking what he called 'the olive branch of toleration', he called on men and women like him to continue to bear the punishments to which they were subjected, envisaging an eventual 'victory, more glorious, than any our adversaries can achieve by all their cruelties'.

Numerous Quakers had travelled already to America, following in the footsteps of Mary Fisher and Ann Austin in the mid-1650s. George Fox went there himself: Penn accompanied him to his ship and carefully studied the epistles he sent home which told of his journeys 'through bogs, rivers and creeks, and wild woods', visiting, administering support and spreading the Quaker message.

While a student at Oxford very early in the 1660s, William Penn wrote later, he 'had an opening of joy as to these parts'. In general these years seemed a time when 'an extraordinary providence' seemed 'to favour [America's] plantation' and to 'open a door to Europeans to pass thither'. The possibility of expansion in this great new western continent was present early on. 'God', he promised, 'will bless and prosper poor America.'

In New England, however, Quakers were treated with even less sympathy than in the old country. Puritans who had crossed the Atlantic in order to escape persecution under Archbishop Laud were little inclined towards toleration themselves. They considered their way the right way, not anyone else's. They would have had little truck with Penn's remark that 'we must give the liberty we ask'. To give liberty to sinners would be absurd, monstrous. When Fisher and Austin first arrived in Boston they were thrown into jail, stripped and examined for marks of witchcraft. Their books were burnt. And the persecution experienced by Quakers there, in the short term, only got worse.[16]

Nevertheless, the creed spread with astonishing speed, all along the east coast of America, parts of which were much more accommodating. In Dutch New Netherland, for instance, while the authorities there did try to ban what they called 'the heretical and abominable sect called Quakers' (and the strict Calvinist Peter Stuyvesant found them abhorrent), they faced a lack of support both from above and below. Back in Europe the company government counselled against persecution, questioning 'whether we can proceed against them rigorously without diminishing the population and stopping immigration, which must be favoured at a so tender stage of the country's existence'. 'Shut your eyes', they advised: 'don't force people's consciences, but allow everyone to have his own belief.'

Much of the population likewise demurred, on more principled grounds. They wished 'not to judge lest we be judged', not 'to condemn lest we be condemned', but rather to 'let every man stand and fall to his own'; doing 'unto all men as we desire all men should do unto us'. This, surely, was 'the true law both of Church and State'. In Jamaica, on Long Island, Daniel Denton and his brother were among those in whom the New Netherland regime protested it had 'put trust & authority' who seemed only to 'connive with the sect called Quakers'. The result, they complained, with a blind eye turned to their 'unlawful meetings and prohibited conventicles', was 'the subversion of good laws, orders and of the protestant religion, and contempt of our authority'. By the early 1660s, the Dentons had to admit to the Dutch governors that 'the majority of the inhabitants of their village were adherents and followers' of this appalling sect.[17]

In old England similarly, although Penn lived relatively quietly during the 1670s, now married with small children, the Quaker cause appealed widely, to 'base and noble, rich and poor, young and old, learned and unlearned, men, women and children'. There were 'glorious, powerful meetings'. In Canterbury – the great ecclesiastical city from which Robert Cushman had earlier escaped – one of countless such gatherings was held by Penn and the 'Friends', who rode away afterwards 'in triumph over all'. 'Truth', it was written, was 'set upon the head of the great city.'[18]

Their very success, though, stirred up opposition. The king was obliged by Parliament to withdraw a grant of indulgence, while a 'Test' Act – intended primarily to weed out Catholics – also barred Quakers from public office. In London they were attacked by great numbers of what they naturally considered 'lying, wicked, scandalous books'. In the wake of the alleged 'popish' plot, revealed (and fabricated) by Titus Oates, anti-Catholic hysteria swelled in England, and the fact that Penn bravely continued to defend toleration even for Roman Catholics, 'for we have good will to all men, and would have none suffer for a truly sober and conscientious dissent on any hand', combined with their refusal to swear the oath of loyalty, made England, for Quakers, an increasingly unpleasant and even a dangerous place to be. His heart was heavy, William wrote, his soul 'unusually sad for the sake of this nation', dominated as it was by 'abominations and gross impieties'. He implored his followers to be ready to move: 'TO THY TENTS, O ISRAEL!'[19]

The problem was that nations, and emigrants, now fought over the American east coast. Even if large swathes were barely inhabited, there were more claims than there was land. For all that the Stuarts were keen to encourage English migration, to secure English dominance of North America, a nonconformist sect was hardly at the head of the queue for favours. As early as 1661 one prominent Quaker had written to George

Fox of the possibility (which they had obviously discussed) of space for the 'Friends' in Maryland, but deemed the land there all taken.[20]

After the Dutch had been obliged to cede the territory of New Netherland to the English, however, a fortuitous chain of events made a grant of land in 'West New Jersey' a genuine possibility. John Berkeley, William's brother, had sold rights that he had been granted by the Duke of York to two Quakers. Penn then became involved, first on account of his legal expertise, and then of his experience administering colonial land in Ireland.

He was quick to insist both on genuine trial by jury, and on absolute liberty of conscience. 'No man nor number of men upon earth', a frame of government decreed, 'hath power or authority to rule over men's consciences in religious matters.'[21] Into a land that was wild, infested with snakes and mosquitoes, Quakers came here by the hundred, skilled and willing to work – husbandmen, tailors, weavers. They brought tools with them, as well as bricks, fired in England, with which to build homes, and they paid native American communities with the manufactured goods which they desired for the land on which they settled.

The fact that King Charles owed the significant amount of £16,000 to William's late father provided the Stuart regime with a cover story; the fact that in the process it would be ridding itself of countless supporters of the opposition gave them added motivation. Beyond the Delaware River – pushing west into the wilderness – lay a vast, fertile territory of which government figures had to admit that 'we know so little'. The regime, William wrote later, was 'glad to be rid of us'. And here, in what he called his 'American country', he and his fellow Quaker emigrants were glad to be rid of England. He sought men of ambition who were willing to work. He asked for it to be called 'New Wales', then 'Sylvania', fearing that the suggested addition of his father's name 'should be looked on as a vanity in me, and not as a respect in the King, as it truly was, to my father'.[22]

The final charter was dated 4 March 1681. Under the Julian calendar, then still in official use in England, this was a Friday – a name which, like the 'heathen' names of the months, was to be replaced in Pennsylvania. (Since the Julian calendar also decreed that 25 March, rather than 1 January, was the first day of the year, March was known as 'First Month'.) Penn's role as proprietor, beholden only to the King of England, was to be recognised by an annual payment of two beaver skins, delivered to Windsor Castle – since moves were already afoot to make this the start of the year – on 1 January.

In designing the government, anxious that it be 'well laid at first', Penn was certain that he wished to deny to himself or to his successors the power to do mischief. 'The will of one man', he wrote, ought never to 'hinder the good of an whole country.' The curses of old Europe – the 'plagues of wars', the class-based society – were all to be abolished. This was a place, as he proclaimed in rapture, which lay '600 miles nearer the sun than England'.

Late in 1682, the *Welcome* carried him to Pennsylvania for the first time. The voyage was in some ways relatively straightforward, taking a little under two months. And as he wrote later, the length of the journey was quite unpredictable, taking anywhere between one month and four, though six to nine weeks was normal. Only the outbreak of smallpox served to make it as terrible as many had feared.

William Penn was not the first to find freedom of religious thought – freedom of any thought – even more tightly curtailed in parts of America, by the 'too strict government' of New England for instance, than it was in England itself, and to be obliged to look elsewhere for the right to worship as seemed appropriate.

Anne Hutchinson was another who found herself, not by choice, on the wrong end of Puritan judgement, as religious anxiety and excitement – among those whose fervour had caused them to emigrate in the first place – reached fever-pitch amid the 'bleak New England wilderness', where life, particularly at first, was hard. 'O how did men and women, young and old [...] beg for Christ in those days', proclaimed one who went.[23] Such fervent religiosity entailed firm opinions and involved, all too often, some explosive disagreements.

Anne had grown up in Lincolnshire during the last years of Queen Elizabeth and the first of King James, in an environment that was evangelical and profoundly immersed in the religious turmoil of the day. She was a self-assured, charismatic and intelligent woman, well-educated and brought up to have confidence in her views. She was part of a large, noisy, opinionated family – the eldest daughter among twelve children – and went on to have one herself, mother to no fewer than fifteen. The environment in which she grew up was certainly not one in which she learnt to shy away from confrontation. Encouraged by her parents, she was immensely knowledgeable regarding the Bible and was happy to disagree with men in positions of authority and seniority, unbowed by what were routine assumptions of feminine inferiority. In England Anne had worshipped in the Lincolnshire church of John Cotton, just as did Anne Bradstreet – and although the latter was a couple of decades younger, the two women almost certainly knew each other.[24]

Anne Hutchinson's father was a Church of England pastor who was often in trouble with ecclesiastical authorities over his uncompromising views: a 'proud puritan knave', as one bishop fumed during his interrogation, 'mad', 'impertinent', 'a very ass'. One doesn't have to look far in order to guess where his daughter might have picked up her unyielding refusal to conform. On several occasions he was slung into prison. He passed his time there making some notes of his trial from memory, and used these subsequently to educate his children, drawing attention to the bishop's folly. What mattered in religious experience, he believed, was not the formal, intermediary role played by a priest – who could easily, just like this bishop, be misguided – so much as an individual's immediate experience of God. It was a conviction that he bequeathed to Anne, to at least one of Anne's sisters, as well as (less directly) to Quakers like William Penn. His sudden death, when Anne was in her late teens, was a shock which made a deep impression upon his daughter.

During the early 1630s Anne felt 'much troubled', just as were Anne Bradstreet and numerous Puritans, by what she called the 'falseness' of the English Church under Archbishop Laud. She was unsettled, she remembered, 'concerning the ministry under which I lived'. And when Cotton, a preacher whom she deeply admired and valued, left for New England along with others of her way of thinking, she confessed that it was 'a great trouble unto me'. She dreamt constantly of emigration, thinking how she would like 'to have turned separatist'. In fact she put aside a whole day, she said, for 'solemn humiliation and pondering of the thing'. She found herself unable to rest, she later admitted, 'but I must come hither'. Unfortunately, though, restlessness was in her soul and emigration from England did not, as it turned out, put an end to the disagreements. Already, on the ship over, she got into heated debate with one cleric. And the reputation for causing trouble clung to her.

Like Anne Bradstreet's parents, and like those in many Puritan families, Anne Hutchinson's had believed in the value of education, for girls as well as for boys. And it is plain from later transcripts of her speech – in which she persistently infuriated and outmanoeuvred her interrogators – that she had benefited from a rigorous, if highly religious, schooling. Not surprisingly, female instruction was something that she herself passionately supported. In New England she worked to help women through childbirth. 'She did much good in our town', remembered John Cotton, who had known her well both in old England and in New. Not only was she 'skilful and helpful' when it came to birth itself, but she also made lasting social and religious contacts in New English society, falling readily 'into good discourse with the women'. The fact that midwifery was widely associated with witchcraft, however, did provide her enemies with an easy brush with which to tar her.

Anne's reputation for wisdom and intelligence led her to begin holding meetings, in which she would discuss the contents of the latest sermons. And while initially these were held purely for the benefit of local women, her analysis proved so compelling and attractive – or so compelling because it was unattractive, persuaded as she was that many of the local preachers were wrong to suggest that good works, as opposed to 'grace', might secure salvation – that before long she was drawing in a wide slice of New England life. She was an excellent communicator, possessed, it was said, of a 'fluent tongue'. Attendance at these meetings soared. And soon as many as eighty people each week were pressing into her house to listen to her thoughts. Husbands, often, were convinced by her through their wives, and all were 'much shaken' by what she had to say. 'All the faithful embraced her conference', it was said, and 'blessed God for her fruitful discourses.'[25]

This was a time when women were not entitled to talk in church, let alone to preach or question the anointed male authorities. The regime in New England could scarcely have responded with greater condescension. To them the commandment to 'honour thy father' seemed clear divine support for their own authority. Surely, they reasoned, no one could expect them to 'deprive ourselves of that dignity, which the providence of God hath put upon us'? This tendency to 'meddle in public affairs' beyond their calling was, they declared, 'the fault of them all': of women as well as of the poor, regardless of gender. Anne, they commanded, should cease activity which they deemed 'not fitting for your sex', in spite of what they admitted was her 'nimble wit and active spirit'. It had never been his intention, Governor Winthrop informed her brusquely, 'to deal with those of your sex'. Women, he advised, should attend to 'household affairs', not 'meddle in such things as are proper for men, whose minds are stronger'.

The fact that she had the nerve to question male leaders on theological questions – that she was at the heart of those 'tumults and troubles' which rocked and divided the young and intolerant colony – made 'Mistress Anne', as her opponents disparagingly called her, an insupportable threat. While she and her husband had a loving relationship, it was clear who was the more dominant personality. 'You have rather been', charged one of her interrogators, a 'preacher than a hearer', 'a magistrate than a subject', 'a husband than a wife'. Outrageously, she refused even to exclude the possibility that men might learn something from listening to her. What if a man were to ask her to 'instruct [him] a little'? she was asked. 'I think I may', was her reply.

It was the very scale of her influence which caused particular concern to leaders in Massachusetts, and which led them to take drastic measures. Numerous colonists – women at first, but men too – followed her lead. And as the colony became increasingly divided, Governor Winthrop admitted in frustration that it was Anne who was 'the head of all this faction', the 'breeder and nourisher of all these distempers'. To him, her popularity was bewildering. It was 'a wonder upon wonder', he exclaimed, 'what a sudden the whole church of Boston', with only a few exceptions, and many from outside Boston too, 'were become her new converts'.

She was summoned to court and was interrogated at length by religious authorities – 'the time now grows late', it was observed, and an adjournment until the morning was requested – just as her father had been in old England. (Among the magistrates who questioned her were both Anne Bradstreet's husband and her father, the latter lamenting that the New England colonists had been 'all in peace' until Hutchinson landed with her 'strange opinions', though Anne Bradstreet herself, whatever her reaction to some of Hutchinson's religious beliefs,

The Short Parliament earned its sobriquet because its duration was three weeks, in contrast to the Long Parliament, which lasted from 1640 to 1660. They were summoned by a king in desperate need of funds, though both had more interest in constitutional reform.

...ies regarding atrocities committed ...Catholics against Protestants during ...Irish rebellion were magnified in the ...ng. The king's willingness to turn ...Catholic soldiers seemed to confirm ...s that he was Catholic already.

A Woman mangled in so horred a maner, that it was not possible shee should be knowne, & after the Villaine washed his handes in her bloode, was taken by the Troopers adiuged to be hanged leaped of the lader & hanged himselfe like a Blooder Tyger.

Companyes of the Rebells meeting with the English flyinge for their liues, falling downe before them, cryinge for mercy. thrust theire Pichforkes into their Childrens bellyes & threw them into the water.

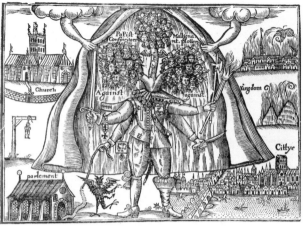

This woodcut from around 1643 portrays the carnage unleashed during the Civil War – the 'unkind differences' watched from America – by an unholy trinity of Irish, papists and 'Malignant [Royalist] plotters'.

The 'black act' of the execution of Charles I caused fervent Royalists like Henry Norwood to leave the country, horrified by seeming proof that God had abandoned England.

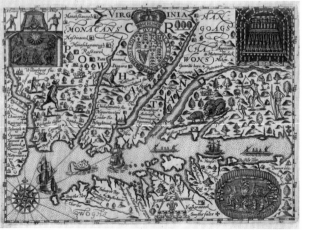

By the 1630s the English colony in Virginia was growing rapidly. A Native American assault soon afterwards killed many, albeit a smaller proportion than the attack in the early 1620s.

*Castor de 26 pouces de longueur entre teste et queue*

rry animals such as beavers,
nted to extinction in Europe but
undant in America, were prized
r their pelts. In settlements like
ew Amsterdam (later New York),
1 beaver skins could buy enough
od to sustain a family for a year.

A contemporary depiction of a
London coffee house, such as
Garraway's of Exchange Alley,
where American furs are known
o have been sold. The dictates of
shion made items like the beaver
hat hugely sought-after.

The Duke's Plan of 1664: a map of New Amsterdam marking its transfer to English rule.

William Penn in armour, aged twenty-two. As a young boy Penn's quiet, thoughtful personality worried his father. Spurning university, the law, and the military, he turned to Quakerism, in whose service he led a mass emigration to America.

# A Further Account

### Of the Province of

# PENNSYLVANIA

### AND ITS

## IMPROVEMENTS.

**For** the Satisfaction of those that are **Adventurers**, and enclined to be so.

IT has, I know, been much expected from me, that I should give some farther Narrative of those parts of *America*, where I am chiefly interested, and have lately been; having continued there above a Year after my *former Relation*, and receiving since my return, the freshest and fullest Advices of its *Progress* and *Improvement*. But as the reason of my coming back, was a *Difference* between the *Lord Baltamore* and my self, about the *Lands of Delaware*, in consequence, reputed of mighty moment to us, so I wav'd publishing any thing that might look in favour of the Country or inviting to it, whilst it lay under the Discouragement and Disreputation of that Lord's claim and pretences.

But since they are, after many fair and full hearings before the *Lords* of the *Committee* for *Plantations* justly and happily *Dismist*, and the things agreed; and that the *Letters* which daily press me from all Parts, on the subject of *America*,

A

In the province named for his father, Penn insisted upon freedom of conscience, urging non-Quakers as well as Quakers to emigrate.

Mary Dyer – escorted to the Boston gallows in June 1660 – was one early Quaker who paid with her life for standing up to intolerant Puritanism in New England.

FRIENDS OR QUAKERS GOING TO EXECUTION.

The contract by which one Richard Lowther agreed to four years of indentured service, 31 July 1627. Such servants had their ocean passage paid for them, often by merchants or investors, and the service they had agreed – usually between four and seven years' labour – was sold on to planters, particularly in southern states like Virginia. In the 1630s standardised, printed indenture documents started to be used.

For the impoverished majority, life in England was desperately hard. Mortality was always high, particularly so during an outbreak of plague.

must quietly have applauded her extraordinary strength in the face of a profoundly chauvinistic male hierarchy.)[26]

These days her civil 'trial' seems a shabby exercise. Plainly, the verdict had been reached in advance. There was no jury. Her accusers were also her judges. If she could not guard her own conscience, the magistrates insisted, 'it must be kept for you'. If her opinions were deemed 'erroneous', they said, 'we may reduce you'. And if she remained obstinate 'the court', they threatened, 'may take such a course that you may trouble us not further'. 'We are your judges, and not you ours', Winthrop, the president of the court, exclaimed, 'and we must compel you'. While secular and sacred authority were distinct in her eyes, well before this had become an accepted tenet in America, her judges were enraged and were provoked to fierce intolerance. Anne, they decreed, was 'unfit for our society' in New England.

She herself, though, was unfazed. Whatever control over her *body* the Massachusetts penal system could claim, she insisted, her *conscience* remained inviolable, her own affair – untouchable by earthly authority, just as William Penn would later insist. 'You have power over my body', she told the magistrates, but only the Lord Jesus 'hath power over my body and soul'. 'I fear not', she said, 'what man can do unto me.' The fear of man was merely a 'snare'. It was a statement which Penn would come to understand and to echo when he languished in prisons in London.

After being convicted in a civil court, Anne was then tried by her church, though the outcome, when the former had already found her guilty (and when many of the same people presided), was scarcely in doubt. Banished from the colony but unbowed, she stood up to walk out of the church, retaining her poise and her dignity. 'Better to be cast out of the Church', she proclaimed, 'than to deny Christ.' Far from being deflated, her opponents observed, it seemed that by contrast she 'gloried in her sufferings'. Ordered to leave Massachusetts, she sought greater liberty in 'a more remote place'. With her family as well as a few loyal friends, she trudged through thick snow and icy winds as an unusually harsh winter began to abate. They were 'stray souls that are gone from us', a delegation from Boston attested, stray souls who had 'stopped their ears against the counsel of Christ to the grief of their brethren'.

First they went to what became the small colony of Rhode Island, an early haven of religious freedom, and there she established a settlement which she and those with her called Portsmouth, after the English coastal town. She was an early and influential resident of a place that was profoundly unusual in its tolerance. But it was not sufficiently distant. And so, when the punitive hand of Massachusetts threatened to reach out for her there, she was obliged to move again, to Long Island under Dutch rule, only months before Daniel Denton. But, unlike him, she was highly unfortunate in the timing of her arrival. There, in the home she had just established, with many of the younger children who still lived with her, she was brutally murdered during an Indian assault in 1643. Her husband had died already. Only one daughter survived the attack. Her blood, one friend lamented, was 'so savagely and causelessly spilt'. Needless to say, for Puritans who were certain of their own views, her bloody demise was interpreted as evidence of divine judgement.[27]

As she had stood to walk out of the church in New England, following the judgement against her, another, younger woman had stood up too, steeling herself – just as Anne did – against the curious but hostile glares of the congregation. Together, the two women walked, upright, looking directly ahead, out of the building for a final time and into the open air. The other woman was called Mary Dyer, helped by Anne during the difficult birth of a deformed stillborn child – dug up and inspected by the colonial authorities, who judged it a sign of her own heresy: 'a most hideous creature', they decreed the poor infant, 'a woman, a fish, a bird, & a beast all woven together'. Grateful and profoundly impressed, Mary insisted not only on leaving the Boston church with Anne, but also on travelling with her to the new community that she established outside the colony.

Subsequently, after Anne's death, Mary joined the group known as Quakers, who in Boston were branded 'a cursed sect of heretics'. When another Quaker recalled the 'sufferings and persecutions which we suffered in New England', she remarked that these Puritan émigrés had behaved worse to them 'by many degrees' than did the bishops of old England. As a result, she said, the Puritan name stank 'all over the world because of cruelty'. Allies and investors in England grew nervous. And in the short term the persecution got worse: penalties against the Quakers in New England grew only harsher.

For the first offence male Quakers were to have one of their ears cut off, while women were to be 'severely whipped'. Repeated offences (and authorities saw no need to distinguish by gender on this one) meant having 'their tongues bored through with a hot iron'. One year later, in 1658, the death penalty was enacted, for Quakers who had been banished and then returned, regardless, to the colony. Mary herself was convicted of this offence, returning with another Mary, who was Anne's younger sister. On that occasion she was reprieved. But when she came back again she was hanged.

Freedom, for the New England authorities, could never mean the right to worship as one chose. To permit this would be to tolerate sacrilege, and to invite God's judgement upon the entire colony: 'so opposite parties could not contain in the same body, without apparent hazard of ruin to the whole'.[28] As it was put by one Puritan emigrant – author of New England's first legal code (which was inappropriately entitled the 'Body of Liberties') – 'enthusiasts' of all stamps had the 'free liberty to keep away from us'. Anne would be banished, declared Governor Winthrop, 'out of our liberties'. He had been put under pressure to be firm, but it accorded well enough with his own instincts.

God would rule in Boston through His representatives, which meant harshly. The colony was a theocracy, not a democracy. The people should 'keep their place'.

If Anne Hutchinson's commitment to liberty of conscience is not always obvious, plainly her ideas on Christianity and on the equality of all believers, male or female, foreshadowed the position of the Quakers. It is no coincidence that her sister – a radical Puritan who, like Anne, had emigrated to America because of her disgust at the constraints which were imposed in England – should have gone on to join the Quaker movement.

William Penn, along with other Quakers, was determined that the ideas he had often advanced, including the liberty of conscience he espoused, could be put into actual practice in an American colony. And then, when they were, that they could be expanded from western New Jersey to the larger territory – the 'good and fruitful land' – of 'Pennsylvania'. None, affirmed the 'Great Law' of that colony, which was drawn up in draft form in England, could be 'molested or prejudiced for their religious persuasion, or practice'. 'Nor', it continued, 'shall they be compelled, at any time, to frequent or maintain any religious worship, place or ministry whatsoever.'

Penn learnt of the worsening persecution that the Quakers were suffering in New England, and the measures against them (as well as against James, the Catholic heir to the English throne) which were taken by the English 'Cavalier Parliament'. In America, he was determined, his ideas could be realised. 'Mine eye', he wrote, 'is to a blessed government, and a virtuous, ingenuous and industrious society.' This would respect Native American inhabitants as all men: 'else what would the great God say to us, who hath made us not to devour and destroy one another, but live soberly and kindly together in the world?' He reassured the Pennsylvania Native Americans that he was 'not such a man': 'I have great love and regard towards you', he promised, 'and I desire to win and gain your love and friendship by a kind, just and peaceable life.'[29] He did gain it. And he maintained it for as long as he lived.

Political freedom, for Penn, was the direct corollary of religious freedom. In the past religious minorities had tended to become political minorities, but only because they were oppressed, and so were given no option but to resist the representatives of the state. In his territory, Penn promised, men and women would not be at the mercy of a governor 'that comes to make his fortune great' (as, by implication, inhabitants had been in other colonies). They would be governed, instead, he assured them, 'by law of your own making'. Here, he promised, 'no law can be made, nor money raised, but by the people's consent'. All inhabitants had a 'right in the government' and should be 'constantly jealous over it'. If they were not party to laws made in their name, he wrote, the outcome would be 'tyranny, oligarchy, and confusion'.[30] It goes without saying that these ideas were of vast importance to the subsequent history of the United States of America.

Socially, too, the ideas which Penn imposed were ahead of their time. It is true that the early laws in Pennsylvania reflected the Puritan influence – the Calvinist influence – upon Quaker thought. Sexual conduct was strictly regulated. Laws also forbade, for instance, a multitude of what now seem harmless pleasures: stage plays, cards, dice, lotteries – in fact all of what were called, 'enticing, vain, and evil sports and games'. Drinking was carefully regulated. All visitors were to be out of public houses by 9 p.m. unless they were lodging there, or had 'very good cause'. Officers would do the rounds to check. And the sale of alcohol to Native Americans, by which often – when drunk – they were duped, was forbidden.

In matters of dress Quakers were urged to keep away from 'vain needless things', as they were to 'renounce immoderate and indecent smoking'. But all the same penalties were dramatically softened, and executions in particular were heavily curtailed. The death penalty was only to be imposed upon anyone found guilty of premeditated murder, at a time when, in England, the number of offences for which capital punishment was applied began to increase considerably, to fifty in the 1680s and well into the hundreds after that, under what has been called the 'Bloody Code'.

The constitution (or 'Frame of Government') which Penn had designed for his province while in England was significantly amended, with Penn's approval, by an Assembly in America. Forty laws were increased to just under seventy. Electoral procedures were established, involving black and white coloured beans placed into a hat, as opposed to paper. But article number one remained liberty of conscience. And Penn continued, to the irritation of many Quakers, to insist upon the equal rights of those many inhabitants whose religious faith was different. 'Employ the sober that are not Friends', he enjoined, 'as well as those that are.' When the persecution of Huguenots grew worse, Penn invited them to Pennsylvania, lamenting what he condemned as the 'great cruelty there [in France]'.

While Quakers certainly did predominate in Pennsylvania, particularly in the upper provinces, Penn never hoped for an exclusively Quaker colony. On the contrary, he wanted difference, and (crucially) the toleration of difference, at a time when this was a highly unusual aspiration. 'If you Quakers had it in your power', he chided one of his own, 'none should have a part in the government but those of your own way.' In the colony's early days he enjoyed sufficient sway that the first law passed by the Assembly, in 1682, guaranteed wide toleration to anyone who 'shall confess and acknowledge one Almighty God to be the Creator, Upholder and Ruler of the world'. (The second law did require that 'officers and commissioners' profess belief in Jesus Christ as the son of God and saviour of the world – a narrowing which excluded Jews, though not Catholics.)[31] What was for the time a remarkable degree of toleration remained a fundamental part of the law in Pennsylvania. In 1701 the provision was transferred by Penn to the Charter of Privileges, with the stipulation that it could never be altered.

Penn was followed to this part of America by a wave of migrants, the majority of whom came from England, though they did also leave Wales, Scotland and Ireland as well as many parts of Continental Europe. Penn wrote shortly afterwards that the colony saw French, Dutch, Germans, Swedes, Danes and Finns, as well as emigrants from Britain, living together 'like people in one country'.[32] Only the flood of Puritans to New England had resembled it in scale. Penn hoped, he said, to be accompanied by those who were 'low in the world', though able – 'ingenious' and 'industrious'. Unusually, for the seventeenth century, he did not see this marriage of poverty and capability as improbable – did not imagine that those who were 'low in the world' were such because God had decreed it this way, or deprived them of the natural potential to advance.

The colony, and its freedom, was actively publicised – in areas of the German states, for instance, where persecution was severe. Those who went persuaded others to follow. Penn himself worked to recruit emigrants, comparing the 'fast fat earth' with that which existed in 'our best vales in England'. The air, he promised, was 'sweet and clear'. The heavens were 'serene'. One Quaker who had remained back in England replied to an emigrant he knew well that he was 'very glad [...] to hear of your welfare & liking of the country'. He regretted, he said, that he had not yet bought lands there himself.[33]

In 1683 alone sixty ships carrying settlers arrived. By 1685 Penn reckoned that ninety had come, not one of which, he said, 'through God's mercy', had been wrecked. The ships' names alone reveal something of the faith of those on board. Among the early vessels to arrive were the *Lamb*, *Providence*, *Submission* and the aptly named *Friends' Adventure*. The thousands of early emigrants included Ellen Cowgill, who sailed with her children John, Ralph, Edmund, Jane and Jennet; Thomas Crosdale, who sailed with his wife Agnes and six children (two boys and four girls); Thomas and Margery Stackhouse, who took their two nephews; Robert and Alice Heaton, who went with their five children; and James Dilworth, with his wife Ann and their son Stephen. Single men, like Stephen Sands, did go. But this was a movement in which young couples, often with children, predominated.

The emigrants came from London but also, often, from elsewhere in England. One of the ships was called the *Bristol Comfort*, another the *Lion of Liverpool*. By the end of 1683 some 4,000 people, Penn reported with satisfaction, had come to the colony. Two years later he estimated the total population of the colony at more than twice that number. Look for a divine command which would be felt in your hearts, Penn urged: 'if an hair of our heads falls not to the ground, without the providence of God, remember, your removal is of greater moment'. And be willing to work hard: 'count on labour before a crop, and cost before gain'. Those who did, he promised, would 'best endure difficulties'.[34]

At first, with no accommodation available, many of the poorer arrivals lived in caves, in the high earthen banks of the Delaware River. Sometimes they even dug these themselves. And they extended them, by digging deeper or by constructing porch roofs of brushwood. Otherwise they camped beneath the tall trees which flourished in this forested region. But the 'capital' of Philadelphia also grew fast. At the end of 1683, again, it had expanded to more than 150 houses – significantly larger than any town in Virginia. And soon, its houses more than doubling in number again, it was the second-largest city, after Boston, anywhere in North America, with a population over 2,000-strong.[35] Some 7,000, by now, were in the colony as a whole.

Many of the houses were constructed for colonists who were well-off – 'brave brick houses'. They were large and well built. Many had 'good cellars' and 'three stories', 'some with balconies'. Quakers, often, were affluent. Many were merchants, with a keen commercial instinct and a desire to exploit business opportunities. By no means all of them lived in caves. A 'fair quay' was soon built in the city alongside which a large ship of 500 tons could berth. Trees, and gardens, were common in the city. With his love for nature, Penn insisted upon it. And he noted the presence of most useful tradesmen: 'carpenters, joiners, bricklayers, masons, plasterers, plumbers, smiths, glaziers, tailors, shoemakers, butchers, bakers, brewers, glovers, tanners, felmongers, wheelrights, millrights, shiprights, boatrights, ropemakers, sailmakers, blockmakers, turners &c'.

Other small settlements – twenty of them, quickly climbing to fifty

– were also formed, and thrived. Penn genuinely liked the climate and setting in this part of North America. (The enthusiasm was not purely to foster emigration.) The air, he wrote, was 'sweet and good', the land fertile, with 'springs many and pleasant'. He had explored quite widely – had been to most of the villages which had sprung up. 'I have made a discovery', he wrote in 1685, 'of about a hundred miles west', and the land if anything only improved, 'richer in soil, woods and fountains'. The weather, admittedly, was changeable – 'constant', he noted, 'almost in its inconstancy' – but it must, for this reason, have been endearingly familiar to an Englishman.

Back in Charles II's England, meanwhile, dark clouds had gathered as the political climate became increasingly fraught and fractious.

During his first visit to America Penn had been separated from what he called 'the greatest comforts of my life' – his wife Guli and their children. And he was anxious to return to them, for all that God, he felt sure, had led both him and fellow Quakers across the Atlantic. As Penn did embark in America he again sent a loving farewell to his wife, lest shipwreck – and this was a perpetual consideration when sailing, for all that so many ships carrying Quakers had crossed in safety – mean that 'the sea be my grave and the deeps my sepulchre'. When he did arrive back, without major incident, he found things in the land of his birth much more 'sour and stern' than he remembered. The king ruled 'with a stiffer hand'. Conditions, in general, he declared, had 'another face than [when] I left them'.

Like his father, Charles ruled, through the final years of his reign, without Parliament. Vicious factional fighting foresaw the emergence of a party system. Unsuccessful plans to assassinate the king (like the Rye House Plot of 1683) had led to increased repression. Prominent figures, some of them Penn's close friends and allies, had been executed, after trials which were often fraudulent and unfair. Hostility towards Catholics in particular had seen the beheading and quartering of an Irish archbishop just before Penn left – 'an utterly harmless man caught up in the wheels of politics and crushed' – who was guilty, according to the judge, of 'setting up your false religion'.[36] Courts, in general, were corrupt. Printed material was heavily censored. And civil liberties were at a low ebb.

The dislike which Quakers harboured for outward class respect – the reluctance to doff their hats, their use of 'thou' rather than 'you' and their refusal to swear oaths, even to the king and the government – made them highly suspicious to the established Church. Almost 1,500 of them had been thrown back into prison. (At least ten times that number, it has been guessed, suffered this fate during the entirety of Charles's reign.) And many others, meanwhile, although at liberty were impoverished by fines, or had their animals or tools – their livelihoods – confiscated.[37] Only Parliament could suspend the operation of penal laws, but this was a path that it was in no mood to pursue.

King Charles himself, meanwhile, was ill, incapacitated, difficult, and little interested in America. He was 'blooded and cupped' by his doctors. His head was 'plied [...] with red-hot frying pans' – 'remedies' which were all too liable to distract him from the sufferings of his subjects. When he died soon afterwards, the frying pans notwithstanding, he was succeeded by his openly Catholic brother James, with whom Penn was on closer terms. But though persecution temporarily improved, it then became worse (both in England and on the European mainland, where Huguenots told of torture and terror inflicted, and of desperate brethren who 'pray to be killed', such was the suffering they were forced to endure).

Another rising in England led to what Penn called a punitive 'effusion of blood'. In London he watched in fascinated horror as one woman was burnt at the stake for her beliefs, pulling the straw closer amid the flames in order to hasten her end. In desperation Penn wrote and published pleas for restraint – in spite of the censors, and often under the (somewhat scanty) cover of anonymity. 'A Persuasive to Moderation', for instance, he addressed to the king and his Council. A gentle line, he promised, was 'ever the prudent man's practice'. But his words fell on deaf ears.

Although rumours of dissension among the colonists in Pennsylvania (of 'scurvy quarrels', and people being 'so noisy and open, in your disaffections') made him want to return, as indeed did word of the glorious horticultural abundance in his own garden in America – the peach trees 'broken down with the weight of the fruit' – Penn felt himself desperately needed in England. Here his court contacts and his personal relationship with James gave him the best hope of trying to have the penal laws repealed, and Quakers released from prison. But remaining in England was not what he wished. He was, in effect, he said, 'a prisoner here'. And so, in place of his personal presence, he wrote and despatched to his American colony pamphlets on the importance of liberty of conscience.

In England King James pardoned Quakers in 1686, and with Acts of Indulgence following, some 1,300 of them were released from prison – moves for which Penn had campaigned personally. On behalf of the 'Friends' Penn took an address of thanks to Windsor. He toured the country, the star speaker at what he called 'mighty' religious meetings, and noted that while he himself had often been arrested, subsequently he was released – a sign of divine mercy, he thought, which boded well for both sides of the Atlantic. 'If it goes well with England', he declared, optimistically, 'it cannot go ill with Pennsylvania.' If God took care of him in one place, He would surely not overlook him in another.

Personally, for his own reasons, King James was anxious to see an end to intolerance. He wished to see the 'Test Acts' repealed, which were directed against Roman Catholics (and Penn's support for this end to discrimination often saw him accused, quite wrongly, of Catholicism himself). Penn rejected advice to disown this royal move. The precepts of liberty of conscience, he declared, were 'cornerstones and principles with me'. And he confessed himself 'scandalized at all buildings which have them not for their foundations'.[38] But the pressure which James exerted caused bitter unrest, nevertheless, among the Protestant mainstream.

Fear mounted when the king remarried a Catholic, producing a male heir whose claim on the throne preceded that of his adult half-sister Mary. She was the safer option for Protestants, married to the Dutch Prince William of Orange, himself a grandson of Charles I. Eventually a secret invitation was sent by a cross-section of political and ecclesiastical leaders, asking Prince William to bring an army to England and to overthrow James's regime.

James's attempts to placate his disturbed subjects were too late. Word of preparations for military action in Holland filtered into England before, in November 1688, William of Orange landed at Torbay in Devon.

With him was a substantial fleet. More than 450 ships carried some

40,000 men, a force significantly larger than the Spanish Armada. When the wind changed suddenly, allowing a landing which had looked impossible, William teased one man good-humouredly: what, he asked, did he think of predestination now? Surely it was obvious that God backed this Protestant landing in opposition to a Catholic king? In the Netherlands the precursor to what has been known in Britain as the 'Glorious Revolution' was called the 'Glorious Crossing'.

William walked on English soil under a banner which promised to maintain 'the liberties of England and the Protestant religion'. Penn was highly unusual in considering that liberty should be extended to *Catholics* as well as to Protestants. Rather than attempting to resist, James, along with his wife and their infant son, fled to France. The revolution was not quite 'bloodless', as tradition has it, but certainly it was peaceful, in comparison, say, with the Civil Wars of the mid-century.

The subsequent coronation of William and Mary did indeed herald increasing liberty, at least for Protestant dissenters who, while not yet assured the right to participate politically, were spared the persecution that they had suffered in the Restoration. In 1689 an act was passed which exempted Protestant dissenters in England 'from the penalties of certain laws' – laws like the 'Conventicle Act', or the 'Five Mile Act', under whose dark shadow they had lived for decades. Although adherence to the Oath of Supremacy was still generally expected, subjects like the Quakers – who remained loyal to the monarchy but whose consciences bade them not to swear such an oath – were granted special consideration: the option to 'declare' their 'fidelity' to William and Mary, to deny that any foreign power (by which was chiefly, of course, meant the papacy) had authority 'ecclesiastical or spiritual within this realm', as well as to profess their Christian faith, their belief in 'God the Father and in Jesus Christ his eternal son'.

The philosopher John Locke, whose *Letter Concerning Toleration* of the same year underpinned the act, urged that the same freedom be extended to the American colonists. 'No man whatsoever ought [...] to be deprived of his terrestrial enjoyments upon account of his religion', he wrote, 'not even Americans': 'if they are persuaded that they please God in observing the rites of their own country, and they shall obtain happiness by that means, they are to be left', he urged, 'unto God and themselves.'[39]

William Penn was in an anomalous position. He could not deny his previous support for James, and did not attempt to do so. However, his passion for liberty and his Quaker conscience were at odds with James's own priorities, and it was of course with real joy that he welcomed the extension of toleration to Quakers and other nonconformists. Above all his first loyalty, he insisted, was to the country of his birth. 'I love England', he declared, and 'ever did so.' His proximity to James, and his refusal to disown that Stuart king, was naturally what his opponents noted. He was duly arrested 'upon suspicion of high treason'. While Penn insisted that he had been 'very much misunderstood', both in his 'principles and inclinations', the subsequent arrival of James in Ireland, and that former king's leadership of a military retinue, did little to placate Penn's enemies.

In spite of the grant of toleration, the 1690s were for Penn a deeply difficult decade. The death, late in 1689, of his four-year-old daughter added profound private grief to his public misfortune. His arrest, once again, the following summer on charges of treason (from which he was also cleared) led him to protest a 'broken health'. His great inspiration, the Quaker founder and leader George Fox, died. And further woes relating to yet another treason charge imposed upon him in Ireland led him to lie low in England for some years – insisting, truthfully enough, that he knew nothing of any Stuart 'invasions or insurrections'. He would be sure, he promised, 'to live very peaceably', and would 'never misuse the liberty I humbly crave'. Freedom was in no way, for Penn and those who supported him, the corollary of anarchy.

'Feel me near you [. . .] and leave me not', he implored his Quaker brethren, many of whom now lived hundreds of miles away across the ocean. But disunity across the Atlantic, as he learnt in letters, only grew worse. He lamented to the colonists what he called their 'divided government', regretting less that they didn't love him than that they didn't 'love one another'. On the international scene, warfare between France and England, in America as well as in Europe, made it increasingly hard for Penn to maintain the Quaker refusal to bear arms. In private, his dear wife Guli grew increasingly ill and died late in February 1694.

It was, to put it mildly, a difficult time. Penn slept little in any case. With his hyperactive, energetic disposition, sleep was not something of which he had ever needed much. And now he found switching off particularly difficult. All this turmoil had, he confessed, 'torn me to pieces', and aggravated such misfortunes as he suffered already. It had made him 'a man of sorrows'. The worst, perhaps, was soon to come, with the premature death of his eldest son – a young man to whom he had grown very close: a young man in whom had lain, as he admitted, 'much of my comfort and hope', a young man 'in whom I lost all that any father can lose in a child'. It had been to him that he had expected to entrust his work in America.[40]

One positive, at least, was that his governorship of Pennsylvania – placed in abeyance while he lay under charge back in Europe – was restored on the proviso that he agreed a moderate relaxation of the territory's non-military policy. (While some Quakers were hardline pacifists, others, Penn among them, were willing to except military *defence* from a blanket proscription.) By the time he eventually returned to America, the long war with France had ended in any case. Colonists blamed Penn for his long absence, and, unfairly perhaps, for any problems that had occurred while he was in England. 'Thou has left us too much to ourselves', they charged – scarcely a very adult admission – and must now 'take speedy care to settle the government.'[41]

When he landed in Pennsylvania at the end of 1699 it was quickly apparent that the growth of democratic sentiment in the colony – including the movement of power away from the Council and towards the Assembly – was entirely in line with what Penn himself had wanted, even if it had diminished the political role that a governor could play. He was distinctly stouter now, in his middle age. He was more prone to ill-health. And he was certainly no longer inclined to run for pleasure through the American wilderness.

The freedom of conscience upon which he had always insisted had duly translated into what, for the time, was an astonishing degree of political freedom. And of course it brought problems as well as advantages. Plenty of his people in Pennsylvania, one ally grumbled, 'neither knew how to use' the freedoms which they had been granted, nor knew even 'how to be grateful for them'. He confessed to finding Penn's 'strange attachment' to the province 'unaccountable'. But Penn, for one, continued to rejoice that the Pennsylvanian colonists were, as he put it in writing to the Assembly, 'strangers to oppression'.[42]

Dangers certainly did still subsist. A move was afoot, though thwarted, for Pennsylvania, as other English colonies in America, to be taken under direct royal control, terminating the indirect, proprietary model. Penn's subsequent heir, after the death of his eldest son, proved a greater worry to him than a reassurance, prone to 'youthful sallies', the amassing of debts and to 'revels and disorders'. And efforts made by Penn, meanwhile, towards a union of the English American colonies, under which they would each, annually, send representatives to discuss issues of mutual concern at a unified American body, proved premature as well as impressively far-sighted.

Although Penn proved willing, ultimately, to negotiate selling his province to the crown – largely because of the vast financial debts which he had accrued – death intervened. The stroke which ultimately killed him is, for the historian, unusually poignant – for it occurred when Penn was midway through writing a letter. His words stop in the middle of a sentence. 'She', he wrote at the bottom of the fourth page, before losing consciousness. It was his second wife who added that her 'poor husband' had not had time to finish the letter 'before he was taken with a second fit'.

Penn did recover sufficiently to add, roughly and unsteadily, that he wanted the letter to be 'ready for the boat', and that he hoped to send more in due course. But in truth he was profoundly affected, and never did regain his old powers, for all that he survived for some years. Those who visited him reported sadly that his memory was 'almost lost', and 'the use of his understanding suspended': how depressing it was, they observed, to see 'what the finest of men are soon reduced to'.[43]

The colony which has remained his monument thrived. By 1700 its population numbered almost 20,000 – an astonishingly rapid increase given that it had only been founded less than two decades earlier. And the ideal in which Penn believed so passionately, of liberty of religious conscience, proved, while ahead of its own time, to be one which was deeply revered by those who came later. It stamped its image on the continent. And it did so gradually on much – on a growing proportion, we may hope – of the wider world.

# VII

# Despair

Edward Furnifull was desperate. His wife Anne had recently given birth. The couple were dreadfully poor. They owned nothing, and they struggled to feed themselves.

Even in London, a city to which like so many others they had probably travelled in search of a livelihood, it proved impossible to find work. It was not long since the devastation of the Civil Wars had finally ceased, but still its effects were everywhere to be seen, in damaged, wounded buildings and damaged, wounded people. Now, if their infant child survived – by no means a certainty – there would be three mouths to feed.

Midway through the 1650s, while Oliver Cromwell presided as 'Lord Protector', Furnifull frantically paced the streets of the capital, searching for any kind of work by which to support his family. But, look as he might, he was unable to find it. There were too many others like him – 'surplus inhabitants' – looking for menial, unskilled labour. Demand for such work far exceeded the supply.

Littering the cobbled streets around the river in London, as well as in Bristol and in other major port towns, were handbills. Posters were glued hastily onto walls, their corners battered and peeling. And all portrayed emigration to America – to the English colonies – in the most positive light, offering 'the most seducing encouragement', both to 'adventurers' on the one hand, and also to the desperate – 'those who are disgusted with the frowns of fortune in their native land' but willing to try 'to court her smiles in a distant region'. It seems unlikely, though, that a man like Furnifull could read. Prospective emigrants – particularly illiterate ones – were rallied at fairs, public gatherings or taverns by drummers, pipers or minstrels and by smooth-talking, well-heeled individuals who flouted expensive-looking watch chains along with their tall stories. Promoters with first-hand experience of the less-alluring truth did what they could to 'hide our defects' and to 'encourage any' to emigrate.[1]

Furnifull got talking to a man called Thomas who was walking the streets with a woman named Christian. The pair seemed kind, concerned and genuine. They behaved, like any in their line of work, 'extraordinarily friendly'.[2] They made astonishing promises to Edward regarding the prospects for the poor in England's plantations in America. This was a place, they said, 'where food shall drop into their mouths', where the population lived happy, energetic lives of 'alacrity and cheerfulness', where 'any laborious honest man may in a short time become rich'.[3] In comparison with the difficulties that Edward faced here at home, the continent sounded a paradise.

His family could sail with him. He had only to sign an indenture – a cross would do – by which he agreed to work as a servant for a few years. (For adults the most common figure was five, the usual range between four and seven.) Then, on the expiry of this term, he would be given land of his own, clothes and supplies: two suits, tools and food. The fact that fewer than 10 per cent of those who signed an indenture survived to claim what was promised was not something that they mentioned.

Edward might become, Thomas and Christian assured him, a rich 'planter' in his own right – a dream of social mobility within a single generation which was beyond his wildest imaginings in England. Even a more scrupulous observer promised the prospective servant that at the end of his time 'he shall be in a flourishing condition' – no longer at the bottom of the pyramid, no longer downtrodden – 'never more to serve any man'.

The climate in America, he was assured, was welcoming. The soil was fertile. Food – fish, birds, animals, crops – was plentiful. For someone who was starving in England it all sounded too good to be true. Even if it was, things would still be better than they were. 'Being thus deluded', it was noted, those down on their luck in England 'take courage, and are transported.'

This was a time when thousands emigrated. In the course of the whole seventeenth century, almost 200,000 arrived in the English colonies in America. Nearly half of them were indentured servants. In a place like Virginia, where the demand for menial labour was high, the proportion was larger: more like three-quarters. And the 1650s were the peak period of emigration from England and Wales throughout that century. More than 7,000 individuals sailed every year. No doubt Furnifull and his family knew others like them who had gone, or who planned to go.[4]

Having agreed to sign the indenture, Thomas and Christian led Furnifull eastward, down narrow, winding, insalubrious backstreets, through slums and past rotting, malodorous heaps of rubbish, offal and excrement. They went beyond London's old city wall (though as the capital had rapidly grown, its wall had ceased to be more than a historical curiosity). They went with the prevailing wind, and the flow of the river, towards what one contemporary called 'the fumes, steams and stinks of the whole easterly pile', eventually stopping at an unremarkable, tumbledown building – often a cookhouse – which was the haunt of indentured servants who were awaiting transportation to one of the colonies across the Atlantic.[5]

In London many of these places were at St Katherine's, a squalid, cramped district on the riverbank just east of the Tower, inhabited by numerous foreigners as well as by impoverished English men, women and children. Its tight, dirty lanes and alleys boasted evocative names like Dark Entry, Cat's Hole, Pillory Lane and Shovel Alley. It was an area, as the English antiquarian John Stow had written at the end of the sixteenth century, 'pestered with small tenements', pressed with more inhabitants than some cities in England (and since his time it had only become more so).[6] A lookout was paid a meagre price to watch for anxious family or friends who might be searching for those they knew who had suddenly gone missing.

The building at which they arrived was much like the one into which a later witness recalled peeping 'at a gateway' and seeing three or four snappy, hustling youths, 'well dressed, with hawks' countenances', along with half a dozen men who looked very different – thin and shambolic, 'showing poverty in their rags, and despair in their faces'. With them was a small crowd of nervous, wild-looking teenagers – no doubt runaway apprentices in fear of capture and punishment, like prisoners who had fled.

Sometimes the thick pall of smoke which hung from the low ceiling made it difficult even to see those inside. The servants' mouths, closely packed together, another wrote, 'resembled a stack of chimneys'. But it was hard to make out faces. Little was discernible beyond the smoke, apart from 'the glowing coals of their pipes'. And there was little to hear, in the anxious silence, beyond benign platitudes and the gasping, sucking and blowing of tobacco.[7]

Having signed his indenture with a shaky cross, Edward's contract had begun immediately. The document was torn in two, with each party keeping half. The corresponding, jagged edge (the 'teeth' or *indent*ure) constituted the legal contract. Servants were strongly advised to keep hold of their portion, to prove the contract if needed. Many who were utterly destitute depended upon and were even motivated by the immediate provisions that signing involved. Edward and his family were provided with clothing and food, with tobacco – the fug within the squalid tenement was generated in large part by the immediate enjoyment of this sweetener – and perhaps with a glass or two of cheap beer. 'We do entertain all comers', proclaimed one of these hawks, 'both men & women.'[8]

When one man listed the provisions required to outfit servants heading to Virginia, he advised that each be provided with a cloth suit, a canvas suit, a pair of woollen drawers and a waistcoat, three shirts, two pairs of stockings, two pairs of shoes, a Monmouth cap, three neckerchiefs, four ells of strong canvas (an 'ell' being an old measure of length, equivalent to just under four feet) with which to make a bed and a bolster, a blanket and a rug which they could share. Those outfitting numerous servants could cut costs by employing a tailor to make multiple items at once. Those to be shipped, who had signed their indentures, were held – 'kept as prisoners' – for a month or more until the ship was ready and a master came to fetch them. Then they were rushed, with others like them, pressed and cramped, on board a ship which was anchored in the dock. (Earlier it had been charged that mortality rates on Virginia Company vessels were high because of the 'stuffing of their ships in their passages with too great a number, for the lucre & gain it seems of the owners of the ships', and little had changed.)[9]

The ship onto which Furnifull and his family were stowed was bound for Virginia. Many, too, went to the Caribbean. A smaller number went further north in America. Furnifull's ship was named *The Planter*, appropriately enough, or at least the servants squashed on board would have been led to believe that the name was appropriate. As soon as she was full she headed downriver to await a favourable wind, and – just as importantly as far as the captain of the ship was concerned – to keep her passengers tightly secured on board, prevented from any second thoughts about leaving their homeland. (Until the ship was ready, as John Winthrop had commented, those paying to take the servants were 'forced to keep them as prisoners from running away'.)[10] A prolonged wait upon the wind might result – in addition to acute seasickness – in the women being put ashore with soap, to wash their own and their menfolk's clothes. If any fled after they had signed, some effort would be made to track them down.

At this point Edward and Anne disappear once more, with their infant child, into the thick fog of the unknown past – into the ship's hold. In their case the clouds only parted at all to allow them, unlike countless like them, to be glimpsed, because Christian and Thomas – the unsavoury pair who lured them to emigrate in the first place – were accused subsequently by another woman of having 'enticed and inveigled' Edward and Anne, of having misled them as to the conditions that they might expect in America. And the legal case was then entered and preserved in the Middlesex county records. In contemporary parlance, Christian and Thomas were accused of being 'spirits' – men or women who made money by gathering up 'men, women and children' on behalf of merchants or boat captains before selling them on, 'against their wills', to be 'conveyed beyond the sea'.

It was a serious charge, and the theft of children in particular was abhorrent even in the mid-seventeenth century, when much which now appals us was not. The very word 'kidnap' was coined at this time to describe the 'napping', or abduction, of poor children – kids – to labour in the colonies.

Late in the 1630s the Mayor and aldermen of London complained bitterly about youths being enticed away, to plantations 'beyond the seas', without the 'consent either of their parents, friends, or masters'. The older cousin of one country boy called John Wise complained (successfully) to the Commissioners for the Admiralty and Navy that, having travelled to the capital, he had been 'deceived and most violently brought on board' – an action sure to cause not only 'the heartbreaking of his parents, but utter ruin for the lad'.[11]

London's leadership claimed that the practice was the cause of 'great tumults and uproars' in the city: uproars which were sufficiently violent to be to 'the hazard of men's lives', at a time when, as we have seen, tensions in the capital were mounting for very different reasons. The term 'spirit' itself was said to have become 'so infamous' that angry crowds had beaten anyone accused of being one badly enough for the person concerned to have been 'wounded to death'.

A few years later, during the Civil Wars, Parliament issued orders that anyone guilty of such abduction should be brought to 'severe and exemplary punishment'. Outgoing ships were to be searched for concealed men, women or children. Charges were made against one ship captain from Bristol for being 'an old rogue', who 'cozened [tricked] many men' before bringing them 'out of the country'. In legal documents from the middle of the century charges of kidnap abound, alongside the usual accusations of robbery, murder, assault, 'bawdery', Royalism or of 'ranting, singing, disorderly' behaviour – testimony both to the fear of kidnap, as well as to the high demand for servant labour among those who had settled in the American colonies.

A year after the monarchy was restored, when an official commission was tasked to look into the subject of servant transportation, it stressed the genuine threat posed by such 'spirits'. 'The ways of obtaining these servants', it concluded, 'have been usually by employing a sort of men and women' – like Thomas and Christian – 'who make it their profession to tempt or gain poor or idle persons to go to the plantations.' In return for a reward from the merchant or the ship's captain who employed them, the report said, they 'persuaded or deceived [the poor and the idle] on shipboard'. One Royalist clergyman had observed a few years earlier that the poor, all too often, were 'cheatingly decoyed without the consent or knowledge of their parents or masters', 'sold to be transported', 'and then resold [...] to be servants or slaves to those that will give most for them'. While it was a practice appropriate enough, he commented, for spirits – for 'the spirits of devils' – it was one 'to be abhorred and abominated' by all men.[12]

A little later, in Germany, agents of this kind were damned as 'soul-sellers'.[13] And it was certainly the case that those who worked as 'spirits' had little thought for the impact of their actions upon either the victims themselves or their families. Parents – 'to their great loss and grief' – had children stolen away from them. And the unsettling effect upon the children themselves, or upon young servants, is hard to imagine. 'For all that he knoweth', blasted the charge in another similar case, the agent on trial was sending a maid servant to her 'utter undoing'.

The basic problem was that a strong economic demand for servant labour existed in America. There simply wasn't that vast pool of cheap, freely available labour which constituted such a worry in pre-Restoration England. Planters were willing to pay well above the cost incurred by merchants in transporting servants. So, for ship-owners looking to fill holds for the outward voyage, which would then be crammed, on return, with colonial goods, the practice made eminent financial sense – even bearing in mind the high rates of mortality at sea. The slave trade, with its terms of servitude unlimited (and extending even to subsequent generations), did not yet exist in the significant form in which later it would. Neither did the judicial sentence of fixed-term transportation from England to the colonies – of 'penal servitude'.

For all that it affected outrage at the appropriate time, the government in England was not genuinely sorry that the impoverished and the desperate should be shipped over the Atlantic to meet this demand, provided that order at home was maintained. It recognised the importance of sending such people. The sort who emigrated voluntarily tended not to be the very poorest, but those who were in what we would call the lower-middle classes. Of the teeming masses of poor, unemployed, uneducated children, the city of London had long been, it was reported, 'desirous to be disburdened'. And the city was delighted – since it did nothing to relieve the problem itself – that private traders did it instead. Not only were sheer numbers the foundation for colonial improvement, wrote the committee of the Council for Foreign Plantations in 1664, but 'people are increased principally by sending of servants'. With hindsight, it was the trade in indentured servants, as one historian has written, which formed 'the backbone of the whole migratory movement'.[14]

It is difficult to say quite how common forceful kidnap was. Probably it was not very common. (At times, of course, it was alleged, having not taken place, while at other times it took place but was never mentioned.) Court books might give the impression, as with all criminal behaviour, that it was more common than it was. But it is noteworthy that the detailed registers of emigrants kept in Bristol from mid-century – of 'Servants Sent to Foreign Plantations' – refer to the books' genesis as a response to the 'many complaints' made to the city's mayor and aldermen 'of the inveigling, purloining, carrying, and stealing away of boys, maids and other persons and transporting them beyond seas [. . .] without any knowledge [. . .] of the parents or others that have the care and oversight of them'. As here, kidnapping – 'stealing away' – was not in general distinguished from deception. And even if the former was unusual, the latter – 'inveigling' – by romantic lies and 'lewd subtleties' regarding the conditions which could be anticipated in America, certainly was widespread.

In the case of children, even the infamous promise of sweets seems to have been used in order to lure them on board a departing ship – a gift which, if it was delivered at all, may have tasted sweet for a moment and bitter for the remainder of a life. Fear of this crime struck understandable horror into parents, as it did also into the many owners of servants or apprentices who lived in England's major port cities.[15]

For some, who had been led, or carried, on board while drunk – perhaps lying literally in the gutter – it may have been easier to pretend that they had been forced, than that they were incapable, and now sorely regretted their incapacity.

Often, though, little deception was necessary. Perhaps some – purloined, tricked, even physically kidnapped – were left 'crying and mourning for redemption from their slavery' as their ship sailed away. Sometimes the behaviour of 'spirits' truly did deserve the charge that it was 'so barbarous and inhumane' that anyone, whatever their faith, 'cannot but abhor'. But at the same time life in England then could be exceptionally hard.

So while some undoubtedly wanted to emigrate for personal reasons – 'husbands that have forsaken their wives', 'wives who have abandoned their husbands', 'children and apprentices run away from their parents and masters' – many who crossed the Atlantic from England did so not to escape *someone* but out of a general sense of hopelessness and compulsion. They looked not for a promised land in a religious sense (as Anne Bradstreet and other Puritans had done) but simply for a place in which they could live. The 'one design' with which many of the emigrants went, it was said, was 'to patch up their decay'd fortunes'.

So while John Wise was extracted from one ship sailing for the New World during the first half of the 1630s at the bidding of his cousin, the following year – far from being grateful for the rescue – he tried again. This time, furthermore, he was successful. He reached Virginia. There he hoped, it was said, for 'better fortune'. And this time, far from protesting his cousin's capture, his cousin sailed with him.[16]

Most of these profoundly impoverished men and women were what the Puritans called 'profane people'. Even if their broader worldview, inevitably, was religious, the considerations which motivated them were primarily material ones. Emigration, Richard Hakluyt had argued, would help those 'not able to live in England'. It would save many from the sad end they would otherwise meet on the gallows. It would be the solution – the only solution – for those who were made 'rusting and hurtful by lack of employment'.

One contemporary writer in Virginia made sad reference to his 'poor spirited countrymen in England', under no illusion but that such people were duped – told tall stories about the colony to which they would travel. But he insisted, nevertheless, that for many the move remained worthwhile. Because the alternative was bleaker still. It might be true that often insufficient allowance was made for the nature of the commitment that they had undertaken, for 'the slavery they must undergo for five years, amongst brutes in foreign parts'. But in England severe poverty afflicted more than half the population.[17]

With hindsight, it is clear that the English economy during this period was undergoing profound structural change, as wage labour – less personal, more faceless – took the place of older, feudal interaction which depended more on a hierarchical human relationship and far less on the exchange of money. The increased enclosure of woods, fields and wasteground, along with a rising population, saw a rapid growth in the numbers who were landless and moved from place to place in desperate search of a livelihood. Prices rose. Wages, in real terms, fell sharply. Travelling to America – major step as it undoubtedly was – was only one further stage in the far greater tramping which went on internally.

In remaining woodland, or on the fringes of cities, makeshift temporary encampments sprang up (as they have done elsewhere in more modern times). Quickly these places came to be seen, particularly by those who weren't in them, as bleak, lawless and alarming: as 'out of the view of God or men'. Begging children, meanwhile, were ever more present and noticeable and seemed like a biblical plague, like 'the caterpillars, frogs, grasshoppers and lice of Egypt'.[18]

For many, England simply offered no way out. Paupers, it was noted, would be 'labouring, and sweating all days of their lives', most only to 'end their days in sorrow, not having purchased so much by their lives' labour, as will scarce preserve them in their old days from beggary'. So desperate were many that they had little choice but to 'beg, filch, and steal for their maintenance'. Dependence upon the annual harvest meant that years in which it failed – years when burials exceeded baptisms – spread panic and even psychosis, as well as actual starvation.

The dreadful famine of 1623, for instance, when 'many died in the streets and on highway sides, for very want of food, famished', remained infamous. The 1630s saw only one good harvest in the course of the entire decade. (Four out of ten was the normal ratio.) Then, for five awful years in a row, harvests failed at the close of the 1640s. Again, the years between 1657 and 1661 were ones of recurrent crop failure, as well as a time of very high emigration. When harvests failed, food prices became prohibitive, as one would expect. As tensions, and the competition for resources, rose, riots became widespread: there were ten in 1629, as many as fifteen two years later; between 1586 and 1631, it has been calculated that rural England saw more than thirty of them.[19]

The cloth industry, that bulwark of England's economy, was sickly and collapsing – failing to provide work for the many who depended upon it.[20] The salaried employment which it could offer was prone to periods of depression, and wages were far too low in the 'good' times to compensate for unemployment in the bad. Meanwhile, recurrent pestilence – devastating, incomprehensible epidemics – caused 'a great death of many', often in precisely the counties from which many were leaving for America, from which an exit route did, for some in dire need, exist. Social and religious innovations, imposed by the Stuart kings, were profoundly unsettling to many, wedded as they were to customs that were hallowed by time.

Everything in the country, one man lamented, was 'in a heap of troubles and confusions'. As a result the best option was certainly 'to go out of the world and leave them'. 'I have seldom seen the world', John Chamberlain agreed, 'at so low an ebb.'[21] 'These times', commented another, bring 'nothing out but fears – fears of sickness, fear of famine.' For a population rarely much above the breadline, these were ever-present concerns.

In spite of everything, though, the size of communities grew, and this expansion seemed a large part of the problem. For the first two-thirds of the seventeenth century, at least, England's population continued to climb. From three million in the sixteenth century, it rose to four million, then five million. And with no corresponding rise in the production of food or in the number of opportunities for work created by the economy, increasing numbers of desperate vagrants, shifting and shiftless, were engaged in a frantic search for employment. Vagrancy – wandering – classed a person in itself as 'undeserving', on the wrong side of the simple moral division of the poor, unlike those *unable* to work, the elderly, say, or the disabled.

Those guilty of it, particularly if they also begged, might be publicly whipped, imprisoned, branded (with a letter 'V') or 'set to hard labour', while repeat offenders were to be 'executed without mercy'. Suburbs and slums expanded outside major towns and cities: particularly, of course, outside London. Those who pushed the idea of emigration to America deplored the way in which people in England would 'crowd and throng upon one another, with the pressure of a beggarly and unnecessary weight'. They should 'remove to another country', it was pronounced, should 'give their neighbours more elbow-room'. They should avoid (as if the thought never occurred) 'a slavish, poor, fettered, and entangled life'. The middle decades of the seventeenth century were, as it has been said, the hardest through which England – the England, at least, of known history – has ever passed.[22]

The concept of legal 'indenture' – of a commitment to work off an initial investment made by an 'owner' which covered shipping, housing and food – was familiar enough in Tudor and Stuart England. The common practice of apprenticeship was scarcely different, after all. One indentured servant in America wrote to his brother who was an apprentice in London that the two of them were 'very near in the same condition': 'I know you have a chain about your leg, as well as I have a clog about my neck'.[23]

The idea of indenture had been suggested back in the late sixteenth century. Many would agree to go to colonial settlements, it had been proposed, in return only for their food and clothing, in the hope that in the long run they might 'amend their estates'. From early in its existence the Virginia Company was promising servants who were willing to be shipped to the colony that they would receive 'houses to live in, vegetable-gardens and orchards, and also food and clothing at the expense of the company', as well as a share of products, profits and land to enjoy, along with their heirs, 'forever more'.[24] By the 1620s the custom was widespread, and it was becoming rapidly more so.

Soon, such servants constituted well over a third of Virginia's population. The process was further accelerated, during the 1630s, by the use of standardised, pre-printed indentures, with blank spaces left for names and for any special provisions. One man, who clearly worked as a 'spirit', promised that he could provide forty servants to be shipped to Virginia at a day's notice.[25] Impoverished servants like Edward Furnifull could pay for their travel not in cash, which they could certainly not have afforded, but by 'signing' one of these indentures. Thus they bound themselves to work for a period of years for a temporary 'owner' (in the short term, often, the merchant, an emigrant 'agent', or the owner, or captain, of the ship, until the servants, with their commitment to work, had been sold on to a planter). And in return this 'owner' promised to fund his or her shipping, to provide 'meat, drink, apparel and lodging with other necessaries during the said term', along with a single payment, a house, land and tools at its conclusion. In somewhere like the tobacco fields of Virginia, as well as in sugar plantations in the Caribbean, indentured labour flourished before slavery became widespread.

Many who were desperate did not pause to worry whether promoters might have been over-selling a plantation, or to weigh the respective merits of one plantation over another. Exaggerated promises found a ready audience. The poor were easy prey, and one should not read too much into their destinations: they sought merely to escape. Whether they ended up in Bermuda, Barbados, Virginia, Maryland or New England depended largely upon who these men, women or children happened to meet.

Usually these were young single men. But young single women, or wives – often young mothers with children – also went, in lower numbers, sometimes to toil in the fields alongside the men, more often to be set to 'householdwork'. Ships were further filled with unaccompanied children – again, largely male children – drawn from what was called the 'superfluous multitude'. Early on, in 1618–19, the Virginia Company raised around £500 to send 200 of them, rounded up 'starving in the streets' of London prior to being shipped over the Atlantic and distributed among the colonists as apprentices. Such seizures became routine. By the late 1620s one account was speaking of 'many ships now going to Virginia', carrying many hundreds of children who were 'gathered up in diverse places'. And far from seeming disreputable, the Privy Council warmly commended the city fathers for 'redeeming so many poor souls from misery and ruin'. It was, wrote an eminent observer, 'one of the best deeds that could be done'.[26]

Colonists themselves, furthermore – with no access to the pools of cheap labour which existed in England – wholeheartedly supported the scheme. 'Our principal wealth', wrote one emigrant, '[...] consisteth in servants.' Take boys rather than adults, planters were advised: 'good lusty youths'. They might provide eight or nine years of service, perhaps even more, where an adult by contrast would offer only four or five. Many of the boys ferried to Virginia in 1619, or those at least who survived their first few years, would no doubt have been murdered in the massacre which took place shortly afterwards.[27]

Joane Robinson of Droitwich in Worcestershire – known formerly as 'Saltwich' because of the naturally occurring salt in the town – is one of some 10,000 names of émigré indentured servants entered in the Bristol port books: in her case, early on in the period when such records were kept, on 9 October 1654. Joane may well have trudged the sixty-odd miles south to Bristol already, in search of work. People's first reaction, before they committed to crossing an ocean, was often to try the big town or city.

She must certainly, when it came to it, have known others who had likewise decided to leave the country at a time of such high emigration, and been influenced by their decision. Travelling to Virginia, she bound herself for five years, secured by an agent named Richard Allen, who is listed as being a surgeon – it being common for 'spirits' to do this work in addition to a main job.[28]

At the end of that term, her master committed to providing her with 'one axe, one house, one year's provisions and double apparel'. The fact that the axe came first in that list – that it was included at all – is an indication of how wooded and difficult the terrain there was liable to be. Possessing an axe as well as a house mattered.

'When ye go aboard', one enthusiast for emigration advised servants, 'expect the ship somewhat troubled and in a hurliburly, until ye clear the land's end.' But afterwards, he promised, once things were put to rights, 'the time' would be 'pleasantly passed away'.[29]

Now, however, this seems a ludicrously upbeat assessment, even by the standards of the time. Ships, in the early- or mid-seventeenth century, were scarcely comfortable places for anyone, least of all for the crowds of indentured servants. The imperative for owners was simply to press as many people on board as possible. And many, at that time of high emigration, were available. So closely packed were they, indeed, that servants were often obliged at night to sleep in shifts, sometimes literally on top of each other. One petition delivered to Parliament months before the Restoration of the monarchy told of more than seventy servants being locked below deck, 'amongst horses' – the treatment of the two species scarcely different – for the course of an entire five- to six-week voyage. As the weather warmed up, it was protested, so 'their souls, through heat and steam under the tropic, fainted in them'. One servant who sailed to Virginia referred from personal experience to 'the heat of the hold'.[30]

Hygiene barely existed at the best of times, but in this environment any outbreak of disease – such as that which William Penn experienced on board the *Welcome* – could prove deadly. Mortality rates of half the passengers were not unusual. The bodies of those who died were thrown into the sea, accompanied by a perfunctory prayer, mourned only by those who had known them. But nevertheless, it was said, 'the sighing and crying and lamenting on board the ship continued night and day'.

For another thing, any remotely 'pleasant' passage of time – and a 'pleasant' time does seem a remote contingency – depended upon calm conditions. But nobody could tell how rough or prolonged the voyage might be. It was possible to get to America in about five weeks. But more was usual. And often it took significantly longer: upwards, sometimes well upwards, of two months. One emigrant lamented what had been 'a five months dangerous passage' to this 'remote continent'. The sheer uncertainty and helplessness were part of the torment. It was a question simply of admitting that one would be 'entering for some time' a separate world, a world in which one would 'dwell under the government of Neptune'.

Storms and seasickness affected most passengers, even if worse misfortunes were relatively uncommon (As with aeroplane flights today, the prospect may have seemed more alarming to many than was justified by the statistics – particularly to those who had never been on a boat before.) Even those who heartily recommended emigration admitted 'the roughness of the ocean'. Plenty of those who emigrated had 'a blowing and dangerous passage of it', hardly able, when eventually they reached land, 'to tread an even step'.

Popular songs memorialised the 'claps of roaring thunder' which characterised the 'bitter storms and tempests poor seamen must endure'. People could not help but worry that there was 'a great sea' between them and America, prone to a great 'violency of storms', a sea which contained 'not only fishes but great fishes' – whales, indeed, that could upset a ship with 'one blow with his tail'. Indentures admitted that the voyage would require 'God's assistance'.[31]

At the end of the century one who experienced an Atlantic storm wrote that 'from all the corners of the sky there darted forth such beams of lightning [...] with such volleys of thunder, from every side, that you would have thought the clouds had been fortified with whole cannon'. 'Such an excessive rain' lashed down, meanwhile, that 'as we had one sea under us, we feared another had been tumbling upon our heads'. One passenger commented on the activity below decks as consisting of 'some sleeping, some spewing, some damning'. On another occasion, one preacher was so seasick simply waiting for the wind to allow his ship to leave England's shores that he made, it was vividly recalled, 'wild vomits into the black night'. Groundlessly, as it happened, it was feared that he would not survive at all.[32]

A voyage extended by poor conditions meant that supplies of food or drink could run dangerously low, and a lack of supplies would be a particular hazard for poorer emigrants whose provisions were basic at the best of times. One emigrant, a century later, wrote of being 'almost starved' by the 'ill usage' imposed by the captain during the passage.

Henry Norwood's voyage, as we have seen, was so tormented by storms – day after day after day – that those on board took first to catching rats to eat (for which the price of exchange soared), before desperation drove them to consume those who had had, Norwood wrote, 'the happiness to end their miserable lives'. It would scarcely have been of much consolation to know that conditions, for slaves, or for convicts, would only get worse.[33]

As well as bad weather and disease, moreover, there were other dangers: such as piracy, with the risk that those on board might be wounded in a fight or captured and sold into slavery. With one threat replaced by another, wrote one voyager, he and his fellow shipmates were 'now in as great danger of being knock'd on the head, or made slaves, as we were before of being drown'd'. For those who were desperate in any case, fear of any of these developments was probably lower than it was for those with more to lose.

How much did the shipment cost the ship-owner? In general, seventeenth-century writers assumed that the cost of passage was around £5 or £6. But since this included a cut taken by the merchant who sold them, the real cost must have been lower. Naturally, the cost of provisions provided to indentured servants depended not only upon their quality – which was not high – but also upon the length of the voyage, which was very variable and dictated largely by the weather conditions.

The first sight of 'America' must have been exciting, as well as nerve-racking, if often a relief. Here was the land about which so much had been promised: the land where their fortunes would be transformed. It was low-lying and thickly forested. Birds – absent, over the Atlantic – now circled and called. One could smell, even across the water, the sweaty odour of pine oil in the heat. Trees, as became obvious when the ship drew close to the shore, were taller than they often were in England. But unfortunately, upon arrival things did not in the short term get much better.

Once the ship docked in Virginia, Edward and Anne Furnifull (assuming, of course, that they had survived the voyage) would have been displayed by the *Planter's* captain on deck, in order that the genuine planters might come on board to inspect them. Numerous patches of the land had been cleared, the pines, oaks, cedars, walnuts, along with the vines and tangled undergrowth, cut down, or eaten down by grazing herds of goats, to allow the soil to be cultivated.

Any attempt at cleanliness – any washing, any cutting of hair or beards – was carried out shortly prior to the ship mooring, the captain having a much keener eye on the saleability of his product than he did on passenger hygiene. The date of the ship's arrival would have been noted on Furnifull's indenture certificate. The arrival of a ship, and a forthcoming sale, was proclaimed locally. 'Just arrived at Leedstown', one paper later announced: 'the ship Justitia, with about one hundred healthy servants, men, women, and boys [...] the sale will commence on Tuesday the 2nd of April.'

Lined up, Edward and the other servants were prodded and examined by each potential owner – their feet, their legs, their teeth. 'I never see such parcels of poor wretches in my life', one London weaver observed some years later, as these servants, all 'set in a row' and 'sold in the same manner as horses or cows in our market or fair'. Auctions were conducted. And Furnifull would have been sold to the highest bidder, then led away to begin his period of slavery. A note of the sale and its date was made on the back of the indenture certificate. One mid-seventeenth-century planter even observed that it was the servants in the New World then, and not the relative minority of slaves, who had 'the worser lives'.[34]

It is true that these men and women had the comfort of being able to regard their suffering as finite and non-hereditary, although in the country they had known, of course, economic status certainly was assumed to pass from parent to child, even without any compulsion involved. But with no long-term interest in their welfare, masters who were inclined to cruelty could, and did, put them 'to very hard labour'. Their lodging was 'ill'. Their diet was 'very slight'.

In somewhere like Virginia, furthermore, the climate was different and unhealthy – certainly at first – whatever promoters had led them to believe. Masters factored into the length of the indentures for which they paid the fact that few servants were able to work productively during the hottest part of their first year. Such was the impact of the 'seasoning' to which they were prone that most were ill for much of that time. Native communities were 'apter', it had been noted, 'to work in the heat of the day'. Perhaps 40 per cent of emigrants did not survive their first year in America at all. Indeed, the fact that deaths caused by the hot climate were noticed to be higher among English white servants than they were among blacks from Africa was a significant motivating factor in the later emergence of the slave trade, although tobacco's call for greater skill in cultivation than sugar meant that this transition took longer in Virginia than it did in the Caribbean.[35]

In addition to the physical sickness which often accompanied moving from England to somewhere like Virginia, there was – at least for many – the emotional dislocation. 'More do die here', one emigrant reported, 'of the disease of their mind than of their body', life in America having been wildly oversold to them, the reality prompting bleak depression.[36]

A few decades before Edward and Anne Furnifull had found themselves targeted by 'spirits', a poor boy from eastern London, not far from the Tower – a boy of only around twelve years of age – was indentured by his parish to be shipped to Virginia (under the terms of the 1601 Poor Law, which had enforced the quite novel idea that the poor had a personal moral responsibility for their deprived condition – that poverty was a sure sign, provided by God, of degeneracy).

For a boy of his age the terms of an indenture were often significantly longer than they were for an adult. It was not uncommon for them to be expected to work for a master for more than a decade. In England, in well-to-do circles, at least for the first half of the century, the general strategy of shipping away those whom Richard Hakluyt had termed the 'offals' of the population was thought highly beneficial, both to the colony and to the beleaguered, overcrowded home country. When it was put to the House of Commons, the scheme was welcomed 'with a very great and grateful applause'.[37]

Richard Frethorne was clearly educated: enough to read, enough to realise how poor, how relatively downtrodden were his circumstances. He managed to send letters back to England, both to his parish churchwarden and to the 'father and mother' who he called 'loving and kind' – though whether he genuinely felt such tenderness, in light of his grim position, might be doubted. He told them, and no doubt he intended it to be painful reading, that 'your child', hundreds of miles across the sea in America, was 'in a most heavy case'. His literacy was uncommon, and the existence – and the survival – of letters which describe his condition much more so.

Richard came from a large, religious household – too large, plainly, for the parents to support. ('I hope all my brothers and sisters are in good health', he wrote home.) His siblings had names, like Obedias, Dorcas or Mary – names for which the inspiration was clearly biblical. And he was expected, though unable, to fend for himself, at a desperately difficult time. He was immersed in the text of the Bible, to which he turned naturally for reference and allusion, astute enough to pepper the letter that he wrote to his churchwarden in particular with precise references: 'remembering', as he put it, for instance, 'what Solomon sayeth in the 35th Chapter of Ecclesiasticus and the 20th verse'. He sailed on the first ship to bring settlers to Virginia after the devastating assault on the English settlements early in 1622 which had left almost 350 dead. The ship docked at the end of that year, around ten months afterwards. Thoughts among members of the Virginia Company were dominated by the attack. And the ship's hold, as a result, was better packed with armour and weaponry than it was with food.

The fact must have occasioned a certain amount of disappointment among settlers who had survived the attack. For provisions were scarce, and settlers – hungry and desperate – were dependent once again upon food supplies shipped from England. We are, wrote one settler to his brother shortly afterwards, 'in great danger of starving'. Life, another confessed, was 'very miserable'.[38] The promoters' talk of fabulous numbers of fish, fowl and deer in America was drivel, settlers protested, put about in England by 'some lying Virginians'. 'I can assure you', one complained, that 'poor servants' had not had any of these things since they arrived in the country. How on earth were they going to catch them?

Since he had been in Virginia, Frethorne wrote, he had not so much as laid eyes on a deer. And while it was true that there was a great deal of birdlife, it was scarcely likely at the time to embellish a table like his. 'We are not allowed', he said in the nervous aftermath of the massacre, 'to go, and get it.' The truth, he wrote home, was that he toiled all day, 'early, and late', on a diet of 'peas' and a thin, watery gruel known as 'loblolly', with at best the occasional mouthful of bread or beef. (Another servant likewise reported labouring 'from sun rising to sun set at felling of trees', with very little food.) John Smith had said the same. For all the abundance of fish, fowl and animals, he wrote, 'we cannot much trouble them'. One settler who was there with Frethorne complained that in the dire conditions, human sympathy died entirely. Men became 'base all over'. Those who were dying were simply left to 'lie down & starve'. 'Nobody', he lamented, would 'come at him'. And those who had died already were not buried. They were simply left to 'rot above ground'.[39]

Frethorne felt himself becoming weaker. He estimated that he was barely an eighth 'so strong as I was in England'. It would be much more useful if the company, rather than talking airily about natural abundance, was to send butter or cheese – foodstuffs that did not first have to be caught. In addition to the lack of food, disease was rife. The ship itself seems to have suffered an outbreak of plague from which many died, their bodies being cast overboard – and the contagion was then spread by the new arrivals to the colony's survivors. Frethorne was lucky, perhaps, to have reached Virginia at all, even if he might not have seen it that way.

Settlements, meanwhile – which had become increasingly scattered and unprotected during the false security of the 1610s, when relations with the neighbouring Native Americans were decidedly relaxed (a fact which can be seen today in the large quantity of native-produced artefacts from the time found during archaeological investigation of Jamestown) – were now fewer and more bunched. Gone, for the time being, were the days of widely dispersed private settlements which boasted, along with the names simply drawn from familiar places in England, evocative ones like Jordan's Journey, or Warwick Squeak.[40]

Nevertheless, primitive towns remained, or were soon revived. Frethorne himself lived ten miles to the east of Jamestown, downstream, on land known as 'Martin's Hundred', perhaps in the small, rough settlement of Wolstenholme Town which, though it had been temporarily abandoned after the massacre, was resettled about a year later. The country here still bore clear witness to the assault. It was 'ruinated', Frethorne reported sadly, 'and spoiled'.

No crop at all had been grown during the last year. Sickness was widespread. Houses were ramshackle hovels, scattered, wooden and quickly thrown up, requiring 'continual repairs'. In marked contrast to England, land was in such abundance that it was easier to live in impermanent huts, then move when the soil became exhausted, than it was to settle, but the quality of building certainly suffered as a result. And if his master did what he had threatened to do and turned his indentured servants out, into the woods to scavenge for tree bark or 'moulds on the ground', more would surely die. A greater number had died since, as a result of disease and deprivation, wrote one settler who lived through both, than 'were slain in the massacre'.[41]

Among those who had survived the attacks but who were starving, the sudden, desperate indulgence in the ship-brought supplies was calamitous. If they had not been murdered already, Frethorne observed – their houses and possessions largely burnt by the Native American 'rogues' – they 'fell to feeding so hard of our provision that it killed them'. This frantic gorging, in those nearly starved, was no less dangerous than were conditions like the scurvy or 'bloody flux' among those newly arrived: among 'us new "Virginians"'. As for the latter, in a matter of a few months, Frethorne lamented to his parents, some two-thirds of the 150 settlers who had arrived with him had died.

All in all he was, he said, 'in a most miserable and pitiful case' – without food, almost without clothes. And he lived in constant fear of the Native American 'enemy', in a small, almost defenceless settlement miles from significant reinforcement. Only recently, Frethorne told his parents, he and the settlers in St Martin's Hundred had had 'a combat with them', capturing and enslaving two, but the truth was that he and his fellow English colonists felt 'in great danger', massively outnumbered as they were. Where they were 'we are but 32', he wrote, 'to fight against 3,000 if they should come'. Should they want to – were God not merciful (and it has to be said that his letters do not abound in examples of this mercy) – they could 'easily take us'. The native communities had learnt how to use European guns: 'pieces', as they were called. And all the time death and sickness continued to weaken them. Frethorne listed some of the many who had died already, though it was only to the adult men that he thought it appropriate to give names: John Sanderford, Thomas Howes, 'one woman', 'one child'.

'Release me from this bondage', he pleaded – from a place that he thought of naturally as 'Egypt' – 'and save my life.' Both by day and in the dead of night, he said, he would hear tired but starving servants crying out that they would prefer to be back in England without their limbs, hauling themselves, begging, from door to door than to remain here. He had not thought a head would hold so much water as 'doth daily flow from mine eyes'. Never, he told them desperately, had he 'felt the want of father and mother till now'.

One might almost think that he exaggerated – that he laid it on thick – but he was still, it should be remembered, a child. He openly asked for his indenture to be redeemed so that he could return to England. But Frethorne never was relieved. He never did sail back across the Atlantic. Mercy never did come, as Solomon had suggested that it would, 'in the time of affliction'. He died in America, not long afterwards. But for him this, perhaps, *was* mercy.

His parents, moreover (and perhaps, again, for the best) never did read about their son's unhappiness and deprivation. Both had died, almost at once, around the time that Richard arrived in Virginia – perhaps of the same rampant infection which spread among those on board his ship.

Frethorne was one of some 8,500 poor children from London who were indentured and sent overseas to Virginia between 1619 and 1625. It was a time when rates of emigration, certainly from the English capital, were rapidly increased, and Frethorne was part of this surge.

Unfortunately, though, the timing for the servants themselves was very bad, even as important men in the colony raked in profits large enough to '[flaunt] it up and down the streets', if and when they returned to London. ('Neither the Governor nor Council could or would', it was muttered, 'do any poor men right.') Supplies with which the servants came were grossly inadequate to sustain them, while too little was produced in the colony itself. Most did not survive for more than a year or two.

Thousands of those who had arrived by the time of the massacre in 1622 had died even before that fearful event, and the alarmingly high mortality rate continued in its aftermath. Far fewer suffered violent deaths at the hands of the Native Americans than perished of natural causes, even if the fact that the land was 'destitute of food' was certainly in part a result of this deliberate damage.[42] (Official inquiry into the appalling state of affairs led, in 1624, to the dissolution of the Virginia Company.) Few indeed of the servants who went with Frethorne – fewer than one in ten – could have hoped to see out the long terms of their indentures.⁴³ At least before the birth of Maryland in 1633, the possibility of escape for any miserable and mistreated servant in Virginia was small, given the distances involved, particularly after the massacre over a decade earlier had made retreat to native settlements seem a much more dangerous and less attractive option.

John Smith's claim that England's poor could live 'exceedingly well' in the American colonies – that English parishes and towns should all send those unable to make ends meet – was scarcely true in reality of Virginia early in the seventeenth century, as he of all people must certainly have known (though he did admit that living in Virginia was 'not a work for everyone'). Sadly, such advice to leave the country was misguided, even when it was well-intentioned – when it came from those who truly wished 'that the poor of England might be so provided for as none should need to go a begging within this realm'. Virginia was not, at the time, 'a [city] of refuge for poor impoverished persons', even when it is allowed that life at home, for the many who called themselves 'soldiers, mariners, glassmen, potmen, peddlers, petty chapmen, cony-skinners, or tinkers' but who to those who rubbed shoulders with them were simple vagrants, was also desperately hard.⁴⁴

In spite of the dreadful suffering late in the 1610s and very early in the 1620s, however, improvements did gradually begin. Discipline started to become slightly less harsh, even if it would certainly still seem so today. (Previously most servants had experienced what was charged, even then, to be 'intolerable oppression and hard usage'.) Since the dictatorial rule of the 1610s, the regime had become a little more liberal. Its intention now, it was proclaimed, was 'to take away all occasion of oppression and corruption'. Settlers were granted more economic liberty, to benefit personally from their activity. The demand for servant labour remained very high.⁴⁵ And during the 1620s prices for tobacco in particular – a plant whose cultivation was extremely labour-intensive – boomed.

During the first half of the subsequent decade, about ten years after Frethorne, one feisty, entrepreneurial emigrant called John Hammond arrived in Virginia. He stayed there for almost twenty years. And then he lived in neighbouring Maryland for two. It seems likely that, initially at least, he was an indentured servant himself. Certainly he sympathised deeply with the plight of the downtrodden in a manner that would have been unusual had he not once been one of them himself.

Subsequently, in the course of the interregnum, he was forced to return briefly to Republican England, and while he was there he wrote his own experiences down in order to encourage others to go. He hadn't simply survived. He had thrived.

He had risen to be an innkeeper, and to run a ferry. His allegiances, though, were also plainly Royalist, and as the conflict in England spilt subsequently into the English territories across the Atlantic, the upheaval had obliged him, all of a sudden, to flee. 'God knows', he said, to do so was 'sore against my will'. And given his hostility towards the Puritans, towards those who 'wore black coats, and could babble in a pulpit' (as well as 'roar in a tavern'), and given what he described as his 'carping enemies in London', this is not hard to believe.

When he returned to England, he published a book entitled *Leah and Rachell, or the two fruitful Sisters of Virginia and Maryland*, which is one of the best such accounts of life for an English colonist in America. The meaning of the biblical analogy was obvious to all its readers. As was its intended audience. Leah and Rachel are sisters, whose hands in marriage, successively, are offered to Jacob after he has travelled, with almost nothing, into a foreign country and served there a term of indenture.

Only after long years of toil does he reap his rewards, with Rachel's hand and a rise from poverty to substantial wealth. It was strange, Hammond commented, that so many 'deceived souls' chose to remain in England, rather 'to beg, steal, rot in prison, and come to shameful deaths, than to better their being by going thither'. These were men, women and children 'whose miseries and misfortunes by staying in England are much to be lamented, and much to be pitied'. To an active soul like Hammond such passivity seemed regrettable, to say the least. Many, he noted sadly, seemed to prefer to follow 'desperate and miserable courses' here, rather than to take the chance of travelling to live in America.

How did those who at present pushed fretful, creaking trolleys of 'trifling' merchandise – matches, coal, pens, laces – who barely made ends meet, who dressed in dirty rags, expect that 'age or sickness' would not, with grim inevitability, push them towards 'beggary'? For three hours, he said, he had followed a man heavily laden with faggots trudging, crook-backed, through the streets, sweating, crying out to advertise his wares, but seldom making more than a pittance. In all this time, he wrote, not a single person bought his goods. It was, he thought, a 'pitiful life'. What 'dull stupidity', he observed – especially in the young – to 'itch out their wearisome lives', reliant on charity, stuffing prisons with their 'carcases', putting up with 'almost perpetual and restless toil and drudgeries', rather than to 'remove themselves'.

For in America, he promised, there existed 'plenty of all things necessary for human subsistence'. 'Such preferment hath this country rewarded the industrious with', he wrote, that the very meanest had risen here to become 'great merchants'. Many who suffered now in England were wrong to think their situation immutable. 'To their ruins' they were 'deluded'. There was hope. And an avenue of escape *did* exist. The book is one of the first clear statements of what has become known since – only since, of course – as the 'American dream'. The poor, by initiative and hard work, could make good.

Hammond would not, he promised, describe an unrealistic utopia, as some had done. He would not over-praise these places, 'as if they were rather paradises than earthly plantations'. He had no desire, he said, to 'spirit' anyone across the Atlantic. In fact it was, he admitted, a 'dangerous' business to encourage anyone to travel in order to better themselves, 'for fear of the cry of "a spirit, a spirit"'. It was true, of course, that vulnerable people had been – and were being – misled. He urged the poor not to be 'seduced by those mercenary spirits that know little of the place', and whose 'foisting and flattering' expressed no genuine concern but was aimed, in reality, only at their own 'reward'.

Let no one, he cautioned, 'rashly throw themselves upon the voyage'. He recommended that anyone unable to 'defray their own charges' sign only a covenant that secured them for a fortnight in Virginia, to allow them to 'enquire of their master' and to establish his 'honest repute' – though whether in practice this would have proved possible is debatable. He detailed the contractual terms which might be expected. But at the same time he lamented the bad press – the 'odiums and cruel slanders', voiced by so many 'black-mouthed babblers' – that this part of America had received of late in England. Forget the caution, he said. Of all the places to which he had travelled – and he had been, he declared, to many – this was where 'I desire to spend the remnant of my days, in which I covet to make my grave' (a wish that he achieved).

He did admit that Virginia had, when first he went there early in the 1630s, deserved much of the criticism that it received. Some of the early 'adventurers' had indeed been known for what he called their 'avarice and inhumanity' – the sort of heedless, frantic, gold-seeking about which John Smith had complained. It was true that, once the profit to be made from it became clear, people had then grown tobacco to the exclusion of all else, fostering a dangerous reliance on England for the provision of food. The regime had unquestionably been tyrannical. Complaints were 'repaid with stripes', while tortures were 'made delights'. The 'owners' of indentured servants were renowned for their cruelty. Attacks by Native Americans certainly had gravely harmed, and weakened, the settlements, bringing them 'to such want and penury, that diseases grew rife'. It was little wonder, in consequence, that the place had been widely criticised – that those who lived there were regarded, sometimes, as 'an indigent and sottish people'.

Substantial improvement, though, had since taken place. Some of Virginia's inhabitants – 'honest and virtuous' – had now enacted laws for the 'severe suppression of vices', 'tending to the glory of God' and obliging the planting of corn ('the main staff of life') as well as tobacco. Cattle and pigs had become 'innumerable'. Better diet and 'wholesome lodgings' had ensured that people enjoyed much better health, and even if emigrants could still expect some sickness at first while they acclimatised, there was now, he promised, 'little danger of mortality'. Native American communities, accepting defeat, had been 'glad to sue for peace', and were now 'in absolute subjection to the English'.

Colonists, he said, had grown ashamed of 'that notorious manner of life' in which 'they had formerly lived and wallowed'. Even those accustomed to being 'lewd and idle' in England were inspired by the example of others to reform their habits, to 'wipe off those stains they have formerly been tainted with'. And the country as a whole, he wrote, 'which had a mean beginning', which had experienced 'two ruinous and bloody massacres', had 'by God's grace out-grown all' and become 'a place of pleasure and plenty'. Nor was it merely pleasant for the well-off. The complaints of servants too, he promised, were 'freely harkened to'. Letters written home by those who had gone there of late, he observed, inclined invariably to 'commend and approve of the place'.

Virginia was now secure and growing. Not all, of course, would make good there. By no means was this a dream world. Life anywhere – for anyone – in the middle of the seventeenth century was tough, and especially so for the type of people who made up most of those who peopled America. (More than half of all those who moved to live in the English colonies south of New England were servants.) But those who continued to damn the place were, Hammond wrote, like the dog who barked at the moon. The moon, heedless, would 'pass on her course'.

'Oh that God', he exclaimed, 'would stir up the hearts of more to go over.'

Later still in the century, opinion in England turned against the outflow of the desperate. Where the consensus had been in favour of offloading those who seemed unproductive, and who seemed a dangerous drain on resources – who were merely 'surplus inhabitants' – mercantilist thought began to see a shift in attitude towards emigration.

Now, instead of being a ball and chain pulling back on the body politic, that reservoir of poor, unemployed labour which undoubtedly existed was perceived as being a good thing, for the country as a whole even if not for the individuals concerned. 'No country can be truly accounted great and powerful by the extent of its territory', declared one writer in the late seventeenth century, or by the 'fertility of its climate', but only 'by the multitude of its inhabitants'.[46]

The result was that people were discouraged from leaving the country who once had been positively pressured to go. In the time of Charles II, the regular trade in English servants duly diminished. From its height in the 1650s, it came to constitute a much smaller proportion of the total emigration to America than it had once done. Increasingly, many servants travelled not from England but from Ireland, Scotland or Germany, since the strong demand for such basic labour, not freely available in America, persisted. By this time, though, the fundamentally English nature of the east coast colonies had been established. English was the language spoken by the settlers. And later arrivals knew that they would have to learn it.

It had always been, and continued to be, the case that impoverished servants went generally to the more southerly colonies (or to the Caribbean), rather than to New England, where there was not the same demand for labour. In the middle of the century it was written that where 'Virginia thrives by keeping many servants, and these in strict obedience', the colonists in New England 'conceit they and their children can do enough, and so have rarely above one servant' – a practice damned by this writer as a 'gross and foolish indulgence'.[47]

Even as the intellectual climate moved against the decision to relocate permanently from England, however, the outward flow continued to be high during the early years of the Restoration – still running, during the 1660s for instance, at over 4,000 per year, even if this was a significant reduction from the number who had left the country late in the previous decade. And many of those who went continued to be poor and disadvantaged. By the final decades of the century, though, numbers do seem to have fallen quite considerably.

Plenty did still leave, however. When Elizabeth Silvester, for instance, took ship from London for Jamestown, Virginia, towards the end of Charles II's reign, she was only fifteen years old. By then it was November 1683 – a year, for the king, of uncertainty and of plots on his life. Elizabeth committed to work for six years as an indentured labourer in order to pay for her voyage to America. She was persuaded and encouraged by an agent named John Ingham, who (just as many had before him) promised real opportunity across the Atlantic, and who acted as witness as she 'signed' the form – even if in fact she could not write and held the quill in an awkward, unpractised fashion. (Where the book in which, at the time, emigrants were recorded, reads 'signature' a note has been made in another hand that the ledger was 'marked', indicating that she had given her assent by what must have been a shaky cross.)

Elizabeth's parents were no longer around. (Their occupation – one that was full-time – is listed simply as 'ded'.) And no one at all survived to look out for her. Not only had her father and mother died, the ledger declares, but she had 'no friends or relations living', no reason at all to remain in England. Ingham saw an easy opportunity. And he duly delivered her to a London ship captain called John Purvis. What became of her afterwards, in Virginia, assuming that she survived the crossing, is not known, as all too often it isn't.

Meanwhile, agents naturally knew that prisoners as a group, before the introduction of the penalty of penal servitude, were more likely than most to agree to serve an indenture. Often they had nothing to keep them in England. Not only did they tend to be people little favoured in life, with nothing and nobody to persuade them to stay in the country, but they were hobbled by a bad reputation which they knew (and were forcefully reminded) that they could cast off at a stroke. The prospect of a chance to start again, even if it involved a few years' of indentured labour, was one which greatly appealed.

So when Thomas Poyner and Mary Tate were approached, having been slung, together, late one night into the New Prison in Clerkenwell – drunk, perhaps, and disorderly – they were more than willing to agree to be shipped and to serve an indenture in Maryland. They had not been charged with a criminal offence. They were not married (to anyone else, that is), and neither of them were apprentices. Neither, in other words, had any legal obligation to another person who might have resented their departure. It was 21 July 1685 when they signed. The shipping agent who recruited them was a mariner from Wapping named John Furle.

Such people came to America in droves. We cannot know much about them. Few left any testimony of their lives. Many, like poor, ill-fated Richard Frethorne, died soon after they crossed the Atlantic. But even those who did not – even those who both survived *and* who flourished – tended to establish themselves in professions which left few written records: as farmers, or shop-keepers, tavern-keepers (like John Hammond) or schoolteachers. They influenced those around them. They shaped the colonies. But they left little mark upon the history that we tell hundreds of years later.

Much, as George Eliot observed, was dependent upon 'unhistoric acts', and upon those who rest now in 'unvisited tombs'.

# CONCLUSION

From early in the seventeenth century, even after the halting, hesitant steps made during the preceding decades, English colonialism made what turned out to be its first enduring advances. The men and women who crossed the Atlantic to live in Virginia, New England and Newfoundland were impelled by motives which were bewilderingly diverse.

While many – most in fact – went because in England they had little hope, because they were desperate, others went out of a blind optimism that America was a promised land, metaphorically or even literally: a land of opportunity, of boundless riches, and one, perhaps, favoured by God in this chapter of the world. The truth, of course, was that its northern parts were none of these things. Particularly during the first half of the century, they offered neither safety and opportunity nor riches. They were not a promised land. Standards of living were no higher – were perhaps even lower – than they were in England. And they were not good there. Or so many would certainly not have left the country in the first place.

Others went, more realistically perhaps, to escape a country in which what seemed the divinely established monarchical order had been rudely and bloodily upended by the mid-seventeenth-century Civil Wars. They went also to pursue valuable trades in a commodity like fur: mammals which had the misfortune to bear desirable coats had been overhunted in Europe but were abundant in America. Emigrants went to take advantage of the liberty, in this new world, of *affording liberty*, of permitting individual men and women to think, and to worship, as seemed appropriate to them – of the assurance, alien in most parts of Europe, that provided that they did not disturb others, no established power would disturb them.

Motivation was different, of course, for every colonist. Each had his or her personal reasons, plenty of which are incapable of being categorised: like the sixteen-year-old boy who emigrated to America because his father had beat him angrily with a stick 'after I went to dancing school to learn to dance'. English dancing tuition was not, in general, a cause that underpinned emigration. But even when reasons are grouped, there were many. The Atlantic world then – even on the narrow coastal strip which constituted English America at the time – was, as one historian puts it, just 'as chaotic and disconnected as the distracted nation that spawned it'.[1]

There was more than enough room in America for variety. The northern parts seemed then, even considering the limited knowledge which existed of the inland regions, unimaginably, incalculably large. Englishmen who were used to regarding good land as a finite and easily exhausted commodity spoke in awe of America's 'large extending arms', and of the endless diversity to be found within a continent of breath-taking expanse. How far could one head west before one again reached the sea? No one even knew.

It was straightforward enough here for colonists to grow a nutrient-hungry crop like tobacco for a few years until the soil was exhausted, and then simply to move. But while some commodities, like land itself, or the wood which grew thickly upon it, certainly did exist in greater abundance, others (like labour) were in considerably shorter supply in the New World than in the old. And there were also hazards which did not exist in England, like the particular threats to health presented by a different climate or by hostile natives.

While it may be the case that it is impossible to find a single factor which aligns perfectly with figures for emigration from certain English regions, it *is* broadly true that rising population in England during the first half of the seventeenth century coincides with rising emigration. From four million the population climbed to five million (having risen already from only three million midway through the sixteenth century). With a stagnant economy failing to produce either more jobs or more supplies, pressure built and was bound to seek a release. It *is* broadly true too, of course, that rising emigration required the possibility of easy departure, and the fact that England was an island with many large ports, inhabited by numerous ship-owners looking to stow paying emigrants on an outward passage in space in the hold which would be used, subsequently, to bring produce back from the New World, provided the opportunity for a large-scale movement of people that would otherwise simply not have been possible.

As well as the rising population, of unquestionable importance was the changing nature of England. While the economy might have been stagnant productively, society certainly was not. The rise of what were known as 'masterless men' – men enmeshed in a new 'wage economy', as opposed to in an older web of feudal relationships – led to what was an increasingly polarised world, a world in which more floated free of permanent contracts, unable to make ends meet, and prey to the siren calls made by emigration agents to leave the country for another one in which life was allegedly easier. In England the social fabric disintegrated. The fact that the country's political capital, London, was also both its economic hub and its major port, from which the majority of the ships carrying settlers departed, served strongly to strengthen the trend.

Then, as population growth tailed off during the latter third of the century, so too did emigration, which now, for the first time since very early in the century, was officially discouraged (though not forbidden). The tentative beginnings, moreover, of an agrarian revolution meant that the pressure which was exerted by food supplies upon population grew smaller. After centuries of maintaining a stranglehold, famine in England began to become a thing of the past.

The tragedy, of course, for so many emigrants was that the promises which they had been willing to believe were simply not true, particularly during the first half of the century.

Emigrants to America did not find a land of milk and honey, any more than did Dick Whittington, for instance, find that the streets of London he walked on were paved with gold. If things were desperately bad in England (and they were), they were desperately bad too in seventeenth-century America. Rates of morbidity for European migrants there were shockingly high, especially in Virginia as opposed to further north in, say, New England.

Almost half of the men and women who sailed there were dead within a few years of their arrival. In parts the death rate for new immigrants was as high as 80 per cent. Sadly, for these profoundly poor and profoundly deprived people, there was no solution. Very simply, it was a bad time to be born, a fact that was true for everyone but particularly so for the unprivileged majority. Death rates had been high too, lest we forget, back in England, in what has been called 'a sickly nation', and at least in Virginia the fact that people settled in a much more dispersed fashion reduced the impact of epidemics.[2]

Perhaps there was more reason in America than in England to *hope*, and hope for many had been a commodity in short or even entirely exhausted supply. A few – and it was only a few – did get lucky on the western side of the Atlantic. Either an early death or a life of painful drudgery might remain by far the most likely outcomes, the former more probable in fact in the New World than it was in the old. But the latter was less of a certainty in America than it was in England. There were no mines of gold or silver: not where the English were. The mountains of Virginia were not 'gold-showing', just as the streets of London had not been paved with the stuff. That was the sort of nonsense peddled by 'spirits' to the easily deluded.

But Dick Whittington did, many years after moving from Gloucestershire to London, become the Lord Mayor. This was not just a fairytale. And it was the same sort of mobility that had impelled him to walk to London which fostered ongoing movement, when ongoing movement (long after Whittington's time) was possible, from English ports across the seemingly, but not actually, endless waters of the Atlantic – to a land which did offer opportunity (as well, of course, as risk), and even if the exploitation of this opportunity was a matter of fortune as well as of endeavour.

In periods of high emigration, which first exploded during the late 1620s and 1630s, when around 80,000 English people left the British Isles, almost 60,000 of them for the New World, many thousands of men, women and children sailed every year. For several decades during the middle part of the century the pattern continued, reduced, as it was, by the massive changes in English government after the Civil Wars and the execution of the king. It was during this period that an English North America ceased to be tenuous and uncertain, and became assured.

The population there – which grew far more as a result of the large flows of migrants than it did because of the birth rate – expanded during the 1630s an astonishing five times, from just under 10,000 to some 50,000 souls. Many did die early deaths in America. But it was then, nevertheless, that England's Atlantic world, which would shape so much of the next three to four centuries of history, was truly born, even if the two hemispheres were not in the short term integrated economically in the way that they would later become.

It is quite true, as has been written, that the lives of the great majority who were colonists then are, and will remain, hidden to the historian. They move in darkness, these people, and the best we can hope is to catch what one writer has called 'a brief glimpse of a colonist during public moments' – during an appearance in court, a profession of faith or the presentation of a will.[3] On such formal occasions some, not all, will flash into view. But these are not times, as we know ourselves, which are perfectly representative of our personalities or our lives.

Nevertheless, we have to make do with the little we have – to be grateful that we have this much. And this, after all, is what makes it possible to catch sight, even if only for a moment, of Edward and Anne Furnifull: the fact that the 'spirit' who lured them to emigrate was arrested and faced legal charges. Most of those treated here, though, with the exception of many in the chapter on 'despair', have left more on which we can base an account of their decision to move across the Atlantic. And the understanding of the factors which motivated these few to start life again on the western shore of the ocean does allow for a more nuanced appreciation of this major ingredient in the shape of the modern world.

Even if it is true that northern America became, in the eighteenth century, markedly more ethnically diverse than it was in the seventeenth – that English colonists were joined by many from other places, from Ireland, Scotland and Germany, from diverse parts of Africa, of course, and from elsewhere – the numbers of the non-English were not then sufficiently large to swamp or change very significantly what was already a predominantly English region.[4] As America began to expand to the west, to impose itself (with devastating consequences) on the native populations which it encountered, it was substantially an English region which did so, and the wars that English America then fought with the French territory further to the north and west – one that was very significantly less populated just as it was significantly larger geographically – ensured that it remained so.

The emigrants of the seventeenth century changed their world, and in doing so they changed ours. And in that sense the promises made by the 'spirits' – the promises that these notorious men and women thought themselves, in their heart of hearts, were far-fetched and unfounded – were not only right: they were not bold enough.

# NOTES

## Introduction

1 'Such loud noise', Archbishop William Laud, quoted in C. Bridenbaugh, *Vexed and Troubled Englishmen*, p. 450; 'multitude of people', Sir Robert Heath in the 1629 Carolina patent, quoted in C.L. Tomlins, *Freedom Bound: Law, Labor, and Civic Identity in Colonizing English America*, p. 169.

2 See for instance L. Irving, *Arctic Life of Birds and Mammals: Including Man*, pp. 16–18.

3 G. Alsop, *A Character of the Province of Maryland*, p. 73.

4 E. Richards, *Britannia's Children*, p. 25.

5 Ibid., p. 2.

6 Estimates can be found in many studies, but see for instance E. Richards, *Britannia's Children*, p. 49.

7 'Huge flow', James Horn, cited in J. Brooks, *Why We Left*, p. 36. Emigration figures, see C.J. Erickson, 'English', in S. Thernstrom (ed.), *Harvard Encyclopedia of American Ethnic Groups*, pp. 320–22. The 'Swarming of the English' is used as a chapter heading by Carl Bridenbaugh. See also Richards, *Britannia's Children*, p. 43.

8 Some other examples of the continued use of words in America after vanishing from the English spoken in England are in D. Freeman Hawke, *Everyday Life in Early America*, pp. 101–2.

9 Brooks, *Why We Left*, pp. 34–5.

10 Alsop, *A Character of the Province of Maryland*, pp. 89–91.

11 The author was Michael Drayton, poet to Prince Henry.

12 Freeman Hawke, *Everyday Life in Early America*, p. 4. Brooks, *Why We Left*, pp. 13, 24. E.S. Morgan, *American Slavery, American Freedom*, pp. 111–12. 'Take fast hold and root', Richards, *Britannia's Children*, p. 40.

13 'Miserable poor people', quoted in P.W. Coldham, *The Complete Book of*

*Emigrants: 1607–1660*, p. 220. 'Late unspeakable increases'; 'diminution of the people', quoted in Richards, *Britannia's Children*, pp. 61, 63.

14 'Vivid people', quoted in Freeman Hawke, *Everyday Life in America*, pp. 1–2. 'Choice grain', quoted in Richards, *Britannia's Children*, p. 52. Eburne, quoted in Bridenbaugh, *Vexed and Troubled Englishmen*, p. 396.

## Fish

1 Hakluyt, quoted in W. Bolster, *Mortal Sea*, p. 43. Henry VIII is quoted in a well-informed Venetian account of 1536, cited in D.B. Quinn, *England and the Discovery of America*, p. 142. 'One Elizabethan writer': Robert Hitchcock. See P.E. Pope, *Fish Into Wine*, p. 20.

2 Tobias Gentleman, DNB. The fishing industry was the country's third most lucrative, after the cloth and tin industries. 'Nation of the sea', R. Whitbourne, *A Discourse and Discovery*. p.1.

3 32 Hen VIII: J. Raithby, *The Statutes Relating to the Admiralty, Navy, Shipping, and Navigation of the United Kingdom*, p. 17. Maps of the time routinely showed rivers much larger than they were in life, for the same reason that roads are often shown in the same way today: because these were what most people wanted, and needed, to see.

4 https://www.britannica.com/place/Grand-Banks

5 See W. Childs and M. Kowaleski, 'Fishing and Fisheries in the Middle Ages', p. 26, in D.J. Starkey, C. Reid and N. Ashcroft (eds), *England's Sea Fisheries*.

6 Sir Francis Walsingham (November 1583): 'America and West Indies: Addenda 1583', in W. Noel Sainsbury (ed.), *Calendar of State Papers: Colonial Series: Vol. 9, 1675–1676 [America and West Indies] and Addenda 1574–1674*, pp. 17–24. British History Online. http://www.british-history.ac.uk/cal-state-papers/colonial/america-west-indies/vol9/ pp. 17–24.

7 A.L. Rowse, *The England of Elizabeth*, pp. 494–7.

8 He had, it was said, 'a tongue at liberty to utter what he thought', D.B. Quinn, *The Voyages and Colonising Enterprises of Sir Humphrey Gilbert*, pp. 431–4.

9 'Large and excellent', Whitbourne, *Discourse and Discovery*, p. 3.

10 Ibid., p. iv.

11 Ibid., p. iii.

12 The figure in 1610 was 200 according to company representatives: G.T. Cell, *English Enterprise*, p. 53.

13 J. Aubrey, *Brief Lives* (ed. A. Clark), p. 277.

14 John Mason, 'A Briefe Discourse', in G.T. Cell (ed.), *Newfoundland Discovered*, p. 94.

15 Ibid.

16 Guy's letter to Sir Percival Willoughby of 6 October 1610 is printed in full in Cell (ed.), *Newfoundland Discovered*, as is an inventory of provisions left with the settlers in August 1611, pp. 60–67.

17 Pope, *Fish Into Wine*, pp. 66–7.

18 Ibid., p. 51 and references therein; p. 65 for Thomas Povey's report of 1660.

19 Ibid., pp. 72–3. This was after the Treaty of Utrecht, 1713.

20 Ibid., chapter 3 and *passim*.

## Gold and Smoke

1 See the biography by Augustus Jessopp at www.thepeerage.com/e692.htm

2 'All devouring', Smith, quoted in D.A. Price, *Love and Hate in Jamestown*, p. 76.

3 'Neither knew nor understood', ibid., p. 52. 'Most apt and securest', ibid., p. 34. John Smith, 'A True Relation', in P. Barbour (ed.), *Complete Works of Captain John Smith*, vol. 1.

4 'Boughs of trees', Smith, quoted in Price, *Love and Hate*, p. 52. The river was later called the James.

5 Quote in ibid., p. 49.

6 Ibid., p. 71.

7 Ibid., p. 94.

8 S. Purchas, *Hakluytus Posthumus or Purchas his Pilgrimes*, vol. 15, p. 70.

9 Price, *Love and Hate*, p. 42.

10 Smith background and quotes, see Price, *Love and Hate*, pp. 3–13; 43.

11 J. Auriol Jenstad, '"The Gouldesmythes Storehowse": Early Evidence for Specialisation', p. 43. Lazarus Erckern, translated in Sir J. Pettus, *The Laws of Art and Nature in Knowing, Judging, Assaying, Fining, Refining and Inlarging the Bodies of Confin'd Metals*.

12 The play was co-written by George Chapman, Ben Jonson and John Marston. The fact that the finding, and the obsession, with gold, were here satirical does not affect its importance as social commentary: a genuine tendency was being satirised.

13 The 'spy' was a man named William Brewster: not the man of the same name who sailed, soon afterwards, on the *Mayflower*. See his undated letter: P.

Barbour, *Jamestown Voyages*, vol. 1, p. 107. He too, of course, was desperate for life in Virginia to prove lucrative, though he was soon to die of a wound inflicted by a Native American. J.G. Hunt, 'William Brewster, Gent., of Virginia', *The Virginia Magazine of History and Biography*, pp. 407–9.

14 F. Fernández-Armesto, *Columbus on Himself*, p. 83.

15 'Ravening appetites', quoted in A. Hadfield, 'Peter Martyr, Richard Eden and the New World: Reading, Experience and Translation', pp. 3–4. 'Only gold can cure', quoted in C. Nicholl, *The Creature in the Map*, p. 204. Price, *Love and Hate*, p. 124.

16 A.L. Rowse (ed.), *The First Colonists*, pp. 8, 142; Sir Richard Grenville, quoted in ibid., p. 80.

17 Pedro de Zúñiga to Philip III, 22 September 1607, doc. 23, P. Barbour, *Jamestown Voyages*, vol. 1, pp. 114–16; Zorzi Giustinian to the Doge and Senate, 29 August 1607, in H.F. Brown (ed.), *Calendar of State Papers Relating to English Affairs in the Archives of Venice*, vol. 11 (1607–10), p. 27.

18 K.R. Andrews, 'Christopher Newport of Limehouse, Mariner', p. 30.

19 K.R. Andrews, *Elizabethan Privateering*, p. 85.

20 B. Woolley, *Savage Kingdom*, p. 43.

21 Quoted in ibid., p. 82.

22 P. Barbour (ed.), *Complete Works of Captain John Smith*, vol. 1, p. 219.

23 Sir Thomas Smythe to Lord Salisbury, 17 August 1607, document 20, Barbour (ed.), *Jamestown Voyages*, vol. 1, p. 112.

24 The recipient was the contrastingly unambitious John Chamberlain.

25 Price, *Love and Hate*, p. 76.

26 Ibid., p. 54. Woolley, *Savage Kingdom*, p. 93.

27 Barbour (ed.), *Complete Works of Captain John Smith*, vol. 1, p. 218 [The Proceedings of the English Colony in Virginia...].

28 Price, *Love and Hate*, p. 85.

29 On the map of New England published with Smith's later account: see D.B. Heath (ed.), *A Journal of the Pilgrims at Plymouth*, pp. xxiv–xxv.

30 The quotations from John Smith are in his *Generall Historie of Virginia... of 1624*, for which see Barbour (ed.), *Complete Works of Captain John Smith*, vol. 2.

31 Smith, *Generall Historie*, chapter 7: Barbour (ed.), *Complete Works of Captain John Smith*, vol. 2, p. 157 and *passim*. J.C. Jeaffreson (ed.), *Middlesex County Records* notes, pp. 334–5.

32 Price, *Love and Hate*, pp. 91; 111; 145. 'Cloud of smoke' quoted in J. Rolfe, *True Relation*, Note on Manuscript by Francis L. Berkeley Jr, p. 22.

33 Price, *Love and Hate*, p. 84. Woolley, *Savage Kingdom*, p. 191.

34 Price, *Love and Hate*, p. 95.

35 Ibid., pp. 96; 108–9.

36 Ibid., p. 126.

37 Ibid., p. 129.

38 See A. Brown, *Genesis of the United States*, p. 570.

39 Chamberlain to Dudley Carleton, 9 July 1612. The full reference can be found here: www.british-history.ac.uk/cal-state-papers/colonial/america-west-indies/vol1/pp13–14

40 Newport, DNB, which also refers to a row he had had with Thomas Dale as a possible cause.

41 Memorial brass, quoted in Rolfe, *True Relation*, character portrait by John Melville Jennings, p. 11.

42 W. Camden, *Annales*, no. 32 for the year 1585.

43 'So frequent', W. Camden, cited in James I, *The Essayes of a Prentise, in the Divine Art of Poesie: A Counterblast to Tobacco*, p. 86. 7,000 tobacco shops in London: Barnaby Rich in *The Honestie of this Age*, p. 26.

44 Sylvester Jourdain.

45 Price, *Love and Hate*, pp. 130ff.

46 Strachey, *History of Travaille*, cited in John Rolfe, DNB.

47 First shipment, Price, *Love and Hate*, p. 186. 'Pleasant, sweet and strong', R. Hamor, *True Discourse of the Present State of Virginia*, p. 34.

48 John Smith, quoted in Price, *Love and Hate*, p. 66.

49 Quoted in ibid., pp. 151–2.

50 Regarding her visit, see ibid., pp. 174–6. Mention was made by Chamberlain of her being well placed at a Twelfth Night masque.

51 Price, *Love and Hate*, p. 173.

52 A.M. Brandt, *Cigarette Century: The Rise, Fall and Deadly Persistence of the Product that Defined America*, pp. 20–21.

53 Hamor, *True Discourse of the Present State of Virginia*, cited in John Rolfe, DNB. For much of this see http://archive.tobacco.org/resources/history/Tobacco_History16.html; 'sealed the success', N. Zahedieh, *The Capital and the Colonies*, p. 199.

54 Price, *Love and Hate*, p. 170.

55 Smith, *Complete Works*, vol. 3, pp. 270–72, quoted in Price, *Love and Hate*, pp. 228–32.

56 Smith, *Complete Works*, vol. 3, pp. 382–3, letter to Bacon, quoted in Price, *Love and Hate*, p. 223.

## Equality Before God

1 R. Cushman, *The Sin and Danger of Self-Love* (notes p. 2).

2 The phrase is that of a Puritan divine called Thomas Cartwright. See, in general, A. Hunt, *The Art of Hearing: English Preachers and their Audiences, 1590–1640*.

3 P. Collinson, 'The Jacobean Religious Settlement: the Hampton Court Conference'.

4 J.D. Bangs, 'The Pilgrims, Leiden, and the Early Years of Plymouth Plantation', www.sail1620.org; Collinson, 'Jacobean Religious Settlement'.

5 Patrick Collinson, cited in F.J. Brenner, *Puritanism*, p. 10.

6 Collinson, 'Jacobean Religious Settlement'.

7 Ibid.

8 The records of the diocesan Court of High Commission in Canterbury list numerous similar cases, see Canterbury Cathedral Archives, DCb/PRC/44/3.

9 H.M. Dexter and M. Dexter, *The England and Holland of the Pilgrims*, p. 426.

10 Genesis 12:1. The translation here and throughout is that of the Geneva version which was immensely influential and was particularly beloved of Puritans of the time, and of those who felt compelled to leave the country. The Geneva New Testament was published in 1557. The complete Bible was published in 1560. Crucially, this was the first Bible to use chapters and numbered verses. It also had extensive marginal notes by eminent Protestant scholars.

11 R. Cushman, 'Reasons and Considerations touching the lawfulness of removing out of England into the parts of America', in D.B. Heath (ed.), *A Journal of the Pilgrims at Plymouth. Mourt's Relation*, p. 95.

12 John Robinson, quoted in Dexter, *England and Holland*, p. 410.

13 This site includes a mid-century design for a dramatically enlarged city: an 'Amstelo-Damum Amplificatum': https://www.rijksmuseum.nl/en/rijksstudio/timeline-dutch-history/1600-1665-amsterdams-prosperity; 'innumerable sects', T. Harris, *Rebellion*, p. 106; 'vend their toys', 'common harbour', in Dexter, *England and Holland*, p. 419.

14 W. Bradford, *Of Plymouth Plantation*, pp. 23–4.

15 Ibid., p. 364.

16 Ibid., pp. 16–17. 'Subject to stinking', from F. Moryson, *Itinerary*, p. 90.

17 www.leidenamericanpilgrimmuseum.org/Page31X.htm

18 Bradford, *Of Plymouth Plantation*, p. 20.

19 'Obstinate and incessant', C. Wolley, *A Two Years' Journal in New York*, p. 20. Bradford, *Of Plymouth Plantation*, *passim*.

20 Bradford, *Of Plymouth Plantation*, p. 27.

21 Winslow, *Hypocrisie Unmasked*, pp. 88–91, quoted in J.D. Bangs, *Pilgrim Edward Winslow*, pp. 12–13.

22 It was a valid concern, of course, for those of their community who remained behind in Holland were in fact entirely submerged, in a matter of decades, within the native population.

23 'Youngest and strongest', quoted in the Cushman Genealogy, p. 22: https://sites.udel.edu/wvg/files/2015/01/Robert-Cushman-Biography-25punar.pdf; Bradford, *Of Plymouth Plantation*, p. 24.

24 Bradford, *Of Plymouth Plantation*, p. 25. (This reference applies only to these last quotes. The others are from Cushman.)

25 Bradford, *Of Plymouth Plantation*, p. 25.

26 Ibid., p. 27.

27 Ibid., pp. 32–3.

28 In his *Description of New England*, John Smith wrote of having read the 'relation printed by Captain Bartholomew Gosnold, of Elizabeth's Isles'. See P. Barbour (ed.) *Complete Works of Captain John Smith*, vol. 1, p. 298.

29 D.R. McManis, *European Impressions of the New England Coast, 1497–1620*, pp. 37–40. See also the Edward Wright world map of 1599 and the Velasco map of 1611, reproduced in D.B. Quinn (ed.), *The Hakluyt Handbook*, pp. 62–3. Smith felt obliged to maintain, in the face of many who insisted that it was, that Virginia was not an island either (*Works*, pp. 325–6).

30 William Bradford, quoted in N. Bunker, *Making Haste from Babylon*, p. 273.

31 'Very low' quotes, from Samuel de Champlain, see D.B. Heath (ed.), *A Journal of the Pilgrims at Plymouth. Mourt's Relation*, pp. xix–xxii.

32 J. Hensley (ed.), *Works of Anne Bradstreet*, pp. 240–41.

33 In 1622 the Bullion Ordinance forbade the export of bullion from the country. See D. McNally, *Political Economy and the Rise of Capitalism*, p. 29.

34 M. Kishlansky, *A Monarchy Transformed*, pp. 92–3, 99–100.

35 T. Harris, *Revolution*, p. 289 and p. 277.

36 Frontispiece to T. Webster, *Godly Clergy in Early Stuart England*. Quote from Jeremiah Burroughes (1638).

37 Harris, *Revolution*, p. 235.

38 Ibid., p. 236.

39 Ibid., pp. 289, 283, 298.

40 D. Purkiss, *The English Civil War*, pp. 31–5.

41 Harris, *Rebellion*, pp. 266, 280.

42 Bridenbaugh, *Vexed and Troubled Englishmen*, p. 455.

43 S.E. Morison, *Builders of the Bay Colony*, pp. 320–21; Hensley (ed.), *Works of Anne Bradstreet*, p. 241.

44 C. Creighton, *A History of Epidemics in Britain*, vol. 1, pp. 463–7.

45 *Four Ages of Man*, Part III, 'Youth'.

46 'Reasons for the Plantation in New England'. See also Bridenbaugh, *Vexed and Troubled Englishmen*, p. 436.

47 Proverbs 22:3.

48 Harris, *Rebellion*, p. 318.

49 J. Winthrop, *History of New England 1630–49 with notes by J. Savage*, Margaret Winthrop letter, 1631, p. 382.

50 The Puritan divine in question was Cotton Mather.

51 John Rous in his *Diary*, 7 June 1630: in C.E. Banks, *Winthrop Fleet*, p. 23.

52 Genesis 12: 1. See, in general, A. Zakai, *Exile and Kingdom: History and Apocalypse in the Puritan Migration to America*.

53 One of their ships was even called the *Mayflower*, a common name for ships at the time, though it was not the same one.

54 2 Samuel 7:10; Bridenbaugh, *Vexed and Troubled Englishmen*, p. 445.

55 John Cotton, *The Way of the Congregational Churches Cleared* (1648), Part I, p.102, quoted in Bridenbaugh, *Vexed and Troubled Englishmen*, p. 460.

56 Bridenbaugh, *Vexed and Troubled Englishmen*, p. 450.

57 Ibid., p. 448.

58 H.C. Shelley, *John Underhill: Captain of New England and New Netherland*, pp. 126–7. Hensley (ed.), *The Works of Anne Bradstreet*, p. x.

59 Hensley (ed.), *Works of Anne Bradstreet*, pp. 293–4.

60 Savage (ed.), *Works of John Winthrop 1630–49*, p. 382.

61 Bridenbaugh, *Vexed and Troubled Englishmen*, p. 463.

62 Harris, *Rebellion*, p. 280.

63 Bridenbaugh, *Vexed and Troubled Englishmen*, pp. 472–3.

64 Ibid., pp. 434, 449, 450, 455, 460–61, 464, 468–9. 'Old way to heaven': letter to John Buxton, November 1640, B. Schofield (ed.), *The Knyvett Letters (1620–1644)*, p. 30.

65 John Winthrop: W.L. Sachse, 'The Migration of New Englanders to England, 1640–1660', p. 251.

## *King*

1 P.H. Hardacre, 'The Further Adventures of Henry Norwood', p. 282.

2 Quotes in W.C. Wooldridge, *Mapping Virginia*, p. 15.

3 Wooldridge, *Mapping Virginia*, pp. 5, 15, 21.

4 Population estimate, Anon., *Perfect Description*, no. 41. Moss reference, see G. Callam, *The Norwoods III: A Chronological History*, p. 105.

5 'Virginia in 1650 (Continued)', *The Virginia Magazine of History and Biography*, vol. 17, no. 2 (April, 1909), pp. 136–7.

6 'Guests' quote is in H. Norwood, *Voyage to Virginia*, p. 186.

7 J.H. Trye, *Colonel Henry Norwood*, p. 116.

8 DNB, John Hampden. Purkiss, *English Civil War*, p. 24. Regarding Hampden's moderation, see Kishlansky, *Monarchy Transformed*, p. 138.

9 'Scholar' reference was made by a Puritan, John Barkstead, in 1659: Hardacre, 'Further Adventures', p. 282.

10 S.R. Gardiner, *History of the Great Civil War*, vol. 1, p. 38.

11 'More war than we expected', R.E. Sherwood, *The Civil War in the Midlands*, chapter 16; 'those who are not with them', Gardiner, *History*, vol. 1, p. 39.

12 'Rotten sheep', quoted in J. Day, *Gloucester and Newbury 1643*, p. 3. The anonymous account of the siege of Bristol is printed in full in E. Warburton, *Memoirs of Prince Rupert*, vol. 2, pp. 237–64. This extract is on p. 252. Of 4,000 to 5,000 foot of the Oxford army who had taken part in the attack, only some 1,400 were able to be mustered afterwards: a sign of the terrible impact the assault had had on the attacking army as well as on the defenders. King Charles himself was appalled, and the destruction played a part in Royalists refusing to attack other cities, like neighbouring Gloucester. See J. Barratt, *Sieges of the English Civil Wars*, chapter 4.

13 K. Roberts, *First Newbury 1643: The Turning Point*, p. 7 and *passim*.

14 D.L. Smith and J. McElligott (eds), *Royalists and Royalism*, p. 91.

15 'Fearful visitation', J.F.D. Shrewsbury, *A History of Bubonic Plague in the British Isles*, p. 408.

16 A. Tinniswood, *The Rainborowes*, p. 187.

17 G. Smith, *The Cavaliers in Exile 1640–1660*, p. 20.

18 S. Elliott Hoskins, *Charles the Second in the Channel Islands*, p. 300.

19 Account of Ann Fanshawe. See D.E. Underdown, *Royalist Conspiracy*, pp. 10–12; R. Hutton, *Charles II King of England, Scotland, and Ireland*, pp. 40–41; Smith, *Cavaliers in Exile*, p. 19.

20 Smith, *Cavaliers in Exile*, p. 20.

21 Sancroft, letter cited above.

22 'Surely God Almighty...', J. Stubbs, *Reprobates*, p. 353. 'That unhappy time' quotes from Sir John Reresby, Smith, *Cavaliers in Exile*, p. 36. Smith estimates that more than 300 men spent over two years living in exile, most in 'the prime of life', and often with families, and households, in tow, and that more than 1,000 shorter-term exiles came and went (p. 52). 'General massacre', Clarendon; 'my own native soil', John Page: Smith, ibid., pp. 59, 62.

23 W. Billings, *Sir William Berkeley and the Forging of Colonial Virginia*, p. 21.

24 Berkeley swore his oath of office in the Privy Council chamber in London on 10 August 1641, but did not take up the role in Virginia until some months later, in March the following year. 'Whole genius', A. Fea, *Memoirs of the Martyr King:* Tract IV: The Narrative of Sir John Berkeley, pp. 163–4.

25 Edward Hyde, quoted in I. Altman and J. Horn (eds), *'To Make America'*, p. 108.

26 Norwood, *Voyage to Virginia*, quoted in Trye, *Colonel Henry Norwood*, p. 115.

27 'Western hemisphere', Billings, *Sir William Berkeley*, p. 32. 'New western world', Sir William Berkeley, *Discourse and View of Virginia*, passim.

28 Smith, *Cavaliers in Exile*, p. 30.

29 John Gauden, published by 'a rural pen' in 1649.

30 W.F. Craven, *White, Red and Black*, pp. 14–15.

31 William Sancroft (a future Archbishop of Canterbury) to his father, 10 February 1649.

32 Smith, *Cavaliers in Exile*, p. 20. Failure of the Royalist cause did prompt a wave of returnees too, though, who disliked life in exile and despaired now of the situation in England ever becoming more hopeful.

33 Report of Lord Loughborough's arrival, in Smith, *Cavaliers in Exile*, p. 23.

34 David Underdown; Eva Scott; references in ibid., pp. 3–4.

35 Translated from the Latin: 'Et Amicis Regis quaquaversum dispersis', the full text of which as it relates to Norwood is printed in Hardacre, 'Further Adventures', pp. 282–3.

36 Hyde, quoted in J.T. Peacey, 'Order and Disorder in Europe: Parliamentary Agents and Royalist Thugs 1649–1650', p. 967.

37 Quoted in ibid., p. 955.

38 DNB, Margo Todd, 'Isaac Dorislaus'.

39 One recent historian indeed has described it as a 'hornet's nest of outraged royalist exiles': Peacey, 'Order and Disorder', p. 955.

40 Many agreed, perhaps, with the Venetian ambassador at Munster who wrote of Dorislaus's 'well merited punishment'.

41 'Formerly sprung', quote in DNB on Dorislaus. 'This law . . .', Walter Strickland, Peacey, 'Order and Disorder', p. 964.

42 The physical description of Norwood was made by a Puritan observer: Hardacre, 'Further Adventures', p. 282. Re. ghosts, see D. Purkiss, 'The English Civil War and Male Identity', p. 222.

43 R. Ligon, *A True and Exact History of the Island of Barbados*, p. 40.

44 W. Thornbury, 'The Royal Exchange', pp. 494–513.

45 Charles was crowned King of Scotland at Scone on 1 January 1651. He had longer to wait to be crowned in Westminster, but Royalists, of course, considered him their king nonetheless.

46 Billings, *Sir William Berkeley*, p. 102.

47 E.S. Morgan, *American Slavery*, p. 147.

48 R.L. Morton, *Colonial Virginia*, vol. 1, pp. 169–70.

49 Billings, *Sir William Berkeley*, pp. 109–10. Morton, *Colonial Virginia*, vol. 1, p. 172.

50 O. Ogle, W.H. Bliss, W.D. Macray and F.J. Routledge, *Calendar of the Clarendon State Papers*, cited in Hardacre, 'Further Adventures', pp. 273 and *passim*.

51 Pepys diary, Monday 22 April 1661. The same entry refers to the attendance of William Penn and his son (see chapter 6).

52 D. Hackett Fischer, *Albion's Seed*, pp. 212–14.

53 Purkiss, *English Civil War*, p. 18.

54 W. Billings, J.E. Selby and T.W. Tate (eds), *Colonial Virginia: A History*, pp. 52–3. Reference is made to personal aggrandisement as 'the guiding precept' in Virginia, which offered 'nearly perfect freedom to hunt for private gain' – 'like some great magnet, Virginia attracted a disproportionate share of ruthless, avaricious men who were callous in their exploitation of others'.

### Fur

1 Quotes from Cotton Mather, *The Great Works of Christ in America*, vol. 1, pp. 398–9.

2 'Not too many at once', John Winthrop, quoted in V.D. Anderson, *New*

*England's Generation: The Great Migration and the Formation of Society and Culture in the 17th Century*, p. 54. 'Nursery of lust', Lucy Hutchinson, *The Memoirs of Colonel Hutchinson*, p. 59. 'New American world', A. van der Donck, *Description of New Netherland*, p. 1.

3 'Hurried into New England', Cotton Mather, ibid. P. Ha, *English Presbyterianism, 1590–1640*.

4 'Naturally beautiful...', A. van der Donck, *Remonstrance*, p. 15. Beautiful rivers, bubbling fountains, quote in E.J. Dolin, *Fur, Fortune and Empire*, p. 34. The colony of New Haven was subsumed by surrounding Connecticut in 1665. Connecticut also laid claim to Long Island until 1664, but the claim was strongly resisted by the Dutch.

5 B. Fernow, *Documents relating to the History of the Early Colonial Settlements*, vol. 14, pp. 76, 416.

6 Ibid., p. 26. Ref. to 'Peter the Chimney Sweep' is re: Long Island, ibid., p. 49. D. Denton, *A Brief Description*. B. Bailyn, *The Barbarous Years*, pp. 245–6. Re: protection against the Native Americans, see H.C. Shelley, *John Underhill*, p. 305. The 'superior to all the rest' quote is from Der Donck, *Remonstrance*, p. 17.

7 Fernow, *Documents*, p. 466.

8 S.D. Middleton, *From Privileges to Rights*, p. 11. The Dutch generally knew the Hudson River as the North River. See http://www.ianchadwick.com/hudson/hudson_03.htm

9 American languages lacked a word for drunk: Der Donck, *Description*, p. 76. Wolley, *A Two Years' Journal*, p. 18. 'All lustily drunk', Dankers' and Sluyter's 'Journal', pp. 273–5, cited in Wolley, *A Two Years' Journal*, p. 24. The word 'hoochinoo' did not, as it happened, come from this particular part of America, but the native enthusiasm for alcohol was widespread.

10 'Impertinent fellows', Fernow, *Documents*, p. 120. 'General ruin', ibid., p. 71.

11 Multiculturalism: E. Homberger, *The Historical Atlas of New York City*, p. 28.

12 E.G. Burrows and M. Wallace, *Gotham: A History of New York City to 1898*, p. 70. An attempt was made to anglicise Harlem by renaming it 'Lancaster', though this never took root: M.G. van Rensselaer, *History of the City of New York*, vol. 2, p. 38.

13 'To come and settle', Fernow, *Documents*, p. 76; 'come daily', ibid., pp. 85; 41. 'Dutch neighbours', ibid., pp. 34–5, talking actually of the English on the Connecticut River not in Long Island. Ibid., pp. 85, 109. 'Hand of God' etc., Denton, *A Brief Description of New York*.

14 See Middleton, *From Privileges to Rights*, chapter 1.

15 Fernow, *Documents*, p. 470.

16 Denton, *Brief Description*.

17 Fernow, *Documents*, pp. 469–71.

18 For the tail alone', Thomas Morton, *New English Canaan*, cited in Dolin, *Fur, Fortune and Empire*, p. 15. For the city's and the province's various flags and seals, see: http://blog.nyhistory.org/of-seals-and-rampant-beavers-new-york-citys-flag-on-its-100th-birthday/

19 Dolin, *Fur, Fortune and Empire*, pp. 6–8. 'From beyond the sea', Philip Stubbes, *The Anatomie of Abuses*, quoted in M. Harrison, *History of the Hat*, p. 104.

20 'Great injury' and 'on both sides' from the 1643 'Proclamation of Peace with the Indians', Fernow, *Documents*, pp. 44–5. The phrase 'our enemies' is used often of the Native Americans in Dutch documents. See for instance ibid., p. 54.

21 Collapse of temporary alliance, Shelley, *John Underhill*, pp. 307–24. 'Fools of them', Der Donck, *Remonstrance*, p. 17.

22 Fernow, *Documents*, pp. 79, 106. F.M. Kerr, 'The Reverend Richard Denton and the Coming of the Presbyterians', *New York History*, vol. 21, no. 2 (April 1940), p. 183.

23 Quoted in M.W. Goodwin, *Dutch and English on the Hudson: A Chronicle of Colonial New York*, p. 7.

24 Van Rensselaer, *History*, vol. 1, p. 473.

25 Fernow, *Documents*, pp. 106, 126.

26 Van Rensselaer, *History*, vol. 1, pp. 467, 473, 492, 508. Fernow, *Documents*, p. 454. 'Smokers', Wolley, *A Two Years' Journal* p. 20.

27 Van Rensselaer, *History*, vol. 1, pp. 472, 479. On the decline of class and its maintenance in New England, for instance, see Freeman Hawke, *Everyday Life in Early America*, p. 111.

28 Fernow, *Documents*, pp. 76, 98, 121, 123.

29 Kerr says they built a stockade (ibid., p. 184). Bailyn, *The Barbarous Years*, p. 246. 'High and Mighty Lords', Fernow, *Documents*, p. 24. Ibid., p. 270.

30 Bailyn, *The Barbarous Years*, pp. 245–6. Fernow, *Documents*, p. 85.

31 Der Donck, *A Description of New Netherland*, pp. 65–6. Der Donck refers to 'such an abundance of wood that it will never be wanting', *A Description of New Netherland*, p. 22.

32 Fernow, *Documents*, p. 425. Der Donck, *Description*, p. 68.

33 Fernow, *Documents*, p. 96. Denton, *Brief Description*. Shelley, *John Underhill*, pp. 350–51.

34 Kerr, 'The Reverend Richard Denton', p. 184. Francis J. Bremer, 'Richard Denton', DNB. A longer extract of this quote is in P. Haring Judd (ed.), *Genealogical and Biographical Notes on the Haring-Herring, Clark, Denton, White, Griggs, Judd, and related families*, p. 149. It is notable that disputes between the English at Hempstead and the local Native American communities became more severe after Denton had departed – the latter alleging that what they had sold was the grass, not the land upon which it grew (Fernow, *Documents*, p. 474).

35 Fernow, *Documents*, p. 339.

36 At a village called Hempstead.

37 J.F. Jameson (ed.), *Narratives of New Netherland*, p. 466.

38 Van Rensselaer, *History*, vol. 1, pp. 495–8.

39 Fernow, *Documents*, pp. 295, 506.

40 Van Rensselaer, *History*, vol. 1, pp. 454, 508.

41 Fernow, *Documents*, p. 467. 'Mad for war', quoted in van Rensselaer, *History*, vol. 1, p. 500.

42 Burrows and Wallace, *Gotham*, p. 71.

43 Earthquake quotes and facts, see http://heritagetoronto.org/the-earthquake-of-1663/.

44 Fernow, *Documents*, pp. 534–8; 546, 548. 'Malignant' English, in van Rensselaer, *History*, vol. 1, p. 516.

45 Fernow, *Documents*, p. 553. Van Rensselaer, *History*, vol. 1, pp. 491, 505. 'Great men', Fernow, *Documents*, p. 546. 'Desolate condition', Fernow, *Documents*, p. 542.

46 M. Pennypacker, 'The Duke's Laws: Their Antecedents, Implications and Importance', p. 24.

47 Fernow, *Documents*, p. 555. Denton, *A Brief Description*.

48 Jameson (ed.), *Narratives*, p. 460.

49 Ibid., p. 462.

50 'General ruin', Rev. Samuel Drisius to the Classis of Amsterdam, 15 September 1664, in Jameson (ed.), *Narratives*, pp. 415–16. Burrows and Wallace, *Gotham*, p. 73. 'It has pleased the Lord', Jeremias Van Rensselaer, quoted in Burrows and Wallace, *Gotham*, pp. 78–9.

51 His official report is in Jameson (ed.), *Narratives*, pp. 455–66.

52 Fernow, *Documents*, pp. 570, 574, 581. Van Rensselaer, *History*, vol. 2, p. 12.

53 The cases came to trial at all only by the defendants being charged with murder by witchcraft.

54 S. Saunders Webb, *Lord Churchill's Coup: The Anglo-American Empire and the Glorious Revolution Reconsidered*, p. 27.

55 Fernow, *Documents*, pp. 562, 574.

56 'Six beavers', Wolley, *A Two Years' Journal*, pp. 26, 43. Burrows and Wallace, *Gotham*, p. 84. In general Governor Andros reported that the volume of shipping coming to and from New York around 1680 was 'at least ten times' higher than when he arrived (in 1674).

## *Liberty*

1 'Epidemical and contagious', A. Westwood, *De Variolis & Morbillis: Of the Small Pox and Measles*, p. 6. 'Cruel and impartial', quoted in C. Creighton, *A History of Epidemics in Britain*, vol. 2, p. 463. On the background to the history of smallpox, see D. Shuttleton, *Smallpox and the Literary Imagination 1660–1820* and A.M. Behbehani, 'The Smallpox Story: Life and Death of an Old Disease', *MMBR* vol. 47, no. 4 (December 1983), pp. 455–509 (1 December 1983). 'Florid', 'damask rose', J. Pechey, *Collections of Acute Diseases in Five Parts*, p. 4.

2 '. . . not had this disease already', Pechey, *Collections*, p. 1.

3 W. Penn, *A Further Account of the Province of Pennsylvania and its Improvements*, pp. 18–19. C.O. Peare, *William Penn*, pp. 245–6. Bridenbaugh, *Vexed and Troubled Englishmen*, p. 8.

4 'Mighty lively' in John Aubrey, *Brief Lives: A Selection*, p. 243.

5 M.M. Dunn and R.S. Dunn, *The Papers of William Penn*, vol. 1, pp. 54–5 (letter of George Bishop, 30 November 1667).

6 Aubrey, *Brief Lives: A Selection*, p. 243.

7 Dunn and Dunn, *Papers*, vol. 1, pp. 33–4 (WP to father, 23 April 1665); p. 41 (WP to father, 4 July 1666).

8 Ibid., pp. 59–60.

9 Ibid., p. 43.

10 40,000 in 1660s, Peare, *Penn*, p. 74. 'Our seventh persecution', quoted in D. Harris Sacks, *The Widening Gate*, p. 270.

11 Matthew 5:33–7. 'Kick up the heel', quoted in Sacks, *The Widening Gate*, p. 290.

12 Peare, *Penn*, pp. 66, 75, 109. 'Frantic doctrines', quoted in Sacks, *The Widening*

*Gate*, p. 271. Dunn and Dunn, *Papers*, vol. 1, pp. 68; 73. 'Meeting for Sufferings', M.M. Dunn, *William Penn: Politics and Conscience*, pp. 12, 25.

13 Dunn, *William Penn: Politics and Conscience*, p. 5. S. Porter, *The Plagues of
London*, p. 254.

14 On this case, see B.R. Nager, 'The Jury That Tried William Penn'.

15 Peare, *Penn*, pp. 111, 116 and chapter 7 *passim*.

16 Ibid., pp. 199, 218. Penn, *Further Account*, p. 2; p. 19.

17 Fernow (ed.), *Documents*, pp. 402–3, 492, 515.

18 Peare, *Penn*, pp. 157, 151. Penn's third surviving child, a son named William
after his father, was born on 14 March 1680, but in the Old Style (OS) dating
system used in England and Wales (as well as in the American colonies) until
1752 this still counted as 1679 since the new year started on 25 March.

19 *To the Children of Light in This Generation* (Nov. 1678), quoted in Peare, *Penn*,
p. 202. Many Protestant dissenters, it should be said, insisted that their beliefs,
unlike those of Catholics, should be tolerated because they had no political
significance (Dunn, *William Penn: Politics and Conscience*, p. 28).

20 Peare, *Penn*, p. 169.

21 Ibid., p. 173.

22 Ibid., pp. 209, 211–12, 214–15.

23 D.D. Hall, *The Antinomian Controversy, 1636–1638*, p. 11.

24 There were twenty-one years between them; Anne Hutchinson was born in
1591, Anne Bradstreet in 1612.

25 E.C. Huber, *Women and the Authority of Inspiration*, pp. 78–9.

26 Hall, *The Antinomian Controversy, 1636–1638*, pp. 317–18.

27 It has been suggested that this assault was directly encouraged by the New
England hierarchy: M.J. Lewis, 'Anne Hutchinson', pp. 46–7. Anne had had
fourteen children before she left England and a fifteenth soon followed in
America. 'So savagely', Samuel Gorton in ibid., p. 47.

28 Hall, *Antinomian Controversy*, p. 10.

29 Peare, *Penn*, pp. 223–4.

30 E.B. Bronner, *William Penn's 'Holy Experiment'*, pp. 10–11; 24–6.

31 'The sober . . .'; 'great cruelty', 'officers and commissioners', Bronner, *Holy
Experiment*, pp. 26–7; 36. Peare, *Penn*, p. 263.

32 Before 1700 the settlers in Pennsylvania were 68 per cent English, 10 per cent
Welsh, about 10 per cent Irish, 5 per cent Dutch and Rhenish, along with a
small number of others: Peare, *Penn*, p. 272. Penn, *Further Account*, pp. 2–3.

33 W. Penn, *A Letter from William Penn, Proprietary and Governor of Pennsylvania*

in America, to the Committee of the Free Society of Traders of that Province, residing in London.

34 http://www.olivetreegenealogy.com/ships/tousa_pa.shtml These names are from the *Lamb* arriving in October 1682. Penn, *Further Account*, pp. 2, 20.

35 Bronner, *Holy Experiment*, pp. 31–2.

36 R. Hutton, *Charles II*, p. 407.

37 Bronner, *Holy Experiment*, pp. 15–16.

38 Peare, *Penn*, p. 306.

39 The text of the act is here: www.british-history.ac.uk/statutes-realm/vol6/pp74-76#h2-0010 – see section X for the special declaration acceptable to the Quakers. Also: www.encyclopediavirginia.org/Act_of_Toleration_1689#start_entry

40 Peare, *Penn*, p. 350.

41 Ibid., pp. 359–60.

42 Ibid., pp. 390, 410.

43 Ibid., pp. 413–14.

## *Despair*

1 '. . . frowns of fortune', William Eddis, quoted in A. Emerson Smith, *Colonists in Bondage*, p. 54. '. . . hide our defects', Peter Arundell, quoted in M. Gaskill, *Between Two Worlds*, p. 68. David Cressy suggests a rate of *illiteracy* among men in rural England of 1642–4 of about 70 per cent, with those in the home counties and metropolitan areas 'somewhat better', but even if it was as low as 50 per cent, Furnifull was certainly in the bottom half. Rates for women were markedly lower still. See D. Cressy, 'Literacy in Seventeenth-Century England: More Evidence'.

2 During the eighteenth century Christian – in the wake of John Bunyan's vastly successful book *The Pilgrim's Progress* – became common as a man's name but previously it had tended rather to be feminine. 'Extraordinarily friendly', quoted Emerson Smith, *Colonists in Bondage*, pp. 69–70.

3 'Alacrity and cheerfulness', quoted in Gaskill, *Between Two Worlds*, p. 58. '. . . in a short time', ibid., p. 68.

4 See figures in S.L. Dahlberg, '"Doe Not Forget Me"', p. 1. Sacks, *The Widening Gate*, notes pp. 2, 6. '. . . flourishing condition . . .', W. Bullock, *Virginia Impartially Examined*, p. 63.

5 William Petty in 1662, quoted in R. Porter, *London: A Social History*, p. 69.

6 For 'Dark Entry' etc., see P. Ackroyd, *Thames: Sacred River*, p. 195. Porter, *London: A Social History*, p. 67, notes that around a third of London's population was now settled in its eastern suburbs.

7 *The English Rogue* (1665), quoted in Emerson Smith, *Colonists in Bondage*, pp. 69–70.

8 Emerson Smith, *Colonists in Bondage*, p. 64.

9 Clothes; 'Kept as prisoners', Bullock, *Virginia Impartially Examined*, pp. 36, 39. '...stuffing of their ships...', quoted in Dahlberg, '"Doe Not Forget Me"', p. 22.

10 Quoted in Emerson Smith, *Colonists in Bondage*, p. 85, note 45.

11 J. Cropper Wise, *Col. John Wise of England and Virginia*, pp. 29–30, quoted in A. Games, *Migration and the Origins of the English Atlantic World*, p. 1.

12 Lionel Gatford, quoted in Sacks, *The Widening Gate*, chapter 10.

13 Emerson Smith, *Colonists in Bondage*, pp. 58, 71, 85.

14 '...increased principally...', quoted in ibid., p. 4. Ibid., p. 25. 'Desirous', Sir Edwin Sandys in 1619, quoted in Dahlberg, '"Doe Not Forget Me"', p. 8.

15 See, for instance, J.C. Jeaffreson (ed.), *Middlesex County Records*, vol. 3. Consult the multitude of references in the index under 'kidnap'. 'Lewd subtleties', quoted in S. Christianson, *With Liberty for Some*, p. 14. Bristol quote in Harris Sacks, *The Widening Gate*, chapter 8.

16 'Husbands that have forsaken...', Mayor of Bristol in 1662, quoted in Emerson Smith, *Colonists in Bondage*, pp. 82–3; '...decay'd fortunes', N. Ward, *A Trip to Jamaica*, p. 10; re: John Wise, see Games, *Migration*, p. 1.

17 Bullock, *Virginia Impartially Examined*, p. 44. 'Brutes in foreign parts', *The English Rogue*, quoted in Emerson Smith, *Colonists in Bondage*, pp. 69–70. More than half: Gregory King calculations for 1688, see ibid., p. 43.

18 '...lice of Egypt', quoted in Brooks, *Why We Left*, p. 31.

19 Emerson Smith, *Colonists in Bondage*, p. 44. 'Labouring, and sweating', Bullock, *Virginia Impartially Examined*, pp. 14, 44. 'Beg, filch, and steal', quoted in Bridenbaugh, *Vexed and Troubled Englishmen*, p. 378. 'Many died in the streets', quoted in A.B. Appleby, *Famine in Tudor and Stuart England*, p. 152; other harvest failures, ibid., p. 155. Also see Craven, *White, Red and Black*, p. 20. Food riots 1586–1631: Brooks, *Why We Left*, p. 30.

20 J. Walter, *Crowds and Popular Politics in Early Modern England*, p. 69.

21 'Heap of troubles', quoted in Freeman Hawke, *Everyday Life in Early America*, p. 4. Quoted in Bridenbaugh, *Vexed and Troubled Englishmen*, p. 361.

22 Alsop, *A Character of the Province of Maryland*, pp. 60, 63.

23 Alsop, *A Character of the Province of Maryland*, p 86.

24 Might 'amend their estates', Sir George Peckham. Heirs 'forever more', Emerson Smith, *Colonists in Bondage*, p. 9.

25 Ibid., pp. 17, 58–9.

26 'Superfluous multitude'; 'misery and ruin', quoted in Christianson, *With Liberty for Some*, p. 11. 'Many ships', quoted in Brooks, *Why We Left*, p. 37. 'Starving in the streets', '... best deeds', John Chamberlain to Sir Dudley Carleton, quoted in Dahlberg, '"Doe Not Forget Me"', p. 9.

27 Emerson Smith, *Colonists in Bondage*, pp. 12–13. Bullock, *Virginia Impartially Examined*, p. 61.

28 When testimony was given shortly afterwards of 'spirits' in London they included a shoemaker, a waterman, a haberdasher, a brewer's servant and numerous others. Often these people were despatching many hundreds of people every year. But few, nevertheless, made their whole living by the trade: Emerson Smith, *Colonists in Bondage*, p. 74.

29 J. Hammond, *Leah and Rachel, or the two fruitfull Sisters of Virginia and Maryland*, p. 7. This is, in general, to be fair, an honest and reliable account.

30 Frethorne, 20 March 1623.

31 Alsop, *A Character of the Province of Maryland*, pp. 55, 62, 96. 'Bitter storms and tempests', in 'Neptune's Raging Fury', Penny Merriments: Street Songs of 17th Century England: http://www.naxos.com/sharedfiles/PDF/8.557672_sungtext.pdf. 'One blow', Alsop, *A Character of the Province of Maryland*, pp. 55, 62.

32 '... such beams of lightning ...', Ward, *A Trip to Jamaica*, p. 12; 'wild vomits', quoted in Bridenbaugh, *Vexed and Troubled Englishmen*, p. 6; 'Some sleeping, some spewing', Emerson Smith, *Colonists in Bondage*, p. 215.

33 One witness recalled seeing a convict – 'this poor man' – 'chained to a board in a hole not above 16 feet long, more than 50 with him; a collar and padlock about his neck, and chained to five of the most dreadful creatures I ever looked upon': Christianson, *With Liberty for Some*, p. 27.

34 Ibid., pp. 36–7. 'Worser lives', Richard Ligon, quoted in M. Parker, *The Sugar Barons*, pp. 61–2 (though, as Parker notes, the claim was not supported by Ligon's own evidence; it is fair to say that either fate, in most cases, was diabolical). Ligon's *True and Exact History of the Island of Barbadoes* was published in 1657.

35 Emerson Smith, *Colonists in Bondage*, p. 34. Native communities 'apter', quoted in Morgan, *American Slavery*, p. 99.

36 '. . . disease of their mind', George Thorpe, quoted in Gaskill, *Between Two Worlds*, p. 58.

37 '. . . applause', Dahlberg, '"Doe Not Forget Me"', p. 10.

38 Ibid., p. 18.

39 Henry Brigg, quoted in ibid., p. 18. Smith quoted in Freeman Hawke, *Everyday Life in Early America*, p. 14. 'Base all over' etc., quote of John Baldwin, 1623, cited in Brooks, *Why We Left*, p. 11.

40 Gaskill, *Between Two Worlds*, p. 57.

41 Dahlberg, '"Doe Not Forget Me"', p. 21. Houses: 'continual repairs', see quote in Morgan, *American Slavery*, p. 112.

42 Morgan, *American Slavery*, pp. 101, 104, 122, 126.

43 7 per cent, Brooks, *Why We Left*, p. 40.

44 Smith, *Description of New England*, p. 348, quoted in ibid., p. 8. '. . . cony-skinners, or tinkers', Bridenbaugh, *Vexed and Troubled Englishmen*, p. 386; '[city] of refuge', ibid., p. 403, in Michael Sparke's *Grievous Grones for the Poor*.

45 Intolerable oppression', Nathaniel Rich, quoted in Dahlberg, '"Doe Not Forget Me"', p. 23. 'All occasion', quoted in Morgan, *American Slavery*, p. 97.

46 Charles Davenant, quoted in P.J. Stern and C. Wennerlind (eds), *Mercantilism Reimagined: Political Economy in Early Modern Britain and its Empire*, p. 62.

47 Quoted in Emerson Smith, *Colonists in Bondage*, pp. 28–9.

## Conclusion

1 '. . . learn to dance', quoted in Freeman Hawke, *Everyday Life in Early America*, p. 4. 'Distracted nation', Games, *Migration*, p. 6.

2 Carl Bridenbaugh, quoted in Freeman Hawke, *Everyday Life in Early America*, pp. 73; 22.

3 Games, *Migration*, p. 7.

4 It was only really in the case of the Africans that North America was, in the short term, a true 'melting pot', because they were not permitted to settle with their own kind – by masters who were blind to the cultural differences: not permitted to continue speaking the language with which they were familiar, or to be immersed in the same culture.

# BIBLIOGRAPHY

## *Primary*

Alsop, G., *A Character of the Province of Maryland* (ed. J. G. Shea) (New York: William Gowans, 1869).

Aubrey, J., *Brief Lives* (ed. A. Clark) (Oxford: Clarendon Press, 1898).

Aubrey, J., *Brief Lives: A Selection Based upon Existing Contemporary Portraits* (London: The Folio Society, 1975, 1996).

Barbour, P., *The Jamestown Voyages under the First Charter 1606–1609: Documents relating to the foundation of Jamestown and the history of the Jamestown colony up to the departure of Captain John Smith, 1609* (2 vols, London: published for the Hakluyt Society by Cambridge University Press, 1969).

Barbour, P. (ed.), *The Complete Works of Captain John Smith (1580–1631)* (3 vols, Chapel Hill, N.C.; London: University of North Carolina Press, 1986).

Berkeley, W., *A Discourse and View of Virginia* (Norwalk, Conn.: W. H. Smith Jr, 1914).

Bradford, W., *Of Plymouth Plantation* (ed. S.E. Morison) (New York: Knopf, 1953).

Brown, A., *Genesis of the United States* (New York: Russell & Russell, 1964).

Bullock, W., *Virginia Impartially Examined* (London: John Hammond, 1649).

Calendar of State Papers:

M.A.E. Green (ed.), *Calendar of State Papers: Domestic Series, of the Reign of James I. 1603–1610; 1611–1618; 1619–1623; 1623–1625 (London: for HMSO, by Longman, Green, Longman & Roberts, 1857–9).*

J. Bruce (ed.), *Calendar of State Papers: Domestic Series, of the Reign of Charles I. 1625–1626; 1627–1628; etc. (London: for HMSO, by Longman, Green, Longman & Roberts, 1859–69).*

W. Noel Sainsbury (ed.), *Calendar of State Papers: Colonial Series, 1574–1660 [America & West Indies] (London: for HMSO, by Longman, Green, Longman & Roberts, 1860).*

W. Noel Sainsbury (ed.), *Calendar of State Papers: Colonial Series: vol. 9,*

*1675–1676 [America and West Indies] and Addenda 1574–1674* (London: for HMSO, by Longman, Green, Longman & Roberts, 1893).

H.F. Brown (ed.), *Calendar of State Papers and Manuscripts Relating to English Affairs, Existing in the Archives and Collections of Venice and in Other Libraries of Northern Italy, vol. 11, 1607–1610* (London: for HMSO, by Mackie & Co. Ltd, 1904).

Camden, W., *Annales Rerum Gestarum Angliae et Hiberniae Regnante Elizabetha:* see the online edition at http://www.philological.bham.ac.uk/camden/

Cell, G.T. (ed.), *Newfoundland Discovered: English Attempts at Colonisation, 1610–1630* (London: Hakluyt Society, 1982).

Cushman, R., *The Sin and Danger of Self-Love Described, in a sermon preached at Plymouth, in New England, 1621* (New York: J.E.D. Comstock, 1847).

Dankers, J. and Sluyter, P., *Journal of a voyage to New York and a tour in several of the American Colonies in 1679–80* (New York: Charles Scribner's Sons, 1913).

Denton, D., *A Brief Description of New-York: formerly called New-Netherlands* (New York: William Gowans, 1845).

Dunn, M.M. and Dunn, R.S. (eds), *The Papers of William Penn* (Philadelphia, Pa.: University of Pennsylvania Press, 1981–7).

Fea, A., *Memoirs of the Martyr King: Being a detailed record of the last two years of the reign of his most sacred majesty King Charles the First* (London and New York: John Lane, 1905): in particular, 'Tract IV: the Narrative of Sir John Berkeley'.

Fernow, B. (ed.), *Documents relating to the History of the Early Colonial Settlements principally on Long Island* (Albany, N.Y.: Weed, Parsons & Co., 1883).

Hakluyt, R., *The Principal Navigations, Voyages, Traffiques & Discoveries of the English Nation* (12 vols, Glasgow: James Maclehose & Sons, 1903).

Hammond, J., *Leah and Rachel, or the two fruitfull Sisters of Virginia and Maryland* (London: T. Mabb, 1656).

Hamor, R., *A True Discourse of the Present State of Virginia* (London: J. Beale for W. Welby, 1615).

Heath, D.B. (ed.), *A Journal of the Pilgrims at Plymouth. Mourt's Relation, a relation or journal of the English plantation settled at Plymouth in New England* (New York: Corinth Books, 1963).

Hensley, J. (ed.), *Works of Anne Bradstreet* (Cambridge, Mass.: Belknap Press of Harvard University Press, 1967).

Hitchcock, R., *A Politique Platt for the honour of the Prince, the greate profite of the publique state, relief of the poore, preservation of the riche, reformation of Roges and idle persones, and the wealthe of thousands that knows not how to live, etc.* (London: Ihon Kyngston, 1580).

Hutchinson, L., *Memoirs of the Life of Colonel Hutchinson* (Cambridge: Cambridge University Press, 2010).

James I, *The Essayes of a Prentise, in the Divine Art of Poesie: A Counterblast to Tobacco* (London: Edward Arber, 1869).

Jameson, J.F. (ed.), *Narratives of New Netherland, 1609–1664* (New York: Barnes & Noble, 1959).

Jeaffreson, J.C. (ed.), *Middlesex County Records*, vol. 3 (Clerkenwell: Middlesex County Records Society, 1888).

Ligon, R., *A True and Exact History of the Island of Barbados* (ed. K.O. Kupperman) (Indianapolis, Ind.: Hackett Publishing, 2011).

Mather, C., *The Great Works of Christ in America (Magnalia Christi Americana)* (2 vols, Edinburgh: The Banner of Truth Trust, 1979).

Moryson, F., *An Itinerary* (Amsterdam: Theatrum Orbis Terrarum; New York: Da Capo Press, 1971).

Norwood, H., *A Voyage to Virginia*, vol. 6 of *A Collection of Voyages and Travels, some now first printed from Original Manuscripts, others now first published in English in Six Volumes . . .* (London: Henry Lintot, 1746).

Pepys, S., *Diary* (London: The Folio Society, 1996); the text is also reproduced by an excellent website: www.pepysdiary.com.

Penn, W., *A Letter from William Penn, Proprietary and Governor of Pennsylvania in America, to the Committee of the Free Society of Traders of that Province, residing in London* (London: Andrew Sowle, 1683).

Penn, W., *A Further Account of the Province of Pennsylvania and its Improvements* (London: s.n., 1685).

Pettus, J., *The Laws of Art and Nature in Knowing, Judging, Assaying, Fining, Refining and Inlarging the Bodies of Confin'd Metals* (London: s.n., 1683).

Purchas, S., *Hakluytus Posthumus or Purchas his Pilgrimes* (20 vols, Glasgow: James Maclehose & Sons, 1905).

Quinn, D.B. (ed.), *The Voyages and Colonising Enterprises of Sir Humphrey Gilbert* (London: Hakluyt Society, 1940).

Raithby, J., *The Statutes Relating to the Admiralty, Navy, Shipping, and Navigation of the United Kingdom, from 9 Hen. III to 3 Geo. IV inclusive* (London: G. Eyre & A. Strahan, 1823).

Rich, B., *The Honestie of this Age* (London: T.A., 1614).

Rolfe, J., *A True Relation of the State of Virginia lefte by Sir Thomas Dale Knight in May last 1616 . . .* (New Haven, Conn.: Yale University Press, 1951).

Rowse, A.L. (ed.), *The First Colonists: Hakluyt's Voyages to North America: A Modern Version* (London: The Folio Society, 1986).

Sainsbury, W.N. et al. (eds), 'Virginia in 1650 (Continued)', *The Virginia Magazine of History and Biography*, vol. 17, no. 2 (April 1909), pp. 133–46.

Schofield, B. (ed.), *The Knyvett Letters, 1620–1644* (London: Constable & Co., 1949).

Sparke, A., *Greevous Grones for the Poore. Done by a Well-willer, who wisheth, That the poore of England might be so provided for, as none should neede to go a begging within this Realme* (London, 1621).

Van der Donck, A., *Remonstrance of New Netherland, and the occurrences there addressed to the High and Mighty Lords States General of the United Netherlands, on the 28th July, 1649* (ed. and trans. by E.B. O' Callaghan) (Albany, N.Y.: s.n., 1856).

Van der Donck, A., *A Description of New Netherland* (eds C.T. Gehring, W.A. Starna, D.W. Goedhuys and R. Shorto) (Lincoln, Neb.: University of Nebraska Press, 2008).

Various, *The Geneva Bible: A Facsimile of the 1560 Edition* (introduction by L.E. Barry) (Madison, Wis.; London: University of Wisconsin Press, 1969).

Warburton, E., *Memoirs of Prince Rupert, and the Cavaliers: including their private correspondence, now first published from the original manuscripts* (London: R. Bentley, 1849).

Ward, E., *A Trip to Jamaica: with a true character of the people and island* (London: s.n., 1698).

Ward, E., *The London Spy. By the author of the Trip to Jamaica* (London: J. Nutt, 1698–9).

Westwood, A., *De Variolis & Morbillis: of the small pox and measles, with their definitions … prognosticks, and cures, etc.* (London, 1656).

Whitbourne, R., *A Discourse and Discovery of New-found-land* (Amsterdam: Theatrum Orbis Terrarum; New York: Da Capo Press, 1971).

Winthrop, J., *The Journal of John Winthrop, 1630–1649* (eds Richard S. Dunn, James Savage and Laetitia Yeandle) (Cambridge, Mass.; London: The Belnap Press of Harvard University Press, 1996).

Wolley, C., *A Two Years' Journal in New York and part of its territories in America … Reprinted from the original edition of 1701* (ed. E.G. Bourne) (Cleveland, Ohio: Burrows Bros Co., 1902).

## *Secondary*

Ackroyd, P., *Thames: Sacred River* (London: Vintage, 2008).

Altman, I. and Horn, J. (eds), *'To Make America': European Emigration in the Early Modern Period* (Berkeley, Cal.; Oxford: University of California Press, 1991).

Anderson, V.D., *New England's Generation: The Great Migration and the Formation of Society and Culture in the 17th Century* (Cambridge: Cambridge University Press, 1991).

Andrews, K.R., *Elizabethan Privateering: English Privateering during the Spanish War, 1585–1603* (Cambridge: Cambridge University Press, 1964).

Appleby, A.B., *Famine in Tudor and Stuart England* (Stanford, Cal.: Stanford University Press, 1978).

Bailyn, B., *The Barbarous Years: The Conflict of Civilizations, 1600–1675* (New York: Vintage Books, 2013).

Bangs, J.D., *Pilgrim Edward Winslow: New England's First International Diplomat; A Documentary Biography* (Boston, Mass.: New England Historic Genealogical Society, 2004).

Banks, C.E., *The Winthrop Fleet of 1630: An Account of the Vessels, the Passengers and their English Homes from Original Authorities* (Baltimore, Md.: Genealogical Publishing Co., 1976)

Barratt, J., *The Royalist Army at War, 1642–1646* (Stroud: Sutton Publishing & Co., 2000).

Barratt, J., *Sieges of the English Civil Wars* (Barnsley: Pen & Sword Military, 2009).

Billings, W., *Sir William Berkeley and the Forging of Colonial Virginia* (Baton Rouge, La.: Louisiana State University Press, 2004).

Billings, W., Selby, J.E. and Tate, T.W. (eds), *Colonial Virginia: A History* (White Plains, N.Y.: KTO Press, 1986).

Bolster, W., *The Mortal Sea: Fishing the Atlantic in the Age of Sail* (Cambridge, Mass.; London: Belknap Press of Harvard University Press, 2012).

Brandt, A.M., *The Cigarette Century: The Rise, Fall and Deadly Persistence of the Product that Defined America* (New York: Basic Books, 2007).

Brenner, F.J., *Puritanism: A Very Short Introduction* (New York; Oxford: Oxford University Press, 2009).

Brenner, F.J., *Puritan Crisis: New England and the English Civil Wars, 1630–1670* (New York: Garland, 1989).

Bridenbaugh, C., *Vexed and Troubled Englishmen, 1590–1642* (Oxford: Clarendon Press, 1968).

Brogan, H., *The Penguin History of the United States of America* (London: Penguin Books, 1990).

Bronner, E.B., *William Penn's 'Holy Experiment': The Founding of Pennsylvania, 1681–1701* (New York: Columbia University Press, 1962).

Brooks, J., *Why We Left: Untold Stories and Songs of America's First Immigrants* (Minneapolis, Minn.: University of Minnesota Press, 2013).

Bunker, N., *Making Haste from Babylon: The Mayflower Pilgrims and Their World: A New History* (London: The Bodley Head, 2010).

Burrows, E.G. and Wallace, M., *Gotham: A History of New York City to 1898* (New York; Oxford: Oxford University Press, 1999).

Callam, G., *The Norwoods III: A Chronological History* (Bexhill-on-Sea: G. Marion Norwood Callam, 1997).

Cannadine, D. (ed.), *Oxford Dictionary of National Biography* (Oxford: Oxford University Press, 2004).

Cell, G.T., *English Enterprise in Newfoundland, 1577–1660* (Toronto & Buffalo, N.Y.: University of Toronto Press, 1969).

Christianson, S., *With Liberty for Some: 500 Years of Imprisonment in America* (Boston, Mass.: Northeastern University Press, 1998).

Coldham, P.W., *The Complete Book of Emigrants: 1607–1660* (Baltimore, Md.: Genealogical Publishing, 1987).

Craven, W.F., *White, Red and Black: The Seventeenth-Century Virginian* (Charlottesville, Va.: University Press of Virginia, 1971).

Creighton, C., *A History of Epidemics in Britain from A.D. 664 to the Extinction of Plague* (Cambridge: Cambridge University Press, 1891).

Day, J., *Gloucester and Newbury 1643: The Turning Point of the Civil War* (Barnsley: Pen & Sword, 2007).

Dexter, H.M. and Dexter, M., *The England and Holland of the Pilgrims* (Boston, Mass.; New York: Houghton, Mifflin & Co., 1905).

Dolin, E.J., *Fur, Fortune and Empire: The Epic History of the Fur Trade in America* (New York; London: W.W. Norton & Co., 2010).

Dunn, M.M., *William Penn: Politics and Conscience* (Princeton, N.J.: Princeton University Press, 1967).

Elliott, J.H., *The Old World and the New, 1492–1650* (Cambridge; New York etc.: Cambridge University Press, original edition 1970, this Canto reprint 1992).

Elliott Hoskins, S., *Charles the Second in the Channel Islands: a contribution to his biography and to the history of his age* (London: s.n., 1854).

Emerson Smith, A., *Colonists in Bondage: White Servitude and Convict Labor in America, 1607–1776* (Chapel Hill, N.C.: University of North Carolina Press, 1947).

Fagan, B., *Fish on Friday: Feasting, Fasting and the Discovery of the New World* (New York: Basic Books, 2006).

Fernández-Armesto, F., *Columbus on Himself* (London: The Folio Society, 1992).

Freeman Hawke, D., *Everyday Life in Early America* (New York: Perennial Library, 1989).

Games, A., *Migration and the Origins of the English Atlantic World* (Cambridge, Mass.; London: Harvard University Press, 1999).

Gardiner, S.R., *History of the Great Civil War, 1642–1649* (4 vols, Gloucestershire: The Windrush Press, 1991).

Gaskill, M., *Between Two Worlds: How the English Became Americans* (Oxford: Oxford University Press, 2014).

Goodwin, M.W., *Dutch and English on the Hudson: A Chronicle of Colonial New York* (New Haven, Conn.: Yale University Press, 1921).

Ha, P., *English Presbyterianism, 1590–1640* (Stanford, Cal.: Stanford University Press, 2011).

Hackett Fischer, D., *Albion's Seed: Four British Folkways in America* (New York: Oxford University Press, 1989).

Hall, D.D., *The Antinomian Controversy, 1636–1638: A Documentary History* (Middletown, Conn.: Wesleyan University Press, 1968).

Haring Judd, P. (ed.), *More lasting than brass: a thread of family from revolutionary New York to industrial Connecticut, by Peter Haring Judd, members of the Haring, Herring, Clark, Denton, Phelps, White, Griggs, Judd and related families* (Boston, Mass.; Newbury Street Press and Northeastern University Press, 2004).

Harris, T., *Restoration: Charles II and his Kingdoms, 1660–1685* (London: Penguin Books, 2006).

Harris, T., *Revolution: The Great Crisis of the British Monarchy, 1685–1720* (London: Allen Lane, 2006).

Harris, T., *Rebellion: Britain's First Stuart Kings, 1567–1642* (Oxford: Oxford University Press, 2014).

Harris Sacks, D., *The Widening Gate: Bristol and the Atlantic Economy, 1450–1700* (Berkeley, Cal.; Oxford: University of California Press, 1991).

Harrison, M., *The History of the Hat* (London: Herbert Jenkins, 1960).

Homberger, E., *The Historical Atlas of New York City* (New York: Henry Holt & Co., 1994).

Huber, E.C., *Women and the Authority of Inspiration: A Re-examination of Two*

*Prophetic Movements from a Contemporary Feminist Perspective* (Lanham, Md.: University Press of America, 1985).

Hunt, A., *The Art of Hearing: English Preachers and their Audiences, 1590–1640* (Cambridge: Cambridge University Press, 2010).

Hutton, R., *Charles II King of England, Scotland, and Ireland* (Oxford: Clarendon Press, 1989).

Hutton, R., *The Restoration: A Political and Religious History of England and Wales, 1658–1667* (Oxford; New York: Oxford University Press, 1987; 1990).

Irving, L., *Arctic Life of Birds and Mammals: Including Man* (Berlin: Springer, 1972).

Jaffe, S.H., *New York at War: Four Centuries of Combat, Fear, and Intrigue in Gotham* (New York: Basic Books, 2012).

Kishlansky, M., *A Monarchy Transformed: Britain 1603–1714* (London: Penguin Books, 1997).

Kurlansky, M., *Cod: A Biography of the Fish that Changed the World* (London: Vintage, 1999).

Mattingly, G., *The Defeat of the Spanish Armada* (London: The Folio Society, 2002).

McManis, D.R., *European Impressions of the New England Coast, 1497–1620* (Chicago, Ill.: University of Chicago Press, 1972).

McNally, D., *Political Economy and the Rise of Capitalism: A Reinterpretation* (Berkeley, Cal.; London: University of California Press, 1988).

Middleton, S.D., *From Privileges to Rights: Work and Politics in Colonial New York City* (Philadelphia, Pa.: University of Pennsylvania Press, 2006).

Morgan, E.S., *American Slavery, American Freedom: The Ordeal of Colonial Virginia* (New York: W.W. Norton, 1975).

Morison, S.E., *Builders of the Bay Colony* (Cambridge: The Riverside Press, 1930).

Morison, S.E., *The European Discovery of America: The Northern Voyages A.D. 500–1600* (New York: Oxford University Press, 1971).

Morison, S.E., *The European Discovery of America: The Southern Voyages, A.D. 1492–1616* (New York: Oxford University Press, 1974).

Morton, R.L., *Colonial Virginia* (Chapel Hill, N.C.: for the Virginia Historical Society by the University of North Carolina Press, 1960).

Nicholl, C., *The Creature in the Map: Sir Walter Raleigh's Quest for El Dorado* (London: Vintage, 1996).

Pagden, A., *Peoples and Empires: Europeans and the Rest of the World, from Antiquity to the Present* (London: Phoenix, 2002).

Parker, M., *The Sugar Barons* (London: Windmill, 2012).

Peare, C.O., *William Penn: A Biography* (London: Dennis Dobson, 1959).

Pechey, J., *Collections of Acute Diseases in Five Parts* (London: Licentiate of the College of Physicians, 1691).

Penrose, B., *Travel and Discovery in the Renaissance* (London: The Folio Society, 2001).

Pope, P.E., *Fish Into Wine: The Newfoundland Plantation in the Seventeenth Century* (Chapel Hill, N.C. and London: University of North Carolina Press, 2004).

Porter, R., *London: A Social History* (London: Penguin Books, 2000).

Porter, S., *The Plagues of London* (Stroud: History Press, 2008).

Porter, S., *The Great Plague of London* (Stroud: Amberley, 2012).

Price, D.A., *Love and Hate in Jamestown: John Smith, Pocahontas, and the Heart of a New Nation* (London: Faber, 2005).

Purkiss, D., *The English Civil War: A People's History* (London; New York; Toronto; Sydney: Harper Perennial, 2007).

Quinn, D.B., *England and the Discovery of America, 1481–1620* (London: George Allen & Unwin, 1974).

Quinn, D.B. (ed.), *The Hakluyt Handbook* (London: Hakluyt Society, 1974).

Richards, E., *Britannia's Children: Emigration from England, Scotland, Wales and Ireland since 1600* (London; New York: Hambledon, 2004).

Roberts, K., *First Newbury 1643: The Turning Point* (Oxford: Osprey, 2003).

Rowse, A.L., *The England of Elizabeth* (London: The Reprint Society, by arrangement with Macmillan & Co., 1953).

Saunders Webb, S., *Lord Churchill's Coup: The Anglo-American Empire and the Glorious Revolution Reconsidered* (New York: Knopf, 1995).

Shelley, H.C., *John Underhill: Captain of New England and New Netherland* (New York; London: D. Appleton & Co., 1932).

Shorto, R., *Amsterdam: A History of the World's Most Liberal City* (London: Little, Brown, 2013).

Sherwood, R.E., *The Civil War in the Midlands, 1642–1651* (Stroud: Sutton, 1992).

Shrewsbury, J.F.D., *A History of Bubonic Plague in the British Isles* (London: Cambridge University Press, 1970).

Shuttleton, D., *Smallpox and the Literary Imagination 1660–1820* (Cambridge: Cambridge University Press, 2007).

Smith, D.L and McElligott, J. (eds), *Royalists and Royalism during the English Civil Wars* (Cambridge: Cambridge University Press, 2007).

Smith, G., *The Cavaliers in Exile, 1640–1660* (Basingstoke: Palgrave Macmillan, 2003).

Stern, P.J. and Wennerlind, C. (eds), *Mercantilism Reimagined: Political Economy in Early Modern Britain and its Empire* (New York: Oxford University Press, 2013).

Stubbs, J., *Reprobates: The Cavaliers of the English Civil War* (London: Penguin Books, 2012).

Taylor, A., *American Colonies: The Settling of North America* (New York, London etc.: Penguin Books, 2002).

Thernstrom, S. (ed.), *Harvard Encyclopedia of American Ethnic Groups* (Cambridge, Mass.; London: Belknap Press of Harvard University Press, 1981).

Tinniswood, A., *The Rainborowes: Pirates, Puritans and a Family's Quest for the Promised Land* (London: Jonathan Cape, 2013).

Tinniswood, A., *By Permission of Heaven: The Story of the Great Fire of London* (London: Pimlico, 2004).

Tomlins, C.L., *Freedom Bound: Law, Labor, and Civic Identity in Colonizing English America, 1580–1865* (Cambridge: Cambridge University Press, 2010).

Underdown, D.E., *Royalist Conspiracy in England, 1649–1660* (Hamden, Conn.: Archon, 1971).

Van Rensselaer, M.G., *History of the City of New York in the Seventeenth Century* (New York: Macmillan Co., 1909).

Walter, J., *Crowds and Popular Politics in Early Modern England* (Manchester: Manchester University Press, 2006).

Webster, T., *Godly Clergy in Early Stuart England: The Caroline Puritan Movement c.1620–1643* (Cambridge: Cambridge University Press, 1997).

Whitbourne, R., *Crosses & Comforts: Being the Life and Times of Captain Sir Richard Whitbourne (1561–1635) of Exmouth in Devonshire* (St John's, Newfoundland: Great Auk Books, 2005).

Wooldridge, W.C., *Mapping Virginia: From the Age of Exploration to the Civil War* (Charlottesville, Va.: University of Virginia Press; London: Eurospan, 2012).

Woolley, B., *Savage Kingdom: The True Story of Jamestown, 1607, and the Settlement of America* (New York: HarperCollins, 2007).

Worden, B., *The English Civil Wars, 1640–1660* (London: Phoenix, 2009).

Zahedieh, N., *The Capital and the Colonies: London and the Atlantic Economy, 1660–1700* (Cambridge: Cambridge University Press, 2010).

Zakai, A., *Exile and Kingdom: History and Apocalypse in the Puritan Migration to America* (Cambridge: Cambridge University Press, 1992).

## Articles / Chapters

Andrews, K.R., 'Christopher Newport of Limehouse, Mariner', *The William and Mary Quarterly*, vol. 11, no. 1 (January 1954), pp. 28–41.

Behbehani, A.M., 'The Smallpox Story: Life and Death of an Old Disease', *MMBR*, vol. 47, no. 4 (December 1983), pp. 455–509.

Childs, W. and Kowaleski, M., 'Fishing and Fisheries in the Middle Ages', pp. 19–28, in D.J. Starkey, C. Reid and N. Ashcroft (eds), *England's Sea Fisheries: The Commercial Sea Fisheries of England and Wales since 1300* (London: Chatham, 2000).

Collinson, P., 'The Jacobean Religious Settlement: the Hampton Court Conference', in H. Tomlinson (ed.), *Before the English Civil War* (London: Macmillan, 1983), pp. 27–51.

Cressy, D., 'Literacy in Seventeenth-Century England: More Evidence', *The Journal of Interdisciplinary History*, vol. 8, no. 1 (Summer 1977), pp. 141–50.

Dahlberg, S.L., '"Doe Not Forget Me": Richard Frethorne, Indentured Servitude, and the English Poor Law of 1601', *Early American Literature*, vol. 47, no. 1 (2012), pp. 1–30.

Auriol Jenstad, J., '"The Gouldesmythes Storehowse": Early Evidence for Specialisation', *The Silver Society Journal*, vol. 10 (1998), pp. 40–43.

Hadfield, A., 'Peter Martyr, Richard Eden and the New World: Reading, Experience and Translation', *Connotations*, vol. 5, no. 1 (1995–6), pp. 1–22.

Hardacre, P.H., 'The Further Adventures of Henry Norwood', *The Virginia Magazine of History and Biography*, vol. 66, pp. 271–83.

Hunt, J.G., 'William Brewster, Gent., of Virginia', *The Virginia Magazine of History and Biography*, vol. 75, no. 4 (October 1967), pp. 407–9.

Kerr, F.M., 'The Reverend Richard Denton and the Coming of the Presbyterians', *New York History*, vol. 21, no. 2 (April 1940), pp. 180–86.

Lewis, M.J., 'Anne Hutchinson', in G.J. Barker-Benfield and C. Clinton (eds), *Portraits of American Women from Settlement to the Present* (New York; London: Oxford University Press, 1998), pp. 46–7.

Nager, B.R., 'The Jury That Tried William Penn', *American Bar Association Journal*, vol. 50, no. 2 (February 1964), pp. 168–70.

Peacey, J.T., 'Order and Disorder in Europe: Parliamentary Agents and Royalist Thugs 1649–1650', *The Historical Journal*, vol. 40, no. 4 (December 1997), pp. 953–76.

Pennypacker, M.,'The Duke's Laws: Their Antecedents, Implications and Import-ance', *Anglo-American Legal History Series*, series 1, no. 9 (1944), pp. 1–64.

Purkiss, D., 'The English Civil War and Male Identity', in C.J. Summers and T.-L. Pebworth (eds), *The English Civil Wars in the Literary Imagination* (Columbia; London: University of Missouri Press, 1999), pp. 220–41.

Sachse, W.L., 'The Migration of New Englanders to England, 1640–1660', *The American Historical Review*, vol. 53, no. 2 (January 1948), pp. 251–78.

Thornbury, W., 'The Royal Exchange', in *Old and New London: Volume 1* (London, 1878), pp. 494–513.

Trye, J.H., 'Colonel Henry Norwood of Leckhampton, Co. Gloucester', in *Transactions of the Bristol and Gloucester Archaeological Society*, vol. 47 (1926), pp. 113–21.

# ACKNOWLEDGEMENTS

I am not an emigrant myself. I was born in the county of Surrey, and now live in London. It is true that in seventeenth-century terms the two places are some distance apart. (Even now, a photo taken in 1995 hangs upon our wall of an old lady from southern Surrey who lived there, in the country, for almost a century, without ever travelling further than the eight miles to Guildford, and to whom the capital city was a strange and distant world.) But plenty did make the journey, of course, as well as very much longer ones, as this book shows.

During the past couple of years, moreover, migration has been regularly in the news. Thousands of men, women and children have been – and are – compelled to leave their homes, particularly in the Middle East, to head, often, for what seem relative havens in Europe. The risks they have been obliged to take, and their personal stories when one hears them, are regularly horrific. For an affluent country like modern Britain, it is *immigration* that has become a permanent subject of interest: a powerful theme during the recent referendum upon membership of the European Union. It is difficult to imagine now that people, not so long ago, were far more likely to want to leave the place than they were to enter it.

Meanwhile, in the modern United States of America – a country built upon the promise of opportunity for all, wherever they should have originated – a president has been elected promising the construction along one border of a physical barrier to unrestricted immigration, with strict limits on entry at other points. This was the divisive political background as I looked in depth at years when the English in particular crossed the Atlantic Ocean in what then were vast numbers: at years when it was the English who were less inclined to worry about immigrants than they were to be emigrants themselves.

ACKNOWLEDGEMENTS

I am indebted to my former editor at Weidenfeld & Nicolson, Bea Hemming, for honing the original idea, as well as, of course, to Alan Samson, my editor there now. I am in no doubt at all that the latter has significantly improved my text with his intelligent and perceptive observations. I am indebted to my excellent copy editor, Linden Lawson, for picking up any number of small inconsistencies or repetitions which I had failed to notice. And I am indebted too to my agent, Jo Cantello, who has encouraged me as a writer from the outset, and who has also read and offered very useful comments upon early drafts of this book.

My father has often been the first reader of preliminary versions of the text, and I am enormously grateful for his comments as well as for his general wisdom and advice. More fundamentally, I am immensely thankful to both my parents for providing – from love, kindness as well as from good fortune – the warm and stable home from which I had the inestimable luxury of being free to leave, or to stay, as I chose.

Most of all I dedicate this book to my own family – to my wife, Nicola, who has been loving and supportive throughout, and to my three children. I might not, thus far, have been obliged to live in distant places, but I can say quite honestly that I would be happy to emigrate anywhere (within the bounds of responsible parenting) provided that they came with me.

# INDEX

Acosta, José de, 58–9
Acts of Indulgence (1687), 232
agriculture, 7, 46, 246
alcohol, 176, 226–7
America, 2, 3, 5–8, 266–7
    and John Cabot, 16–17
    and death rates, 268–9
    and England, 26–7, 270–1
    and France, 234, 235
    and indentured labour, 237–9, 243,
        247–50
    and 'Pilgrim Fathers', 112–14
    and population growth, 269–70
    and precious metals, 65–8
    and Puritans, 127–31
    and Quakers, 215–18
    see also colonies; New England;
        Pennsylvania; United States of
        America; Virginia
Amsterdam, 106–8
Anglo-Spanish War, 68, 69; see also
    Armada
animals, 45
anti-Catholics, 4
Appalachians, 60
Armada, 28, 37–8, 52
Asia, 2, 3, 16, 26
Assembly, the, 227, 235
Atlantic Ocean, 9, 12, 16, 23, 27–8,
    251
auctions, 253
Austin, Ann, 215, 216

Bacon, Sir Francis, 86
Balboa, Vasco Núñez de, 59
Bancroft, Richard, Archbishop of
    Canterbury, 102
Banks, the, 15, 20, 21–2, 27
Barbados, 164
bears, 45
beavers, 11, 179, 180, 181–2
Belfield, Richard, 72
Bennitt, Nicholas, 83
Berkeley, John, 148, 157, 192, 218
Berkeley, William, 143–4, 148, 154–6
    and Royalism, 163, 164, 165, 166, 168
Bismarck, Otto von, 6
boat-building, 23
Boston, 9, 132, 222, 224, 225, 229
Bradford, William, 7
Bradstreet, Anne, 1, 8–9, 118–19, 120, 121
    and emigration, 127, 128–9, 130–1
    and Anne Hutchinson, 222–3
    and New England, 132–3, 135–6
    and poetry, 136–9
    and smallpox, 124–5
Bradstreet, Simon, 125
Bristol, 13, 16, 21, 23, 41–2, 43
    and civil war, 149, 150, 151
    and servants, 244, 249
British Empire, 34, 266

Cabot, John, 2–3, 15–17, 26
Canada, 3, 6, 192; see also Newfound-
    land

Canterbury, 95–7, 98–9, 100, 102–3, 217
capital punishment, 225, 227
Caribbean, the, 2, 5, 26, 55, 69, 248
Carleton, Dudley, 72
Carolina, 169
Catholics, 27, 28, 29, 37, 136, 230
   and Canterbury, 96–7, 98–9
   and Charles I, 122–3, 145
   and Ireland, 147
   and James II, 232
   and 'popish' plot, 217
   and resurgence, 171
   and wars, 119
Cavaliers see Royalists
Cecil, Robert, 51–2, 53–4, 63, 64, 65, 70–1
censuses, 48, 183
Central America, 3
Chamberlain, John, 247
Charles I, King, 121, 122–3, 124, 138
   and civil war, 148–9, 150, 151, 154
   and execution, 156, 158–9, 169
   and Parliament, 130, 133, 146, 147–8
   and religion, 145
   see also Royalists
Charles II, King, 11, 144, 151–3, 154, 212
   and death, 231
   and Quakers, 217, 218–19
   and repression, 230
   and Restoration, 167, 168, 169, 191, 210
   and Royalists, 158
   and Virginia, 155, 163, 164, 166
Charter of Privileges, 228
Chesapeake Bay, 8, 141, 143, 169
children, 241–2, 243, 244, 246, 249; see also Frethorne, Richard
Churchill, Winston, 6
class, 186, 201–2, 212, 215, 231
cloth industry, 246
cod, 16, 17–18, 39, 40, 45, 50

colonialism, 266
colonies, 30, 32–3, 93–4, 174–5
   and criteria, 54
   and indentured labour, 256–7
   and Newfoundland, 34–6, 38–9, 40–1, 42–9
   and union, 236
   see also Jamestown; New Netherland
Columbus, Christopher, 2, 26, 65, 84
'conventicles', 100, 101, 212
Cope, Sir Walter, 64–5, 70–1
copper, 66, 67
Cotton, John, 120, 129, 130, 134, 220
Council for Foreign Plantations, 192, 195, 243
Cromwell, Oliver, 154, 167, 168, 191, 237
crops, 7, 46, 246
curiosities, 69
Cushman, Robert, 1, 95–7, 99–101, 102–3, 104–5
   and America, 113–14, 115, 117–18
   and Leiden, 108–9, 110–12

Dare, Virginia, 4
Dawson, William, 72
death rates, 268–9, 270
democracy, 172
Denton, Daniel, 170, 171, 173, 178, 200
   and the Dutch, 194–5
   and England, 196, 197
   and fur trade, 180, 181
   and Jamaica, 189
   and New Netherland, 201–2, 203
   and Quakers, 216–17
Denton, Nathaniel, 189
Denton, Richard, 170–1, 172–4, 184, 187, 189–90
der Donck, Adriaen van, 179–80, 181, 182
disease, 56, 80, 246, 256; see also smallpox
Dorislaus, Isaac, 159–60, 161

Drake, Sir Francis, 3, 52, 66
Duke's Laws, 200
Dutch West India Company, 176, 177, 184, 186, 190, 192–4
Dyer, Mary, 224, 225

earthquakes, 193
East India Company, 82
Easton, Peter, 41, 46, 47, 49
*Eastward Ho* (play), 63
Elizabeth I, Queen, 3, 28–9, 31, 32, 37, 39, 118
  and Protestantism, 97, 99, 100–1
emigration laws, 4
England, 1, 3, 4–7, 144–7, 119–20, 230–2
  and America, 26–7, 30–3, 270–1
  and Catholics, 37
  and Charles I, 121–3
  and civil war, 137–8, 147–54, 183–4
  and Commonwealth, 157–8, 164–5, 209–10, 211–12
  and emigration motives, 8–13, 105–6, 171–2, 244–7, 266–8
  and fish, 18–20, 22, 23–5, 47
  and land patents, 174
  and the Netherlands, 188, 191–2
  and New Netherland, 192–201
  and Newfoundland, 33–6, 38–41, 50
  and precious metals, 66–8, 77
  and Quakers, 228–9
  and religion, 212, 217
  and tobacco, 84–6, 88–9, 91–2
  *see also* Bristol; Canterbury; Lincolnshire; London; Plymouth
English language, 6–7, 263
equal rights, 227

famine, 246, 268
fish, 9, 18–25, 30–1, 32–3, 135
  and Newfoundland, 37, 40, 42, 46–7, 49
  *see also* cod

Fisher, Mary, 215, 216
Fort Orange, 176
Fox, George, 213, 215, 217–18, 234
France, 3, 5, 13
  and America, 26–7, 31–2
  and Canada, 192
  and Catholicism, 28
  and Charles II, 152
  and fish, 18, 25
  and Newfoundland, 49
  and tobacco, 84
  and war, 234, 235
Frethorne, Richard, 8, 254–6, 257–8, 265
Frobisher, Sir Martin, 70
fur, 11, 175–6, 177, 179–82, 202
  and Native Americans, 203–4
  and Richard Nicolls, 199
Furnifull, Edward, 237–8, 239, 240–1, 248, 252, 253

geography, 29
Germany, 19, 228, 242–3, 263
Gilbert, Sir Humphrey, 27–8, 29–35, 36–7
Glanfield, Francis and Richard, 69
'Glorious Revolution', 232–3
gold, 10, 58–60, 62–3, 64–7, 74–7
  and tests, 69–71
Gorges, Fernando, 52–4
governance, 117, 184–5, 200–1, 226–8
Great Britain, 4–5; *see also* England; Scotland
'Great Case of Liberty of Conscience, The' (Penn), 215
Great Fire of London, 214
Great Plague, 213–14
Guy, John, 41–6, 47
Guy, Jonathan, 48
Guy, Nicholas, 47–8

Hakluyt, Richard, 23, 67, 245
Hammond, John, 259–63

Hampden, John, 145–6
Hanseatic League, 19
Hempstead, 174, 176, 178, 183, 187–8, 189
    and the Dutch, 195
    and Richard Nicolls, 200
Henrietta Maria, Queen, 122–3, 145, 157
Henry VII, King, 17
Henry VIII, King, 17, 19, 28, 97
herring, 18–19, 27
Holland *see* Netherlands, the
Hudson, Henry, 175
Huguenots, 95, 99, 227, 231
Hunt, Robert, 55
Hutchinson, Anne, 219–24, 225
Hutchinson, Mary, 225

Iceland, 17, 27
indentured labour, 12, 92, 238–44, 247–50, 263
    and Virginia, 252–4, 255–9, 264–5
    and voyage, 250–2
Ingham, John, 264
Ireland, 4, 5, 147, 158, 263
    and William Penn, 210, 211, 218, 234

Jamaica (colony), 181, 189, 193
James I and VI, King, 4, 39, 41, 69, 82
    and death, 121
    and Puritans, 101–2, 103–4, 107
    and Spain, 72–3
    and tobacco, 86
    and wars, 119–20
James II and VII, King, 157, 158, 194, 226
    and 'Glorious Revolution', 232–3
    and Richard Nicolls, 195, 196, 201
    and William Penn, 231–2, 234
*James* (ship), 170, 171
Jamestown, 55–7, 61–3, 73–5, 78–9, 88–9
Johnson, William, 72

kidnapping, 241–4

labour, 12; *see also* indentured labour
land rights, 11, 174–5
Laud, William, Archbishop of Canterbury, 123–4, 130, 133–4, 138, 172
    and Anne Hutchinson, 220
    and reforms, 145
    and Scotland, 146
*Leah and Rachell, or the two fruitful Sisters of Virginia and Maryland* (Hammond), 260
Leiden, 108–12
*Letter Concerning Toleration* (Locke), 233–4
liberty, 212, 214–15, 216, 233
    and Pennsylvania, 225–6, 227, 232, 236
Lincolnshire, 118–19, 120–1, 124, 125–6, 219–20
literacy, 186
Locke, John, 233–4
Locker, Capt John, 161, 162
London, 237–40, 241–2, 243, 268
Long Island *see* New Netherland
lotteries, 80–1

Manhattan, 176, 177, 194, 197
Martin, John, 58, 60, 62–3, 70, 71, 74, 76
    and John Smith, 75
Mary II, Queen, 232, 233
Maryland, 169, 259
Massachusetts Company, 93, 130
*Mayflower* (ship), 9, 113, 115–16
'Mayflower Compact', 117
Merchant Adventurers, 32–3
migration, 2
multiculturalism, 177, 228, 270

Naseby, battle of, 149, 151
Native Americans, 7, 8, 60–1, 262
    and alcohol, 176, 227

and attacks, 182–3, 257
and disease, 3, 129
and fur trade, 179, 182
and gold, 65
and New Netherland, 178
and Newfoundland, 42, 49
and Henry Norwood, 141–3
and Pennsylvania, 226
and Puritans, 128
and Peter Stuyvesant, 188–9
and trade, 175
and Virginia, 57, 59, 74, 79–80, 163, 169
*see also* Pocahontas; Powhatan
navigation, 23, 29
Navigation Act (1651), 165
navy, the, 19, 37
Netherlands, the, 19, 106–12, 120, 169
and Isaac Dorislaus, 159–60
and England, 183–4, 188, 191–2
and fur trading, 175–7
and Royalists, 152–3
and trade, 164, 165
New Amsterdam, 173, 174, 176, 177
and England, 194, 197–9
and fur trade, 179–80, 182
and growth, 185–6
*see also* New York
New England, 8, 10–11, 114–18, 131–3, 134–6, 172
and Anne Hutchinson, 221–4
and Puritans, 219
and Quakers, 216, 224–5
and servants, 263–4
New Netherland, 172–4, 177–8
and attacks, 182–3, 224
and England, 190–201
and fur trade, 179–82
and governance, 184–5, 186
and Quakers, 216–17
*see also* Hempstead; New Amsterdam
New World *see* America; Canada

New York, 199, 200, 201, 202–4
Newfoundland, 2, 3, 16, 22, 24–5, 42–9
and England, 30, 33–6, 38–41
and trade, 49–50
*see also* Banks, the
Newport, Christopher, 51–2, 53, 54–7, 61, 82
and Walter Cope, 65
and gold, 58, 59–60, 63, 71–2, 76
and Jamestown, 73–4
and privateering, 68–9
and John Rolfe, 87
and Virginia, 78
Nicolls, Richard, 195–6, 197, 198, 199–201
Nicot, Jean, 84
North Sea, 18–19, 27
North West Passage Company, 82
Norway, 27
Norwood, Henry, 1, 140–4, 147, 167–8
and Royalism, 148, 149, 150, 152–3, 157, 158, 159
and Virginia, 155, 160–3

Oates, Titus, 217

Pacific Ocean, 59
Papacy, the, 28, 29
Parkhurst, Anthony, 20–3, 25, 27, 28, 34, 35
Parliament, 25, 64, 99, 135, 146, 147
and Catholics, 37
and Charles I, 122, 123, 130, 133, 145
and civil war, 149, 151–2, 154
and kidnappings, 242
and Virginia, 164–6
Penn, William, 11, 205–6, 207, 208–12, 213–15, 217, 223
and America, 216, 218–19
and England, 230–2, 234–5
and native languages, 7
and Pennsylvania, 225–30, 235–6

Pennsylvania, 205, 208, 218–19, 225–30, 235–6
Pepys, Samuel, 167, 192, 213
persecution, 100, 228
   and Huguenots, 95, 99, 227, 231
   and Quakers, 205, 212, 213, 214, 215, 216, 224–5
'Persuasive to Moderation, A' (Penn), 231
Philadelphia, 208, 229
Philip II of Spain, King, 29–30
Philip III of Spain, King, 81–2
'Pilgrim Fathers', 9, 99, 113–18
piracy, 40, 41, 46, 47, 49
plague, 118, 121, 123, 213–14
plantations, 12, 91, 248
Plymouth, 51–3
Pocahontas, 1, 89–91, 92
politics, 13–14, 226, 235; see also governance
Poor Law (1601), 254
population growth, 236, 245, 247, 267, 268
Portugal, 3, 4, 17, 25, 37
poverty, 12, 237–8, 239–40, 242, 243, 260–1
   and emigration, 244–7
Powhatan, 74, 78, 89
Poyner, Thomas, 265
Presbyterians, 172, 174
prisoners, 264–5
privateers, 39, 40, 68–9
Protestants, 27, 28, 31, 32
   and Charles I, 122–3
   and Newfoundland, 34
   and persecution, 95
   and William III, 232–3
   see also Puritans
Prynne, William, 145
Puritans, 9, 10–11, 97–105, 118–22
   and America, 112–13, 127–31
   and Anne Bradstreet, 125–7
   and Anne Hutchinson, 219–24

   and William Laud, 144–5
   and the Netherlands, 105–12
   and New England, 131–3, 134–6
   and Quakers, 216
   see also 'Pilgrim Fathers'

Quaker Act (1662), 213
Quakers, 205–6, 207, 210, 211–13, 214–15
   and America, 215–19
   and New England, 224–5
   and Pennsylvania, 225–30
   and repression, 231–2
   and toleration, 233, 234

Raleigh, Sir Walter, 25, 28, 120
   and tobacco, 85, 91
Ransack, Abram, 72
Reformation, the, 27, 99, 106
religion, 9, 10–12, 123–4, 146
   and fish, 30
   and tolerance, 200, 227–8, 233–4
   see also Catholics; Presbyterians; Protestants; Quakers
Rhode Island, 224
Roanoke, 3–4, 85
Robinson, Joane, 249–50
Rolfe, Bermuda, 87
Rolfe, John, 1, 83–4, 86, 87–90, 92–3
Royalists, 11, 140–4, 147, 148–54, 195
   and exile, 156–8
   and Restoration, 168
   and vengeance, 158–60
   and Virginia, 154–6, 160–6, 169
Russell, Walter, 80
Russia, 182
Rye House Plot, 230

St John's, 33
Salem, 131–2
salt, 22, 49, 135
Scotland, 5, 146, 147, 158, 263
Sea Venture (ship), 83, 86–7

servants, 12, 237–44, 247–50, 263
  and Virginia, 252–4, 255–9
  and voyage, 250–2
settlements *see* colonies
Sharplisse, Thomas, 81
'ship money', 122, 145–6
shipping, 13, 19, 135
  and disease, 206, 207–8
  and indentured labour, 250–2
shipwrecks, 36–7
silver, 62, 65–7
Silvester, Elizabeth, 264
slave trade, 5, 20, 92, 94, 135, 243, 254
smallpox, 124–5, 206–8, 219
Smith, John, 57–8, 61–2, 93–4, 78–9, 259
  and gold, 75–7, 82
  and New England, 114, 116
  and Pocahontas, 89, 90
South America, 3, 26
Spain, 3, 4, 5, 37, 39, 72–3
  and America, 26, 31
  and Catholicism, 28, 29–30
  and the Netherlands, 109, 110
  and silver, 66, 67
  and Virginia, 81–2
  *see also* Anglo-Spanish War
*Speedwell* (ship), 113, 115
'spirits', 241, 242–3, 244, 249
*Squirrel* (boat), 36–7
'Starving Time', 80, 88
Stuyvesant, Peter, 184–6, 188–9, 190, 192–4, 216
  and England, 196, 197, 198–9

Tate, Mary, 265
Test Acts (1673), 217, 232
tobacco, 10, 21, 84–6, 135, 259
  and Native Americans, 61
  and the Netherlands, 109
  and Quakers, 227
  and John Rolfe, 87–9
  and Virginia, 91–3, 155

Toleration Act (1689), 233
trade, 49–50, 66, 67, 164–5
  and fish, 135
  and New Amsterdam, 185–6
  and New York, 202
transportation *see* indentured labour
*True Relation of the State of Virginia, A* (Rolfe), 91

unemployment, 245–6, 247
United Provinces *see* Netherlands, the
United States of America, 13–14, 226

vagrancy, 247
Vikings, 2, 3
Virginia, 8, 10, 42, 67–8, 81–2
  and gold, 58, 59–60, 62–3, 71–3, 74–7
  and improvements, 259–63
  and indentured labour, 252–4, 255–9, 264–5
  and Native Americans, 79–80
  and Royalists, 142–4, 153, 154–6, 163–6, 168–9
  and tobacco, 91–3
  *see also* Jamestown
Virginia Company, 64, 77–9, 80–1, 258
  and indentured labour, 248, 249
*Virginia Merchant* (ship), 161, 162

wage labour, 245, 268
wampum, 179
wealth, 9–10, 66, 67
weather conditions, 15, 35–6, 42, 43–6
  and indentured labour, 253–4
  and New England, 116
  and sea, 86–7, 140–1, 170, 251–2
  and Virginia, 73
*Welcome* (ship), 205, 206, 219

West Indies *see* Caribbean
Whitbourne, Richard, 9, 37–8
    and Newfoundland, 34, 35, 38–9,
        40–1, 48
Whitgift, John, Archbishop of Canter-
        bury, 98, 102
Whittington, Dick, 268, 269
wildlife, 45
William III, King, 232–3
Winthrop, John, 9, 127, 130–1, 133,
        215, 241
    and Hutchinson, 222, 223, 225

Wise, John, 245
witchcraft, 200, 216
women, 32, 46, 93, 137
    and Anne Hutchinson, 221–2
    and indentured labour, 248–50
    and Puritans, 118, 120, 127
    and rights, 186
wood, 11, 25, 43, 76
Worcester, battle of, 165

York and Albany, James, Duke of *see*
        James II and VII, King